# Arti-fact-ual

Duke University Press
*Durham and London* 2023

Printed in Canada on acid-free paper ∞
Project Editor: Liz Smith
Designed by Courtney Leigh Richardson
Typeset in Warnock Pro, Clarendon, Source Variable Code, and Flood by Copperline Book Services

Library of Congress Cataloging-in-Publication Data
Names: Davis, Elizabeth Anne, [date] author.
Title: Artifactual : forensic and documentary knowing / Elizabeth Anne Davis.
Other titles: Experimental futures.
Description: Durham : Duke University Press, 2023. | Series: Experimental futures | Includes bibliographical references and index.
Identifiers: LCCN 2022044167 (print)
LCCN 2022044168 (ebook)
ISBN 9781478019886 (paperback)
ISBN 9781478017202 (hardcover)
ISBN 9781478024453 (ebook)
Subjects: LCSH: Committee of Relatives of Turkish Cypriot Missing Persons. | Forensic sciences—Social aspects—Cyprus. | Documentary films—Political aspects—Cyprus. | Cyprus—History—1960—Documentation. | Cyprus—Social conditions—1960—Documentation. | Cyprus—Politics and government—1960–2004. | BISAC: SOCIAL SCIENCE / Anthropology / Cultural & Social | HISTORY / Europe / General
Classification: LCC DS54.9 .D37 2023 (print) | LCC DS54.9 (ebook) | DDC 956.9304—dc23/eng/20230105
LC record available at https://lccn.loc.gov/2022044167
LC ebook record available at https://lccn.loc.gov/2022044168

Cover art: From exhibition on the Black Bible of the Missing, 1974. Reproduced with permission from the Press and Information Office in the Republic of Cyprus.

This publication is made possible in part with support from the Barr Ferree Foundation Fund for Publications, Department of Art and Archaeology, Princeton University.

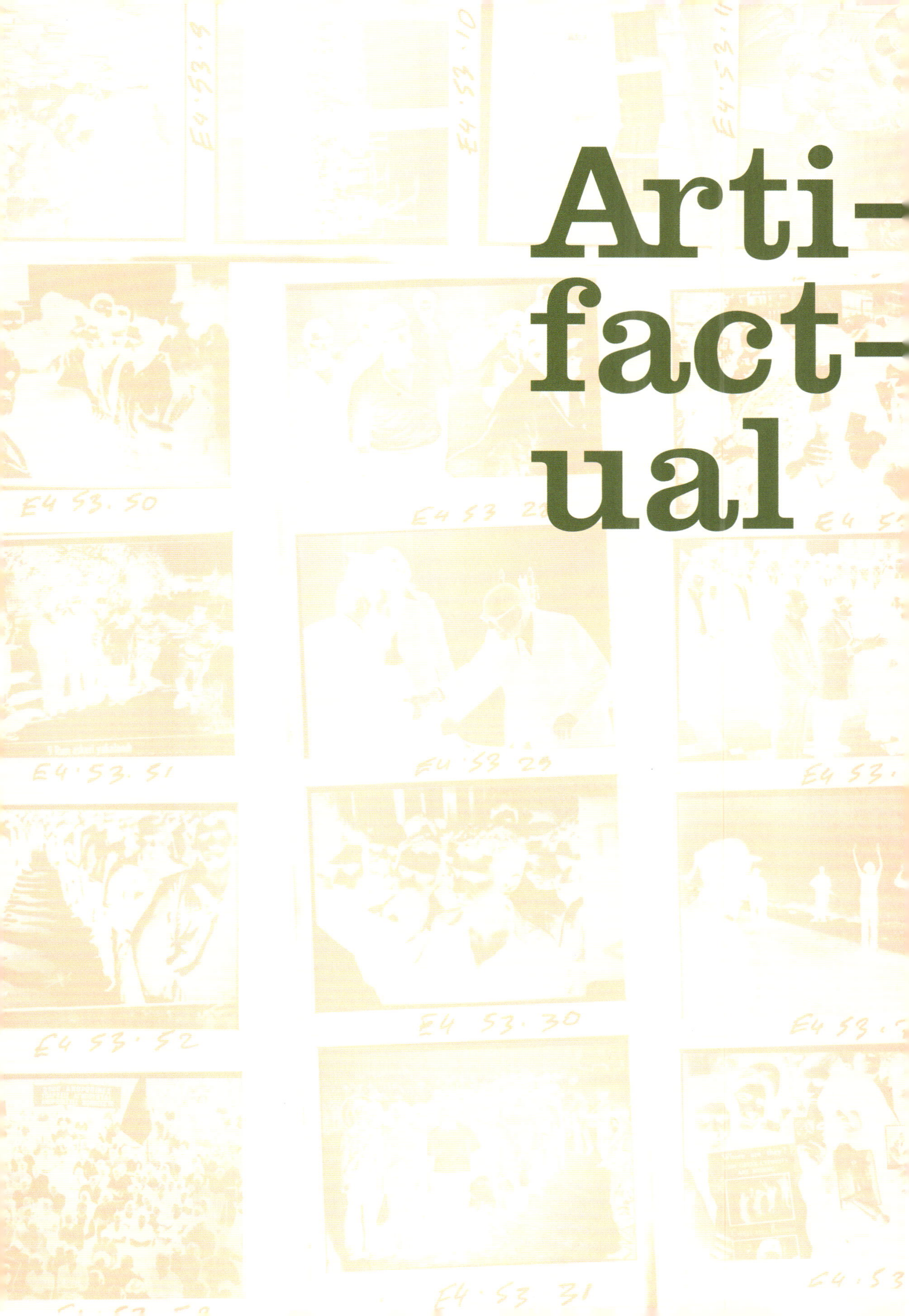


# Arti-fact-ual

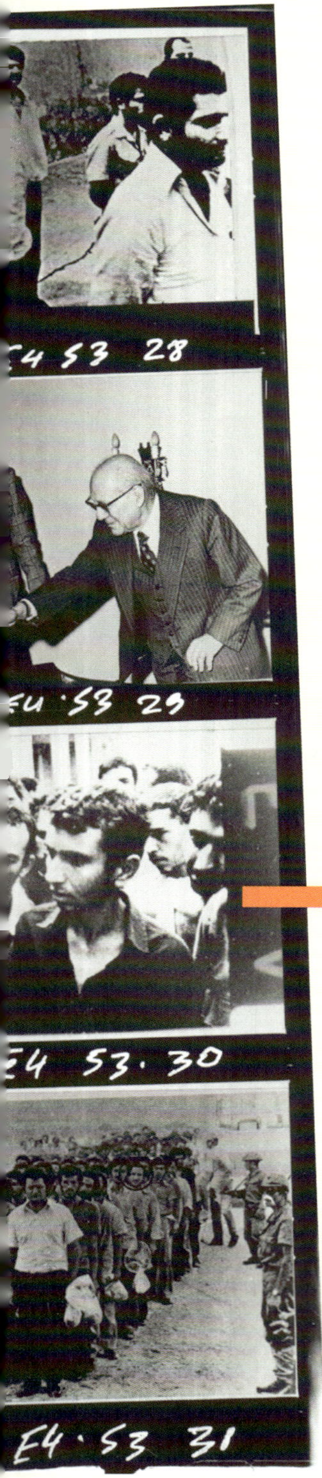


# Forensic and Documentary Knowing

Elizabeth Anne Davis

EXPERIMENTAL FUTURES
Technological Lives, Scientific Arts, Anthropological Voices
*A series edited by Michael M. J. Fischer and Joseph Dumit*

for Ruby

Since Aphrodite this island has turned into
  a rubbish dump of love.
Our feet tangled in the roots of invaders
bone piles crack as we move
under our weight.

The earth so over-saturated with death syrup
the only escape
        is not poetry . . .
                    water!

Gür Genç, from "Not Poetry . . . Water" (2000)
translated by Aydın Mehmet Ali

# Contents

1

## Forensic — 45

# 2

## Documentary — 173

# Acknowledgments

I owe a debt of gratitude that I cannot measure or repay to my interlocutors in the Cypriot context, some of whose own work has become my "material." I deeply appreciate their willingness to engage with me so seriously, and to meet my questions with their own curiosities, thus opening a shared horizon of knowledge making. Others whose work is not discussed in this book nevertheless shared precious insights, great stories, and their wonderful company with me; this book bears their good influence. Some of my interlocutors have become close friends; our conversations have been going for years, and I hope they will never come to an end. Many have read parts of this text and helped me, as only they can, to develop and improve it. Along with others I have renamed in the text, I warmly thank Alev Adil, Umut Bozkurt, Rebecca Bryant, Panicos Chrysanthou, Costas Constandinides, Olga Demetriou, Karen Emmerich, Ellada Evangelou, Leslie Frost, Antonis Hadjikyriacou, Evi Haggipavlu, David Hands, Mete Hatay, Murat Erdal Ilican, Alana Kakoyiannis, Ruth Keshishian, Iosif Kovras, Yael Navaro, Argyro Nicolaou, Kyriakos Pachoulides, Yiannis Papadakis, Despo Pasia, Nicos Philippou, Stephanos Stephanides, Theopisti Stylianou-Lambert, and Konstantina Zanou.

Due to the conditions of confidentiality to which I agreed, and which bind them as well, I cannot name the scientists and staff at the Committee on Missing Persons with whom I worked in 2011–12, some of whom I visited on later trips to Cyprus. Many are no longer with the CMP, though some are. I wish I could thank each one of these people individually for their patience and generosity, for giving me their time, sharing meals and stories and jokes and complaints with me, inviting me out, teaching me their practices, and showing me their world. I have enormous respect for the work they do and how they do it, especially in dealing so judiciously with the limitations and pressures they face in that work.

I am, however, very glad to be able to thank by name the former Third Member of the CMP, Christophe Girod, long since departed from Cyprus, without whose understanding of the project and gracious guidance in navigating the CMP I would never have been able to conduct fieldwork as I did. I am grateful, too, to Linda Marquardt, in the Third Member's office, for her consistent help and kindness, as well as to Florian Von Koenig and Bruce Koepke, who facilitated my access to CMP photographs and my permission to use them, long after my fieldwork was done.

I have been writing and rewriting this book for more than ten years, and many brilliant and generous people have helped me in the process. I am especially grateful to friends who took precious time to read closely and share their feedback on the evolving text: Yelena Baraz, Karen Emmerich (again!), Jessica Goldberg, Mark Greif, Belinda Haikes, Liz Harman, Eben Kirksey, Pamela Mazzeo, Shannon Novak, Anand Pandian, Lauren Silver, and Melissa Yates. My dear Diane Nelson also belongs in this list, though engaging with my writing is only one of the countless ways she helped me think and enriched my life.

My profound thanks go, as well:

To the graduate students with whom I had the pleasure and privilege of working as I was writing this book, who helped me conceptualize and communicate better and from whose own work I learned so much. They have all moved on to bigger and better things by now. I have in mind especially Tyler Adkins, Jessica Cooper, Thalia Gigerenzer, Onur Günay, Sebastián Ramírez Hernández, and Igor Rubinov.

To the participants in the "Ethnography and Theory" working group organized by Didier Fassin at the Institute for Advanced Study in 2013–14; in the workshop organized by Susanna Trnka and Catherine Trundle at the Radcliffe Institute for Advanced Study in 2014, "Beyond Neoliberal Responsibilisation: Rethinking Anthropological Approaches to Responsibility"; and in the long-format conference, "The Anthropology of Becoming," organized by João Biehl and Peter Locke at Princeton in 2014. My comrades in these groups gave discerning and open-minded attention to my work early on, when it made the most difference. Among them, I especially want to thank Mike Fischer for his searing and imaginative commentary; Laurence Ralph for offering a crucial thought about narrative in this text; and especially João, for painstakingly reading my book manuscript as it was then, introducing me to William Connolly's work on time, and suggesting the resonance of Nicole Loraux's writing on civil war—right on the nose.

To Dimitris Gondicas, my colleague and mentor in Hellenic studies at Princeton, who has given me tremendous and indispensable support for this project from the earliest phase of research onward (and has tirelessly clipped Greek news items related to the Cypriot missing for me, when I could not keep up); to Stefania Pandolfo, whose influence on my thinking and sensibility as an anthropologist is beyond reckoning, and who first brought Damir Arsenijević's writing to my attention; to Joe Masco, whose work on secrecy has provided me ongoing inspiration, and whose incisive reading of my writing in progress opened new avenues of thought; to Jody McAuliffe, whose critical perspective and wit have sharpened my own, and whose stunning theatrical adaption of Don DeLillo's *The Body Artist*, which she directed at Duke University in 2018, offered me a way to think about the phenomenology of time that made possible my writing of this book this way; to Vangelis Calotychos, whose insight into the Cypriot context and whose ongoing commentary on the shapes and legacies of conflict there have helped me ask better questions; and to my colleagues in the Department of Anthropology at Princeton, especially Carol Greenhouse and Rena Lederman, who, in their different ways, offered me human support when I needed it, and modeled practices of anthropology to which I continue to aspire; as well as Carol Zanca, Mo Lin Yee, and Patty Lieb, who have provided so much vital and multifaceted help over the years that enabled me to keep going with this project in the interstices of everything else.

To the audiences, participants, and organizers of the talks and workshops where I have presented portions of this writing over the years, including at the University of Auckland, the University of Chicago, Duke University, Washington University, the Seeger Center for Hellenic Studies at Princeton University, and the Joukowsky Institute for Archaeology and the Ancient World at Brown University. Sharing my work with people in these settings, and learning from their generative and provocative questions and comments, has been the most enjoyable and productive part of the writing process. In the same spirit, I thank the two anonymous reviewers at Duke University Press, who probably spent more time with this text than they had bargained for and gave me rich, thoughtful feedback that made it much better.

To my editor at Duke University Press, Ken Wissoker, who supported this book project unstintingly from beginning to end, in its many forms and tempos, and who offered crucial advice and guidance all along the way; as well as to Elizabeth Ault and Ryan Kendall, who graciously and expertly played key roles in the editing and production process.

Finally, to my family. To Rob Vogt, who has shared my life in Cyprus as well as the United States and has supported me as I have stolen time over the years to travel and write. His exquisite artistic sensibility has shaped and enriched my own sense of the visual and material world of Cyprus. He also taught me how to take good photographs and provided essential technical support in producing the images in this book. And to Ruby Davis, who was born a few years into this project and has grown as the book has grown: she is ever becoming, densifying my own belonging to time in the most joyful and surprising ways.



I have been very fortunate to receive generous support at Princeton University for my research and writing in this project, including a Stanley J. Seeger Hellenic Studies Sabbatical Research Grant, a Richard Stockton Bicentennial Preceptorship, a Behrman Faculty Fellowship in the Humanities, and research grants from the University Committee on Research in the Humanities and Social Sciences. I have also enjoyed the immense benefit of two sabbaticals at the Institute for Advanced Study (IAS) in Princeton—first, in the School of Social Science, and later, in the School of Historical Studies—where I found a by turns stimulating and serene environment in which to read, write, think, and learn from truly remarkable colleagues. My second year at the IAS was made possible by a Frederick Burkhardt Residential Fellowship for Recently Tenured Scholars awarded by the amazing people at the American Council of Learned Societies; I thank them and the panel of reviewers sincerely. I also want to thank Didier Fassin and Joan Scott in particular for their warm hospitality and helpful engagement with my work while I was at the IAS.

The excerpt from Gür Genç's poem, "Not Poetry . . . Water," that appears on the dedication page is reproduced with permission. The full poem was originally published in Turkish in his collection *Yolyutma* (Nicosia: Işık Yay, 2000). I thank Gür for his generosity and trust, and for the inspiration of his work.

Early versions of some material in this text were previously published in chapters of edited volumes: "Time Machines: The Matter of the Missing in Cyprus," in *Unfinished: The Anthropology of Becoming*, edited by João Biehl and Peter Locke (Durham, NC: Duke University Press, 2017); "'The Information Is Out There': Transparency, Responsibility, and the Missing in Cyprus," in *Competing Responsibilities: The Ethics and Politics of Contemporary Life*, edited by Susanna Trnka and Catherine Trundle (Durham, NC: Duke University Press, 2017); and "Archive, Evidence, Memory, Dream:

Documentary Films on Cyprus," in *Cypriot Cinemas: Memory, Conflict, and Identity in the Margins of Europe*, edited by Costas Constandinides and Yiannis Papadakis (London: Bloomsbury, 2015). I am grateful to João, Peter, Susanna, Catherine, Costas, and Yiannis for inviting me to participate in these extraordinary collective projects, and for patiently and assiduously shepherding the writing to publication.

This publication was made possible in part with support from the Barr Ferree Foundation Fund for Publications, Department of Art and Archaeology, Princeton University. I thank the Barr Ferree Committee for their immense generosity.

# Prologue. Nobody Knows a Thing

Why must we know what we don't want to know? Why would we claim to know what we don't know, or not to know what we do? These questions flash through the documentary film *Birds of a Feather*, made in Cyprus by Stefanos Evripidou and Stephen Nugent in 2012. The film features interviews with Cypriots who lived through episodes of civil and state violence in the 1960s and '70s, as well as Cypriot researchers, activists, and educators who study those events. These figures rarely appear in the film in conventional talking-head interviews; instead, they are filmed together, already in dialogue about Cyprus's history of violence and division, and it is their conversations—with all the contradictions, tensions, and elaborations they contain—that form the overt subject of the film.

The film opens in Peristerona, a farming village in the foothills of the Troodos Mountains, just west of Nicosia, the capital city of Cyprus, and just south of the so-called Green Line, the de facto cease-fire line that has divided the Greek-Cypriot region in the south from the Turkish-Cypriot region in the north since the war in 1974. Although Peristerona had been a so-called mixed village, inhabited by Greek Cypriots and Turkish Cypriots, for most of its modern history before the division, its residents today are exclusively Greek Cypriots—those who had lived in the village before the war along with those who arrived afterward as refugees, forcibly displaced from their homes in the north. In the opening sequence, the camera follows Salih Niyazi, in his sixties, in an elegant suit, identified as a Turkish-Cypriot former resident of the village. He explains in a voice-over that, since the opening of the border, he has returned every day to Peristerona to visit his old friends, to eat and talk with them. As he makes his way through the village mosque, now empty and encrusted in dust—there is no one to use it—he speaks, in Greek, of the suffering of Turkish Cypriots before 1974 and the suffering of Greek Cypriots during 1974: "I believe that we shouldn't hide behind our fingers, all us Cypriots. We should speak the whole truth, Turks and Christians. That's what I believe."[1]

Salih joins Andreas Kyriakides and other residents of the village who have gathered around a café table in the bright courtyard of the mosque. They speak in Greek, Andreas's native language; in his youth, Salih, like many Turkish Cypriots from mixed villages, had mastered the dominant language. They argue over an incident in 1964, when their neighbor, Arif Çağal, was shot by a Greek-Cypriot police officer. Andreas suggests that Arif had been a member of a Turkish-Cypriot militia group at the time and had been trying to cut the village's phone line to the police when he was shot; Salih disputes his account, contending that Arif had innocently been harvesting olives in his field when he was targeted by the police. They argue over where the shooting took place and who saw it. They argue over what each has told the other about the incident in the past. "You don't know!" Andreas shouts. "Of course I know!" Salih shouts back, laughing. They argue over each other's qualifications to testify: Andreas was a few years older than Salih and therefore "knows better"; but Salih was "in the events" and heard the story directly from Arif's sister, mother, and grandmother, all witnesses to the shooting. The two men interrupt each other, pointing, flicking their worry beads. Their voices rise and fall; their sight lines connect and move apart. A third man, an old friend of the other two, finally intercedes: "Anyway. It's over!"

Peristerona is one of the legendary sites of the Cyprus conflict—a village of storied beauty, built on the banks of Peristerona River among shimmering olive groves and flowering, redolent citrus and almond. I have seen it. I visited because it is one of the places celebrated by peace-minded Cypriots as a symbol of harmony between Greek Cypriots and Turkish Cypriots, as they lived there together for generations before it was riven by violence in the 1960s. The PRIO Cyprus Centre,[2] a nongovernmental research center in Nicosia that explicitly brands itself as bicommunal—meaning it employs Greek-Cypriot and Turkish-Cypriot researchers and disseminates materials in Greek and Turkish as well as English on both sides of the divide—gives a quick sketch of the events in its report for Peristerona, which a PRIO research team mapped as part of the project "Internal Displacement in Cyprus" (PRIO Cyprus Centre 2011b). According to the PRIO report, Peristerona was a mixed village of about 1,200 people in 1964; that February,

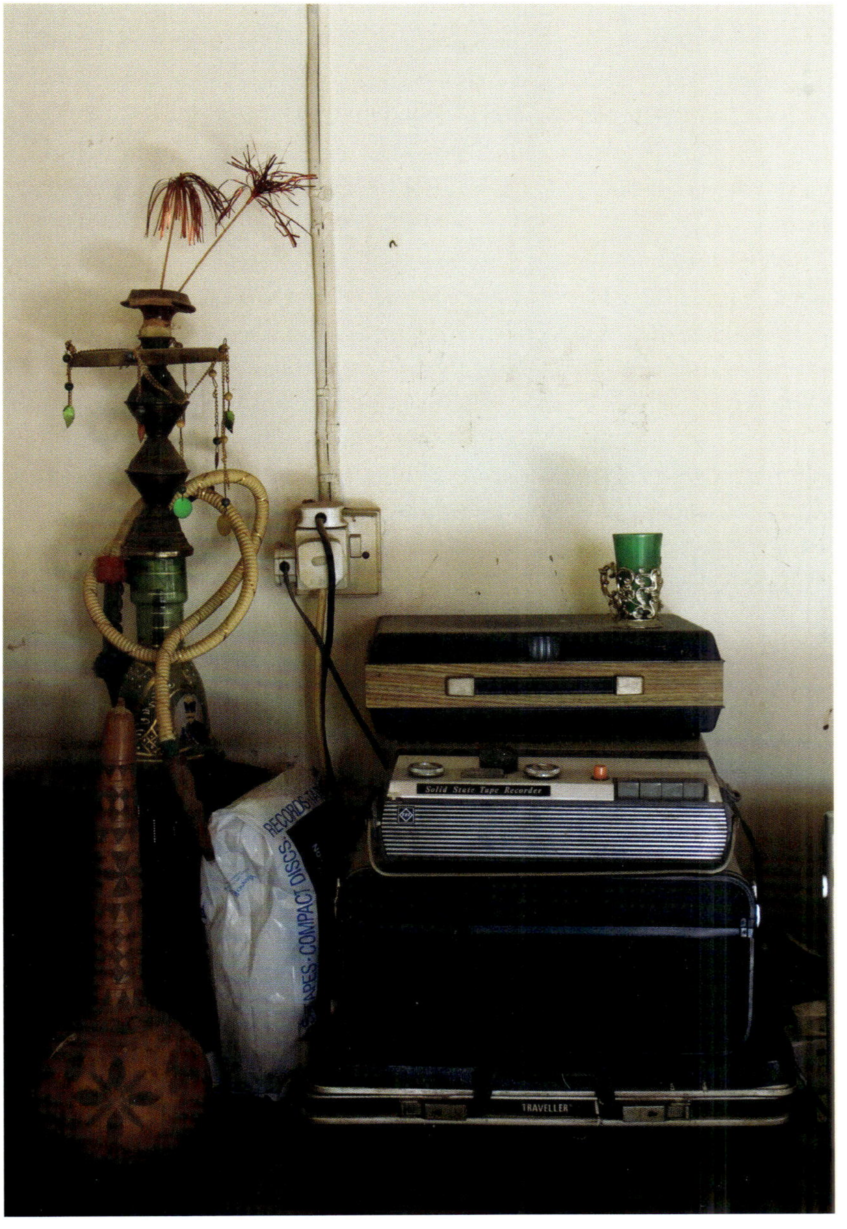


*NO.*

**P.1**

after two Turkish-Cypriot police officers were shot, almost all the Turkish-Cypriot residents fled—about five hundred people altogether, two-fifths of the village—and settled in enclaves in Nicosia, or in towns under Turkish-Cypriot control in the north. Those who returned to the village during a phase of calm in 1968 left again, for good, in 1974, when two Turkish-Cypriot residents were killed by Greek-Cypriot irregulars from a local paramilitary group.



Before I visited, I had already encountered Peristerona in another film, which framed the village as a place of exodus and exile. The village was the addressee of a melancholic poem by Neşe Yaşin, a Turkish-Cypriot poet and peace activist born in Peristerona who, as a young child in 1964, fled with her family to Nicosia. Her return to her village as an adult, "a woman broken by life," as she describes herself, was recorded by the Greek-Cypriot filmmaker Panicos Chrysanthou for *Our Wall*, the documentary film he made in 1993 with Niyazi Kızılyürek, a Turkish-Cypriot friend, a political scientist at the University of Cyprus and, at the time of this writing, a member of the European Parliament: the first Turkish Cypriot to be elected from Cyprus. *Our Wall* was the first bicommunal film to be made in Cyprus about the events of the conflict, and, as such, it is considered by many of my interlocutors in the Cyprus film world to be groundbreaking in its time. I saw it at a screening in January 2012, with about thirty other people, in a municipal gallery on the southern edge of the so-called dead zone in the center of divided Nicosia. Chrysanthou was there, and, before the screening began, he explained to the audience (in Greek) how the film had come about. He said he had always imagined the film through a poetic frame, but it was not until he met Neşe Yaşin that he had figured out how to do it. This was in 1988, long before the checkpoints between the northern and southern regimes opened in 2003, a time when it was nearly impossible for Turkish Cypriots and Greek Cypriots to meet; but they had both gotten formal permission to attend a cultural event in Nicosia, and they got to talking there about their childhood experiences of fleeing their villages, he to the south and she to the north. He remembered her for a long time afterward, he said, and eventually managed to get a letter to her through Kızılyürek, a mutual friend, inviting her to appear in the film they were then planning to make together.

In the sequence, Yaşin travels to Peristerona by bus, passing along the Venetian fortress walls enclosing the old city of Nicosia, topped with barbed wire and shadowed by the flags of Greece, Turkey, Cyprus, and the UN. The bus follows a long, dusty road to the village, crossing over a dry riverbed, passing by a rusty van half-buried in a sandy field and old buildings left half-constructed and crumbling. Ambling dreamily through the village, Yaşin speaks the lines of her poem in voice-over, in Turkish, as English subtitles spell out a translation:[3]

I remember when I was a little girl.
Everything changed quickly then between joy and sadness.
They brought me into this world to live through a story.
I had a mother and father then.
I remember the day I saw the almond-tree for the first time,
the sun rays caressing the flowers and my face
and a village kept deep inside me as the joy of life.

People there had beautiful faces.
They thought that this child was born to be happy.
Peristerona, the child who called out your name
didn't know that this was going to be a sad story.
When she discovered the first bullet,
when she heard the grown-ups whispering with tears in their eyes,
she tasted a great pain and was scared.
The mother could have died with the baby still in her womb.

Peristerona, you became a village more distant than the stars.
Who remembers today the little princess of the flowers who once
lived here?
What life took without pity out of her arms each day
was turned into tears wetting the pillow every night.
Little girl from Peristerona.

Hello, Peristerona. Do you remember me?
I've grown up, haven't I?
Do you remember when I used to walk along
your narrow streets holding my doll with the red hat?
Was that a fairy tale?
Was it a fairy tale, that I ran through the daisies?
Maybe I loved you so much because they forced us to part.
I always thought of you, Peristerona.
Happiness was with you.
My tears began after you.
There was always a place in the world that I always wanted to reach.
It was you, Peristerona.
A village more distant than the stars.

Yaşin enters the gated courtyard of an old house where she might have lived as a child, though the film does not say so. She encounters a very old woman dressed in black—a widow—who greets her with shaking hands, in mixed Turkish and Greek, and remembers her grandmother: "We harvested together. We had a very, very, very good time together." Yaşin's voice-over continues:

> Here I am, Peristerona.
> I've grown up and they say that I look like my mother.
> I think I am as old as she was when she left you.
> The war turned her first into a captive and then an unhappy and ill woman.
> By her grave I think of you.
> You are a dream-land village, Peristerona.
> You are the joys left behind, a house that was looted and set on fire,
> a place in the throes of death.
>
> When they brought our few belongings to our little house in exile
> they said our house had been looted and burned down
> and that my dolls were no longer there.
> With sadness I stared at what they were unloading from the truck
> and I cried inconsolably for my dolls.
> My dolls, poor captives of the war.
> I was forbidden to cry for you when at that time people were losing their lives.
>
> Oh, Peristerona, how much both of us have been wounded by wars.
> The joyful cries of the child are no longer heard in this house.
> I came to you as a woman broken by life, like all the other women,
> those who cried in two different languages from the same pain.
> On their faces is printed a story steeped in blood.



During Yaşin's voice-over, the camera has already moved slowly through the doorway of an old house in Peristerona, down its creaking wooden steps into its basement, landing at last on the dour face of a middle-aged woman sitting stiffly on a wooden chair. The next sequence cuts between this woman and another, older woman sitting on the porch of another house. They recount, in Greek and Turkish, respectively, the atrocities they witnessed and experienced themselves in the summer of 1974—not in Peristerona but in villages so much like it that their names do not seem to matter. Where Yaşin is burdened by a melancholic attachment to her lost childhood village, which she remembers in a poetic reverie, these women seem to be trapped in traumatic repetition, each reliving her experiences of the war by herself, unable to forget or move on. Separately, each breaks down in tears and covers her face; they "die every day"; they "can't go on." This series of cuts yields a series of metonyms: the pain of these women comes to stand for the pain of "all the other women" named in Yaşin's poem, and more, the pain of all Cypriots. The intimate knowledge of violence conveyed in their testimony comes to stand for the history of war in Cyprus. And Peristerona comes to stand for all the villages of Cyprus destroyed by that history. It is a very specific place and also a generic anyplace of destruction and haunting.

*Birds of a Feather* returns to Peristerona in its closing sequence. The debate between Salih and Andreas about the shooting incident suddenly resolves into quiet consensus:



ANDREAS (*looking off-camera as he speaks to the filmmaker Evripidou, who appears briefly in the left foreground*): My friend, nobody knows a thing.
SALIH: They know nothing at all. Nothing.
ANDREAS: Nothing. (*He points to his left, off-screen, and the camera follows his gesture to show the face of a younger man, sitting silently.*) Costas here, he's forty years old, and if you ask him, he has no idea what happened.
SALIH: Nobody knows, nobody knows.
ANDREAS: Nobody. Us, we're the last generation from the '70s. . . .
SALIH: We're the last generation who knows.
ANDREAS: But when we go kaput—then, as a society, we can recover. Why wouldn't we?[4]

Every position one could take in recounting and accounting for a history of violence is taken by these old friends in the opening and closing sequences of the film. Propositions of knowledge contend with accusations of not knowing: of ignorance, credulity, confusion, dissimulation. The opening sequence gives the lie to the premise that historical knowledge—what happened, who, and why—can be discovered; that someone knows for sure; that the facts to compose a coherent consensus can be ascertained. Positions become ways of seeing, modes of partiality, habits of refusal. In the closing sequence, disagreement and contradiction are assimilated into a larger story of how knowledge relates to history. Salih and Andreas know what happened, even if they do not agree on the facts; what matters is that they carry this knowledge with them into a present from which the incident in question recedes further every day. The younger generations *don't know*; they do not bear with them, embodied in their very persons, the poisonous, destructive knowledge of violence that is essentially retrograde, drawing people back to the past in their emotions and arguments. These old men are "the last who know," they say; their knowledge will die with them, and perhaps the conflict will die as well. Even if their deaths are the cost of peace, then, it is perhaps a hopeful question that Andreas asks in his final line: Why wouldn't society recover after that? Why wouldn't history begin again?

I attended the premiere of *Birds of a Feather* at the Lemesos International Documentary Film Festival in August 2012. Theatro Ena, a historic theater in the old municipal market area by the waterfront of Lemesos (known in English as Limassol), was full beyond capacity, with about 150 people seated in folding chairs and another few dozen standing. The audience included many people I knew—teachers, activists, academics, and artists I had seen at cultural events in Nicosia as well. After the closing credits, the festival organizers invited Stefanos Evripidou, the producer and codirector of the film (also a prolific and well-known journalist for *Cyprus Mail*, the only English-language daily newspaper published in Cyprus), to stand and take questions. Thirty seconds of silence ticked by before a man in the back of the theater asked him, in English: *What was your motivation for making this film? So many films have been made about the Cyprus Problem. Do you have a new perspective?*



Evripidou laughed good-naturedly. *Maybe the economy is more important now than the Cyprus Problem!* Two days earlier, *Children of the Riots*, a film by Christos Georgiou about young people involved in street protests in Greece during the early days of the economic crisis, had screened to a packed house; that crisis was on its way to Cyprus as we watched. Evripidou continued, *What was our motivation? It seemed like no one could actually talk about history. We got tired of Greek Cypriots and Turkish Cypriots doing bicommunal work, or doing nothing, but not having conversations, and not listening. Rather than trying to change opinions, we hope this film just gives some perspective.*

The next question came from the front, in Greek: *Have you seen the documentary made by Christopher Hitchens,* Cyprus: Stranded in Time*? That film gives a tit-for-tat perspective on the conflict. What do you think of that? Do you think Cyprus is an occupied country?*

Evripidou demurred, repeating the question in English for the audience, and answering that he had not seen the film. *I can't give an opinion on that,* he said. *But it's from here that dialogue starts!*

What could he have said? The questioner's reference to Hitchens was, it seemed to me, a challenge to Evripidou to abandon the assiduously even-handed perspective he had achieved in his film and sustained in his address to the audience—his invitation to dialogue rather than opinion. Hitchens, a notoriously contrarian polemicist, had spent years in Cyprus as a foreign correspondent for the *New Left Review* and the *New Statesman*, during and after the war. In 1984, he authored one of the internationally best-known works on the Cyprus conflict, *Hostage to History: Cyprus from the Ottomans to Kissinger*, considered by some a work of conspiracy theory, as it doggedly mounts the case, with much evidence from confidential sources, that NATO powers—the United States, the United Kingdom, Turkey, and Greece—colluded in the division of Cyprus in the service of their own Cold War geopolitical interests. The film to which the audience member had referred—a BBC television documentary made in 1989 as part of the *Frontiers* series—followed the same line as Hitchens, the narrator and central character of the film, who travels throughout the island, itemizing the "absurdity" of the division and its disastrous consequences for the people he calls "ordinary" Cypriots.[5]

*Do you think Cyprus is an occupied country?* The question, its blunt abruptness so out of keeping with the measured tone of Evripidou's film, implied that Cyprus was indeed a hostage—of Turkey, perhaps, or the UN, or, as Hitchens had it, history itself. The questioner seemed to be pushing Evripidou to take a position, to say what he knew about who was to blame for the war and the long-standing division, and not to retreat, in bad faith, behind dialogue and listening. The filmmaker had, after all, already expressed his frustration with the inefficacy of bicommunal work—activist cooperation between Greek Cypriots and Turkish Cypriots that endlessly rehearsed the ideology of peace while turning a deaf ear to factual disputes and demands for accountability. Evripidou said he wanted his film to "give some perspective"; the first audience member to speak had wondered whether he had a "new perspective" to give. Was there something more this film could be made to say—something this audience wanted to know and did not already know about the Cyprus conflict?

*Birds of a Feather* was, at that moment, a party to a conversation taking place throughout Cyprus by way of documentary films and their public screenings: a conversation in which familiar places, people, and stories were reassembled from historical fragments and re-presented for collective recognition and inquiry. It was a conversation about the good of knowing Cyprus's history of conflict, in two conflicting senses. In one sense, the good of knowing described an ethical orientation: a valorization of truth as a prerequisite for recovery and reconciliation. The other sense, borne of a more suspicious sensibility, took the form of questioning. What was the good of knowing, when knowledge itself was so fragile, partial, and debat-

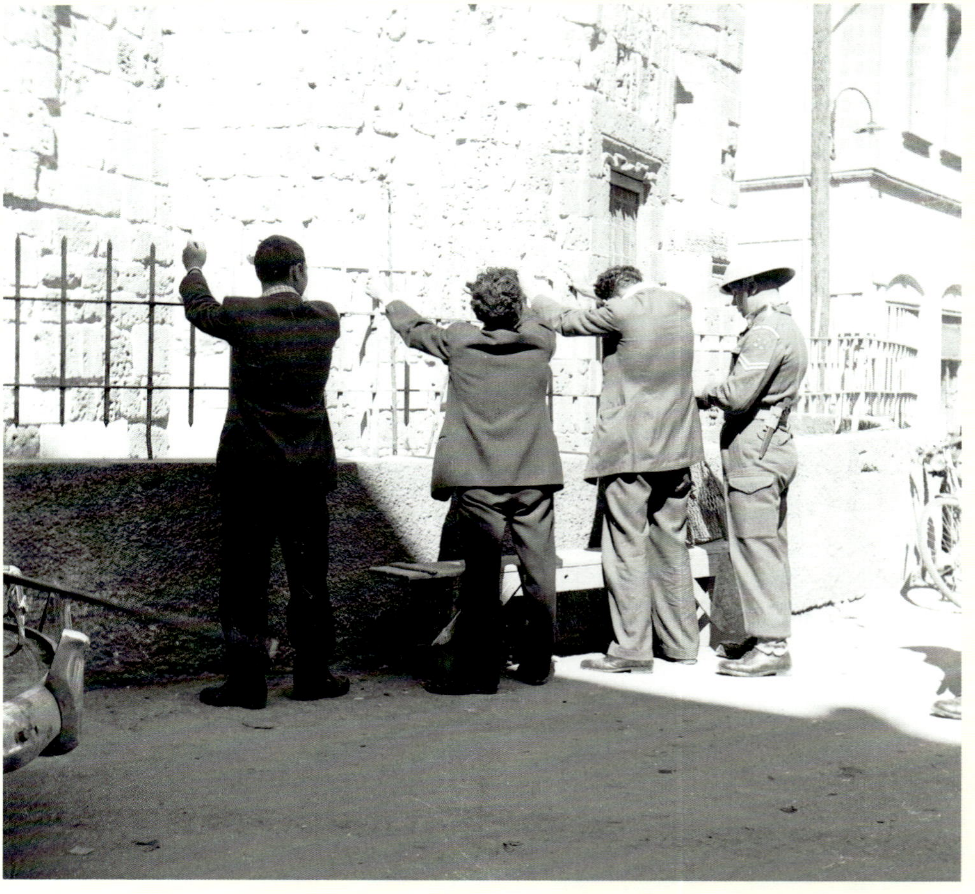

NO.

P.2

able; when it carried the memory and the threat of harm; when it inexorably pulled people into conflicts they had not yet and might never overcome; or when it merely disclosed, again, what everyone already knew? This tension within the good of knowing conditioned, I think, how many Cypriots came to understand themselves as subjects of history, forty years after the war and counting. This book is about the many ways in which they made knowledge and assimilated knowledge in that process of understanding—and the existential challenge posed to them by the indeterminate status of knowledge that cannot be shared.

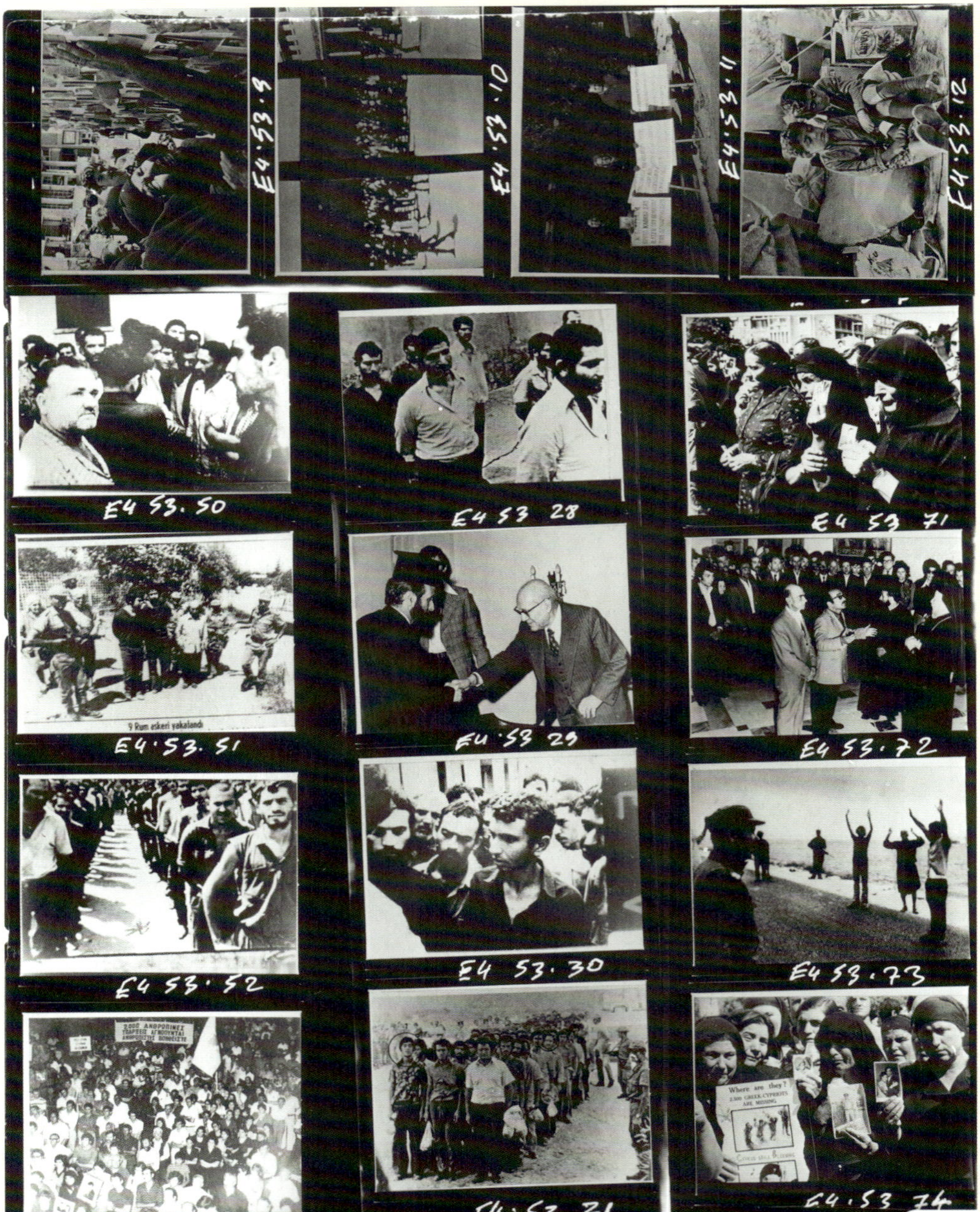
E4'53.9
E4'53.10
E4'53.11
E4'53.12
E4 53.50
E4 53 28
E4 53 71
9 Rum askeri yakalandı
E4'53.51
E4'53 29
E4 53.72
E4 53.52
E4 53.30
E4 53.73
Where are they?
ARE MISSING
E4'53 31
E4.53 74

NO.

P.3

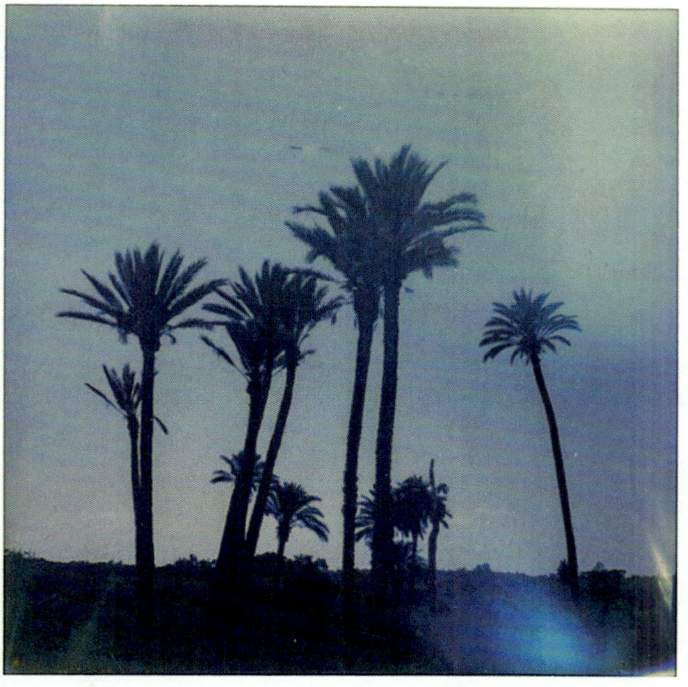

NO.

P.4

# Introduction

## Conflict as Such

The facts of the past are contested, however often they are repeated. The line of division across Cyprus—known as the Green Line, and also, by some and not others, as "the border"—first marked the separation of Greek-Cypriot and Turkish-Cypriot municipal authorities in Nicosia, the capital city, in 1958. It was designated as a UN cease-fire line following devastating episodes of paramilitary and civil violence in 1963, and became a permanent de facto partition after the war in 1974. For the period between 1963 and 1974, when the cease-fire line definitively separated these populations, authorities in the north reported 1,800 Turkish Cypriots killed and 492 missing; authorities in the south reported 3,000 Greek Cypriots killed and 1,510 missing.[1] During the same period, almost 215,000 Cypriots were displaced: about a third of the Greek-Cypriot population and half the Turkish-Cypriot population.[2]

The Republic of Cyprus is the de facto name of the regime in the south, which claims continuity with the sovereign nation declared independent from Great Britain in 1960, and which enjoys international recognition as well as membership in the European Union; I call it "the Republic" or "the south" in this book, knowing from experience that even these terms will offend or even outrage some who would just call it "Cyprus," as if plain and simple. The regime in the north, which unilaterally declared itself an independent sovereign nation in 1983 but is recognized as such only by Turkey, is officially named the Turkish Republic of Northern Cyprus; I call it "the TRNC" or "the north" here, though in the south it is commonly known as "the occupied territories" (τα κατεχόμενα), in contrast to "the free areas" of the Republic. The territory of the TRNC—though not the regime—also belongs to the European Union, in theory if not in practice. In thus referring to the sides of the division, I am following the minority practice of some of my interlocutors, honed with much painful trial and error, and designed to facilitate respectful communication and mutual understanding among people living on one side or the other, who have survived or inherited one history of violence or the other and aspire—perhaps impossibly—not to reproduce those histories in their use of names and terms.

As I write these opening lines, I recall the remarks of a Cypriot friend some years ago, as we were spending a blistering summer afternoon in the shady backyard of his father's house in north Nicosia. At that time, my friend had just finished his dissertation on the history of property in Cyprus. One of his advisers had suggested that he remove an early chapter detailing the history of the Cyprus conflict, since it was not directly pertinent to his research on Ottoman and British policies of land tenure. But my friend had fought to keep the chapter: *Every Cypriot thinks he has to write a treatise explaining the Cyprus conflict from the beginning,* he said to me, laughing. *It's my birthright to write it!*[3]

How far back must we go, to give an account of the Cyprus conflict from the beginning? To the founding of the Republic of Cyprus in 1960, following four years of guerrilla warfare waged against British authorities as well as Turkish Cypriots by Greek-Cypriot radicals? To the British, ruling from 1898 to 1960, who introduced an ethnonational division between Greek Cypriots and Turkish Cypriots as a critical tactic of divide and rule? To the Ottomans, ruling from 1571 to 1898, who governed the inhabitants of Cyprus as discrete and unequal religious communities? To the Venetians, ruling from 1489 to 1571, who militarized the island and built its fortress geography? To the Lusignans, ruling from 1192 to 1489, who introduced feudal government, dispossessing Indigenous residents and concentrating massive estates in no-

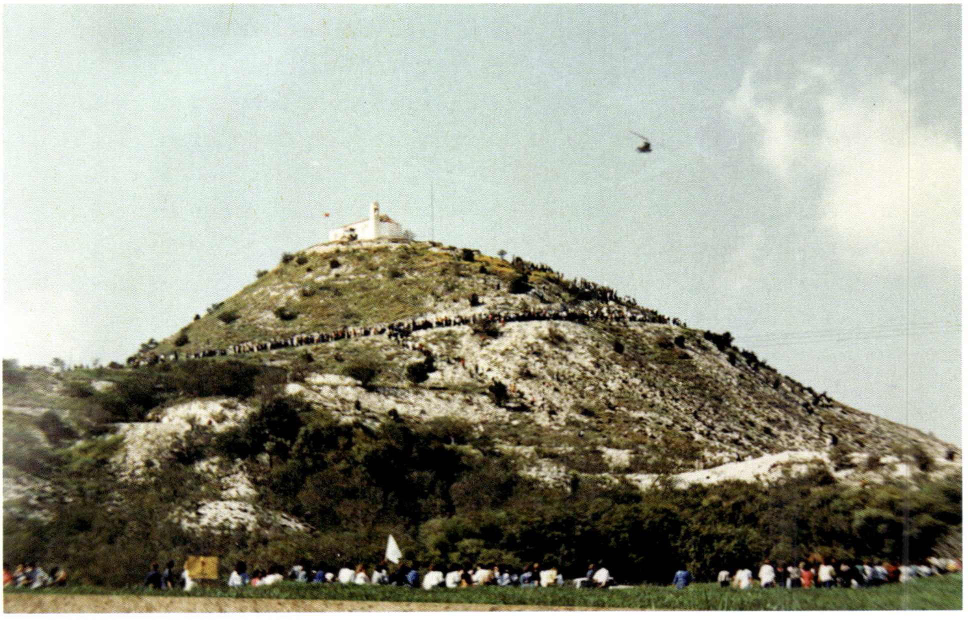

NO.

I.1

ble and foreign hands? To the Byzantines, ruling from 330 to 1191, who administered the growth of Orthodox Christianity throughout the island, in bloody wars with European Catholic and Arab Muslim crusaders and invaders? To the ancients—the Mycenaeans, Assyrians, Egyptians, Persians, Ionians, Hellenes, and Romans—the earliest inhabitants of this "island of Aphrodite" and the earliest war makers, whose artifacts are still being excavated and celebrated in Greek-Cypriot nationalist claims to the origins of Western civilization? How far back in historical time, and through how many imperial formations of culture and political economy, should the division of Cyprus be traced?

When I first conceived the idea for a research project on the so-called Cyprus conflict, and began to educate myself about the many debates that remained unresolved, I armed myself with what I thought were urgent questions about the nature of conflict and prospects for reconciliation. But the more I read, and the more I learned from those who became my interlocutors and friends in Cyprus, the less solid the conflict became as grounds for my research. Giving an account of the Cyprus conflict was not, of course, my birthright, but my position as a foreigner was equally delimited by this task. The unremitting focus on conflict on the part of Cypriot and foreign researchers quickly showed itself as a trap for my own work, mostly conducted inside a peace-minded community of activists, writers, teachers, artists, journalists, scientists, and academics.[4] These people, my interlocutors, defined their aspirations in opposition to conservatives, the majority of Cypriots, who resisted reunification for different reasons in the north and the south; and especially to ultranationalist and neofascist groups like the Grey Wolves in the north, and ELAM (Εθνικό Λαϊκό Μέτωπο)—the National Popular Front party, closely linked with Golden Dawn in Greece—that emerged in the south in the early 2000s. The rise in auto and pedestrian traffic between north and south since the opening of checkpoints in 2003, and the revivification of the dead zone at the center of divided Nicosia, had fostered the growth of an antinationalist, multicommunal political culture whose origins can be traced to bicommunal groups active since the 1980s—something like a "minor" community, perhaps, in Deleuze and Guattari's ([1975] 1986) sense of an essentially political collective that speaks in a majority language from a marginal (in this case, postcolonial and antinationalist) position. In my experience, members of this community for the most part took for granted that multiple perspectives on the conflict—and indeed multiple histories entailing incompatible factual claims—were present and arguable. At the same time, they often expressed frustration and even boredom with the perennial posing of the Cyprus conflict as such. The chronic impasse in regard to a political settlement, the perpetual reiteration of entrenched positions, the stale terms of discussion, the occlusion or outright exclusion from consideration of other political problems in Cyprus, and the intractable self-congratulatory demeanor adopted by people across the political spectrum: all these features of the Cyprus conflict played a part in disposing progressive Cypriots to disaffection with activism and activist production of knowledge and culture.

*Artifactual* is born of this impasse: a situation of crisis, of opening, and still, of waiting. Although a plan for reunification has persisted as a dominant issue (if not *the* dominant issue) in Cypriot politics since 1974, the Green Line remains in place at the time of this writing. I have heard many Cypriots say that the division has become more entrenched and normalized—as well as more profitable—since the opening of checkpoints between north and south in 2003, and Cyprus's accession to the European Union in 2004 as a divided country.[5] United Nations–mediated negotiations between Greek-Cypriot and Turkish-Cypriot authorities in 2008–10, 2010–12, 2014, 2015–17, and 2021 opened and closed, quickly folded into a history of the same. But beyond this terrain of official state politics, an undeniable cultural shift has taken place in Cyprus in the last twenty or so years: a post-ethnonationalist vision of Cyprus's future has emerged along with a vigorous, multivocal questioning of its past.[6]

Such questioning is by no means a priority in all areas of governance in Cyprus. Other grave matters have provoked protests, rumors, and demands for change, but not widespread, organized calls for investigation and reform or intensive research and creative projects: matters such as human trafficking, the multiplex precarity of migrant workers, black markets for weapons and drugs, offshore banking, the prison system, and the political activities of religious institutions. The Cyprus conflict is one area where transparency is valorized and actively pursued by Cypriots across the political spectrum—perhaps because, as Marios Constantinou (2006), Olga Demetriou (2018), and Demetriou and Ayla Gürel (2008) have shown, the division has so thoroughly determined the structure and operations of government since the founding of the Republic in 1960. It has also oriented demands for reform toward supranational organizations—the UN and the EU, especially—which helps to explain why claims for information about the events leading up to the division are often framed by Cypriots in human rights language, in terms of their "right to know" (Bryant 2010; Demetriou and Gürel 2008; Kovras 2008; Kyriakou 2011, 2012a, 2012b; Sant Cassia 2005; Yakinthou 2008).

Why do Cypriots want to know what happened, so many years after the violence? What kind of knowledge do they seek? And is that knowledge effective? In this book, I take up these questions, exploring two interrelated areas of knowledge production about the violence of the 1960s–1970s: forensic science and documentary film. My ethnography follows the forensic archaeologists and anthropologists who work to locate, exhume, identify, and repatriate the remains of Cypriots killed in episodes of violence and buried in secret graves before and during the war, from 1963 to 1974, as well as filmmakers who use archival photographs and film footage from this period in their contemporary films, installations, and publications. In my analysis, I work through the dynamics of secrecy and revelation that animate the production of these knowledges and their reception, exploring the aims and ends to which they are differently tied. I examine how these knowledges interact in Cypriot political and cultural life: how they reinforce, supplement, or undermine each another. And I show how these knowledges about their history of violence have come to inform the hope some Cypriots feel for an open, democratic, unified society; or the certainty, felt by others, that this will never come to pass.



Artifacts are the special matter shared by the forensic scientists and documentary filmmakers whose knowledge making I document in this book: material remains (or remainders[7]) that are exhumed or otherwise uncovered, examined, and made to reveal something about the past. Bones and archival images are the artifacts, in this sense, that anchored and molded the knowledge projects pursued by my interlocutors. But I use the term "artifact" in this book as more than a commonplace label for this kind of matter. I do not want to place much conceptual weight on definitions, especially etymological ones; language is dynamic, and it would be foolish to equate meanings with origins, as Michel Foucault (1980, 140) argued in his essay on Nietzschean genealogy—a historical method that is categorically opposed to the search for origins.[8] In any case, the significance of a concept exceeds the semantic resources of any language in which it might be expressed, which makes translation a much more interesting context for conceptual work than etymology. That said, I chose the title *Artifactual* for this book in part because I wanted to amplify the double entendre of "fact" (from the Latin *factum*, any number of etymological sources tell me, meaning an act or fact) as something both done and known. "Art(i)-" accentuates the doing of the fact, the process of skillful crafting: the art of making facts.

This notion of artifacts as skillful works of knowledge will, I hope, redistribute into a different conceptual form what Bruno Latour long ago observed as "the 'dialectic' between fact and artifact": an "impossible antinomy," as he put it, that deeply vexed both the realists and the constructivists he caricatured, who were unable either to hold to the purity of their positions or to resolve what they perceived as the paradoxical nature of experimentally "made up" scientific facts, being both "manmade" (in contingent, situated lab settings) and decidedly "*not* manmade" (but rather "out there" in the world), both "fabricated and not fabricated" (Latour 1999, 125). Even longer ago, pursuing a "usable doctrine of objectivity" for feminists seeking "a better account of the world" than positivist science had yet offered, Donna Haraway also rejected "the radical social constructionist programme" that framed the "artefacts and facts" of "manufactured" scientific knowledge as nothing more than "parts of the powerful art of rhetoric" in which "truth claims of hostile science" were made, debated, and accepted (Haraway 1991, 188, 187, 186–87, 185, 184, 185, 186). The "feminist critical empiricism" proposed by Haraway (1991, 188), and the ever-proliferating vocabulary developed by Latour and others—starting with "actants" and "propositions"—were meant to accommodate and resolve the apparent paradox of scientific artifacts by reconceptualizing the entities and relations that populate and structure the networks that characterize the events and situations in the world that we care about and thus care to know about. This undertaking in science studies and adjacent fields has, over a few generations, helped to destabilize the boundaries between ontology and epistemology that were once commonsensical in the history and anthropology of science, at least on Latour's account.[9] The destabilization of those boundaries—our living and thinking with the intractable, irreducible mutual entanglement and entailment of what a thing is and how we know what we know about it—has in turn made many other analytic moves possible (or, if they were already possible, more intelligible), including one that is key to this book: the understanding of artifacts as temporal operators.

Raised (partly) in this tradition of science studies myself, in describing my interlocutors' work throughout this book, I routinely refer to knowledge making, knowledge production, and knowledge projects, rather than to truth or, in a specifically Foucauldian register, truth games or truth regimes, which concern the very means by which truth as such is discursively established and distinguished from what is false, irrelevant, or nonsensical.[10] This is largely because, in the practices of my interlocutors, I do not think their onto-epistemological premises or procedures were being challenged or transformed by failures or alternatives; the way facts should be made in human biology, physical anthropology, archaeology, ecological science, and history (by which I mean historicism; more on this, below)—the knowledge fields most often in play here—was not being questioned. That does not mean the knowledge my interlocutors produced was not questioned; indeed, it was. But that questioning was conducted in the terms of the domi-

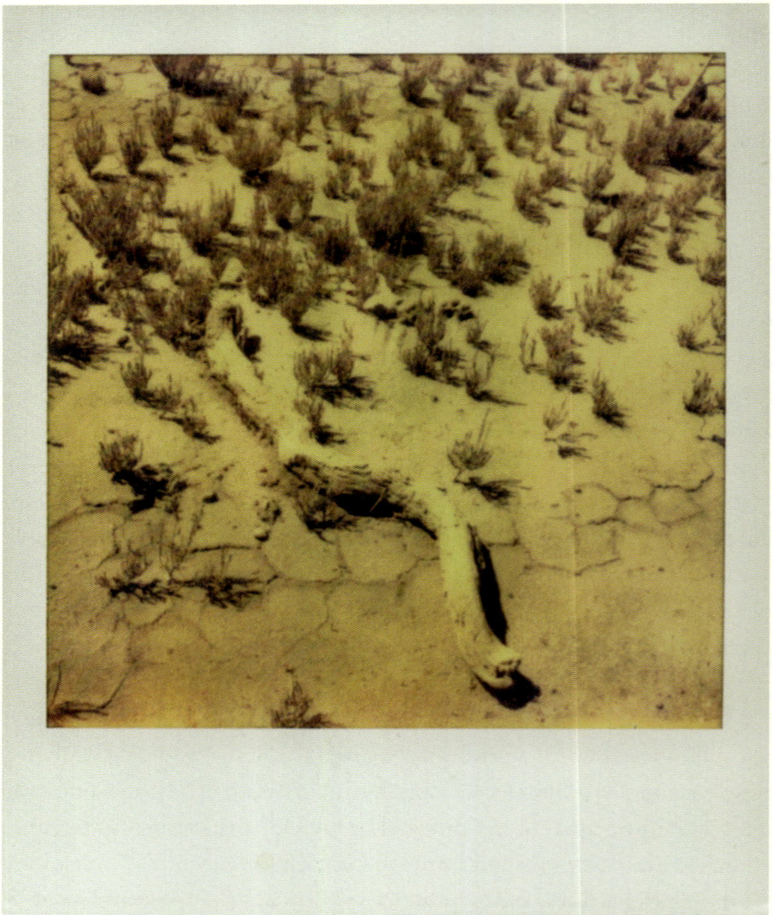

*NO.*

**I.2**

nant truth game: on grounds of suspicion that something was being hidden, distorted, or otherwise misrepresented, and thus that the true facts could be revealed or concluded without changing the onto-epistemological rules of the game. (I have more to say on suspicion, too, in the last section of this introduction.)

Thus, the forensic scientists and documentary filmmakers whose work I examine here often had specific and discrete goals that they could meet with the onto-epistemological tools at hand: to determine the singular identity of a set of human remains, to learn what had happened in a particular village on a particular day, to map the movement of people and things and money, to recover a memory or confirm the details of a story. The tools they used to investigate and analyze the artifacts they handled were important and effective insofar as they prepared those artifacts to link up with narratives about the past that were already at work in Cypriot public culture, shaping consensus reality—even if, on the unstable grounds of enduring conflict, consensus reality was especially hard to affirm, or enlarge, with such pieces of empirical knowledge. As a descriptor, then, "artifactual" conveys not only how knowledge is made (from what materials, with what tools, in what circumstances and time frames) but also, and more important, why knowledge is made: to what ends, in the service of which stories.

In the context of long-enduring social division in Cyprus, and therefore the long-enduring coexistence of incompatible narratives about the past, the artifactuality of knowledge signals its special fragility and falsifiability: again, not in onto-epistemological terms, but rather in social and political ones. These are the stakes of studying conflict as such, as I came to understand when I began conducting my own research in Cyprus. "Conflict" itself was a negotiated term, I learned—one of many by-products of self-censorship on the part of Cypriots who did not want to appear to be taking sides in the division they had inherited. The negotiated safe vocabulary for discussing conflict was delicate and sometimes sardonic; for some terms known to cause offense, there were "no agreed alternatives," as noted in *Words That Matter: A Glossary for Journalism in Cyprus*, authored by Turkish-Cypriot and Greek-Cypriot journalists in 2018 (Azgın et al. 2018).[11] I found many progressive Cypriots reluctantly but resignedly describing the actions of Turkish armed forces in the summer of 1974, for example, as a "military intervention" rather than an "invasion" or "occupation" (terms used commonly in the south) or a "peace operation" (a term used officially in the north). Violence done to people and property was often named "tension," and its agency as "ethnic" or "intercommunal" rather than "state" or "paramilitary." I found myself broaching conversations in this intricate, frail, fraught idiom that sometimes seemed to me to be uncompelling to Cypriots themselves—people so rehearsed in the terminology of the conflict that I suspected it might be more interesting for them to discuss other issues with me. Not to discuss the conflict at all, however, would be to accede to the normalization of the division—a position that many found untenable, not only politically but also morally and socially.

Was there any room for discovery in this double bind? How could I pursue knowledge in a context where everything that could be said had already been said, and the people I sought out as experts were reluctant to say it all again? And who was I to aspire to discovery, anyway? The overly well-trod ground of conflict studies in Cyprus came to stand, in my mind, for critical questions about the innovation, authorship, and ownership of knowledge that I could not answer. I wondered how to tell the difference between wanting to know and wanting to be "in the know," as Diane Nelson puts that ambiguous, burdensome insider status in her work on reckoning with the history of genocide in Guatemala (Nelson 2009, e.g., xxxiii, 30, 153). As I began my own research in Cyprus, some of the people I sought out as experts warned me that I might encounter difficulties picking my way through the turf claims of Cypriots who had worked so hard to carve out even the smallest corner of expertise on the conflict. Competition for the attention of a small public, and for scant funding to launch education projects, archive projects, oral history projects, and art projects, raised the guard of Cypriot researchers and activists. *People don't talk to each other here,* a political scientist told me, during my second trip to Cyprus in 2010. She had been working for several years at a nongovernmental organization that was about to fold, for financial and personnel reasons. *You have to be very careful not to threaten anyone. You have to stroke their egos. Treat them like kings—that's what Cypriots want!* And then, laughing, but not offering to play this role herself: *What you really need is a godfather, to vouch for you and open doors.* In many of my other conversations with Cypriot researchers and activists, they described Cypriot culture as crippled by scandal, clientelism, and conspiracism: sheepish or melancholic descriptions that gave them space to disidentify with aspirations to knowledge even as they were actively, if ambivalently, pursuing it themselves. In my own research, I did encounter a few gatekeepers who declined to talk with me, discouraged my curiosity, or disparaged my naïveté (or perhaps my arrogance) in trying to "do something" in Cyprus. I also found a few godparents, who did open some doors for me, in time.

One of these was a Cypriot art historian whom I met in November 2011, and who ultimately became a close friend. At our first meeting, I found him friendly and good-humored; he had spent many years in the UK and could adopt, he said, an outsider's perspective on Cyprus. Over lunch, we talked about conspiracy theories and a recent documentary film about the so-called children of the division in Cyprus. When we got around to the question at hand—namely, what I wanted to know from him—I told him that I was interested in studying knowledge about the conflict. *Which conflict?* he asked me, pointedly. I paused, realizing I must have taken something for granted. *There are many conflicts in Cyprus,* he explained. *They're obscured by the focus on the conflict between Greek Cypriots and Turkish Cypriots. But there are many other kinds of difference here.* He told me about the long-standing Armenian and Maronite communities in Cyprus, who had been forced to side with a majority community—Greek-Cypriot or Turkish-Cypriot—after the division in 1974. The Maronites had chosen the Greek-Cypriot side, he said, but had also developed their own nationalist politics, celebrating their Lebanese ancestry and identifying Lebanon rather than Cyprus as their homeland. Yet they were never discussed as part of the Cyprus conflict.

Then there was class conflict. The historian detailed for me the formation of the Communist Party of Cyprus (KKK) in 1926 and its abolishment by the British following the October Revolt against colonial rule in 1931. But the party continued to operate in the shadows, he said, founding trade unions and fostering working-class and peasant solidarities—including all ethnic and religious communities—through the 1930s–40s. The unions remained the only legal vehicles for leftist organization until AKEL, the new (and current) communist party, was founded in 1941. *This struggle has been completely forgotten in Cyprus,* he observed, noting that class-based cooperation and mutual assistance between Greek Cypriots and Turkish Cypriots were derailed by intercommunal tension and violence from the 1950s onward.

Then, too, there was conflict over immigration. *Surely you've noticed the presence of migrants here?* the historian asked me. He described the movement to Cyprus of people from the Philippines, south Asia, eastern Europe, and west Africa since the 1990s, occasioned by the collapse of the Soviet Union and intensifying since 2004, when Cyprus joined the European Union. *These people are victimized in many ways,* he told me: sex trafficking, exploitative employment, hazardous housing, police harassment, the state's informal policy of refusing all asylum claims. *But they're blamed for everything.*

In laying out these additional axes of conflict in Cyprus for me, the historian seemed to be pushing for their equal footing with the conflict between Greek Cypriots and Turkish Cypriots. In that push, the door he had opened for me led back to the Cyprus conflict. The division between Greek-

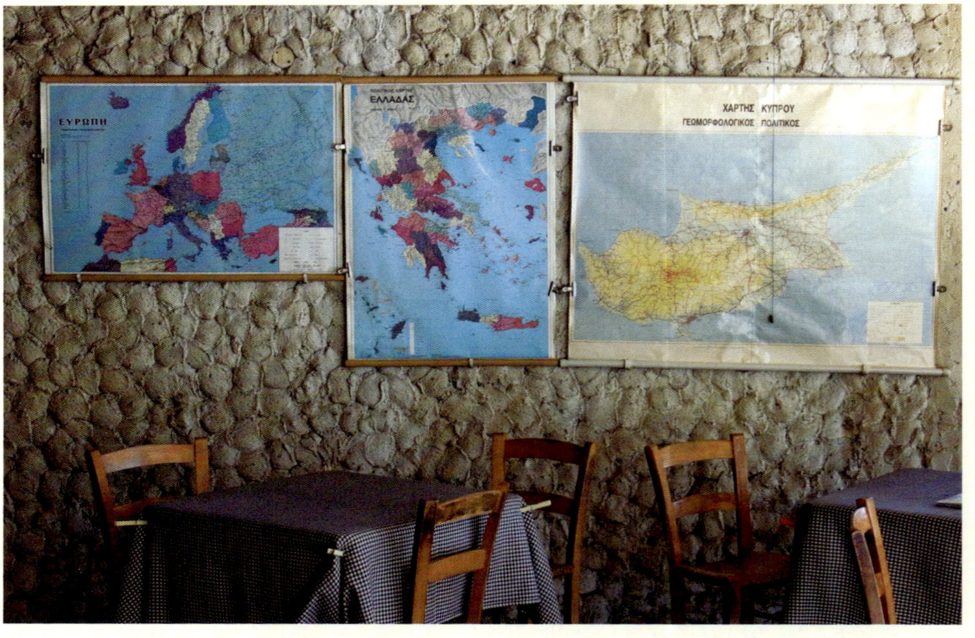


NO.

I.3

Cypriot and Turkish-Cypriot communities had already so thoroughly colonized social and political life in Cyprus that other struggles and divisions inevitably appeared in relation to it: as dimensions and effects of it or, on the other hand, as social and political problems in their own right that the division mystified and obscured—what anthropologist Olga Demetriou has called "minor losses" (Demetriou 2018, e.g., 2, 22, 56). As I got to know Cypriot researchers and activists who addressed other such problems in Cyprus—poverty, corruption, sexism, xenophobia, the broken system of political asylum—I became increasingly self-conscious about my own focus on the Cyprus conflict. Perhaps it was only by way of justifying that focus that I began to see the closed horizon of conflict as, itself, an artifact of conflict: an effect of living in enduring division, an experience that yielded urgent desires to know what had happened and how, but that determined all such knowledge as a repetition of division.

That repetition was most obvious to me in the intractability of the positions my interlocutors occupied (and still occupy) in relation to the division, despite the aspirations many expressed to overcome those positions somehow. I knew no one engaged in knowledge projects in Cyprus who did their work with equal or comparable depth, reflexivity, and creativity on both sides of the divide; I knew no one who was neutral, no one who was fully mobile between north and south, and no one who claimed to be. Their projects conveyed "situated knowledges," as Donna Haraway names a kind of knowing counterposed to the rationalist detachment that she associates with modern science, but also to relativism—both being "god tricks promising vision from everywhere and nowhere equally and fully" (1991, 584). Marilyn Strathern ([1991] 2004, xvi) framed this problem of situatedness in anthropological knowledge making as an artifact of the historical shift she was observing in the 1980s from a "perspectival" to a "postplural" anthropology—from, that is, a relativism necessitated by the fact of multiple perspectives (I see the world from my perspective, you from yours) to a partiality necessitated by the fact of fractal perspectives (I see infinitely multipliable and recombinant facets of worlds, rather than one whole world—and you do, too). This postplural epistemology does not speak to or about wholes, social or otherwise. Situated knowledges, likewise, Haraway says, take "the view from a body, always a complex, contradictory, structuring and structured body, versus the view from above, from nowhere, from simplicity" (1991, 589). In arguing for feminist objectivity as a modality of knowledge making, she raises the question of how to see from the body—how to establish a vantage "from below" that is not one perspective relative to others but rather an avowed partiality that cannot stand alone, though it can link up with other partialities in "webs of connection" to form "shared conversations" (Haraway 1991, 191).

With this question in mind (a question of such long standing, now, that we might sometimes forget to pose it), I am tempted to suggest that the knowledge projects I studied in Cyprus were, in their partiality, no different from any other—and tempted, then, to reject the kind of exceptionalism I find in so much scholarship on Cyprus that emphasizes its uniqueness and anomalous status on any given register and thereby undercuts the comparative thinking that would facilitate its cultural and political theorization, as I argue elsewhere (Davis, n.d.).[12] And yet I cannot ignore the unyielding presumption of wholeness as an end point for the knowledge projects pursued by many of my interlocutors—their retrojection of one Cypriot society before the division, and their projection of one Cypriot society into the future after reconciliation—as they lived in division and lived out its consequences. The division of Cyprus, enduring throughout their lifetimes without reunification nor definitive separation, contributed a specific and determinate social form to the situatedness of their knowledge. They had grown up on one side of the divide or the other; their friends, families, and professional worlds, their memories and comforts, their fears and desires and blind spots, were rooted on one side or the other. Most spoke either Greek or Turkish natively, but not the other language; even those few who did know both found their options to speak limited by the presence of interlocutors who did not. By consequence, the compulsion to operate in English—also a Cypriot language, established as such in the 1960 Constitution, but no one's primary language except for some visitors and expatriates—was strong and relentless.

As a researcher myself, I was specially (perhaps especially) limited; an outsider by any measure, unrooted on either side of the division, I nevertheless had my biases and preferences. Before coming to Cyprus, I had lived long-term in Greece but not Turkey; I spoke Greek (though not Cypriot Greek) well, but only a little Turkish, and English natively; although I spent time all over the island while conducting my fieldwork, I lived on the south side of divided Nicosia, where Greek and English were the dominant (not to say only) languages, enjoying all the cosmopolitan conveniences of Cyprus's European Union membership that had flowered there since the early 2000s. My limitations joined up with the limitations of my interlocutors to narrow and distort my questioning and learning, in some ways that I believe I can account for, but also in some that, I presume, I cannot. No one I know—least of all me—has achieved a view of a whole Cypriot society. Any attempt to present a balanced picture would thus be an empty gesture; from what vantage, after all—by what "god trick"—could balance be judged? This text, then, can only represent my partiality, in all senses, as I belatedly share in the peculiarly faceted conversation that my interlocutors in Cyprus have been conducting for a very long time.

## Overview

This book is based on field research that I have been conducting in Cyprus since 2007 and as recently as 2021. My fieldwork included a period of ten months in 2011–12, when I worked with the forensic teams of the Committee on Missing Persons (CMP), a bicommunal organization established under UN auspices that is charged with determining the location and identity of the bodies of over two thousand Cypriots who went missing during the violence of the 1960s–1970s. With the CMP, I worked both on field excavations throughout Cyprus and in the laboratory in central Nicosia where human remains were examined and identified. During that same period, I involved myself in the activities of several organizations and institutes for public media recently established in Nicosia's dead zone, and attended dozens of documentary film screenings and exhibitions of art and archival photographs in Nicosia and other cities. I thus came to know well a number of filmmakers, photographers, and archivists whose work has been critical to the development of a public, visual vocabulary of conflict and peacemaking in Cyprus.



Part one of this book addresses the forensic investigations conducted by the CMP. For decades, as investigative journalists on both sides of the division have shown, state authorities in the north and the south blocked the CMP's investigations, concealing information about the deaths of the missing and the location of their bodies, and either encouraging relatives to put the past behind them (in the north) or cynically nurturing the hope among relatives that their loved ones might still be alive (in the south).[13] Since 2004, when the recovery of the missing was separated from other issues relating to political settlement and newly framed as a nonpolitical humanitarian project, the CMP has been conducting investigations at a rapid pace with the controversial mandate, laid down in its terms of reference, not to "attribute responsibility for the deaths of any missing persons or make findings as to the cause of such deaths."[14] This mandate is grounded in an ideology of closure—an expectation that confirming the deaths of the missing and returning their remains to their families, and thus naming the bodies of the missing but not the perpetrators of their deaths, will suffice to heal the wounds of the past and clear a path toward reunification.

Reckoning with the deaths of the missing, then, to the extent that it happens today, takes the form of mourning rather than accounting.[15] The concealment of evidence that could be used to seek justice for these deaths is a constitutive part of the investigation process, which proceeds from the anonymization of witness testimony, to the destruction of gravesites through excavation, to the storage of forensic photographs and findings in confidential archives. Despite this secrecy surrounding the precise fate of missing persons, the CMP has received a great deal of media coverage in Cyprus in recent years, and the forensic teams have featured in a number of television broadcasts and documentary films. Images of scientists working with bones have become as commonplace as those of anguished relatives in representations of Cyprus's violent history, while forensic evidence has replaced grief as the public form of positive knowledge of that violence: empirical evidence determining the fact of death. But this evidence radically delimits what it means to know what happened: to be certain of death without knowing its cause and circumstances. In exploring the material, social, and imaginary dimensions of these forensic investigations in Cyprus, I show how this process participates in an ideology of transparency that sometimes reproduces secrecy, suspicion, and impasse rather than resolving unanswered questions.

In part one, then, I pay special attention to the dynamic activity of the artifacts of death, the hard evidence of violence at the center of so much concealing and revealing (and concealing again). The bones and belongings of the missing, exhumed painstakingly from mass graves and laid out on tables for analysis, identified and photographed, cataloged and archived before their reburial, are scripted in the narrative of healing and closure promoted by the CMP as the brute facts of death to be ascertained—and thus as substitutes for other truths that cannot be disclosed publicly. These artifacts objectify knowledge about the violence of the past that remains ever present in the ongoing division of people and places in Cyprus. Exploring this process of objectification—the transformation of suspicion into material objects, and of those objects into objective proof—I examine the intimate and complex work scientists do to "see" a missing person in his or her bones: a work of reconstruction, simulation, imagination, and humanization. And I consider what this knowledge does to the scientists, in turn.

Part two of this book addresses the visual archive of violence in Cyprus, and how this archive has been used in artistic and political projects of reckoning with the past through documentary film. Venues for film production and screening have proliferated in urban Cyprus since the checkpoints opened in 2003: places where filmmakers collaborate with one another and connect with audiences, and where relationships take shape among filmmakers, artists, journalists, scholars, and other producers of knowledge and culture. Public screenings of documentary films in Cyprus have formed a new social space where intergenerational and intercommunal encounters with the past can happen; indeed, these screenings seemed to me, during the time of my fieldwork, to be among the most popular and productive spaces for discussion and debate about the history of division. But the affective dynamics of identification and catharsis in these encounters often deflected examination of the archive as a source of evidence. Those filmmakers who turned to archives to learn something about the past that they did not already know often found themselves trading in stock images and footage, offering generic depictions of war and the peaceful times before, and thus reproducing the very narratives they sought to contest.



In part two, then, I consider how documentary filmmakers in Cyprus have tried to resolve this archival dilemma—this tension between conventionality and novelty—using footage and photographs of the events of the 1960s–1970s to experiment with the visual representation of Cyprus's violent history. Archival material is flexible, available for resonance with viewers not only in the forensic register of evidence but also in the phenomenological register of experience: of time, confusion, shock, reverberation. I explore how Cypriot filmmakers have tapped into these different registers, presenting archival materials as transparent, uncontested evidence of the events in question; as enhancements of the personal or collective memories of the events belonging to personae in the film; or as open-ended explorations or poetic reveries of the events, without clear veridical stakes or claims to historical truth. I trace the development of an aesthetics of the archive in Cypriot films, both in debates over the terms of use and interpretation appropriate to archival material, and in the cultivation of a taste for such material in documentary film. Notably, some Cypriot filmmakers have deferred the evidentiary problem of the archive, seeking instead an edge to cut through convention in its phenomenological resources—reworking its resolution, speed, palate, clarity, sequencing—in order to engage the sensorium of the audience, not so much to inform as to disturb and to imagine. Other filmmakers have probed the problem of archival evidence from a different direction, fictionalizing historical events and sites of collective memory in their works while refusing documentary classification. What all these approaches share—in their incorporation of archival images, in their visualization of artifacts like ruins and bones, and in their treatment of archival images as artifacts—is a preoccupation with the material presence of the past.

This text is, thus, organized in two main parts, addressing processes of knowledge making that I encountered in my fieldwork as somewhat distinct domains, phenomenally and socially. Their separation in the book, however, is artificial, contrived to set intelligible parameters for my ethnographic exploration and analysis—to set contexts, in other words. Forensic investigation and documentary film are mutually implicated in Cyprus, in terms of their shared artifacts—bones and images—and, in some ways, their onto-epistemologies. I have designed this book to manifest both the distinctiveness and the imbrication of these artifacts and onto-epistemologies, highlighting moments when markers of one kind of knowledge appear in the context of another—as in the archaeological metaphors of time (burying and digging the past, for example) that pervade documentary films about the division, and, likewise, the understanding of bones as pictures of the past that framed forensic analysis at the lab. Beyond the special affinities between forensic and documentary investigation expressed by these commonplace metaphors, I also track the many ways in which documentary and forensic knowledge directly fed into and extended each other, as in documentary filmmaking about the forensic investigations, and the use of archival photographs and footage by forensic teams to find clues to the location of hidden graves and the identity of missing persons.



Interspersed throughout the book, readers will also find a series of images —I call it an archive—that amplifies my discussion of archives throughout the main text and especially in part two. In constructing this archive, I drew inspiration from several experiments ventured by ethnographers and other writers to perform, in textual form, an experience of archival recursivity.

Key among these experiments are Neni Panourgiá's *parerga*, or "work[s] alongside another main work" (1995, xx), as she writes in her introduction to her first book, *Fragments of Death, Fables of Identity*. On the website for her second book, *Dangerous Citizens: The Greek Left and the Terror of the State*, Panourgiá (2009) describes *parerga* as "alternate stories about the main narrative, or interpretations of events."[16] In these books, her *parerga* include her own commentary on the main text; her memories and stories she has heard from others; archival photographs and documents; letters, lists, poems, and fragments of writings by other authors—all placed obliquely to the main text, either in a parallel text running across the lower portion of each page (in *Fragments of Death*) or in the side margins (in *Dangerous Citizens*), rather than in footnotes or endnotes (although she uses those, too). The archive in my book takes a different form, but I give it a similar rationale; it is, as Panourgiá describes *parerga*, an "additio[n] . . . meant to complete, expand, and augment the main discussion" (1995, xix–xx).[17]

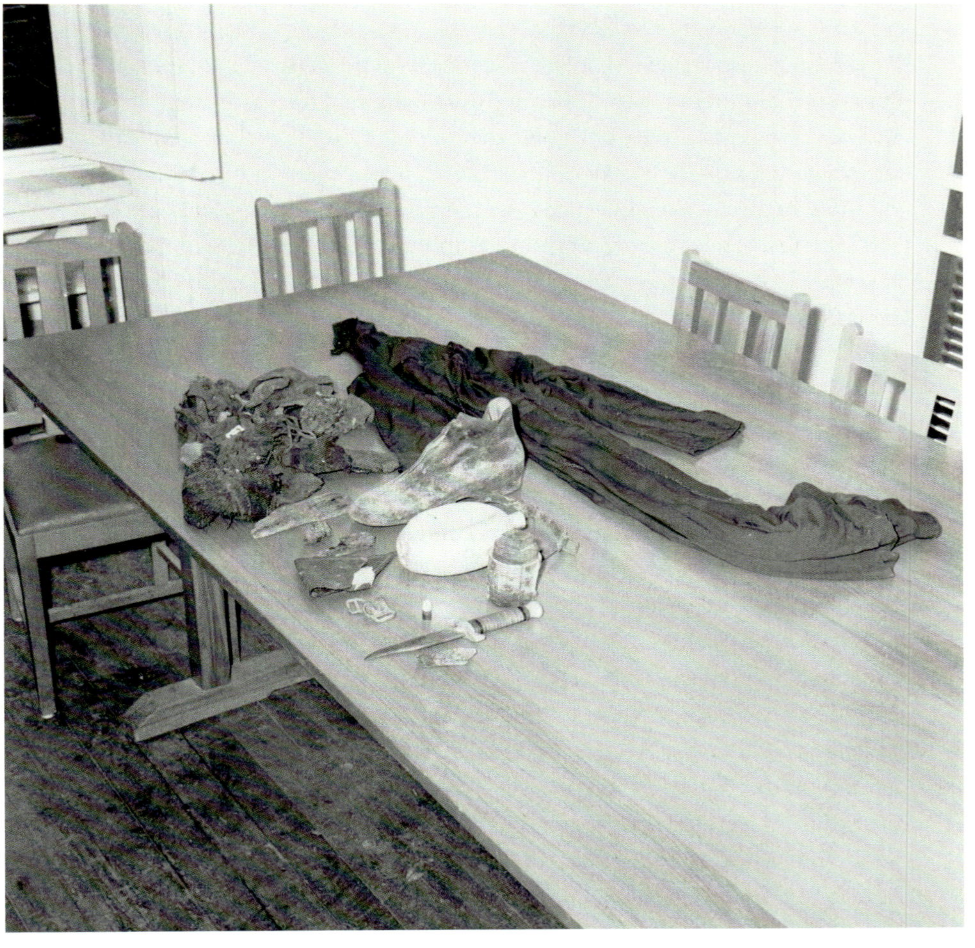

NO.

I.4

Another source of inspiration for this archive is the experimental text *The Wind under My Lips*, composed by Stephanos Stephanides (2018), a Cypriot poet, translator, and comparative literature scholar. The bilingual English/Greek text intercalates Stephanides's poems between passages of autobiographical prose evoking his early childhood in Cyprus in the 1950s; his abrupt, unwanted move at the age of eight to Great Britain after the dissolution of his parents' marriage; and the rambling life of curiosity, creativity, and melancholy that followed.[18] In addition to the visual impression of English facing Greek in the bilingual text, what struck me when I first picked up a copy, newly stacked in a Nicosia bookshop immediately after its publication in 2018, were the images that appeared, every so often, along the top quarter or half of a page: black-and-white photographs of Stephanides and his family members (I gathered) during his early years in Cyprus, printed on the ivory archival-paper pages of the book in the same black-and-gray ink as the text, but without captions. And then, in the last part of the book, interspersed within the pages of one long poem titled "Postcards from Cyprus (Made in India)": pairs of facing pages printed with three color images each, again uncaptioned, depicting scenes of everyday life in contemporary Cyprus. Stephanides notes in his acknowledgments: "The colour photographs were generously contributed by Indian filmmaker Anandana Kapur. The black and white photographs were for the most part taken by my father, Demos Stephanides, in the 1950s" (2018, 8).



This lightest touch of contextualization, making clear that he is not the author of the images, is all that Stephanides offers to indicate to readers how they might receive them. Without captions, the images trouble their own penchant for iconic reference. For readers, they may shape-shift from snapshots of Stephanides's childhood and places in Cyprus where he has lived or visited to images much more loosely articulated with his experience: a genre of imagery whose commonplace familiarity—whose availability to readers as their own experience, or that of someone they know—emphasizes their indexicality; their reference depends on their context. With this technique, Stephanides invites readers to identify with the text: to feel his loss of childhood and home as theirs in some way, to remember and dream and wander with him through the text, without staking this most intimate experience on the singular facts of his biography. It is that kind of experience that I hope the archive in my own book will open for readers.

I compiled this archive from a number of sources: photographs from the Press and Information Office in the Republic of Cyprus, photographs from the CMP in Cyprus, stills and screen grabs from documentary films and art performances, the artworks of Nicos Philippou and Panicos Chrysanthou, my own and others' photographs of places and events and people, and scans of ephemera I collected during fieldwork. Their order in the text and their placement on the page matter, but I hope they will not be received as mere illustrations of the text in whose interstices they appear. Rather, they form a sequence whose reference is internal to the archive; it is another story, told visually.

That story is about the mediation of time, memory, and knowledge by images—a mediation that I would call amnesiac or, with Jacques Derrida (1995, 10, 11), archiviolithic. It is an ongoing process of editing (framing, cutting, concatenating), repressing, repeating, decaying, decontextualizing and recontextualizing, altering and repurposing, that describes both the circulation of these images and the condition of their recognizability and efficacy. My emphasis on this mediation would be undermined by any straightforward captioning—any attempt, that is, to pinpoint their evidentiary value through their iconic representation of events, places, and people. Their reference is more complex, unstable, and problematic than any such captioning might convey. Without captions to stabilize that reference artificially, I hope they may resonate with different readers for different reasons. For some, perhaps especially some Cypriots, their iconic reference to historical events and collective memorial sites in Cyprus may be privileged. For others, they might evoke events, places, and people far afield in time and space from those under discussion in this text; for yet others, they might suggest indeterminate elsewheres and elsewhens, anytimes and anyplaces, familiar from stock footage of other wars.[19] That these images can represent both specifically and generically—as the photographs in Stephanides's text do—is precisely what enables them to perform the mediation I am exploring in this book. Instead of captioning the images on the page, then, I offer an appendix where I attribute copyright, marking the ownership or custody of each image (which may be quite different from its origin or author). In some cases, too, I append commentary that embellishes the main text in a different key or voice (sometimes not my own), more like notes than captions; in this way, the images may refer to and help make sense of the main text without merely illustrating it.

What I want to foreground, by emplacing this series of images in the text, is their metareferential meaning: their common condition of being images that thematize images. Their sequencing generates reference to the production and selection and circulation and repetition of images over time, and thus to how these images have animated and shaped Cypriots' (and others') reckoning of their history of violence and division. In other words, the sequencing of these images constitutes an archive out of an array. Like all archives, this one is essentially incomplete and misleading in its incompleteness if readers expect it to stand for a situation of which it is but a set of fragments, contingently gathered together by the accidents of my own research and writing.

My research for this book was conducted partly in Greek and to a very limited extent Turkish, but also partly in English, an official language in Cyprus and the lingua franca of bicommunal groups whose members did not share a native language. The multilingual environment in which I worked is represented in the text in my attentiveness to the spoken languages of my interlocutors and to problems of communication among Turkish Cypriots and Greek Cypriots—including contestations over the terminology of conflict—as well as to the special vocabularies of bicommunal discourse, which I take to be a novel feature of post-ethnonationalist Cypriot culture. That is not to say that I celebrate bicommunal discourse and ideology in this book, however. In Cyprus, as in many other postconflict contexts in which multiculturalism has been waged against the violent racism or ethnonationalism of the past, bicommunalism sometimes seems to reify and naturalize the very divisions in Cyprus that it is intended to heal.[20] I recall, in this vein, talking over coffee with two Cypriot friends, a philosopher and a poet, who had joined me after attending a poetry reading in Nicosia. They were discussing what it was like for them to do intellectual work in Cyprus; both participated often in conferences and public readings, and both had dense dealings with the organizers of cultural events in Nicosia. The philosopher railed against the multiculturalist "peace culture" under whose aegis such events transpired, a culture that obliged every Cypriot to represent the community to which she "belonged" in strictly identitarian terms—that is, to "be ethnic." The poet added that there were only two choices in this scenario: *You can't be a citizen of Cyprus. You have to be a member of one of the two communities; there's no other option. I suppose that's a good way to make sure there will always be two governments, two bureaucracies—everyone can keep their jobs!*

Inspired by these friends and many other interlocutors who likewise distanced themselves from bicommunal terms of engagement, I do not, in this book, take for granted the entrenched nature of communal, intercommunal, ethnic, or national bonds and divisions in Cyprus. Instead, I leave open the question of how such bonds and divisions are produced, reproduced, or disrupted in the present, in dynamic interaction with different kinds of knowledge about conflict and division. I use the terms "Greek Cypriot" and "Turkish Cypriot" to designate individuals only when these terms circumscribed the context in which I knew them—as with CMP employees, who were explicitly hired to represent these communal categories on the forensic teams, and used them in reference to one another—or when people consistently used these terms to identify themselves, most often the case with Cypriots of the immediate postwar generation, who grew up during and immediately after the division in 1974.[21] Many of the younger Cypriots I knew were more interested in non-ethnonational categories of identity, such as "citizen" and "migrant," around which they sought to build broader solidarities. My circumspection about the ethnonational and bicommunal grounds for contextualizing the knowledge projects of my interlocutors in Cyprus is thus informed and conditioned by experiments with identity and community that Cypriots from post-postwar generations were developing at the time of my fieldwork.



## Emergence and Recursion

The morning of April 7, 2012, I was up with the sun and walking through old Nicosia to meet a friend at her home on the north side of the city. I approached the checkpoint at Ledra Street, a narrow pedestrian road lined with shops that were already buzzing and open for deliveries at that hour. Since the previous autumn, a small group—a couple dozen people at their peak—had been living here, in the area of about a block, extending from the busy shopping area through the empty, ruined buildings of the dead zone between the Greek-Cypriot and Turkish-Cypriot checkpoints. The installation had begun with a few people staging weekly demonstrations and grown into a permanent camp, where many more came to live—sleeping, cooking, debating, gathering for assemblies, music, and films—first in tents and then in an abandoned building that they cleaned, repaired, painted, and equipped with generators. They were a diverse group: Greek Cypriot, Turkish Cypriot, immigrant, expatriate, antiauthoritarian, anarchist, Marxist, Green, undeclared. Their movement developed in dynamic alignment with Occupy movements worldwide but on the very particular ground of Cyprus, installed as they were on the edge of the dead zone between the north and south sides of old Nicosia, just a few steps from the checkpoints and the area in between, patrolled by UN troops. Inhabiting this no-man's-land, an ostensibly safe space—a buffer zone—between the two regimes, they aimed to develop a different relationship to land and property from that which they had inherited from what they called the "war generation." On October 15, 2011, in solidarity with mass protests from the Arab Spring to the Spanish Indignados, they had issued a press release and a Facebook posting, and handed out leaflets to passersby:[22]



> Description
>
> The 15th October Movement: Occupy the Buffer Zone
>
> This is an inclusive movement functioning within some principal umbrella concepts for which we initially united, these are:
>
> —
>
> The reunification of Cyprus
> To raise awareness of how the Cyprus Problem is but one of the many symptoms of an unhealthy global system
>
> —
>
> It is important to elaborate on the intended inclusiveness of the last point.
>
> We have occupied the space of the buffer zone to express with our presence our mutual desire for reunification and to stand in solidarity with the wave of unrest which has come as a response to the failings of the global systemic paradigm. We want to promote understanding of the local problem within this global context and in this way show how the Cyprus Problem is but one of the many symptoms of an unhealthy system.
>
> In this way, we have reclaimed the space of the buffer zone to create events (screenings, talks etc.) and media of these events, which relate to the system as a whole and its numerous and diverse consequences.
>
> Opinions expressed in this manner are not necessarily of the entire group, only the umbrella points of reunification and solidarity with the global movement can be assumed to be.

Performing their entitlement to inhabit this small piece of Cyprus's immense stock of abandoned property—specifically, a building owned by the Greek Orthodox Church in Cyprus, which declined to evict them—they contested the sovereignty of both the Republic of Cyprus (in the south) and the Turkish Republic of Northern Cyprus (in the north), as well as the occupation of Cyprus and the management of its buffer zone by UN peacekeeping forces since 1963 (Erdal Ilican 2013). For months, I passed through their installation every few days as I crossed the checkpoints; I passed a few evenings as well at their general assemblies, film screenings, and parties, in the company of dozens of others attracted to the movement. Occupy the Buffer Zone (OBZ) endured the cold, dank winter of 2012 and came to seem—to me, at least—as permanent a part of the urban environment as the ruined buildings among which they camped. Despite derision and attacks in the press, and surveillance and harassment by UN peacekeepers, the Turkish army, and the Greek-Cypriot police, OBZ held their ground for seven months.



That morning in April, they were gone. I learned later that an antiterrorist squad of the Greek-Cypriot police had raided the installation, seriously injuring seven people who lived there (along with several dogs) and arresting twenty-eight. All at once, tents were pulled down, furniture and equipment removed, banners and photographs torn from the walls. Members of OBZ returned the next day to reinhabit the area, issuing a call to supporters to regroup and give a show of strength. I joined almost a hundred people gathered that night to discuss strategies for continuing the movement—and also to eat, drink, smoke, and listen to a rembetiko trio whose spirited minor key wound all the way up and down Ledra Street. I heard rumors that the raid had been coordinated at the top—that is, by the UN; the ongoing unity talks between Greek-Cypriot and Turkish-Cypriot authorities mediated by the UN had reached a critical point, and the high international profile of OBZ might have been perceived as an obstacle to the negotiation process. Another factor identified by those gathered that night was the upcoming EU presidency, set to move to Cyprus in June: "It's time to clean up," a Greek-Cypriot politician had said at a press conference only a few days before. Later that week, a demonstration to protest police brutality started in the main square on the south side of the walled city and proceeded up Ledra Street to the checkpoints where OBZ had dwelled. They made many signs of resistance, duly noted by the press. But within a month, the movement as such had moved on to other venues and tactics.

Less than a year after the police raid that shut OBZ down, in March 2013, the Republic of Cyprus entered the company of Eurozone states in crisis: banks closed, foreign capital withdrew, corruption scandals erupted, and parliament was presented the forced choice of a European bailout (which came to be known as the "haircut"). Bearing out OBZ's foreboding about global neoliberal governance in Cyprus, a new era of austerity began, in which the gift of membership in the European Union—from which the north had largely been excluded, in practice if not in policy—turned out to be poisonous. Austerity had come to the north two years earlier, when tax increases, the privatization of public utilities, and massive cuts in public sector salaries were imposed by Turkey. Now, in 2013, the south was swiftly catching up; the once-prosperous side of the division was transforming into a site of economic stagnation, political volatility, and dependency on sovereign patrons.



The going of OBZ and the coming of austerity in Cyprus are potential historical indices of a transformation in the meaning and effects of the division itself, which continued forcefully to shape social and political life in Cyprus during this time as it had for the previous fifty years, but in new directions, with new implications. The human geographer Murat Erdal Ilican, reflecting on his experience in OBZ, describes how he was dislodged from his scholarly habits of "seeing like a state," in James Scott's famous phrase, as he came to realize that writing about OBZ "carries the weight of creating knowledge about a movement whose history is too recent" for the "contours of questions" about it to crystallize in "academic debate" (Erdal Ilican 2013, 56). He associates this inchoateness with the destabilization of identity wrought by OBZ—reckoned through the group's shifting and disavowed boundaries of inside and outside, their claims to "local" and "global"—which appeared, to him, as perhaps the most important question at stake in the movement.

This vocabulary of destabilization and disavowal hints at something incipient and inchoate that is waiting to emerge. Indeed, Erdal Ilican's reckoning with his own complex disruption by OBZ has clear echoes in the recent problematization of "emergence" in anthropology. Michael Fischer, perhaps the most creative and prolific contributor to this discussion, identifies "emergence" in the present—like the past, he suggests—with the appearance of "new ethical and political spaces" with which we are ill equipped to contend by our "traditional concepts and ways of doing things" (2003, 9, 37). His formulation of "emergent forms of life" brings into relation, on the one hand, the "ethnographic datum" that expert knowledge producers increasingly claim that new knowledge is required for us to comprehend and address new situations, and, on the other, the "social theoretical heuristic" of acknowledging that "complex societies, including the globalized regimes under which late and post modernities operate," are not stable formations but rather exist in some complex, shifting temporal relation of proximity and affinity to "historical horizons" (37). One cannot ask about those historical horizons without seeking epistemological and ethical grounds for the tools we have, or make, for posing questions.

In Cyprus, these questions of emergence were impossible for me to disaggregate and distribute between the social-political field of my ethnographic research and my tools for knowing it. Perhaps that is the case everywhere and everytime; but in "the new Cyprus," as Rebecca Bryant dubs the era of open checkpoints and EU membership, the overdetermination and colonization of knowledge production by the Cyprus conflict seemed to me to thematize that impossibility in a unique and especially compelling way.

To say that any emergent form of life, or emergent cultural or political practice, sticks to the tools we already have at hand for analyzing it, and thus might miss analysis in its own terms, is another way of saying that emergence is restrained and dynamically conditioned by recursion. This assertion is not made explicitly but is illustrated beautifully in an article coauthored by Cypriot scholars Olga Demetriou and Murat Erdal Ilican (2018), "A Peace of Bricks and Mortar: Thinking Ceasefire Landscapes with Gramsci." They return here to OBZ, and specifically to the cleaning and restoration of one building within the encampment, in order to compare it with another reconstruction project in central Nicosia: the renovation of a war-torn building inside the buffer zone and its transformation into the Home for Cooperation (H4C), a multifunctional center for bicommunal research and activity founded and managed by the Association for Historical Dialogue and Research. Demetriou and Erdal Ilican minutely document the day-by-day processes of reconstruction entailed by the two projects, and the political ideologies that animated and followed them (their shorthand, which they nuance substantially in the paper, is "liberal/progressive" for the H4C vis-à-vis "anarchist/revolutionary" for OBZ). They construe participants in both projects as "organic intellectuals in the Gramscian sense" (Demetriou and Erdal Ilican 2018, 899); these participants were engaged in "making heritage" in the urban environment of Nicosia's dead zone, in ways that contested not only the division of Cyprus that is symbolized and concretized by the dead zone but also the gentrification of the old walled city, where the dead zone is located, that has been ongoing since the pedestrian checkpoint at Ledra Street/Lokmacı opened in 2003.

That this environment was (and is) characterized, materially, by the debris and ruins of war—abandoned, dilapidated buildings behind fences and barbed wire, riven by bombs and bullets, full of trash as well as the property and other traces of prior occupants—drives the authors to focus on the human labor required to transform the two buildings. They therefore empha-

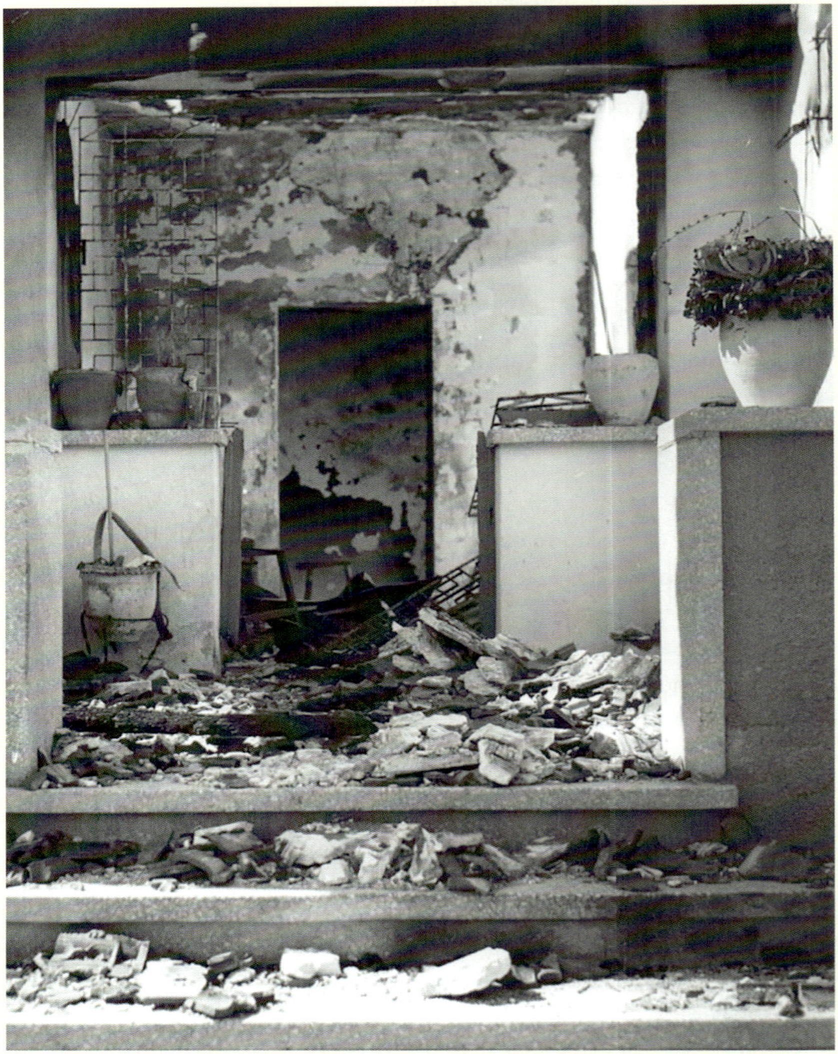

NO.

I.5

size the "embodiment" of the work performed by OBZ participants in particular, which involved occupying the vantages (even the "shoes") of prior occupants, seeing and touching and using their things, but also lifting, sifting, carrying, cleaning, and being vulnerable to the physical environment—being present, in short, in a way that manifested the "intimate connection between intellectual and physical labour" they devoted to their project. These protesters, the authors explain, were "planners, dwellers, builders, cleaners, and thinkers" (Demetriou and Erdal Ilican 2018, 906).

Demetriou and Erdal Ilican end on a skeptical note, pointing to the role gentrification plays in the assimilation of protest by "hegemonic structures" of "capital accumulation" (2018, 911). But I would rather draw attention to their insistence on the "transformative capacity towards a new political situation" that animated the two projects of reconstruction, on their account—not because this capacity represents hope in an affective register (the authors are not hopeful, nor am I, especially), but because it expresses change as it happens, even when it goes unnoticed by most. So, they say, "The war over concepts, ideologies, and their material transformations continues through the new groups, the new ideas, and the new practices that take shape now in communal kitchens, brochures and journals, and protest initiatives" (900, 911). This transformative capacity is not incidental to the projects pursued by the participants in H4C and OBZ, as Demetriou and Erdal Ilican show; rather, it is a constituent feature of reconstruction. The participants encountered the material ruins and debris of war and, through a process of "memorialisation," they "render[ed] it heritage" (908). I cannot think of a better description of the recursivity inherent in emergence, though I adduce other illustrations of the point in the pages that follow.



## Comparison and Context

This book grew out of my previous project on psychiatric reform and community-based care in Thrace, a culturally heterogeneous and politically contested region between the Turkish and Bulgarian borders of northeastern Greece. In my first book, *Bad Souls: Madness and Responsibility in Modern Greece* (Davis 2012), I examined the multifaceted contention over responsibility among patients and therapists in this borderland, focusing on embodied histories of conflict and psychosocial dimensions of governance by way of the power dynamics between Greek therapists and Turkish-speaking Muslim patients from local Turkish, Pomak, and "Gypsy" communities. My research in Thrace thus introduced me to the problematic of minority governance in Europe and its borderlands, including "survivals" of Ottoman imperial rule. Along the way, I developed a vague and tentative comparative perspective on Thrace and Cyprus, with an appreciation for the complex histories they shared of pluralism, hybridity, communalism, and war. From the Ottoman period onward, Cyprus and Thrace appeared to me to be intimately connected, such that conflicts at one border were reflected in increased tension and even militarization at the other. Moreover, they seemed to me to bear important similarities as regions of historically Greek predominance where large Muslim-minority communities maintained ties to Turkey, and where long histories of conflict were expressed through embodied and discursive forms of suspicion.



When I initiated my research project in Cyprus, I was often asked how I had ended up in Cyprus after spending so much time in Greece. I would usually respond with some very provisional articulation of their comparability. I got many blank looks and a few blunt objections. A Cypriot historian tactfully told me once, *I think it would be difficult to draw a comparison like that. Our situation here is very different.* When Anna Fragoudaki and Thalia Dragona, education scholars in Greece, came to Nicosia in March 2012 to speak about their decades-long project to develop bilingual (Greek/Turkish) schools and curricula in the northeastern Greek city of Komotini, they prefaced their presentation with a series of elaborate caveats, distinguishing the majority/minority dynamics of the Greek-speaking and Turkish-speaking populations of Greece from the two-state situation in Cyprus, and distinguishing the history of war between Greece and Turkey from the ongoing division in Cyprus. Similar parameters circumscribed the discussion of *Twice a Stranger*, a documentary film screened at the H4C in 2012, which addressed the population exchange between Greece and Turkey in the wake of World War I. The ethnonational coordinates of history and identity in Greece, Turkey, and Cyprus constituted implicit grounds of comparison with which many Cypriots seemed profoundly uneasy. Respecting this unease as I came to understand it better, I developed a wariness about comparison on the grounds of ethnonational identity that I have maintained in this book.

Even so, as I write about the particular experiences Cypriots have had in reckoning with their history, I show that these experiences are not isolated from other histories or other processes of reckoning. In their inaugural statement, reprinted above, OBZ articulated a compelling vision of Cyprus's embeddedness in a larger world: "The Cyprus Problem is but one of the many symptoms of an unhealthy system." The Cyprus Problem is composed of many parts from elsewhere—parts as abstract as theories and vocabularies, and as material as personnel, equipment, and body parts. I pay close attention, therefore, to the transnational dimensions of the diplomatic, peacekeeping, and transitional-justice apparatuses in Cyprus, including forensic investigations; and those of public culture, especially films and texts, whose production and circulation transpire outside as well as inside the borders of Cyprus. Parts of the Cyprus conflict likewise exist in many other places: in Greece and Turkey, where the enduring division remains a social trauma and a political bargaining chip; in the UK, where the Cypriot diaspora, a crucial political constituency in Cyprus, is approaching the size of Cyprus's own population; and even in Bosnia and Herzegovina, where the Cypriot DNA databank is housed and the DNA of Cypriot missing persons is tested.



Along these lines, I raise the issue of place: that is, what kind of place Cyprus is, and whether it is the place about which I have written this ethnography. The continuities and connections between Cyprus and other locales that I have been describing are more than explanatory; they are constitutive of the Cypriot context, as much as the more familiar features that so often distinguish it, at least in the imagination of foreigners: its smallness and literal insularity, the grayness of its sovereignty and economy, its fusion of western/European and eastern/Levantine cultures, and, of course, its enduring conflict. I do not deny that those features belong to Cyprus, but I want to emphasize that they also belong elsewhere, and tie Cyprus to elsewhere, and are therefore better understood as connections to other locales than as distinguishing features of this one.

It is for this reason that I decided ultimately to take "Cyprus" out of the title of this book, where it had stayed for years as I worked on the research and the text. The decision was in a sense made for me by my friend Nicos Philippou, who subtly suggested not too long ago that I did not need "Cyprus" in the title and that keeping it there might inadvertently limit the book's readership to a specialist audience—that is, those who already care about Cyprus. The suggestion was so subtle, in fact, that I almost thought it was my idea to let "place" operate more ambiguously in this ethnography. But this is an idea that Philippou has been working at for a very long time, both in his writing (Eftychiou and Philippou 2010; Loizos, Philippou, and Stylianou-Lambert 2010; Philippou 2014; Philippou, Stylianou-Lambert, and Wells 2014; Stylianou-Lambert and Philippou 2014) and in his photography (Philippou 2005, 2007, 2016; Philippou and Zackheos, n.d.), which explore Cyprus's colonial history and postcolonial experience. In these works, he shows, place is something whose defining characteristics we are trained to perceive and desire through visual media; in Cyprus, those media have largely been touristic and folkloristic in style, characterized by romantic landscape photography and village pastorals that satisfied British colonial appetites.

To see place differently, one can take familiar tropes in the visual representation of a place and subversively recontextualize them in order to highlight and criticize their conventional reference—a strategy Philippou pursued in *Coffee House Embellishments* (Philippou 2007), taking up the trope of the coffeehouse as a public space of male sociality and agonism in the Mediterranean (and especially the Greek) world.[23] Another kind of intervention is to look at different things altogether, and deploy those things visually in order to redefine the place or broach the problem of defining it—Philippou's approach, I would argue, in his most recent photography book, *Sharqi* (Philippou 2016), from which several images in this book are drawn. Thus, the Cypriot art theorist Elena Stylianou writes, in *Sharqi*, Philippou "revisit[s] existing key symbols of significance for Cyprus" and reenvisions them or altogether displaces them. One such symbol is the olive tree, which Stylianou notes has "ties to herbal remedies and Greek mythology" and, I would add, has long functioned as a key symbol of Greece—the homeland claimed by Greek-Cypriot ethnonationalists and clearly rejected as such by Philippou. "Here," Stylianou observes about *Sharqi*, "the olive tree gives way to the less obvious palm tree," which can be "cultivated almost anywhere in the world. . . . In many ways, it seems like a more appropriate symbol for Cyprus, as the island's identity cannot be traced back to a single historical trajectory" (Stylianou and Philippou 2018, 106, 108). His Polaroids of palm trees, which we might find in Florida or Tasmania or Thailand, were indeed taken in Cyprus and in that sense do iconically represent Cyprus, but they do not particularize it in order to distinguish it from those other places. What these images do is connect Cyprus to those other places and, in doing so, suggest new comparisons that might distinguish Cyprus from those other places differently. In an essay on *Sharqi*, the Cypriot literature scholar Stavros Karayanni describes this comparative perspective offered by the images as "contrapuntal"—Edward Said's term, "whose usefulness," Karayanni explains, "is that it offers a comparative reading of contrasting narratives" (2019, 270).[24] That is the kind of comparative perspective I aim to develop in this book, too, decentering Cyprus as the place of this ethnography, and toggling between its various insides and outsides as I have come to recognize them.

## Time, Secrecy, Artifactuality

When it comes to the definition of place by visual representation, there is no aesthetic that more relentlessly defines Cyprus today than that of postconflict ruin.[25] Deserted villages falling to rot; homes and shops in the dead zone of old Nicosia, the walled city, suddenly abandoned during riots and bombings and left ever after in suspended animation; airplanes grounded and rusting on the tarmac of the old airport of Nicosia, secreted within the UN-controlled buffer zone—such images of environments untouched since 1974, laden with the artifacts of conflict, might be taken to suggest something about the affective life of Cypriots, too: people frozen or stranded in time, almost fifty years after the war and counting, fixed in chronic impasse, trapped in traumatic memory, tired and cynical, waiting, still but tensed, anticipating further harm. Indeed, as I show in part two, such representations are commonplace in recent documentary films about the Cyprus conflict and the ongoing division. If there is motion in these representations, it is in the form of repetition: of reliving violence and dislocation; of rehearsing intricate, sclerotic arguments over property, security, and justice; of going through the familiar motions of settlement negotiations as if hoping for a new development, without any corresponding feeling of hope.



These aesthetics of ruin in Cyprus might be enchanting for many (like me) who see a story of power both in the events of destruction they materialize and in the chronicity of their decay—an "enchantment" that Shannon Dawdy (2010, 761) connects with the by turns romantic and dystopian "fascination" with ruins in the "archaeological turn" taken by anthropological approaches to time and materiality.[26] But, as Dawdy points out, one does not have to adopt a romantic or dystopian perspective on the ruins of modernity to register and appreciate the heterogeneous, nonprogressive, even paradoxical temporalities that their contemplation opens up. Indeed, the "recent ruins" of Cyprus suggest to me an alternative orientation to time—what I discuss, below, as an artifactual mode of historicity—that counters the frozen temporality of postconflict impasse that I advisedly refer to as "paranoid."[27] In the context of the knowledge projects I examine in this book, I understand paranoia not as a clinical pathology (or any kind of pathology) but rather as an epistemology entailing a particular orientation to time: a knowledge practice of rehearsal and repetition, of learning again what one already knows, of anticipating that what has come before will come again or, more precisely, that it is always still happening.

This description of paranoia was of course popularized by Eve Kosofsky Sedgwick in her now-classic essay, "Paranoid Reading and Reparative Read-

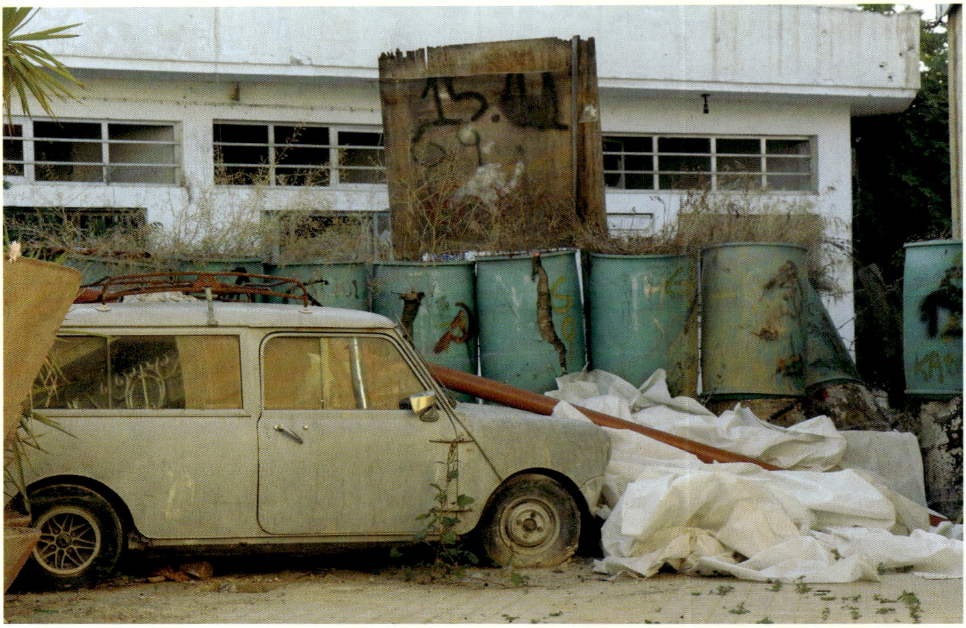

*NO.*

**I.6**

ing," where she examines dominant practices of reading, interpretation, and critique attached to the overdetermination and inevitability of "systemic oppressions" (2003, 124)—and thus, she argues, to an essentially closed temporality. Working from Ricoeur's taxonomy of interpretive styles in which Nietzsche, Marx, and Freud appear as progenitors of the "hermeneutics of suspicion," Sedgwick catalogues the "suspicious" techniques of demystification, revelation, exposure, and decipherment of hidden violence and false consciousness through which paranoid critical theorists acquire a sense of self-protective distance from power and the satisfaction of "smart" analysis with sharp political teeth. In the contagious quality of paranoia—its capacity to generalize and reproduce itself, overtaking other modes of knowing—Sedgwick discerns its distinctive orientation to time: "a rigid relation to temporality, at once anticipatory and retroactive, averse above all to surprise" (146), in which knowing what one already knows generates a sense of proximity to truth: "The unidirectionally future-oriented vigilance of paranoia generates, paradoxically, a complex relation to temporality that burrows both backward and forward: because there must be no bad surprises, and because learning of the possibility of a bad surprise would itself constitute a bad surprise, paranoia requires that bad news be always already known. . . . No time could be too early for one's having already-known, for its already having-been-inevitable, that something bad would happen. And no loss could be too far in the future to need to be preemptively discounted" (130–31).



Sedgwick's interest in this essay lies not so much in assessing the value of paranoid knowing as an approach to truth as it does in questioning paranoia's affective entailments and political commitments: "What does knowledge *do*—the pursuit of it, the having and exposing of it, the receiving again of knowledge of what one already knows?" (2003, 124). She seeks affective and political possibility beyond paranoia in "reparative knowing" (146), characterized by openness to surprises (even bad ones) and in attunement to contingency in the past as well as the future: a sense that things could have been otherwise yielding the hope that things could yet be otherwise. She poses the question of knowledge, here, as one not of access to truth but rather of the efficacy of affect, where affect is intricately bound up in an orientation to time.

Given the intense focus on the history of division and the chronicity of impasse in Cyprus, it is not surprising that time is a central theme in much recent work in Cypriot anthropology. Yiannis Papadakis, for one, has written extensively on the temporal dynamics of division, working through contradictory memories and differential forgetting of the time before war, and analyzing the mythical and historical temporalities structuring Greek-Cypriot and Turkish-Cypriot nationalisms, in cultural productions such as films as well as the material environments of symbolic spaces—neighborhoods in the old walled city of divided Nicosia, and the mixed "UN village" of Pyla, among others (Papadakis 1998, 2000a, 2000b, 2005). Yael Navaro (2012, 7) explores the mutual constitution of space and time in the north after the division but before the opening of checkpoints, showing how the "stunted temporality" of this period materialized in Turkish Cypriots' experience of confinement in a "make-believe" state. She finds essential to this experience the phantomic presence of former Greek-Cypriot residents, exerted through "melancholic objects" such as ruins, piles of rubbish, and looted household objects, temporally keyed to the moment of division and unassimilated through mourning.[28] Rebecca Bryant (2010, 150; 2014, 681) takes a different approach to the materiality of postdivision life in the north, considering history as an expressive register of belonging in the experience of Turkish Cypriots forcibly displaced from their homes in the 1960s–1970s, who both yearn and fail to forget or "pu[t] the past behind" them. She examines their appropriation of different kinds of objects left behind by Greek Cypriot refugees: "remainders," "reminders," and "remains" of an "unfinished history" such as houses, household items, photographs, and other personal effects (Bryant 2010, 149; 2014, 682, 691, 695). It is the "temporal dynamism" of these objects, she argues, that renders them "available for historical work," even in their alterity to the temporality of history in which Turkish Cypriots reckon their belonging to place in the face of a radically uncertain future (Bryant 2014, 683, 684). And Olga Demetriou (2007) examines the formation of political subjectivity in Cyprus in relation to an "event temporality" that has characterized postwar life. Taking the opening of the checkpoints in 2003 as a point of departure, she argues for an understanding of such momentous events (including the division itself) as "supplements" to the truth-making processes whereby people understand the situation they are in, and thus as "mediations" of past and present that open the possibility for novelty and difference to emerge from history—if only temporarily. In Cypriots' reactions to such events, she finds indications of the limits of their subjection to state power in the liminal phase immediately following a "surprise" event, and their formation as subjects of the state in the aftermath, as they consciously make decisions about how to act in relation to change and thus come to understand themselves as already governed in particular ways (Demetriou 2007, 990, 1002).

The event temporality theorized by Demetriou as central to political subjectivity in Cyprus—establishing the division as the foundational event in recent Cypriot history—has, perhaps, overdetermined the pervasive representation of Cyprus as frozen or stranded in time and stuck in the past. But if we look closer, we can see that those ubiquitous images of postwar ruin in Cyprus are not at all what they seem. We do not see images of life in suspended animation; we see the material buildup of time, the process of decay, the pathways of life after the event: war, displacement, opening, closure. The homes and shops and transit points abandoned abruptly all those years ago do not look now as they did then. Dust and debris have accumulated on the surfaces of things; infrastructure has broken down into rotten wood, broken glass, and crumbling stone; plants and flowers are growing through the cracks in floors and windowsills; anthills and spider webs are built and rebuilt. These sites are not frozen in time; on the contrary, the work of time is visible everywhere we look. The aesthetic of postwar ruin in Cyprus thus could not be further from retro aesthetic trends in fashion, music, architecture, and design; this past is not a foreign country we can visit, reenact, and repackage.[29] It is present, unassimilated, and changing. Time passes; life goes on. The effect of the event of war—division—has become a cause of other things. The event itself is radically unstable on a historicist reckoning of linear time.



This situation describes a special mode of historicity: an experience of being in time whose interpretation defines the place and the relative significance Cypriots assign to past, present, and future. In their introduction to a collection of ethnographies of historicity, Eric Hirsch and Charles Stewart describe historicity as a "complex temporal nexus of past-present-future," a "dynamic social situation" that entails "a complex social and performative condition, rather than an objectively determinable aspect of historical descriptions" (2005, 262). In this light, the historicity I associate with the Cypriot situation of enduring division and impasse is artifactual: it describes a temporal experience, and an interpretation of that experience, anchored by objects that survived the war and remain available for study, reuse, and recontextualization. It is not the pastness of these objects (their "historicality," in Hirsch and Stewart's term, 262) that interests me here, but rather the way their presence—their being present—materializes the past and, in doing so, summons a future. This is why, earlier, I characterized the knowledge projects pursued by forensic scientists and documentary filmmakers as, themselves, artifactual in nature: as dealing in facts made artfully that matter insofar as they link up with narratives about the past that figure expectations (especially hopes and fears) of what is to come.

Exploring this artifactual mode of historicity thus requires my ethnographic focus on Cypriots' work with the artifacts of conflict: the bones

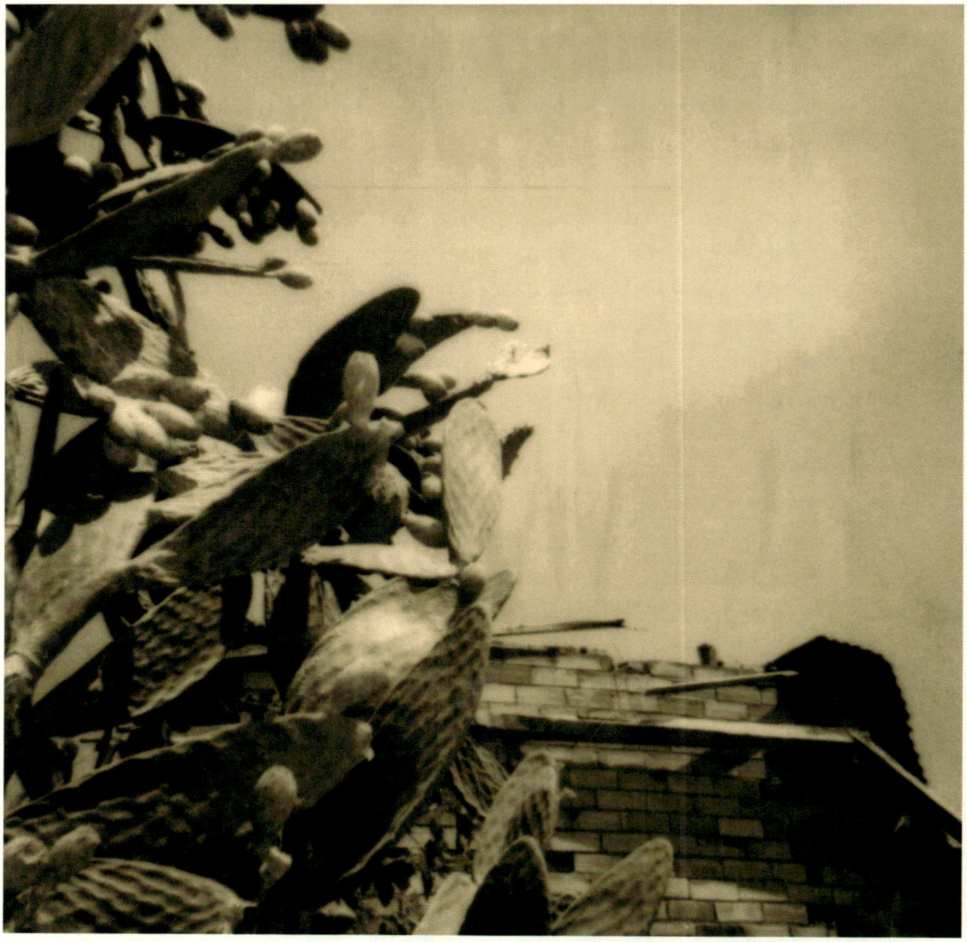

*NO.*

**I.7**

and belongings of the missing, exhumed from fields, wells, backyards, groves, forests, and mountainsides; and photographs and films from the 1960s–1970s, recovered from ghostly public archives and scattered personal collections where they had been stored to wait out the passage of time. These artifacts manifest and materialize what Ewa Domanska conceptualizes as the "non-absent past": an "ambivalent and liminal space . . . occupied by 'ghostly artifacts' or places that undermine our sense of the familiar and threaten our sense of safety" (2006, 346). While Domanska locates the missing bodies of the disappeared (in Argentina, in her case) in this "conceptual space," my interlocutors dealt with the recovered bodies of the disappeared, or photographs and films of the dead or the past, and processed them as remains—thus introducing a material dimension to the enigma of non-absence. Bones and images have entered different regimes of knowledge making from different storage spaces and hiding places in Cyprus, and they have different material properties, sensory affordances, and onto-epistemological implications; but in their unsettling of "the familiar," as Domanska puts it, including historical narratives of conflict and reconciliation, they have all become dynamic temporal operators in a situation of chronic impasse.



In their operation, these artifacts seemed to me, on occasion, to generate what political philosopher William Connolly, riffing on the final scene of the Coen brothers' 1991 film *Barton Fink*, describes as "moment[s] of time without movement, engaging different zones of temporality"—moments that "arrest multiple sites and speeds of mobility that impinge on one another when in motion" (2011, 2). As I understand Connolly, it is the interference among these sites and speeds ("force-fields") that actuates the experience of stopping ("time without movement"), but a focus is required—an image, an object, a "multisensory memory"—around which the past and present may coalesce in that moment (5, 2, 4). In the scene from the film that inspires these reflections, Barton Fink encounters a woman on a beach who sits and looks to the sea, adopting a distinctive posture; the "scene freezes," Connolly tells us, and, in freezing, "recalls" a painting, unremarkable at the time, of that woman in that posture on that beach that had featured in numerous earlier scenes as a fixture on the wall of Fink's rented room (1). For Connolly, it is this "figure of arrested movement"—or rather, this image of this figure—that forms a focus for our momentary experience of "time without movement" at the end of the film (1, 2). It is not time that moves then, nor the woman frozen in her pose, but rather we, the viewers, who "move back and forth between the picture and the closing scene" (2), perhaps (Connolly does not say so) exploring the temporal paradox presented by that scene: the painting, when we recall having seen it earlier, seems to be a representation of the final scene that has not happened yet in the chronological narrative of the film. *What time are we in? When do we belong? Is our world actually less finite than we take it to be?*

The impossibility of the painting, or of the final scene transpiring when it does, is a beautiful illustration of what Connolly discusses later (not with this example) as the powers of the false in Gilles Deleuze's theorization of the time-image in film. In *Cinema 2*, Deleuze broadly historicizes these powers and reads them symptomatically, associating their pervasion of post–World War II cinema with a loss of belief in the world: "The modern fact," he declares, "is that we no longer believe in this world. We do not even believe in the events which happen to us, love, death, as if they only half concerned us. It is not we who make cinema; it is the world which looks to us like a bad film" (1989, 171).[30]



Among the filmic techniques and traits that Deleuze identifies with the powers of the false are "anomalies of movement" and "false continuity shots" (Deleuze 1989, 128); the "indiscernibility of the real and the imaginary" (131); the "simultaneity of incompossible presents, or the coexistence of not-necessarily true pasts" (131); the use of mirrors, forgers, and other trickster characters; and, most generally, "falsifying narration" (133)—all having to do with the decomposition of Euclidean space (and movement within it) as a temporal framework.[31] Deleuze does not take the powers of the false to be destructive, immoral, repellent, or regrettable, even as symptoms; rather, like Nietzsche's conceptualization of the will to power, he sees them as a source of creativity, change—becoming—in ways that are unpredictable, beyond morality and, in some sense, beyond human agency and reckoning.[32] Thus, Deleuze says, "becoming is always innocent" (142); it does not entail or imply moral or political decline or progress; it is neither liberal nor cynical in tenor, but is rather "oppose[d]" to "history" (142).[33]

For his part, Connolly, as I read him, is less interested in demonstrating Deleuze's theorization of time-images in cinema than he is in exploring the ethical and political implications of the experience such images may inspire in viewers. His "experimental intervention," as he frames it, is to try to "amplify the experience of becoming" by harnessing such "protean moments" when they happen—dilated beyond the "punctual time" of decision and action—to new reflections in "ethics, politics, economics, and spirituality" (Connolly 2011, 10, 5, 8). These "protean moments" are not inherent properties of the images and objects that often serve as their focus or anchor, as Connolly makes clear. They are, rather, the effects of one's choice to acknowledge and actively augment their interruptions of punctual time, and thus to appreciate the way these interruptions deepen and complicate our "belonging to time" (5). The dilation of temporal experience he is after may thus enhance one's apprehension and appreciation of the uncertainty and essential openness of the world: a "world of becoming" (8, 5, 10).[34] This appreciation may be a spiritual or therapeutic end in itself, but Connolly also insists that it may activate and galvanize one to move in the direction of "existential attachment and political action" (10). Thus his "agenda," as he calls it (10), being within history (and not "opposed" to it), diverges quite radically from Deleuze's conceptualization of "innocent" becoming.

I find Connolly's philosophy of a "world of becoming" a vitalizing complement to the paranoid epistemology in which the violent history of Cyprus might otherwise seem deeply and exclusively entrenched. What Sedgwick seeks as reparative hermeneutics can be found, I think, in Connolly's theorization of time as becoming. Following Sedgwick's suggestion that paranoia is a chosen disposition to knowledge rather than a privileged path to truth, and that it may thus coexist and fruitfully interact with other dispositions to knowledge, I aim in this book to develop a different understanding of the artifacts that are so often held to symbolize a Cyprus frozen in time. What I describe as an artifactual mode of historicity is, on this understanding, a materially mediated scenario of potential change, inspired by encounters with artifacts and enacted by their recursive recontextualization. My interlocutors, in undertaking artifactual knowledge projects, were seizing on this potential in their anticipation of the future—not a particular future, but what Deleuze calls "irreducible multiplicity" (1989, 145), naming a sense of radical openness, in light of which, whatever future arrives will come as a surprise.

I do not mean, however, simply to substitute "artifactuality" for "paranoia" in my conceptualization of these knowledge projects, as I do not think the matter of time in Cyprus can be understood apart from the problem of paranoid knowing—the problem of learning (again) what one already knows, driven by the suspicion that one has missed something: that something crucial has been concealed or withheld. Orientations to knowledge that I consider paranoid, in this sense—enacted in the unremitting treading over the ground of conflict by Cypriot and foreign researchers that I noted above—were conditioned by public secrecy to a high degree. Cypriots critical of the politics of division have often accused the state (meaning different things: the Republic of Cyprus, the TRNC, the "parent" states of Greece and Turkey) and state-like entities (a range of paramilitary and "deep state" organizations operating in Cyprus, including proxy agencies of Greece, Turkey, the United States, and the United Kingdom) of sponsoring and concealing violence against civilians, surveilling and suppressing journalists and activists, censoring school curricula and artistic productions, and, in these and other ways, "brainwashing" postwar generations of Cypriots. Working actively against these practices of secrecy and their material sedimentations in social and political life, my interlocutors encountered many kinds of opacity in their work: privacy, confidentiality, classified status, censorship, silence, ambiguity, ghostliness, forgetting, confusion. Secrecy shape-shifted and densified and fractured and reassembled itself as both an object and a filter of their research, rendering some knowledge visible while other knowledge was left or kept unseen and, in some cases, encouraging the production of nonknowledge as a phatic activity.



But if secrecy thus expressed power, I am interested, too, in how secrecy denuded and eroded it—for example, by undermining the credibility of state actors and inspiring counternarratives to official discourses. In this book, then, I do not undertake a simple celebration of openness; to say the least, the chronic impasse in Cyprus, continuing at the time of this writing, does not warrant such a celebration. But I do pay attention to moments of openness that I observed in my interlocutors' approach to their knowledge projects about the Cyprus conflict—including their propensity to keep at it, to come back again and again to unanswered questions, to develop new spaces and new languages for communication—which were tempered but not obliterated by their cynicism and despair at other moments.

In this context of knowledge making, fraught and delimited in all these ways, the projects pursued by my interlocutors in Cyprus had ethical and political stakes that were temporal in form, connecting knowledge about the past to prospects of justice, healing, and peace in the future. This book is about how and why they came to address themselves to those stakes. They looked for the remains of long-missing persons and tried to integrate the dead they found into their communities of the living. They sought in archives of all description the traces of hidden violence, secret plans, and untold stories. They became audiences for the memories of "the last generation who knows," as Salih Niyazi described himself and his friends in *Birds of a Feather*: the last generation of witnesses to the violence of division and, for some, participants in it. In this book, I explore what it meant for these Cypriots—forensic investigators, archival researchers, and filmmakers, among others—to wrestle with the ambiguity and the danger of such knowledge. In their wrestling, they sought to "expand the domain of the empirical," as Avery Gordon (1997, 21) describes one way to make room for ghosts in our analysis of social life; and, as part of that process, to try to put a whole society together with pieces of empirical evidence.

At the risk of harping on this point, I want to emphasize here the rarefied nature of the communities and knowledge projects I document in this book. From the beginning, I conceived my own project as working against the hegemonic conditions of discourse on the division of Cyprus; that meant, to me, not giving mainstream ethnonationalist discourses any more attention than they had already received from journalists, activists, and scholars of all sorts. Readers outside Cyprus may have little sense of just how difficult it has been for progressive Cypriots to create and nourish the fragile space of indeterminacy and deferral in which my interlocutors have been trying to work; such a space might seem inevitable and common sense, especially to anthropologists and activists who have long ago passed to the other side of multiculturalism to become trenchant critics of it, and the rigid notions of identity and heritage promoted in its name in so many plural societies. Readers in Cyprus, though, know the difficulty better than I, and may therefore object to how poorly this book represents the actual conditions of political life and knowledge making in Cyprus. I agree, and I can only say in my defense that my goal has never been to write a representative account. My goal is rather to offer a glimpse of an emergent phenomenon from a rare and unstable vantage—to see if that vantage can be substantiated and sustained without dissolving into the double binds that relentlessly push Cypriots to take sides. I do not know if it is possible to distinguish and hold apart the indeterminate and malleable aspects of postwar life in Cyprus from those that are determined and intractable. But, to borrow Sedgwick's framing, I would like to find ways to let paranoid hermeneutics interact with reparative ones in an "ecology of knowing" (Sedgwick 2003, 145)—to document that complex ecology in Cyprus, and perhaps to contribute to it with this book.

# 1

# Forensic

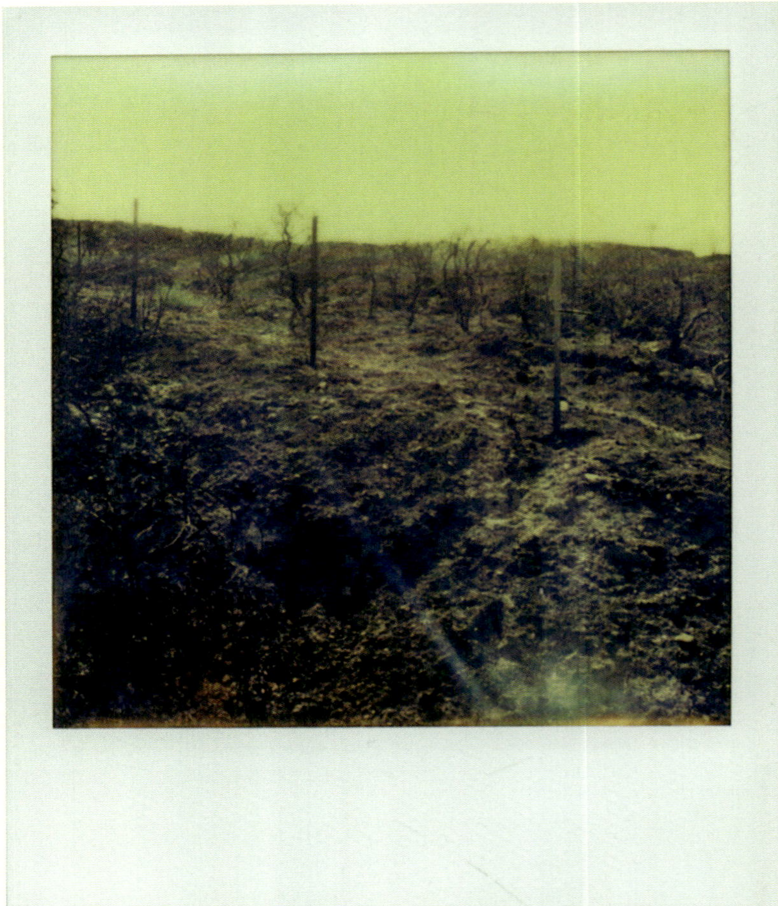

NO.

1.1

Many would stop me in the middle of the street to whisper "secrets," to point out a burial site or to share a story from their past. . . . I have only been their "mouthpiece," publishing what they want to say.

—Sevgül Uludağ, *Oysters with the Missing Pearls*

## The Only Terrorist Is the State

On April 23, 2003, the Green Line bisecting Nicosia opened for the first time since 1974. The crossing began at Ledra Palace, a bombed-out luxury hotel in the center of the city that has served as the headquarters of the UN Peacekeeping Force in Cyprus since 1963, and the site of bicommunal diplomatic and activist meetings from the 1980s up to the present. This was the first pedestrian checkpoint to open in the divided capital city. According to media reports, on that day in April, thousands of Greek Cypriots and Turkish Cypriots turned up, seeking to visit homes on opposite sides of the Green Line that they had been forced to abandon some thirty years before. Many reported, to their surprise, being met with humility and hospitality by those—also refugees and exiles—who had occupied those homes since the division.[1] Additional checkpoints opened across the Green Line in the following months as cross-border traffic began to normalize.



I crossed for the first time a few years later, in July 2007, with members of a bicommunal organization called Stop War in Cyprus. Crossing still carried a charge then—a risk, or sense of risk—that it no longer does, for me or for most Cypriots I know, though some still face harassment from guards.[2] The group had been marching that summer in Freedom Square, in the southern part of the old walled city in central Nicosia, and publicizing their upcoming visit to two mass graves: one on the south side of the Green Line and one on the north side. The dead buried in those graves were Turkish Cypriots and Greek Cypriots counted as missing since 1964 and 1974, respectively; the graves had recently been excavated by the Committee on Missing Persons (CMP) in Cyprus, whose staff worked with information from witnesses and civilian investigators going back more than two decades by then.

About thirty people gathered for the event: Greek Cypriots and Turkish Cypriots, the latter having already crossed the checkpoint at Ledra Palace to meet the group on the south side. Many carried wreaths and flowers to lay on the graves. They were activists, university students, relatives of the missing, former politicians, and others; they had supported Kofi Annan's doomed plan for the reunification of Cyprus before its accession to the European Union in 2004.

D., a woman who arrived at the checkpoint shortly after me, introduced herself as a "Greek Cypriot" and a "private citizen." She told me it had been a cruel practice of the Greek-Cypriot government to allow the relatives of the missing to believe their loved ones might be alive: *The government knew very well they were dead,* she said. *In many cases, they even knew where the bodies were, because they had spies everywhere and close ties to the mili-*

*tia groups who had done the dirty work.* The mystification had persisted for thirty years: relatives of the missing would stage demonstrations at Ledra Palace, petitioning the state for information and progress in the investigations of the missing—and the state would turn these demonstrations to its own uses, jockeying for the moral high ground by accusing the other side of refusing to exchange information. As D. spoke to me of this contrived impasse, she pointed out a line of graffiti on the low wall around the grounds of Ledra Palace, reading aloud, in Greek: ο μόνος τρομοκράτης είναι το κράτος (the only terrorist is the state).

As I learned later, when I conducted fieldwork with the CMP, exhumations of mass graves in Cyprus were conducted occasionally in the late 1990s and early 2000s by international nongovernmental organizations such as Physicians for Human Rights and by consulting agencies like the for-profit British Inforce Foundation and the nonprofit Argentine Forensic Anthropology Team (EAAF).[3] Despite these efforts, and even though the CMP had been established in 1981, it did not begin its own systematic investigations until 2004, when the recovery of the missing was de-linked from the prospect of a political settlement and newly framed as a "purely humanitarian issue," as political scientist Iosif Kovras puts it, attributing this outcome to efforts by officials in the Republic's Ministry of Foreign Affairs, under pressure from the European Union and lobby groups formed by relatives of the missing.[4] Since then, as of this writing, of the 2,002 people counted officially as missing, the remains of 1,177 individuals have been exhumed, and 1,024 individuals have been identified: 733 Greek Cypriots and 291 Turkish Cypriots.[5]

Although the CMP does not emphasize this point, its purview is limited to victims of intercommunal violence—that is, Greek Cypriots killed by Turkish Cypriots or Turkish military personnel, and Turkish Cypriots killed by Greek Cypriots or Greek military personnel. Many victims of violence cannot be counted in these communal terms of identity; it is well known that many Greek Cypriots, mostly leftists and other supporters of President Makarios at the time of the attempted coup in July 1974, were killed in that period by Greek-Cypriot members of EOKA-B, a right-wing ethnonationalist paramilitary organization, or by Greek officers and soldiers.[6] Conversely, I have heard many accounts of the deliberate but secret bombing of Turkish-Cypriot homes and mosques by members of TMT, a Turkish-Cypriot paramilitary organization that in many respects also governed Turkish-Cypriot enclaves between 1963 and 1967, or by the Turkish army, who attributed this violence to Greeks or Greek Cypriots in order to stoke fear and hostility between Greek Cypriots and Turkish Cypriots, and to rally support among Turkish Cypriots for partition.[7] At least two international agencies—the

Inforce Foundation and Physicians for Human Rights—have investigated cases of Cypriots killed by members of their own communities (conceived in ethnonational terms), and a few archaeologists who worked at the CMP at the time of my fieldwork participated in those investigations, but the investigations themselves are organizationally unconnected to the CMP. Intracommunal violence in Cyprus, which has left unclaimed bodies throughout the island, is thus secreted within the mission of the CMP; forensic knowledge of these deaths is not legible to the intercommunal politics of peace and reunification between Greek Cypriots and Turkish Cypriots.

Residents on both sides of the Green Line have long accused the Greek, Turkish, and Cypriot states of fomenting and perpetrating violence in the period from independence in 1960 to the division in 1974. Few members of the police, military forces, and paramilitary groups active at that time have been tried for their crimes. I have heard from Cypriot friends and colleagues about the many such men (they are all men) who enjoy prominence as politicians and magnates today—a public secret that helps to account for the persistent impasse in reunification.



In labeling a "public secret" this widespread knowledge of war crimes committed by prominent Cypriot citizens, I aim to foreground Cyprus's connection to many other postwar contexts where forensic and documentary knowledge projects have likewise taken shape around the revelatory impetus to uncover the truth of political violence. Michael Taussig, in his now-classic work on public secrecy, discusses in these terms the "law of silence" that governed the dirty war in Colombia (for example)—the kind of "smoke-screen" that obscured but did not conceal links between paramilitary violence and the state, which everyone knew that everyone knew: "Knowing it is essential to its power, equal to the denial. Not being able to say anything is likewise testimony to its power. So it continues, each negation feeding the other, while the headlines bleat EL ESTADO, IMPOTENTE" (1999, 5–6).

Public secrecy, as Taussig describes it here, is a shared condition of social life "where the secret is not destroyed through exposure, but subject to a revelation that does justice to it" (1999, 8). What he imagines (with Benjamin) as "doing justice" to the secret is not a matter of exposure, which would destroy the secret as such, but rather a showing of the secrecy of the secret—a kind of revelation that he calls "defacement": a transgressive and mystical act of unmasking and illuminating that "creates sacredness" (51). If the public secret is a "pseudo-secret"—not secret at all, in fact, but rather a "deliberate deceit" known by all (149)—then nothing is revealed in its revelation but the play of surface and depth that gives the impression of a truth behind appearances, and that, paradoxically, continues to give that impression after the play is revealed as such, making truth seem more real and pressing than ever. What Taussig calls the "ideology" of secrecy is this fantasy of a real secret behind the public secret—a real mystery to be solved, driving a "*'drama of revelation' which, like unmasking, amounts to a transgressive uncovering of a 'secretly familiar'*" (58, 51).[8] That uncanny thing, he says, is experienced as sacred in the increase in "spiritual plenitude" generated by its unmasking (149).

In his ethnography of the missing in Cyprus, Paul Sant Cassia (2005, 220, 221) takes up Taussig's formulation of public secrecy to explore the "masquerade" of ignorance regarding the fate of the missing in the south to which D. had drawn my attention. He relates the stories of Androulla Palma and Maroulla Shamishi, Greek-Cypriot women who had actively lobbied the Republic for years to determine the fate of their husbands, who went missing in 1974. Having given up on any resolution by the state, in 1997 they attempted to dig up their husbands' remains from an anonymous mass grave in the Lakatameia military cemetery in south Nicosia, where they believed them to be buried. In 1999, the CMP, not yet conducting its own investigations, hired a forensic team from Physicians for Human Rights to excavate the grave at Lakatameia, where the remains of 126 Greek-Cypriot men—soldiers, reservists, and some armed civilians killed immediately after the second invasion in August 1974—were ultimately found. The names of the dead had been placed on the official list of Greek-Cypriot missing persons in 1974 and confirmed many times afterward, although it is now clear that authorities in the Republic knew not only of their deaths but also of the location of their bodies. The Lakatameia excavation, along with another undertaken by Physicians for Human Rights at the Saint Constantine and Helen military cemetery nearby, followed from a series of stories published in 1995 by Andreas Paraschos, a Greek-Cypriot investigative journalist then writing for the *Phileleftheros* newspaper, as well as by Makarios Drousiotis, writing mainly for *Politis*.

Sant Cassia (2005, 218) takes the publicity around this subterfuge on the part of the Republic—a "simulacrum of knowing" "manufactured" by the state, he says—as a revelation of public secrets: that the missing were in fact not missing but dead and, moreover, that not all the Greek-Cypriot missing had disappeared on the Turkish side at the hands of the Turkish army, as the Republic had insisted since 1974. In Sant Cassia's view, the actions of Palma and Shamishi dismantled those particular forms of public secrecy—Greek-Cypriots could no longer "not know" these truths (though they already knew them)—but not the ideology of secrecy that has contin-

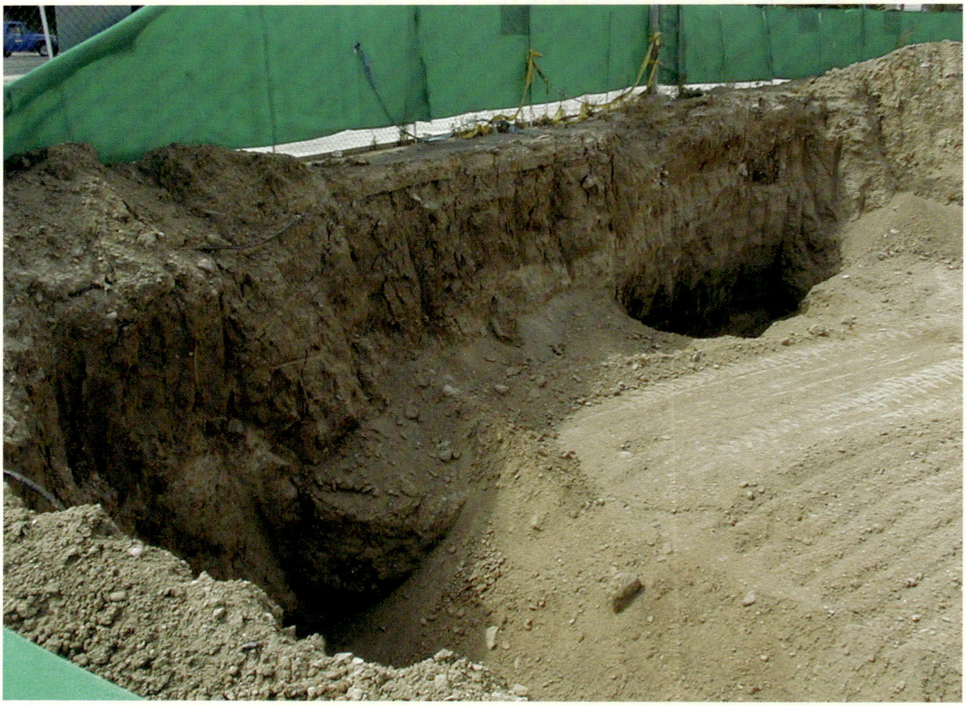

NO.

1.2

ued to sustain a drama of revelation around the missing. Specifically, Sant Cassia points to the insistent centrality of the state in the sacralization of the remains of the missing after their revelation—certifying their identity scientifically, controlling relatives' access to them, and presiding over their ritualized reburial—as durable aspects of the ideology of secrecy that presents transparency as the state's business.[9]

By 2004, some five years after the Lakatameia excavation, the CMP had emerged as the institutional platform on which both state regimes in Cyprus—the Turkish Republic of Northern Cyprus alongside the Republic of Cyprus—could operate their centrality in this drama. Publicity surrounding the CMP's role in investigating the missing, arising out of the coverage of the missing in the 1990s and early 2000s by journalists such as Andreas Paraschos and Makarios Drousiotis in the south and Sevgül Uludağ in the north, has continued in print. During the time I was working with the CMP, in 2011–12, reporters routinely covered the exhumations and funerals of the missing, as well as many scandals at the CMP, including a dispute that led to the transfer of the Cypriot DNA databank from the Cyprus Institute of Neurology and Genetics to a forensic agency in Bosnia and Herzegovina, and an exposé of the purportedly poor qualifications and investigative procedures of CMP employees.[10] The CMP has long run its own public information office and regularly issues press releases in English, Turkish, and Greek, to newspapers in both the north and south—where they are often, however, mobilized for radically different political messages—and on its own website, where all its press releases are archived. Its publicity is addressed, then, to audiences conceived as multiple (including the international community); the style of this publicity is one of neutrality and balance.

In writing (before the advent of the CMP) about the revelation of public secrecy by Androulla Palma, Sant Cassia focuses on the role of publicity in the resolution of the mystery posed by her husband's missing remains. He notes the intense media attention paid to Palma in the days after the excavation she attempted at Lakatameia, and her tortured negotiations with the politicians she held responsible for deceiving her all those years, who now wanted to preside over his public funeral, and prevailed. At the wake she held afterward in her home, where she displayed her husband's remains and belongings, she told the story—different stories, actually, differently told—of how he had been found and identified at last. Sant Cassia (2005, 209), who notes he was the only man who entered the house for the wake, observes the way women relatives and neighbors "gathered" around Palma to listen, "like the chorus in an ancient Greek play," "express[ing] collective feelings, social sentiments" in the tragic drama of the missing. These women, he seems to suggest, are the public of public secrecy—those whose "knowing what not to know," in Taussig's (1999, 6) distillation, describes, in collective terms, both their complicity with secrecy and their drive to expose the truth, if only partially. They did not witness the "action" but "recounted" it, and, in their recounting, they named the accountability of the state.

I suspect that something is being taken for granted, here, in Sant Cassia's assignment of public status to a Greek chorus that could only be located in the Republic of Cyprus. (His interpretive references are to Aeschylus and Sophocles; his research, he notes, was conducted mostly in the south and concluded before the checkpoints opened in 2003; his experience in the north and its world of refence is, thus, extremely limited [see Sant Cassia 2005, x].) The same something may be taken for granted, too, in Taussig's reading of secrecy as a mediation of law—in his swift slipping from law to state to head of state, as he reads Julian Pitt-Rivers's new preface to his old book about a southern Spanish village during Franco's dictatorship, in which preface, Taussig indicates, Pitt-Rivers all too easily recasts his village ethnography as an "ethnographic explication of secrecy" (Taussig 1999, 65). This something is the condition of Taussig's attention to public secrecy as an "arm of statecraft" in the Franco dictatorship, and indeed of his understanding of the "dissimulation" Pitt-Rivers finds characteristic of Andalusian sociality as instead "the very quintessence of the state, occupying the moral high ground of the public secret" (69)—a line of thinking that specifies public secrecy as a modality of state fetishism and thus of (potential) defacement.[11]



In the introduction to this book, noting the impossibility of achieving a coherent perspective on a whole Cypriot society, I gestured toward what I think is being taken for granted in these theorizations of public secrecy: that is, a public isomorphous with the nation of a nation-state or, in a more Foucauldian register, with the population of a state.[12] A modern public of the public sphere, of public discourse, of popular sovereignty. But what if there is no public to hold and behold the public secret? No shared language, no shared media, in which knowledge could be disclosed and debated? No gathering around social divisions, as Sant Cassia sees women gathering around Palma, to recuperate a shared vision of justice and demand it from the gods?

There are reasons to think there may be no such space, no such discourse, no society, no state, that is shared by Cypriots across their profound and enduring division—despite the bizarre staying power of Cyprus as a nation-state with its anomalous status in international law and associated apparatuses of sovereignty and recognition. If that is so, the Cypriots whose knowledge projects I am examining here—peace-minded Cypriots addressing a (re)unified society—perhaps stood in for a Cypriot public retrojected as a loss and projected as an impossible hope. The state (and its fetishism) cannot function as a stabilizing frame for understanding public secrecy in this context, despite the accusation: *the only terrorist is the state.* The predicate of that line is not an answer but a puzzle: what (is the) state? The very nature of the power capacitating and flowing through the social is in question here.

*What state?* In Cyprus, this question certainly has determinate referents: the Republic of Cyprus, the TRNC, Turkey, perhaps also Greece, depending on who is asking. But the very multiplicity of referents makes it clear that one cannot only ask after determinate referents; the question "What state?" is also an ontological one about the nature of the state as such ("What is the state?"). As I noted in the introduction, Occupy the Buffer Zone posed questions about sovereignty, property, territory, and identity as distinctively Cypriot questions and ambitiously general questions about how human life is organized at this moment in history; to answer them, classical liberal and sociological theories of the state that take the stabilizing hyphen in "nation-state" for granted will not do. My research in Cyprus has thus led me to ethnographies and theories of the state that explore its ideological and imaginary dimensions, its margins and borders, and its implication with para-state entities.[13]



Such works on the state have powerfully shaped my perspective on Cyprus, which confounds liberal models of statehood in many quite obvious ways: from the residues of minority corporate governance left by Ottoman imperial and British colonial rule, in which communities rather than individuals were treated as subjects of rights (see Bryant 2016); to the gray economic zones on its southern and northern coastal borders as well as at the internal so-called border between the two regimes, where formally illicit exchange is actively facilitated by both state and nonstate actors (traders, police, customs agents); to the paramilitary groups that perpetrated so much of the violence in the 1960s–1970s that is routinely called intercommunal; to the centrality of refugeehood to the "whole structure of citizenship," as Olga Demetriou (2018, 217) argues in writing about the massive displacement of Cypriots on the island between 1963 and 1974; to the utterly anomalous status of the Republic of Cyprus in international law, produced in part by the establishment of a breakaway state in the north, the TRNC, whose sovereignty and legitimacy are perennially in question.

Indeed, the TRNC appears in much of the political science and social science literature on Cyprus as an archetypal fake state, though anthropologists who have treated it as an ethnographic object have been careful to plumb the intricate complexities of its apparent fakeness. Yael Navaro, for example, offers an ethnographic account of life in the TRNC in the period before the opening of checkpoints in 2003; she locates the state-ness of the TRNC in "phantomic" space (2012, e.g., 13, 15, 18): in both affective forms (haunting, melancholy) and material ones (built environments, household objects, documents) that "exert" affective force, where its being "phantasmatically crafted" (15)—that is, made-up—is most evident.

In their new book, written well after 2003, Rebecca Bryant and Mete Hatay address the peculiar and exceptional but nonunique status of the TRNC as a de facto state—a state, they write, with "de facto police, de facto judiciaries, de facto civil servants, and de facto politicians" (2020, 6). They meticulously document the building of this "state"—marking with scare quotes the heightened factitiousness of the term's referent—from the earliest physical separation of Greek Cypriots and Turkish Cypriots during the 1950s through to the present. They trace three central processes—"territorialization, Turkification, and the creation of a new polity"—that entailed the design and normalization of "a sense of territorial integrity" in the region north of the "border," a "perception of wholeness" there, and "a sense of separateness" from the Republic of Cyprus (33). In their introduction to the text, Bryant and Hatay note that "Greek Cypriots very rarely appear in these pages. . . . [They] tend to enter the picture at particular levels of discourse, especially in the realm of what we call the factitious" (24–25), which is to say insofar as, and exactly when and where, Greek Cypriots make claims to the real status of the Republic of Cyprus in explicit or implicit contrast to the TRNC's pseudo status.

In taking up the paradox of the de facto state in northern Cyprus, and the variety of ways in which Turkish Cypriots have become citizens of that state over the last sixty years, Bryant and Hatay presume as the very condition of their research the inexistence of a single Cypriot state, and likewise, of a single Cypriot society. The division is ineradicable, in their depiction; moreover, the process of division began much earlier than most Greek Cypriots account it, and it was not a shared experience. In an article written not long after the opening of the checkpoints, Olga Demetriou observed "an aporia at the heart of *Greek Cypriot* political subjectivity, whereby 'division' is the knot that binds nationalism and innocence . . . trauma and pride . . . the continuation of the conflict and pursuit of peace" (2006b, 64, emphasis added); she later wrote of a "dwelling on division that has come to define Greek-Cypriot subjectivity" (Demetriou 2018, 3). Bryant and Hatay suggest that division has not been as wounding or foundational for many Turkish Cypriots, for whom there is no going back—not only because the violence before division did too much damage that cannot be repaired; not only because the state and society that have come into being in the TRNC are capacitated and conditioned by the existence of the division; but also, perhaps—it is hard to know—because there was no unified Cypriot society before the division to count now as a loss, or to hold out as a utopic future.[14]

The bicommunal group I accompanied on that visit to mass graves in July 2007 had, on the contrary, a decidedly pan-Cypriot or "Cypriotist" mindset. The many obstacles we faced that day helped them articulate the need for it, starting from the long delay in our visit to the first grave. We waited an hour for police escorts to arrive, and this gave the media time to join as well: newspaper reporters and photographers, and cameramen from four major TV networks. The police rode ahead of our bus on motorcycles, lights flashing and sirens blaring, attracting as much alarmed attention as possible. On the bus, D. talked to me about her motivation for coming along. She was not a member of any of the organizations, she said, but she was interested in bicommunal activities and had many Turkish-Cypriot friends. She noted that a good friend of hers, who was also very active in bicommunal work, had made excuses not to come along that morning; finally, this friend had admitted to D. that she did not want to participate in public events. *She has her own private way of going about her activism, and she doesn't want any of her clients to see her on* TV *or in the news. There's no common, public experience of the new Cyprus: after the checkpoints opened, each person's experience has been individual and isolated.*



The first grave we visited was on the south side, at Strovolos, on the southwestern outskirts of Nicosia, a peri-urban area then being developed as a residential neighborhood. The grave was located along the main road, marked by a tall chain-link fence covered in orange mesh and danger signs. We gathered around two large holes that had been excavated and left open. Speeches began when the cameras were ready; the entire event was recorded and broadcast later that evening on Greek-Cypriot news channels. Several journalists spoke about their involvement in the investigations. Members of Stop War in Cyprus addressed the crowd in Greek, Turkish, and English. They told the story of the graves, formerly wells supplying a small village that had been razed in the 1970s. In 1964, when violence broke out in Nicosia, Turkish-Cypriot residents of the city were rounded up and brought here, shot, and thrown into the wells. So far, three bodies had been found in one of the wells, but there were five grave sites on this same patch of land, and the investigators estimated they might find twenty or thirty victims altogether. Those who had come to memorialize the dead left flowers and wreaths. A banner was laid over them, reading, "Our common pain and common future unite us." Reporters interviewed and photographed the mourners and the speakers.

As we were leaving the first grave, D. struck up conversation with E., a Turkish-Cypriot student at Eastern Mediterranean University in Famagusta who was sitting behind us on the bus. She had come to the event with A., her grandmother. D. had met them both at a public event at a university in the south the previous week, when E. read an essay she had written on the final passing of the missing across the border, now that the checkpoints were open. *It made such an impression on me,* D. told her. *I've been telling all my friends about it.* E.'s grandmother, A., was a vibrant, funny woman, who spoke to us in Greek. She explained that she had grown up in the mixed village of Louroujina, and all her family there had known Greek. A. left the village in 1963, during the first episodes of violence, and moved with her husband to north Nicosia, where they bought a house and raised their children.



E.'s other grandmother was a "sad person," she said. After the war began in the summer of 1974, her grandfather had taken his sisters to the airport so they could leave for Turkey. *He hired a taxi to take him back to the village. They crossed through two checkpoints along the road, but they got lost somewhere before they reached the third. My grandmother still believes he'll come back someday. She thinks maybe he was taken to Greece and he's still alive. But the rest of the family knows he's dead.*

It was on this grandmother's account that E., still a teenager at the time of the referendum on the Annan Plan in 2004, had gotten involved in bicommunal work and advocacy for relatives of the missing. She had recently gone to Brussels with a delegation of Greek-Cypriot and Turkish-Cypriot students, and told us she was surprised at how little the Greek Cypriots knew about their history. *They believe "the Cyprus Problem" is that Turkey invaded and killed Greek Cypriots. They didn't know about the massacres of Turkish Cypriots at Muratağa (Maratha) and other villages. They didn't know that Greek Cypriots and Turkish Cypriots had committed the same crimes.* D. agreed: *It's true. Many Greek Cypriots don't know this history, and that makes it impossible for us to reconcile.*

We traveled by bus to a roadway checkpoint at Agios Dometios, used then for highway traffic through Nicosia. The organizers warned us that we might have trouble with the guards. If they agreed to let us through, we would fill out our visa forms and cross in the bus; if they did not let us through, the Turkish-Cypriot passengers would disembark, cross the border on foot, and continue in a van on the other side. Greek Cypriots who wanted to cross would have to do so in private cars. The organizers had been negotiating permissions for several weeks. One explained that it was better to keep "open relations" than to risk being blacklisted by the Turkish army: *They've been playing this game with us for years, but we will go on!*

In the event, we were stopped at the checkpoint. As we waited, conflicting accounts circulated on the bus: a similar group had been allowed to cross only a few days before, and so this group would also be able to cross; or Greek Cypriots could cross privately, in rental cars, but not as part of a group (one of the organizers asked wryly, *Oh, so we can cross separately, but not together?*); or Greek Cypriots could not cross at all, and, if they tried, their names would be written on the blacklist, and they would never again be allowed to cross; or the reason Greek Cypriots were not allowed to cross was that they were forbidden to participate in demonstrations or "public political activity" in the TRNC. *That's how "demonstration" is defined here,* a young man said: *Any activity that takes place in public. If we wanted to cross to buy Persian rugs, we'd have no trouble at all.*



Eventually, we learned that Greek Cypriots would not be allowed to cross, even in private cars. They decided to stay on the bus. The rest of the group, presumed to be Turkish Cypriots, had been given permission to get out of the bus, cross on foot, and continue in a van on the other side, but they rejected this plan and disembarked in order to stage a protest. It began on the tarmac very close to the northern checkpoint. Blocked in by cars, the protesters held up a banner—*Our common pain unites us*—and chanted, addressing then-presidents Papadopoulos (of the Republic) and Talat (of the TRNC) by name: *Peace in Cyprus cannot be stopped!*

And so the group split, despite their best efforts. The Turkish Cypriots who would continue on—a group of about fifteen people—took flowers from the Greek Cypriots and promised to place them on the mass grave: *The flowers can cross—they have no nationality!* D. stayed behind. With my US passport, I was able to cross on a temporary visa. But the protest was not over. The Turkish Cypriots of the group held out their banner and began walking back toward the checkpoint, chanting, *No police state in Cyprus!* The guards physically blocked them, grabbing for the banner, pushing back the men in the group. One of the young organizers took pictures with his cell phone until it was confiscated by a guard. The protesters sat on the ground to evade physical contact. One of the Greek-Cypriot cameramen filmed from the other side of the checkpoint.

After some negotiations with the guards, the protesters moved on to the van that was waiting for us on the north side of the checkpoint. As we pulled away, members of the group laughed darkly about the scuffle. E. told me

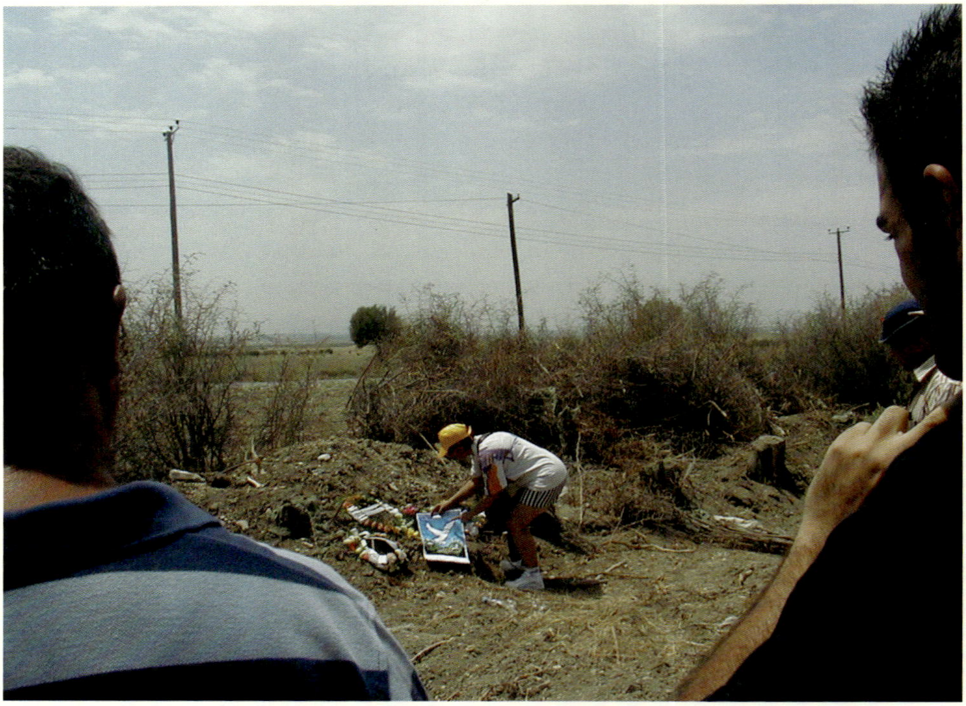

NO.

1.3

that our photographs had been taken by military surveillance as we crossed. *This could cause problems for us in the future*, she said. I asked her how the military would be able to identify us from the photographs, and she told me they already knew who the group members were, since they had attended so many other demonstrations. The military was keeping track, making connections. She joked with me: *If there's a blacklist, you're on it now!* She noted that the border guards were Turkish army, not Turkish-Cypriot police: *If it had been our own police, they would have let us through.*

In the new van, we headed on to the second mass grave near Balıkesir (Palaikythro), a small village northeast of Nicosia. The site was outside the village, in open land. When we turned off the highway onto the country road, the driver lost his way. We had been going aimlessly for some time when two passengers on the bus noticed we were being followed by a white sedan. The drivers were immediately identified as civil police, meaning Turkish-Cypriot police, who had apparently been following us since the checkpoint but only became visible as they repeated our twists and turns on this isolated country road.



Our driver finally found the grave site. Two official Turkish-Cypriot police vehicles were already parked there, lights flashing; they had been notified of our visit in advance. The white sedan parked off in the distance. No media appeared. We got out and gathered around a small pile of dirt marking the grave, which had been excavated and filled in some time before. One of the police officers took photographs of us while some members of the group, including me, photographed the grave. A mourner pointed them out to me: *The Greek Cypriots have more freedom than we do. They have police, but at least they're not secret police.*

The story of the second grave was told by Sevgül Uludağ, the Turkish-Cypriot journalist who had located it. When she began her investigations, she said, no one would speak with her: there was a "law of silence" around the civilian violence of the 1960s, as opposed to the state violence of the 1970s. But eventually, on condition of anonymity, some villagers showed her the site. It had been a mixed village until the invasion, she explained, but less than a month later, in August 1974, a dozen Greek-Cypriot villagers were killed by their Turkish-Cypriot neighbors and buried here—in retribution, it was said, for the rape of their wives perpetrated by other Greek Cypriots who had passed through the village during military mobilizations in the area. Thirty years later, when the grave was excavated, the bodies were removed and identified by forensic teams from the CMP. The hole was filled back in immediately, Uludağ told us, "to cover the guilt." *Can you imagine?* E. asked me. *The families were brought here to see their loved ones, just skeletons, and they recognized them by their clothes—the same dresses, the same shirts they were wearing that day.*

Our visit to the two mass graves that day refracted the border (or "border," as Bryant and Hatay have it) dividing north and south. On the south side of Nicosia, it involved a swift passage through an open checkpoint; a large public event at an open grave that was staged, photographed, and filmed from beginning to end; and a dramatic but protective show of security by official police. On the north side of Nicosia, it involved a protest at the checkpoint, ending in an armed scuffle and the confiscation of cameras; a refusal to allow Greek Cypriots to cross; a formal restriction on public demonstrations; and a small event at a closed grave in an isolated site, closely monitored but not visibly secured by secret police—and the oblique expression of threat: *If there's a blacklist, you're on it now!*



While these two phases of the event might appear as an antithesis between regimes of democratic transparency and repressive secrecy—that antithesis was, after all, expressed by participants, and I believed them, at the time—I rather think that this bicommunal, border-crossing, peacemaking, truth-seeking event shows how an ideology of secrecy works to sustain the enduring division of Cyprus. The revelation of the mass grave in the south was broadcast that evening only to a Greek-Cypriot audience; there was no broadcast at all in the north, though knowledge of the event traveled by other routes and had its effects. If there was a public whose members experienced the same event together, it was instrumental and fleeting. D. had told me earlier that day that the opening of the checkpoints in 2003 had the effect of making people feel "isolated" and "individual"; in this event, the Cypriots who purposively came together in solidarity were forcibly redivided at the border.

In a sense, this event was a reenactment in reverse of a series of public demonstrations that took place during the year before the opening of checkpoints, when Turkish-Cypriot activists attempted to cross the border in Nicosia in innovative ways: "jumping from one of the bastions on the Venetian walls of Nicosia, slipping through buildings on the narrow stretches of the line, using the old sewerage system," as Demetriou (2007, 993) reports. In the repetition of those protests in which I participated in 2007, bicommunal activists showed that "the border" was still a border, even after the opening of checkpoints: that the opening was not the definitive event it had seemed at first, and that the fight against division must go on.

## Time Machines

One afternoon in February, at the Anthropological Laboratory of the CMP—a few days after it had snowed in Nicosia for the first time in fifteen years, and all the scientists had left their tables to run outside in their white lab coats to play on the tarmac—H. and Z. were working together on a case, Z. on "the body," as she called it, and H. on the belongings found with it in the grave. H. held up a watch for us to inspect. It was still in good shape, somewhat small (I thought) for a man's watch, with a simple, round face and a cloth strap. H. pointed out that the watch had stopped when the date read "16." This body had come from a mass grave dating, they thought, to August 16, 1974, immediately after the second Turkish invasion. H. and Z. stopped for a moment and looked at the watch. Z. explained to me that it might have been broken at the same moment when the man was killed. *We see lots of watches,* she said. *Usually, if they're not broken, you have to assume that they just kept working, keeping time long after the person was killed, which is weird—like a heart beating in a dead body. But then you see one like this, and you know it had the same fate as the person. It's like a time machine—it takes you right there.*



In the forensic investigations on which H. and Z. and other scientists worked, and which Cypriot publics followed with more and less avid attention, the CMP reckoned with war through such artifacts of death: the bones and belongings of those who went missing during the conflicts of the 1960s–1970s. The time machine that H. showed me that afternoon at the lab "takes you right there"—"there" being a time as well as a place: the moment as well as the scene of a death. The literality of the watch's representation of time made it, perhaps, an ideal time machine; but in its capacity to materialize and stop time, it was no different from many other objects of forensic work. Layla Renshaw, writing of exhumations of the Civil War dead in Spain, notes the "powerful material and aesthetic properties and affordances of the dead and their associated objects . . . [which] actively shape the responses and representations that can be made by the living" (2011, 27). The key to her insight lies in the "active" shaping of those representations by artifacts of the dead—their lively efficacy, despite their symbolism of death. I see this efficacy in the ways that bones tell time, recording the rhythms, patterns, and accidents of a person's life, in traces left by habits (eating, smoking), repetitive movements, diseases, injuries, environmental elements. They also continue to tell time after death, aging and changing at a different pace once buried in the ground. In this capacity to tell time, bones are perhaps more like mechanical timepieces than they are like other organic matter of the body, such as the flesh, which quickly decomposes and disappears, wholly or partially, after death.[15]

At the CMP's lab, bones objectified knowledge about the deaths of the missing that had been concealed at the time of violence and revealed in the form of evidence during the long-deferred time of investigation—some forty to fifty years later, at the time of my fieldwork. This forensic process of making evidence out of artifacts did not, however, exhaust their activity; the bones and belongings of the missing also came to be dynamic operators in complex time. Jane Bennett, parsing Deleuze, describes "an operator" as "that which, by virtue of its particular location in an assemblage and the fortuity of being in the right place at the right time, makes the difference, makes things happen, becomes the decisive force catalyzing an event" (2010, 9). As operators, in this sense, the artifacts of the missing told many kinds of time, in the performative rhythms of science and ritual; they materialized the temporalities of death, waiting, discovery, analysis, sanctification, and reburial.



In registering this operation of time by bones in the forensic context, I do not mean to imply their agency—though as Krmpotich, Fontein, and Harries suggest in their introduction to a collection of essays on bones, "agency comes in different forms," some of which are not reducible to nor divisible between persons and things. Scholarship and debates on vital materialism, object agency, and nonhuman "actants" over the past two decades, they argue, have brought about a crucial "re-conceptualization of what 'doing' actually amounts to" (2010, 373). It is easy to miss the subtle point they are making (many have missed it in the debates to which they refer), but in this and later sections, I want to dwell on it and extend it ethnographically. Operating time is something that the bones of the missing in Cyprus "do," as I see it, not only because their material properties and sensory affordances endow them with a special capacity to tell time to the scientists who interact with them, but also because those properties and affordances are what manifest the bones' survival of violence and the long time afterward: their materialization in the present of the "non-absent past," in Domanska's term—in short, their artifactuality. These properties and affordances thus compose the sensible, knowable difference immanent in the present that creates the possibility of a kind of time travel for the people who work with the bones; and that, I think, makes all the difference.

An understanding of bones as things that tie the past to the future was implicit in the CMP's ideology of closure; digging up bones in mass grave exhumations was explicitly framed as *Digging the Past in Search of the Future*, the title of a documentary film commissioned by the CMP about its mission.

This notion of the future is possible to think only when the past is conceived in terms of loss, such that the future may be apprehended through healing: a future anterior contingent on forensic investigation. This future was commonplace in public discourse about the CMP's work, even styled for public consumption, and it required no personal encounter with the bones of the missing to understand or anticipate. But, as I observed, working with the bones and belongings of the missing inflected the way the scientists at the CMP understood the past in relation to the future; their work with these artifacts mediated their own belonging to time.

This mediation was effected, in part, by the temporal unfolding of forensic investigations: the way they uncovered and revealed in real time a history of violence that had been buried and concealed through secrecy. As I show in later sections, CMP excavations required many months to complete, sometimes years, demanding extreme endurance and patience on the part of the archaeologists who toiled day after day, doing the painstaking work of delicate searching without knowing if they would ever find a single bone; or, if they found a grave, excavating slowly and deliberately, countering political and financial pressures to work ever faster. The historical and geological processes of sedimentation required this protracted temporality of excavations to undo the work of time and reveal the past. As the artist Francesc Torres writes of his experience photographing the mass grave exhumation of Civil War dead at Villamayor de los Montes, Spain, "When recovering historical memory, we often find ourselves immersed in a literal metaphor, which means a radical contradiction of terms. This happens when the unquestionable certainty that history has taken place emerges at the same time that its sediments are dug up. So, 'digging up memories' is not just a figure of speech" (2007, 15).

But the experience of time in the forensic context was also mediated by the artifacts of the missing in their capacity to effectuate the mode of historicity that I have been calling artifactual. In working with scientists at the lab and in the field, I learned that these time machines, as Z. called them, both filled time and killed time, generating experiences of duration and arrest for the people who worked with them, rendering pasts and presents simultaneous. Time machines seemed to make it possible for the scientists to conceive of the future differently from the clichéd anteriority proffered by "digging the past": not in terms of the telos of reconciliation, but in terms of the difference immanent in the present that was rendered sensible, knowable, by the presence of the past.

I recall here Connolly's notion of time as becoming: "a moment of time without movement, engaging different zones of temporality" (2011, 2). Al-

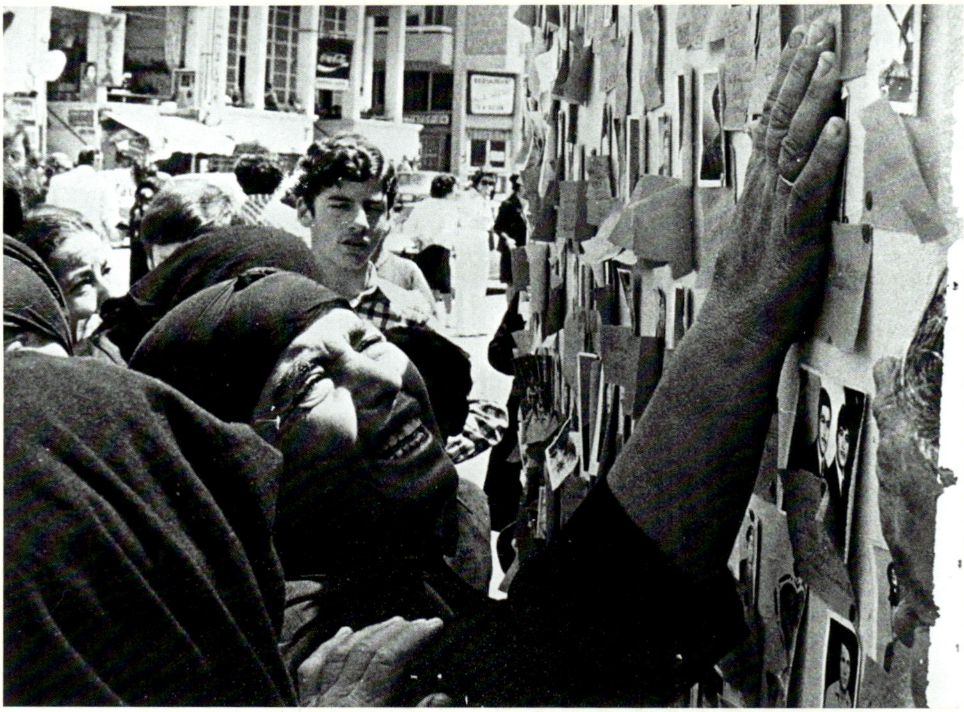

NO.

**1.4**

though, in his text, Connolly finds his way into this experience of time through a personal memory, I suggest that it may be entered as well through objects that do not have mnemonic efficacy. Palmié and Stewart give some indication of this possibility in their discussion of "chronotopic switching," which "activate[s]—often unintentionally and spontaneously—particular pasts in joint or individual attention" and gives one access to "the feel of the past" (2016, 219). That access is often assumed to be restricted to personal memory—typified by Swann's tasting the madeleine in Proust's *In Search of Lost Time* (as indeed Palmié and Stewart have it in their article). But the artifactual historicity anchored for forensic scientists by the bones of the missing does not depend on personal memory, and indeed could not, given that none of the scientists experienced the events whose artifacts they were examining. A focus on personal memory—which has determined so much knowledge production about the Cyprus conflict, by way of testimonials and memoirs—may obscure how much people do not remember, and how much they do not know about the past by way of individual memory. Their not-knowing did not, however, foreclose their "feel of the past," nor their sense of a future to come.



I take some inspiration for thinking beyond the biographical parameters of personal memory from Tiffany C. Fryer's archaeological and ethnographic research in Tihosuco, Mexico, a town on the front lines of the Caste War of Yucatan (1847–1901) that was abandoned after a bombing in 1867 and reoccupied generations later. In her collaborative project to develop a historical knowledge base for the heritage work that current residents seek to do, in a context where historical facts are very hard to come by, Fryer pays close attention to how particular sites and objects in the old town stimulate the communication of "collective remembrance" (2021, 5, 6) on the part of her interlocutors. Collective remembrance, she argues, is not reducible to personal memories; it is, rather, a way of "remembering what we do not know," of "know[ing] the past through a cultivated relationship with things, incorporating newly encountered knowledge about the past in ways that intimate remembrance rather than via fact-oriented learning" (5).

This way of knowing is anchored and mediated by what Fryer calls "unsuspecting materials" (2021, e.g., 5, 7, 24). These materials are not the "usual suspects"—that is, heritage objects already saturated with memorial significance and commodified in various ways for the international heritage industry—but rather the otherwise unremarkable features of the postwar built environment (a mysterious anteroom in a complex of buildings, for example, or the hooks on one wall of an old house) that her interlocutors use to speculate about the past, based on their association with those people who might have lived in and used these sites and objects. Fryer, drawing from Reinhart Koselleck, takes this rich association of the living with the dead as key to collective remembrance; what the living remember in this way exists "within the corpus of experiences that they understand themselves to have access to—those alien moments of the lives of others we are in association with, as Koselleck put it—and that they understand themselves to be allowed to reproduce as cultural or memory authors" (11). For Fryer, "remembering what we do not know" is "an embodied theory of open pasts" that demands our understanding the past as "a set of overlapping timespaces . . . rife with potentiality rather than finitude" (24, 8). This potentiality is mined by her interlocutors as they develop collective remembrance in the present as a basis for knowledge claims about the past.



From Fryer's work I take two points about memory with immediate relevance to the forensic context in Cyprus: first, that remembering can be powerfully materially mediated; and second, that remembering can be collectively experienced through associations between the living and the dead who are related to a site or event. At the CMP, the people who worked most closely with the remains of the missing had no personal memory at all of the violent events recalled by those remains. The memory of those events was discharged to them nevertheless. It was not discharged to just anyone; as I discuss in the next section, the scientists employed at the CMP were all Cypriots, all inheritors of the division, all related in one way or another to someone or to many who had gone missing or been killed or displaced during the violence of the 1960s–1970s. It was through their association with those victims of the conflict that they were eligible to be entrusted with the memory of the missing; and it was through their tactile work with the material remains of the missing that they experienced that memory as knowledge of the past.

In her seminal work on classical law and politics, *The Divided City*, Nicole Loraux dwells on the amnesty granted to the Thirty Tyrants by the democrats after a brutal war for Athens, following the democrats' return from exile and their restoration of democracy in 403 BCE. Taking the sacred oath not to recall the war, on pain of death, was the procedure by which individuals became citizens after war, and by which the city could once again be imagined "as a whole," devoid of division (Loraux 2002, 142, 48). Loraux notes the specific forms of remembering forbidden by this amnesty: not only commemorative plays, which might rouse the anger and resentment of those wronged by the Tyrants, but also, and more urgently, lawsuits against the wrongdoers, since the function of trials was to transform memory (as evidence) into justice (as punishment).

The reasoning behind this enigmatic amnesty unfolds in Loraux's conceptualization of *stasis*, or civil war, as the foundation of politics. She elaborates a domain of the politico-theological in the founding of the city by war, which entailed the domination, assimilation, or exclusion of some by others—a victory sealed and legitimated by sacrifice to the gods. But conflict does not stop with the founding of the city; for Loraux (2002, 30), the city in peacetime also operates through conflict, which it continually represses in the democratic process of prevailing in a vote—the process by which a collective will is wrested from individual differences and the conflict of factions—by privileging "kinship" and "shared community" over divisions.



In Loraux's imagination of politics, the city is thus necessarily and essentially divided; it comes into being through division, which it must continually overcome by forgetting so as not to rekindle wrath and resentment in every democratic debate, since "recollection itself is a wound" (2002, 41). She warns that the "silence" that "surround[s]" *kratos* (57)—a term that, in Homeric sources, denotes "superiority and thus victory," or "to have the upper hand" (69), but that in modern Greek simply means *the state*—marks the "repression" or "denial" of conflict, but not, in fact, its forgetting (68, 70). Indeed, she argues, the victorious democrats remembered all too acutely the violence, horror, and injustice of the war, and "it is precisely because they remembered the past that they forbade anyone to recall it" (263). But, she writes, "conflict cannot be forgotten without consequences. . . . The prohibition of memory may affect the very definition of memory; and the will to memory may take refuge in recalling why memory limited its own existence" (193, 263). In orations after the amnesty, she finds recurrent, insistent traces of this fixation on memory in the democrats' exhortations to all citizens of Athens to remain loyal to the amnesty, and in their ambivalent double-negations justifying it: "We were not unjust" (264).

The resemblances between Athens in the fifth century BCE and Cyprus in the twenty-first century CE—in the politico-theological underpinnings of the city/state, in the reckoning of citizens with civil war, and in their anxiety and ambivalence about their memory of war—are robust but easy to overstate. To identify contemporary Cyprus with the ancient Athens of the amnesty would be to allegorize rather than analyze its political situation. I introduce Loraux here not to suggest such a facile comparison, but rather to extend her reflections on the dangers of forgetting conflict, even in the interest of peace. If amnesty, in classical Athens, wrought a distortion and hypertrophy of memory, fixing on the civil war as an event whose ever-present potential to recur required constant vigilance to avert, then what are the dangers of closure, to which the CMP has been so committed? The work of healing the wounds of war by putting the dead to rest, rather than letting them lie, might appear to be a work of memory rather than forgetting; the funerals of the missing after their remains were found and returned to families certainly emphasized this dimension of the CMP's mission. But in concealing evidence of violence in the name of political neutrality, the CMP did as much work to forget the conflict and to forego justice.

In the scenario opened by this analogy, the forensic scientists in Cyprus are custodians of memory, granted the task of "'hold[ing] memory of evil'" (Loraux 2002, 39), protecting citizens from remembering what they have done to one another as, in Loraux's reading of Aeschylus, Athena entrusted the Erinyes to do for the citizens of Athens after the verdict of Orestes, thereby transforming them into the sacred Eumenides. Loraux implies that, as guardians of dangerous knowledge, the Eumenides were consigned to live with their own rage and resentment, always on the verge of wreaking vengeance and thus destroying the peace of the city. Did their custody of memory take a similar toll on the forensic scientists—Cypriots who had grown up in a divided society, without their own memories of violence or the time before? In performing scientific objectivity in the service of purely humanitarian goals, and in signing confidentiality agreements not to disclose to anyone what they knew, were they pledging not to participate in political life? (And what did the discharge of their own memory to these young people, in the form of forensic knowledge, cost those Cypriots who had lived through the war?)

While these scientists did not experience personal memories of the violent events, they did experience the presence of those events personally and directly, as they handled and studied the bones of the missing and transformed that presence into forensic knowledge. These artifacts thus refracted and reorganized time, summoning and configuring relationships between the past and the present, the dead and the living. In working with them, it seems to me, the scientists were in a special, perhaps unique position to decline the binary terms in which the past was starkly opposed to the present in discourses of division and reconciliation in Cyprus: either to forget (kill the past) or to remember (keep it alive); to sustain the conflict or to end it once and for all. In thus sensing the instability of the past (which did not stay put but went on, in artifactual form) and thereby the heterogeneity of the present (composed of the "now" as well as the "then," which both defamiliarized and enriched it), they might, too, sense an openness, a multiplicity, in the future.

## Circles of Trust

The CMP comprises three political representatives: the Greek-Cypriot Member and the Turkish-Cypriot Member, appointed by their respective governments at the level of minister, and another known as the Third Member, selected by the International Committee of the Red Cross and appointed by the UN. Under the Members' direction, since 2004, teams of Greek-Cypriot and Turkish-Cypriot archaeologists, physical anthropologists, and geneticists have been conducting investigations: exhuming remains on both sides of the Green Line, analyzing them, and confirming their identity with DNA testing. Once a missing person's identity has been confirmed, the remains are returned to the person's relatives, who also receive, if they wish, psychological counseling and financial support for burial. 

In 2011–12, I conducted fieldwork with the CMP, spending several months on field excavations and several at the CMP's Forensic Anthropological Laboratory ("the lab"). The year before, on the advice of the Third Member, I had submitted a formal proposal to the CMP to conduct open-ended ethnographic research with the forensic teams, and was soon granted permission, pending "clearances" on a "case-by-case basis." I was not permitted to work at the Cyprus Institute of Neurology and Genetics (CING), a bicommunal nonprofit medical center where DNA samples were tested until 2012.[16] I visited a number of excavations, spending longer periods of time at three main sites: one in a cultivated field, one in a well, and one on a mountainside, an enormous site connecting several smaller excavations extending from a rocky peak down to a wooded valley. The field and mountain excavations had been going on for years when I joined, and most of the exhumations (when remains were found and removed) seemed to be in the past; the well excavation, on the other hand, was initiated only a week before I was assigned to the team and closed shortly after I left, so I was able to participate in almost the entire process. The teams working at these sites ranged in size from four to over twenty archaeologists—the CMP employed between fifty and sixty archaeologists altogether at the time—of whom some were more or less permanently assigned to the sites, while others rotated in and out as needed.

The lab was located in a fenced-off section of central Nicosia on the site of the old Nicosia airport, now a United Nations Protected Area, part of the buffer zone. Access was strictly limited to UN personnel and CMP employees, who were obliged to show photo ID cards to armed UN guards in order to enter (I got one of these, too). Within the massive airport site, the lab occupied a set of small buildings on a piece of tarmac, surrounded by a chain-link fence that demarcated it as sovereign British territory, according to the terms of the 1960 treaty of independence; the UN rented the facility from the British Forces Cyprus for a nominal fee.[17] When I worked there, the main building at the lab, a cinderblock structure dating to the 1960s, had two large rooms filled with tables where bones and artifacts were cleaned and examined by two teams of anthropologists, about a dozen people altogether. The building also contained a DNA extraction booth, a large storage annex for human remains and artifacts, and a file room. Extending from this main structure were separate prefabricated buildings housing a computer lab, a management office, a kitchen, and a viewing facility. In 2012, plans were being laid to add another building for storage, as the human remains and artifacts exhumed in the field were accumulating faster than the anthropologists could analyze them and prepare them for return to relatives.



I learned that the cases undertaken by the CMP were initiated by investigators, working from the official list of Greek-Cypriot and Turkish-Cypriot missing agreed upon by both sides. Investigators gathered information from witnesses to "known" episodes of violence in which specific missing persons were thought to have been killed, although they often came across other information, relating to other cases or previously "unknown" violence, in the course of their research. The investigators I met were middle-aged Greek-Cypriot and Turkish-Cypriot men with their own experiences of the conflicts between 1963 and 1974. Some worked occasionally with investigative journalists, such as Sevgül Uludağ in the north and Andreas Paraschos in the south, but many worked on their own or with assistants hired by the CMP.[18] These men had extensive kinship and patronage networks, based in their own villages and refugee diasporas—networks they tapped in their research, making relatively easy passage into small "circles of trust," as one explained to me. These circles included people who had been combatants at the time of the conflicts—military personnel, members of paramilitary groups, armed civilians—as well as noncombatants: villagers, farmers, merchants, relatives of the missing. With few exceptions, the investigators worked behind the scenes, quietly and off the record, knowing that many witnesses would refuse to speak if their cooperation were made known even to their neighbors, not to mention the larger publics paying close attention to the work of the CMP. I learned from archaeologists, though, that some witnesses were more open about what they knew; they would often help the forensic teams excavating near their homes and share information.

Unlike the investigators, the scientists at the CMP were young, most under thirty years of age; they had not been born when the war took place in 1974. N., an archaeologist, told me the CMP preferred younger employees for the forensic work, since they were fit and energetic, had few family responsibilities, and could be expected to work long hours for low pay. Some were required to relocate for months at a time in order to live closer to remote excavation sites; only young people were "up for an adventure" like that, she said. A number of CMP scientists were nevertheless married with small children, including a few working in the field who had taken a short time off for childbirth and then returned as quickly as they could. Many of the scientists I knew considered their employment with the CMP to be temporary; by 2012, the project was expected to last no more than a few years. *Everyone knows there's an expiration date on this project*, L. told me. Thus, although positions at the CMP were prestigious and highly sought-after, there was also a high turnover rate; anytime an archaeologist or anthropologist found a permanent position elsewhere—for example, in the Department of Antiquities, a civil service position—they would jump at it. In the meantime, as C., another archaeologist, explained to me, *It's good experience, good training. You make really good friends, working here. And for some of us—not everyone—the mission of the CMP is really important.*



All members of the scientific staff held undergraduate degrees in a pertinent field, most in archaeology—though their areas of specialization ranged from art history and classical archaeology to prehistoric archaeology and geoarchaeology—and fewer in physical anthropology or osteology. No one held a degree in forensic science; no Cypriot universities or institutes offered such a degree program, though a few of the more experienced lab workers expressed interest in earning a forensic science degree through online or distance learning programs offered by British universities. Many of the CMP scientists had attended university outside Cyprus, either in Greece, Turkey, or the UK; quite a few held master's degrees, and some were in the long, expensive process of working toward a master's or doctorate while employed full-time at the CMP. Those who had little university training in physical anthropology acquired expertise as they gained experience in the lab. Everyone I met at the lab had also worked in the field at one time, in some cases for years and in others for only a few months; they had come to the lab either because they had requested the transfer or because they had been asked by their respective Member to fill an empty post.

These transfers were reversible, in theory, and I met more than a few lab workers who were eager to get back to the field. The scientists seemed to me to sort themselves fairly easily into what they called "field people" and "lab people." The field people appreciated the challenge and the concreteness of physical work, and enjoyed the satisfaction of immediate discovery and the camaraderie of teamwork under difficult conditions. The lab people, on the other hand, found themselves better suited to focused analytic work; they were gratified by seeing cases to their conclusion and appreciated a more "normal," office-like workplace and schedule, especially those with children. This division of labor was fairly recent, I learned; in the early years of the CMP, the same personnel (much smaller in number) exhumed remains and then analyzed them in the lab, following cases from beginning to end.



The CMP was required by design to employ Cypriots, exclusively, on the forensic teams. (Other positions—lab managers, equipment officers, IT specialists, support staff—were often held by expatriates, some of them seasoned UN employees who had worked in other countries before their posting in Cyprus.) In practice, Cypriot identity was established by parentage; scientists on the forensic teams had at least one Cypriot parent, and many had both a Cypriot mother and a Cypriot father, defined by their birth in Cyprus. Membership in a Cypriot family, in this sense, was a basic qualification. A few employees were, as they put it, "half Cypriot," with a Greek or Turkish parent. One anthropologist of such mixed parentage told me that, in his job interview, he had been asked whether he held Greek or Cypriot citizenship—a question he refused to answer on the grounds that, regardless of national citizenship (he in fact had dual citizenship), according to EU labor regulations, citizens of any EU country were entitled to apply for the job. He wondered whether it was even legal for the CMP to discriminate against non-Cypriots in hiring for these positions. The criterion of Cypriot identity at the CMP was "purely political," he said.

Another "purely political" factor, the principle of balance, likewise regulated employment at the CMP. Equal numbers of Greek Cypriots and Turkish Cypriots were supposed to staff the forensic teams at all times—this, despite the radical asymmetry between the two populations on the island (approximately 64 percent Greek Cypriot and 17 percent Turkish Cypriot at the time of my fieldwork).[19] Archaeologists often found themselves rotated onto a different site team in order to balance it when a cocommunal team member called out sick or was abruptly transferred to the lab. F., one of the team leaders at a field site where I worked for a time, joked with me about how helpful my collaboration was, in this sense: because I lived in the south and spoke Greek, I could count as a Greek Cypriot if one of the Greek-Cypriot team members were absent. We both found this funny, and silly, but in practice, my informal qualification as a Greek-Cypriot team member did, on occasion, enable him strategically to defuse the daily pressure to balance his team.

L., another archaeologist, told me bluntly that the people who worked at the CMP were "selected for it," for political reasons: *You can't be a na-*

*tionalist and work here,* she said. I never learned how the CMP filtered out nationalists in the hiring process, but I did hear from a number of the scientists that their work at the CMP caused strain in their families; their parents, for example, did not share their sense of the importance of reconciliation, or might fear they would develop friendships or romances with their colleagues, young people from "the other side." Quite a few of the scientists I got to know were leftists whose politics placed them well outside the mainstream, though just as many told me they were "not political" and just wanted peace in Cyprus. In any case, screening out nationalists, even if informally and incompletely, exacerbated the difficulty the CMP faced in finding sufficient numbers of qualified Cypriot anthropologists and archaeologists with good working knowledge of English—the official language of the project and all its documentation. Those who ended up working at the CMP were indeed a select group. *You're in a bubble here,* L. told me. *We're not representative of Cypriots in general.*



Even within this bubble, I heard occasional accusations of "racism" on the part of employees toward those of "the other side"; I understood "racism" in this context as a gloss for ethnonationalism. These accusations were expressed privately to me, never openly among colleagues, nor directly to the colleague in question. As far as I could see, Greek Cypriots and Turkish Cypriots worked together in the lab and the field in a thoroughly mundane way. They were skilled at subduing complaints and stepping around tensions. They shared not only work and workspaces but also rides, meals, and jokes. They brought what they called "typical" Greek-Cypriot and Turkish-Cypriot dishes cooked at home to work and shared them with colleagues, explaining their recipes and cooking techniques. They attended one another's weddings. They gave one another gifts of baby clothes, and sweets on birthdays and name days. They read one another's coffee grounds and smoked one another's cigarettes. If this sociality was, for most, somewhat shallow and merely workaday, some also socialized outside work, traveling across the so-called border to meet up at bars and clubs in Kyrenia (on the northern coast) or south Nicosia; I was aware of a few close friendships that had developed and were sustained across communal lines.

Language was perhaps the most significant division between Greek-Cypriot and Turkish-Cypriot employees, or at least the most obvious to me; especially during meals and coffee breaks, conversations at work often developed in Turkish or Greek, excluding those who did not share the language. English was the official language of the CMP and the only language shared by Greek-Cypriot and Turkish-Cypriot employees, but few of them genuinely spoke it fluently; an uneven sort of "UN English" was the lingua franca, which inevitably constrained and compromised communication. Yet many scientists I knew had picked up quite a bit of their colleagues' language; some had even taken classes at their universities. Trying out the other language, especially slang and traditional Cypriot dialects of Greek and Turkish, was a common form of play at work. In the spring of 2012, the CMP offered classes in Greek for Turkish-Cypriot employees and in Turkish for Greek-Cypriot employees, in addition to English classes for everyone, held at the H4C. Although the classes were scheduled irregularly and after work, when CMP employees were already exhausted and obliged at home, they were nevertheless popular and well attended.



The day-to-day operation of the CMP thus offered many occasions for collaboration and cooperation between Greek Cypriots and Turkish Cypriots. The work environment was decidedly nonpolitical in regard to the Cyprus conflict. That is not to say that CMP scientists did not hold political views about the events of the 1960s–1970s, or the issues at stake in the ongoing negotiations over reconciliation; but they avoided making comments that might anger or hurt their colleagues, and many seemed to share general contempt and mistrust as much toward their own government as toward the people or government of "the other side."

Only rarely did communal divisions seem to bear on the knowledge production these scientists were undertaking at the CMP. When it did, however, the very premise of the CMP—that knowing the fate of the missing on both sides would heal wounds on both sides—was called into question. If the scientists were primed to empathize and keen to socialize with one another, they were also forced by the nature of their work to contend with conflict; as they learned to look past division, they were looking directly at its evidence. One afternoon at the lab, V., a Turkish-Cypriot archaeologist, told me quietly that he had just heard a Greek-Cypriot colleague say, *The trouble all started in 1974*—a formulaic expression I had heard conservative Greek Cypriots use to date the conflict to the Turkish invasion, which victimized Greek Cypriots, and thus to obscure all the violence against Turkish Cypriots that had been perpetrated by Greek Cypriots in the previous decade. Sitting next to us, L., who had gone to school in Greece, pointed out that it had been the official policy of the Republic of Cyprus until the year 2000 to deny the existence of any Turkish-Cypriot missing persons.[20] *People in the south were brainwashed*, she said. *Children learned this in school. But information is starting to come out now. It will take time, but people are becoming more aware*. V. was not appeased. *But my colleagues know better!* he said. *They exhumed Turkish-Cypriot bodies from 1964!* If their exposure to this clear evidence of mass murder did not suffice to educate them about the violence

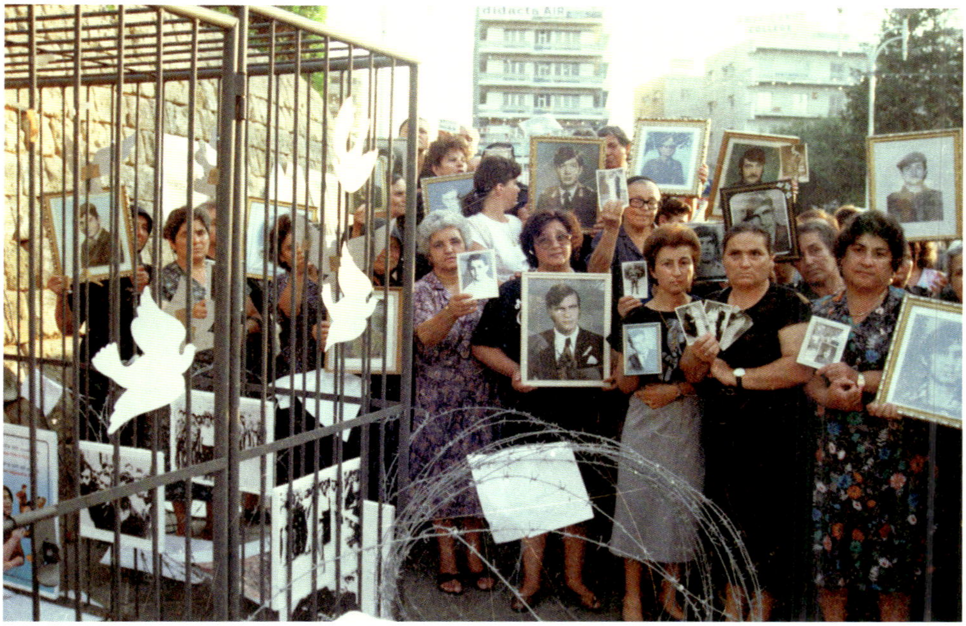


NO.

1.5

committed by "their side," rousing their consciousness of their own complicity in the conflict and their compassion toward "the other side," what would?

Indeed, early in my time with the CMP, I began to sense disappointment in a number of the scientists who carried with them, to the field or the lab, their own family histories of the conflict, which inflected their forensic work and their expectations of their colleagues. V. and P., for example, Turkish-Cypriot archaeologists who had recently been transferred to the lab, shared their family histories with me one day at lunch at the UN cafeteria. Usually, we ate with a larger group, but that day, many of the lab workers had stayed behind; perhaps it was the absence of any Greek-Cypriot colleagues from the table that emboldened V. and P. to talk to me about such sensitive issues. They told me stories they had heard from family members about how Turkish Cypriots had moved into enclaves in 1964—events, V. said, that many Greek Cypriots seemed not even to know about. V.'s father's family had fled from Limassol, a large port city on the southern coast, to an enclave in north Nicosia after his father had been betrayed by a Greek-Cypriot coworker whom he had thought was his friend. P. said, *I can't imagine this. If anything like that ever happened and my colleagues were in danger, I'd do everything I could to protect them.* P.'s mother and aunt had escaped from Paphos, on the island's southwestern coast, in 1964, ahead of their parents, with the aid of a Greek-Cypriot taxi driver who had false papers allowing him to cross the cease-fire line. They managed to pass safely through all six checkpoints between Limassol and Nicosia. Before the last checkpoint, P. said, a Greek-Cypriot soldier had joined them in the taxi and recognized that the passengers were Turkish Cypriots, despite their attempts to conceal their identity. But, contrary to their expectations, he had covered for them and wished them safety. *There were good people and bad*, P. said. *Some helped each other, others betrayed.* Z., who had just joined us at the lunch table, told me about her grandmother's brother, who had gone missing in 1964. *We know he's dead, but we don't know where*, she said. *My grandmother thinks it was their friends, men she and her brother grew up with—they trapped him outside the village and shot him dead. After you learn something like that, it's very hard to trust people.*

## Same Old Shit

One clear morning in March 2012, after a week of heavy rain that had kept most of the field excavation teams indoors, I joined two Greek-Cypriot archaeologists at the Ledra Palace checkpoint, where they gathered each morning to wait for a ride from their Turkish-Cypriot colleagues. We crossed the checkpoint with our UN badges just as one of their team leaders arrived in a pickup truck. We drove north and east on the road to Ercan airport, passing through the outskirts of northern Nicosia, passing by new housing developments, warehouses, and supermarkets, until we reached a farming area in the shadows of the Pentadaktylos Mountains. The site was an open field owned, B. told me, by a Turkish-Cypriot man whose small house sat on the southeast corner.

R. explained a few things about the site to me, asking B. to correct him if he missed anything, since she had spent as much time there as he had. He told me that witness information indicated eight or nine civilians had been buried here in July 1974, as well as twelve or more soldiers about a month later. It seemed to me that B. faintly recoiled when R. said "civilians"—perhaps she was thinking they might have been armed irregulars, and thus combatants rather than civilians—but R. immediately repaired his comment: *That's what the witnesses said. We don't know who the people were.* The first team to excavate, in 2006, had found the remains of at least five people in the middle of the field, which they had exhumed before closing the site. Since those bones were very few, and unarticulated, investigators thought that more remains of those five individuals could be found here, as well as remains of many other people. Excavation resumed in 2011 and had been ongoing for almost a year when I joined the team. During that time, they had found another grave with the remains of at least three individuals—an elderly woman and two children, whom they thought had been hit by tank fire—toward the southern edge of the field. The remains of an adult man were found a few months later near a house on the main road, at the northern edge of the field, and then another two individuals on the southern edge, behind the ruins of a mud-brick house.

T. was the reporter for the site: the team member entrusted each day with taking photographs and recording field notes, drawings, measurements, and findings. She had worked here with the first team in 2006 and returned with the new team several years later. She made a face: *This has been going on much too long!* B. explained their excavation strategy to me. The area was a large subdivided field used for cultivation; the CMP had persuaded the owner to cease planting and harvesting until excavation was complete. The team had started in the area closest to the road and then moved on to the eastern side. Once excavated, those bare tracts had become their staging area, where they parked their trucks and stored their equipment as they extended the excavation toward the western edge of the field. At the southern edge were the roofless ruins of the mud-brick house, cutting a jagged shape against the open sky. I soon learned that the team used the ruins as a toilet. They had excavated all around it but not inside.

The team was pursuing the slow and painstaking process of surface clearing and trenching. B. told me that, initially, they had been one small team with one machine, but when they had found a grave the previous winter, they were given an additional machine and several more people to work. *It's a big site, and they want us to finish it,* she said. *Now we can do two things at once.* One of the machines was a backloader, used to dig trenches and deposit piles of soil along the edges. Two people surveyed this process at all times, one on either side, watching for bones—one to look inside the trench and one to look at the piles of soil. The other machine was a digger, which pulled up soil and deposited it in piles that a group of archaeologists would work through with pickaxes, breaking up the thick clumps of mud and stone. If they managed to find bones in a pile, they would sieve-sift the soil by hand to get a closer look.



That morning, the team was split into two groups; one was deployed to follow the backloader, and I joined the others, who would work at breaking up piles of heavy soil. F., one of the team leaders, distributed small pickaxes to us, some light and some heavy, some with sharp tips and some blunt; F. graciously gave me one of the lightest and sharpest. We chopped into the mud, breaking it apart and scouring it for bones and fragments. It was tough physical work; the mud was hard, heavy, and full of stones. B. showed me the calluses she had grown in the webbing between her thumbs and forefingers: *See how tough I am! You'll get these too, if you stick with us.* The work continued for three hours, broken up by a short coffee break that we took around the open bed of the pickup truck in the middle of the field. It was R.'s turn to make the coffee; others opened up loaves of bread and shared out tomatoes and cheese. Everyone smoked (except me).

During the afternoon shift, after a lunch delivered to the site by a local restaurant, the two groups switched places, and I ended up following the backloader with B. and R. We stood very close to the edge of the trench. I watched their sight lines; they stared intently into the trench as the toothed bucket scooped out soil, and then at the soil as it was redeposited on the ground. Occasionally, one of them would signal to the machine operator to stop, then pick something up from the pile for a closer look and throw it back into the trench when it proved unremarkable. The work was monotonous; after a morning of chopping and picking, I found it restful and sort of mesmerizing, but B. kept saying she was bored. R. listened to something on his iPod. We continued for a few more hours. When we were done for the day, walking back to the truck, I asked R., *So, what are you doing tomorrow?* He laughed: *Same old shit, every day.*

I worked with the team at that site for a month, following machines, looking at soil. One afternoon, I was standing beside F., following the digging machine in its slow progress, staring at the soil it churned up every few feet. F. was quiet; he lit one cigarette after another. I asked him how many he smoked per day. *It depends,* he said. *In the field, on a day like today, I smoke just to pass the time: an hour goes by, I light one, a few minutes go by, I light one, like that—maybe ten during the day. But when we find bones, I don't smoke at all. I get too busy. I get focused on the work and I forget about smoking.* I asked him, *So when are we going to find some bones?* He stared into the trench. *I don't think we'll find any more bones at this site. But we have to try.* 
In the past, he told me, CMP excavations had occasionally been closed with the expectation of opening them up again after further investigation, but he was against this practice. *All it means is that some other team has to come back in the future and do everything all over again that we've already done. Like, this site was excavated in 2006, they found several bodies, and then our team came back in 2011 and found five more. But we started from scratch and it took us a long time to figure out the best approach. I don't think the site should be closed again—we should continue until it's done. And we need to continue, because there's information that more bodies are here somewhere. But I don't think we'll find them. We're looking at everything carefully so we don't miss anything. The point is, we want to make sure that when we close the site, we can really close it for good.*

After another week, I asked to be assigned to a new site. I wanted to see something different; I wanted to see discovery. I ended up on a well excavation in the north where, again, nothing was found after several weeks. I returned to the field site in May for a few days while waiting for another placement. It was hot and humid by then, and working in the open field without shade was getting difficult; I joined the archaeologists in complaining about it, mostly the same group I had gotten to know two months earlier. The team was split into two groups following the two machines as they opened trenches, one from the south end of the field and one from the north. Positioning ourselves with our backs to the sun, we were exposed to the dust raised by the machines, which stuck to our faces and hands and got into our noses and mouths. I felt the grit in my teeth and the back of my throat for days afterward. T. told me they entertained themselves guessing how much dirt they were eating every day. *Eating dirt, that's what this site is about,* she said.

She meant more than she said, and eventually I cottoned onto her meaning. Both trenches were finished by the end of the morning, so after lunch the machines opened two new ones from the center of the field. I noticed a large tractor working over the soil in the next field over, which belonged to the owner of a new luxury villa with a swimming pool, looking completely out of place on the eastern edge of the field. T. told me the tractor driver was just clearing the field, not planting yet. *But they might,* she said. *We don't know what's going to happen with this excavation. In theory, we'll keep going, but the information we have from the witnesses is vague, and it's a big field, and we're not looking in the right places, obviously.* I asked her if she had any idea where the right places were. She laughed. *The people who ran from tanks and guns—where would they go? They'd go to the mud house, of course! They'd try to hide. Wouldn't you? But we're not allowed to excavate inside the house.* I was surprised, and asked her why. *We want to go in,* she said, *but the bosses won't let us. They're playing a different game. We shouldn't be surprised. It's very political at that level—like everything in Cyprus! Things don't get done that should get done, for political reasons.* She told me there was an ongoing discussion at the CMP about whether the excavation should proceed at all. R. and F. were preparing a presentation for the CMP Members, to make the case for continuing.



I looked back across the big field, taking in the hard-packed bare tracts the team had already excavated and backfilled, and the grassy tracts they had yet to touch. It looked empty to me. I turned toward the mud-brick house on the other side of the field. There it stood, open to the sky, grasses and bright wildflowers growing through and all around it. Its floors had crumbled to dust long ago. Perhaps the ground within its walls held everything the archaeologists were looking for: the bones of more civilians and all the soldiers killed here in the summer of 1974. What were the "political reasons" that kept them working a few steps away, trenching empty ground day after day, month after month, pressured to move ever faster, carried forward by the rhythm of the machines, meditating, smoking, looking but not seeing?

In the end, R. and F. made a persuasive presentation, and the excavation was allowed to continue. When I left Cyprus that August, the team was still working at the field, turning over the earth piece by piece.

## The Politics of Bones

As a humanitarian, nonprofit organization with an entirely local scientific staff, the CMP was unique at the time of my fieldwork among the postconflict forensic agencies that have proliferated worldwide since the 1980s. The organization contracted to investigate mass graves in Bosnia and Herzegovina starting in 2000, for example, was a for-profit company with an international staff, which the CMP began paying for DNA testing when its relationship with the Cyprus Institute of Neurology and Genetics ended in 2012. Damir Arsenijević, rejecting the instrumentalization of knowledge generated by postconflict forensic investigations, notes that identifications of those killed in the Bosnian genocide in 1992–95 were "locally driven" but swiftly folded into an expanding international forensic enterprise of postwar reconstruction and multicultural peace management: "In the end, all this money poured into Bosnia following the war is not for nothing. There is something to show for it. But is this the 'target'? Is this the 'deliverable project'? Is this the 'empowerment' or 'building local capacities'? Is the only option for Bosnians to be given a niche in the international service industry as experts, assisting around the world in the identification of mortal remains? To produce material for somebody's Master's thesis? To be a case study? Is that the only way to ensure translatability?" (Arsenijević 2011a, 203).



With a view to disrupting the consolidation of this enterprise, its profitable proliferation of expertise and its presumption of comparability or "translatability" across postconflict scenarios, Arsenijević (2011a, 203) proposes an alternative: to "reclaim the means of knowledge production," which might entail reclaiming the bones themselves, "snatching the sample" back from the scientists. One of the Cypriot investigators I met early in my time with the CMP expressed similar skepticism about the global enterprise of forensic knowledge. *Everyone has their own agendas,* he said. *I don't just mean the politicians. The scientists, too, and the academics.* He smirked at me. *They want to write books, they have their CVs to fill.* I laughed, about to protest somehow my implication in his comments, but he anticipated my defense and waved it away: *This is normal! It's legitimate. Everyone has these concerns about their work. But for me, what we're doing at the CMP isn't work. I expect the scientists to treat their work as a serious obligation, as something to do for the future of Cyprus, for their children, and for the families who have suffered. A lot of them don't have this attitude. They look at their job here as an opportunity to help the people who hired them. Or they look at it as practice for doing something else later on. It's a good job for them, and it's also a way to enter international circuits through the UN.*

Even the nonprofit Argentine Forensic Anthropology Team (EAAF), celebrated as a pioneering grassroots human-rights organization, had a lucrative multiyear contract with the CMP. The EAAF—whose own first teams were trained in the early 1980s by forensic experts from the United States—had been hired by the CMP in 2004 to conduct its earliest investigations, train Cypriot archaeologists and anthropologists in techniques of excavation and analysis, set up its database, and provide ongoing supervision.[21] During the time I worked with the CMP, some EAAF members continued to play a supervisory role, traveling to Cyprus twice a year to audit procedures and give advice on updating equipment, safety standards, and work procedures.



Forensic expertise and the infrastructure of investigation were thus transnational and mobile, yielding striking resemblances among different postconflict scenes of forensic investigation along with tenacious, untranslatable particularities. One of the CMP's distinctive features was its nonpolitical mandate. According to its terms of reference laid down in 1981, the committee "will not attempt to attribute responsibility for the deaths of any missing persons or make findings as to the cause of such deaths."[22] This mission delimited in a particular way the amount and the kinds of evidence to be collected and analyzed by the forensic teams. Scientists at the CMP attempted to recover and identify as much of the remains of the missing as they could, a painstaking process in exhumations as well as at the lab. Introducing me to "the politics of bones," as he put it, the same investigator explained the rationale for this: *In Bosnia, for example, they were collecting evidence of mass violence that they could use to prosecute war criminals. It was all about the scale of violence. So they just collected bone samples they could test for DNA; they didn't even try to recover the bodies. Here, we're not doing prosecutions. We're not collecting evidence for that. And there are important reasons, religious reasons and symbolic reasons, why we want to give the whole body back to families. They're very disappointed with how little we're able to find, most of the time.*[23]

With this mandate, the CMP operated through the "rhetoric of conciliation" rather than the "rhetoric of justice," the two uses of the "truth of the *corpus delicti*"—the body of the crime—that Thomas Laqueur (2002, 81) identifies in contemporary human rights discourse. The forensic process of truth production by the CMP was oriented not to solving crimes but rather to naming bodies: "A person, with an identity and a place within a family and a community, is brought back from the anonymity of a grave and in some sense given back to his or her people," as Laqueur puts it (82). Naming victims' bodies without naming the perpetrators of their deaths defined the radically determinate space of forensic investigation in Cyprus.

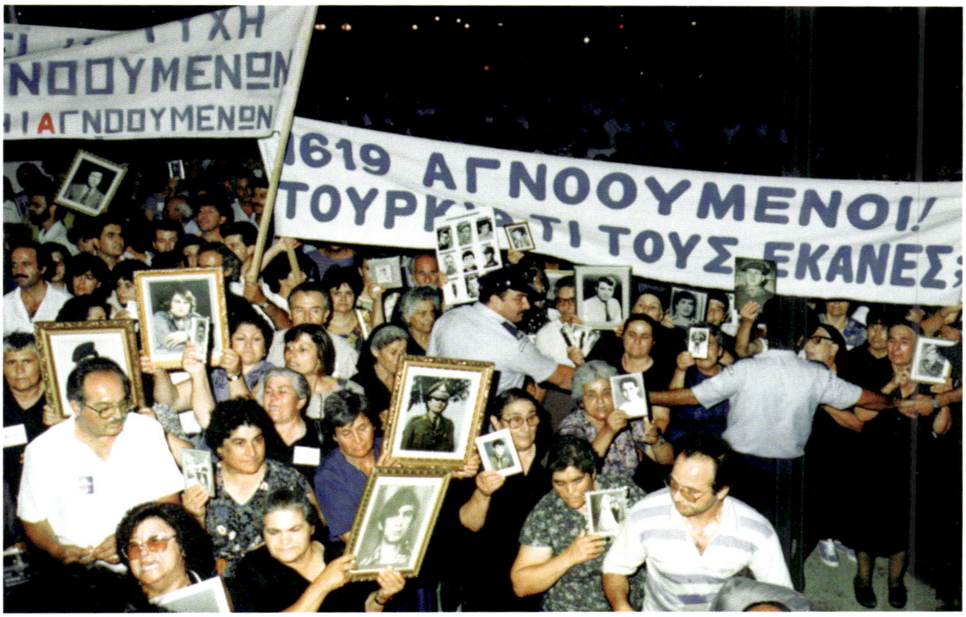


NO.

**1.6**

Another particularity of the CMP was its detachment from its constituencies: relatives of the missing, especially, as well as larger publics in the north and south for whom the resolution of the fate of the missing was the nominal key to moving forward from their history of conflict. In many other post-conflict sites of forensic investigation, such as Argentina and Spain, exhumations of missing persons were initiated by grassroots organizations and conducted by volunteer forensic teams, who worked directly with relatives and witnesses and maintained open access for the public to their excavation sites and forensic findings (Crossland 2000; Ferrándiz 2006; Renshaw 2011).



In both cases, excavations became sites of memorialization as well. Ferrándiz and Baer (2008) examine the elaborate work of "memory recovery" taking place in Spain, for example, in tandem with forensic investigations into the fate of 70,000–100,000 people killed during the Civil War (1936–39) and under Franco in the decades afterward (¶ 2). Excavations undertaken since the early 2000s began, they show, through the efforts of victims' descendants, who organized themselves in groups such as the Association for the Recovery of Historical Memory and others that followed. Ferrándiz documents the complex forms of witnessing, testimonial, and media attention developing out of this memory work: "the appearance and consolidation of a full-scale 'meaning industry' around memories of the Civil War" that he compares to mobilizations in Germany around the sixtieth anniversary of the end of World War II and the Holocaust (Ferrándiz 2006, 10, citing Sztompka 2000). Engaged in their own project of video documentation at these excavation-memorial sites, Ferrándiz and Baer explore the "different modes of recording, archiving and distributing digital images associated with exhumations" that they see as "crucial elements in the process of recovery of 'historical memories' in contemporary Spain" (2008, ¶ 7). They note persistent conflicts among different memorial associations, and between these associations and forensic teams, over how much and what kinds of "visibilization" should be taking place (¶ 18).[24]

These robust efforts to record, broadcast, and archive the forensic excavations in Spain, and the conflicts over the appropriateness of these efforts, together indicate a high level of public involvement in those excavations. In Cyprus, by contrast, the CMP—a hybrid, bicommunal agency in a divided state, hosted and largely funded by the UN—conducted its confidential investigations outside the public eye. Although excavation sites were not hidden, and indeed were quite visible to people living and working nearby as well as to the journalists who reported on them, their locations were not publicized; access was restricted by safety tape and mesh fences, and sites quickly fell back into invisibility once excavations were complete, backfilled and unmarked by signs or plaques. The lab, likewise, was located in a protected UN site without public access; even invited guests and press representatives required special permission and a UN escort to enter.[25]

The extensive coverage in Cypriot newspapers of scandals at the CMP, and complaints about the speed, effectiveness, and correctness of its investigations, signaled to me doubt and suspicion on the part of Cypriot publics. There was no sense of grassroots initiative at the CMP, no place for relatives or others invested in the investigations to play an active role in shaping the CMP's objectives or procedures. The visibility of field and lab work was tightly controlled, even as the CMP engaged in its own strategic self-promotion—a peculiarly synergetic dynamic of secrecy and publicity.



## History Doesn't Belong to Us

Despite the CMP's stance of political neutrality, and its interdiction on attributing responsibility for the deaths it investigated, the forensic scientists informally made findings every day about the causes and circumstances of the deaths of the missing. C., an osteologist who had been working at the CMP for several years, told me that their lab reports were designed to prevent conclusions from being drawn about the cause or manner of death; the forms elicited information in discrete, quantitative chunks, rather than in what she called "narrative" form. But C. had been trained to think in narrative terms, she said, assembling pieces of evidence that would lead to the conclusion that the event of death had transpired in a certain way. *A narrative like that needs a lot of description*, she told me. The CMP lab reports had boxes for recording measurements of each bone according to several different metrics, in order to determine the person's age, osteological sex, injuries, and pathologies, but there were no spaces in which to write descriptions of the bones. Moreover, the forms elicited "differential diagnosis," as she put it; the scientists were asked to note any traumas or pathologies that might be related to the death, supplying evidence for multiple possible causes without drawing conclusions. When I asked C. who would read these reports, she said, *No one! They just sit in the archive.* But she added that she thought the CMP was afraid families might request the reports years down the line, so they wanted to limit and frame the information recorded on the forms in a very particular way.

And thus the production of forensic evidence yielded its own secrets, in turn. These secrets were not only a matter of what was concealed in the

CMP's confidential archives. They were also a matter of what was quite literally destroyed in the process of investigation. When human remains are exhumed, the graves are destroyed. I have learned from archaeologists that such destruction is part and parcel of discovery, and that what is destroyed depends on what investigators are seeking. As the team leader at one excavation site told me: *The first thing I learned about excavations is that they destroy culture. Once you understand that, you understand that the question is how to learn as much as you can from a site while doing the least damage.* According to CMP protocols, material evidence recovered in an excavation would be removed from the site each day, brought to the lab, then washed, dried, cataloged, and stored in the climate-controlled annex until it was time for analysis—a matter of weeks, months, or years. When the analysis was complete, any bones and fragments that could be identified conclusively were returned to the relatives of the victim, along with any associated artifacts. Artifacts that could not be associated with a specific person were retained by the CMP in storage. Any potentially dangerous materials, like munitions, were turned over to the UN to be destroyed by the bomb squad. Thus, according to procedure, most of the material evidence recovered by the CMP was reburied by relatives; some was stored anonymously; and some was destroyed.

In my work with the CMP, I saw nothing to indicate that the excavations conducted by its forensic teams were any more damaging to evidence than other excavations. But archaeologists did question the appropriateness of their excavations in a more general sense. For example, when I joined the team working at a large excavation site on a mountainside in the north, I heard a long debate over lunch between G., who worked part-time curating exhibits at the Archaeological Museum in Nicosia, and N., who said he was altogether "against" excavation and exhibits. G. had started the conversation by announcing her plan that evening to see a new exhibition at the Archaeological Museum, just opened in celebration of the upcoming Cypriot presidency of the European Union. N. asked her, *What is this? You spend all day working on an excavation and then at night you go to the archaeology museum?* G., surprised, asked him, *Don't you like archaeology? Aren't you an archaeologist?* N. told her he preferred archaeological parks, where sites were opened with all the artifacts left in situ and glassed over so that visitors could see the site intact. He complained that the science of archaeology had not progressed much in a hundred years, that excavation techniques were still "very primitive" and did terrible damage to the history embedded in the ground. G. agreed that archaeological techniques were in some ways "too crude for proper excavations," but she contended that was exactly why they needed to continue their work—to improve their methods, and to keep learning about their civilization and their history.

N. replied, *History doesn't belong to us; it belongs to future generations. We should be preserving it for them. We could do that with satellite photography and three-dimensional photography—we don't need to excavate right now. People in the future will have better tools; they'll know what to do.* G. asked him how they would know when that moment had arrived: *How long should we wait? Anyway, there are ways to excavate and preserve at the same time—you can excavate just a corner of a site, rather than the whole thing.* Gesturing across the massive site where they were working that day, N. pointed out, *If you only dig part of it, you don't get the whole picture; you just have little pieces, and little ideas that don't get at the whole. Look at how we do things—do you really think we're taking good care of these bones?*



N.'s criticism was ethical, not methodological. His team followed clear, established procedures as they had been trained to do. Archaeologists working in the field carried with them an acute awareness of the importance of these procedures to ensuring good evidence. They told me they were criticized constantly in the newspapers for doing sloppy work, for not following proper procedures in their excavations, for not storing bones safely, and, in some cases, for destroying evidence out of incompetence or political motivations. O., another archaeologist, told me, *People don't understand why investigations take so long. We're attacked all the time in the media—people say we're too young, we're lazy, we don't take the work seriously. They don't understand how hard it is. . . . On a lot of sites, we just don't have good information from witnesses, and we have to dig around for a long time before we find the grave. They don't understand how meticulous we have to be in order to recover entire bodies, rather than just a few fragments for identification, like they did in Bosnia. And then the analysis takes forever—we have so few people working in the lab, and we have to check and double-check everything to be sure we've got the right person. And then there's a huge backlog for DNA testing.*

O. described the daily push by supervisors to go "faster, faster, faster" before the money ran out. When she first began working with the CMP, she told me, she had heard the project would continue for ten years or more—"as long as it took!" Now, however, the Members were suggesting a much shorter horizon of about three years. (At the time of this writing, the CMP is still doing its work.) This reduction in the scope of the project had almost entirely to do with funding, O. said; the investigations were extremely expensive, and the CMP was wholly dependent on funding from the EU and UN, which were increasingly spare in their contributions. The lab manager told me that, given its short life span, the CMP would consider it an "excellent success" if 80 percent of the missing were found by the time they shut down.

Under these pressures, one of the excavation supervisors was known to complain about the extensive documentation required of field workers according to proper procedure. Recording everything in field notes and photos slowed down the excavations, and he could not see the point of collecting all that data when the important thing was to recover the bones and return them to the families as soon as possible. F., who had worked for several years in the field, objected to this. He told me that when it came to field photography, *More is better! The camera can see things you don't see. The whole process of excavating has to be recorded so that you can reconstruct it years later, if you need to.*



That prospect—reconstructing investigations in the future—was, perhaps, the crux of the matter. When I worked with the CMP, it ensured the anonymity of witnesses and the confidentiality of forensic data, but there was no guarantee of those assurances in the future. Should a political settlement ever be achieved between the Republic and the TRNC, an essentially new federal regime would emerge, with a new justice system. A truth and reconciliation process could be initiated as part of this regime change and, with it, a new form and new role for the CMP, if it survived at all. Its confidential archives could be opened to the public, or at least to police and prosecutors. What were treated at the time of my fieldwork as politically neutral deaths could become murders and assassinations. Field reports of excavations could become records of crime scenes; anthropological analyses could become autopsies. And it was with that uncertain future of the state itself in mind that the CMP kept its secrets.

## Keep the Door Locked

When I first began spending time at the CMP lab, I went without instructions or directives from the Members of the CMP; I was encouraged to find my own place. Eventually, after I got to know some of the scientists, I took that place next to them as they did their work. But in the beginning, not sure what else to do with me, perhaps, the lab manager sent me to the archivist, who organized and maintained all the files kept at the lab. The CMP had massive paper and digital archives, and I spent many weeks reading through them. Access was (otherwise) strictly limited to CMP employees, who were required to sign confidentiality statements prohibiting them from discussing the details of their work with people outside the organization, except for "scientific" purposes, as their contracts put it—purposes that seemed to be worked out on a case-by-case basis, as permissions for my own research were.

For instance, in 2012, a few CMP archaeologists traveled to Atlanta, Georgia, to present papers at the annual meeting of the American Academy of Forensic Science. This was the first time any research conducted by the CMP would be presented in a public forum, and there was some resistance to this among the Members and their assistants. Written and oral versions of the papers underwent extensive editing by the Members—"censorship," as one of the presenters described it to me. Important details such as the location of excavations and the presumed ethnicity of the victims were removed from the papers. Street signs and the faces of CMP employees were obscured in the field photographs. The presenters asked me to help them with their papers, but they were not allowed to email me digital copies, lest I circulate them—despite the fact that the papers would be published in the conference proceedings. There seemed to be both great concern and great confusion over what should and should not be said and shown, and no clear understanding of how context and audience might inflect those questions.



When the CMP group returned from Atlanta, I heard all about their experiences at the conference. Most newsworthy, S., one of the archaeologists, had been approached after her presentation by a forensic anthropologist from an American agency, who was working on a difficult excavation that she thought might be facilitated by the methods S. had described in her paper. S. had obtained permission from the CMP to share her paper with the American anthropologist but told me she did not know whether she should try to publish it in a forensic science journal, as the American anthropologist had encouraged her to do. *It contains confidential information,* she explained. On the other hand, it was already public, as it would certainly be published in the conference proceedings. A few days later, S. was interviewed by a newspaper reporter. She told me afterward, *This journalist wants to show how the knowledge we produce in Cyprus is useful to the rest of the world, too. But it was complicated—I couldn't tell her anything that I didn't say in my conference paper, or give her any other photographs. Nothing specific.* Within a month, though, she had produced a version of the paper that she planned to submit to a forensic science journal, after it was reviewed by an Argentine colleague from the EAAF who had trained and mentored her, as well as by the CMP. She was nervous about the reaction of the Members, who had given her such a hard time before the conference, but she told me she was committed to sharing her knowledge with archaeologists outside Cyprus.

The archives themselves contained dense and voluminous documentation; each step of each investigation was described, imaged, analyzed, checked, and double-checked. Hard copies of all case files were stored in a special annex of the main lab building. The file cabinets were locked, and I was introduced to the annex with a warning: *This is all confidential*, the archivist told me. *You can look at anything you want, but you have to put everything back when you're done reading, and you must keep the door locked*. The files were organized by case number, divided into closed and open cases. Each hard-copy case file contained a folder with antemortem data: a photograph of the missing person near the time of his or her disappearance, attached to a sheet with the person's name, the name and contact information of the "reporting relative" interviewed at the time of the disappearance, a brief description of the circumstances surrounding the disappearance, and a basic physical description, including injuries and medical conditions. Case files also contained original field and lab notes, handwritten on preprinted forms, including inventories of bones and artifacts, hand-drawn maps of excavation sites, and hand-drawn pictures of bones. For the final reports, these handmade materials were transformed into typed narratives and data that could be input into database fields. These final reports were peer-reviewed—that is, checked by at least one coworker—and then edited, printed, bound, and labeled as the official "Archaeological Report" and "Anthropological Report" for each case. The archaeological reports included day-by-day accounts of the excavations, with photographs, measurements, and detailed descriptions of the sites, as well, sometimes, as a sheaf of transparencies showing the location and position of the bones in each stratum, which, seen together, depicted the entire contents of the grave three-dimensionally. The anthropological reports were equally detailed, with photographs of bone arrays and specific bone markers or anomalies, along with drawings of the bones, indicating on a model skeleton those that had been found and analyzed.

Recent case files also contained printouts from the digital database into which all data had been entered. These data included measurements and descriptions of every single bone examined, handwritten onto lab reports and then entered into the ForDisc database.[26] The results of the ForDisc estimates were also written on the lab reports. *The amount of information that goes into these reports is astounding!* the lab manager told me as he explained the process. Each lab report was peer-reviewed—that is, checked by a second anthropologist against the bones; any discrepancies would have to be "reconciled" by a third anthropologist. Once the peer-review process was complete, the lab manager triple-checked the entries for consistency, comparing the original lab report against the peer reviewer's notes.

Each case file also included DNA results from the Cyprus Institute of Neurology and Genetics (CING). These results were represented both visually—in the form of a family tree depicting each relative who had contributed a blood sample in relation to the missing person—and narratively, describing the missing person's kinship relations, the testing process, and the results of analysis, along with an explanation of the parameters of certainty. Accompanying the data and reports were the chain-of-custody forms that traveled with the remains throughout their journey, signed by personnel at every stop—from the field to the lab, from the lab to CING, from CING back to the lab, from the lab to the CMP office, and from the CMP office to the relatives who ultimately received them. Case files might also contain correspondence between relatives and the CMP, and among scientists at the lab and CING. A notice of the viewing with relatives was usually included, along with any press releases issued by the CMP regarding the missing person, and an official memo from the Third Member declaring the identification of the remains as fact.



The lab manager was responsible for designing and updating the digital archive, he told me. The first database used by the CMP had been developed by the EAAF for its use in Argentina, which the lab manager had then adapted to the CMP's purposes, removing some input fields and adding many others. The digital archive at the time I saw it was "in progress"—as it always had been, I came to understand. Forensic teams had been excavating and analyzing remains for several years before the lab manager began working on the database. His job since then, he said, had largely consisted of streamlining and standardizing the information reported by the teams. The CMP had transferred two fieldworkers to the lab in order to edit the archaeological reports, "correcting" the language—the reports were all written in English—and elaborating descriptions of the process and the findings as needed, in line with a "standard of professionalism." *A lot of the archaeologists hate writing reports,* A., one of the editors, told me. *They're in the field. That's what they're good at. It takes all their attention, and they really don't like having to stop and write. They think a lot of things are "self-explanatory" that actually need explanation. And many of them don't have the language skills to write good narratives anyway.* Since both the report editors had extensive field experience, he told me, they understood what was written in the field reports, as well as what was left unstated. Theirs was a work of translation from the field to the archive.

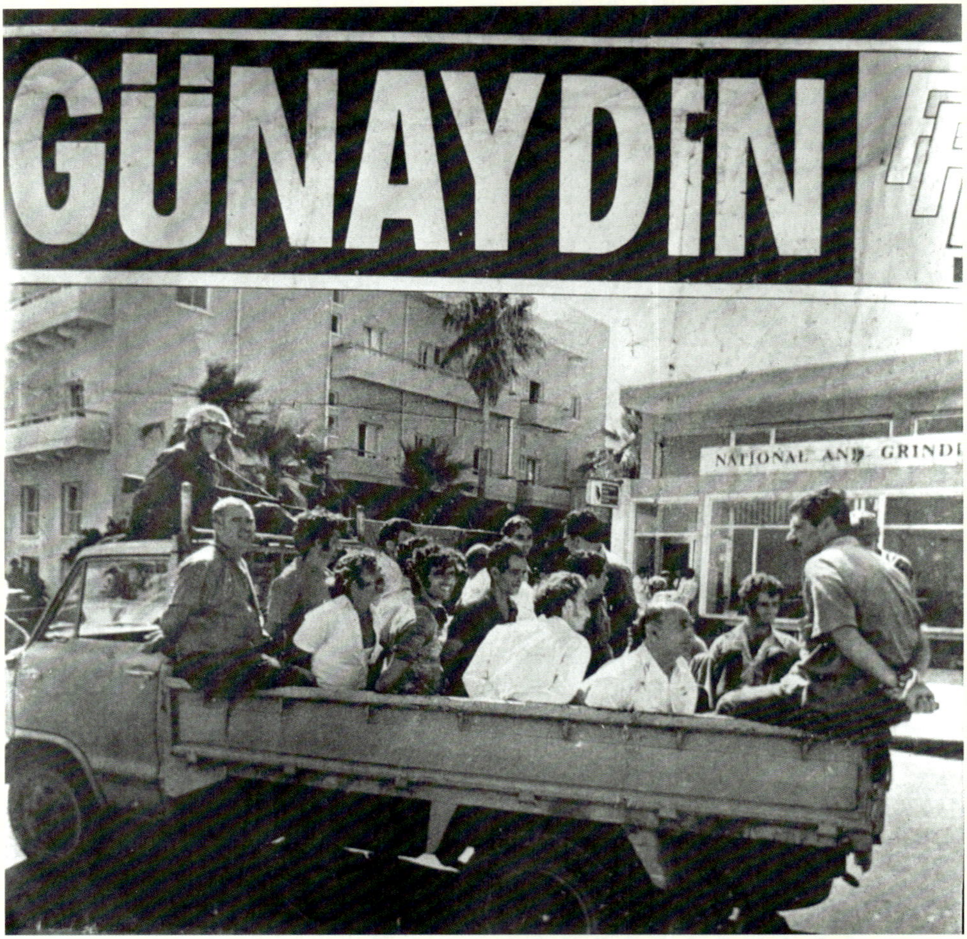


*NO.*

**1.7**

The results of all this immense effort at documentation and clarification—the evidence of the CMP's procedural transparency—were confidential. The lab manager had constructed all the gateways that restricted access to different parts of the database. All the computers at the lab were networked to the database on a secure server—not connected to the internet—but different employees had different kinds of access. For example, geneticists were locked out of lab and field reports, since DNA identifications were required to be carried out blind. Likewise, anthropologists undertaking blind analysis of remains were locked out of the antemortem data in the case file. Only the archivist and the lab manager had access to all the data.

However carefully constructed, the interface between scientists and database was sticky and constantly changing. This became evident to me in a series of discussions I witnessed at the lab over the index of place names in the database. Archaeologists were inconsistent in their use of place names in their field reports: some used only a Greek or only a Turkish name; some used both for villages that had two names, but placed the Greek or Turkish name first according to their own language; and for sites in the north, where place names had been changed after the war in 1974, some used the old Greek or Turkish name and some the new Turkish name.[27] The Members had made a decision the previous year about how to name sites, but no one had told the lab manager, so he had not changed the input fields for place names in the database. This meant that multiple files for one site might be stored under different place names in the database, and anyone searching for a file might not find it where expected. One of the investigators told me, *This problem with the names, it's a political problem but also a practical problem. In the north, they changed all the place names after 1974. But the CMP is a humanitarian organization. We don't care about politics, and we don't care about what happened after 1974. So we all agreed to use the names from the 1960s, the ones people used when the events were happening. The problem is that none of the Turkish Cypriots born after 1974 know the old names. You say "Lysi" and they have no idea what you're talking about. They only know "Akdoğan." They think they're being asked to use a Greek name instead of a Turkish name for political reasons, but it's just the opposite!*

These discrepancies, and the suspected politics behind them, had already generated some conflicts between field archaeologists and the people who edited and filed their reports, and who therefore had to change the names the archaeologists had used if they did not conform to the policy. I found the lab manager—a non-Cypriot UN employee—one morning in the computer lab, fuming as he sorted chronologically through all the files to date and tried to correct and systematize the place names. *People think it's so easy to make a decision like this!* he said. *They don't consider how much it affects the whole database: all the files have to be changed! Anyway, it should be a Cypriot who standardizes everything. I don't know the geography or the names very well, and I can't tell when one site is close enough to another one to go by the same name.*

In a way that was different from the shielding of postmortem data from anthropologists or geneticists conducting blind analysis of remains, the place names of excavated gravesites were data whose availability and intelligibility depended on the identity of the person seeking access. One difference between these two forms of restriction lay in their purposiveness: blind analysis was based on principles of objectivity and confidentiality, while place names arose from an accidental materialization of implicit social disparities. Another difference lay in the delimitation of identity effected by these two forms of restriction—the first determined by a professional-functional category, and the other by ethnonational belonging, which converged in the identities of these forensic scientists. This database, part of a UN international project, was designed with "stranger sociality" in mind, as Elizabeth Povinelli (2011, 156) describes a "way of knowing how to go about navigating and interacting in the world and circulating things through the world" with unknown and often unseen people—that is, in a world of universal public access. But the "social skin" of users—their belonging in "thickly embedded social relations" that conditions their production, reproduction, acquisition, and circulation of knowledge, as Povinelli describes "kinship sociability"—was inadvertently built into the database architecture and "thickened" by its use (162, 156). What users could learn about an excavation site from the database depended on what they already knew about its place in Cypriot geography and history—knowledge that was contingent, in many cases, upon their age and their identities as Greek Cypriots or Turkish Cypriots.

## Those Aren't His Bones

The CMP's mission to promote healing and closure while refraining from politics corresponded to an understanding of mourning the missing as a psychological process, operated—for some Cypriots, if not others—by religious symbolism. When a missing person's remains were identified, a psychologist from the relatives' ethnonational community would be dispatched to counsel them and prepare them for a viewing of the remains. Viewings took place at the lab, where relatives could see the bones and artifacts, meet the scientists who worked on their case, and ask questions. This event was the culmination of a lengthy process of investigation, during which relatives had little if any direct communication with the scientists working on their case. Their first contact was usually the viewing, where scientists could convey what they knew—or some of what they knew—and relatives could come to reframe or translate in forensic terms their grasp of what had happened to their missing person.

These viewings were also, sometimes, occasions for conflict. A. told me that it was at viewings that the bones "became real people" to her; witnessing the emotions of family members as they encountered the remains, hearing their stories about the person, and trying to answer their questions about the death made manifest the ties that had once embedded the person in a family and community, and that had remained, until that moment, abstract for the scientist. But the process did not always work that way for the families, she told me. Interacting with them was difficult, because they often had questions that were "not scientific" in nature or that the scientists could not answer. *Some family members are okay*, she said. *Some are angry; some cry, others don't; some accept the death, others don't. The atmosphere can get tense when they're suspicious of us. You just have to stay calm and keep explaining what you know and what you don't know.*

I saw these dynamics of suspicion and transparency play out in a viewing I attended at the lab; my permission to be there had, I learned later, been negotiated on my behalf with some difficulty. Three missing Greek Cypriots had been identified: two teenaged brothers and their uncle, killed during a raid on their village in August 1974. The investigator had told me that dozens of people were killed that day, but the bodies had been moved from the site later on, presumably to hide the evidence. What the archaeologists found at the original gravesite were just a few dispersed small bones and fragments left behind. At the viewing, the remains of the three people were laid on three separate tables; since very few whole bones had been found, it was mostly fragments, arranged as far as possible in the shape of bodies. Another table held the artifacts associated with the individuals, in clear plastic bags: some scraps of clothing, buttons, shoelaces, a cigarette case. Three small wooden boxes, like coffins, were stacked in another corner of the room; when the viewing was over, the remains would be wrapped and placed in these boxes, then transferred to the CMP office in south Nicosia to await the funeral a few weeks later. Next to the boxes, along the back wall of the room, a sort of family shrine had been assembled, with framed photographs of the three victims, a lit oil candle, an incense burner that would be lit when the family entered the room, and icons of Mary and Jesus. K., one of the anthropologists, told me she always felt strange setting up these shrines, lighting the candles, putting the photographs of the victims in the frames, bringing the coffins into the room: *There's nothing scientific about it! It's much too personal. It makes the viewing feel more like a funeral.* She thought it was inappropriate for her to be involved so intimately in the family's grief. But the CMP psychologist, who had worked with the relatives as the case unfolded and arrived at the viewing ahead of them that morning, insisted it was important for the family to begin the process of mourning when they first encountered the bones: *The symbolism matters*, she said.



Sixteen members of three generations of the victims' family attended the viewing, including the widow of the adult man, who was also the aunt of the two young brothers. The chief investigator introduced himself and the scientists who had worked on the case, and explained the purpose of the viewing to the family. *Our mission is purely humanitarian*, he said (in Greek). *We don't do political work or pursue criminal justice. The role of the forensic teams is very limited; their sole purpose is to find the remains of the missing and determine their identity. We do not investigate the manner of death or attribute responsibility. The purpose of our meeting this morning is for the scientists to explain the investigation, to present their findings, and to answer any questions you have.*

The presentation of archaeological findings began with witness information that had led the team to a site near the victims' village, which they had excavated over a period of several months. The team leader gave a PowerPoint presentation with satellite maps pinpointing the gravesite and a series of photographs of the excavation itself, though none showed any human remains in situ or in evidence bags. She described the progress of the dig, as they had located layers of irregular soil and bone fragments, and then continued to the bedrock level to ensure they had found everything. The bones and bone fragments were small and very dispersed, she said; the archaeologists had had to dig slowly and carefully, mostly with hand tools rather than machines, so as not to miss anything. They had ultimately found the bones of at least ten individuals, of whom three were the relatives of the people in the room.

During the presentation, one of the relatives—a middle-aged man who had survived the raid on his village as a child—asked the team leader a series of questions about the burial. Could they tell if the soil had come from somewhere else? Could they tell if all the bones had been buried there at the same time? Did they know how many people were buried there? Did the presence of so few bones mean that all the people murdered that day in August 1974 were not killed at that site? The team leader was circumspect in her responses. She said they could not know for sure, but the most likely scenario was that all the villagers had been killed and buried at this site at the same time, and then at some later time—*No, we can't tell when*—the bodies had been moved elsewhere, so all that was left were these small bones and fragments. No, she said, they couldn't test the soil to date the different types more precisely; tests could be done on the soil to determine this, but the CMP did not conduct those tests. Later, the archaeologist told me she suspected this man had been trying to elicit scientific evidence that he could use to bring a court case against Turkey. She could tell that he was "skeptical," she said, so she had tried to be very careful in explaining what the team could and could not know about the grave on the basis of their excavation. *The most difficult part is when there's nothing more to say*, she told me, *but the family just keeps asking for more.*



Another relative, an elderly woman, asked the team leader about the possibility of establishing a time frame: how precisely could they date the burial? She said that someone in the nearby village had seen "our people" alive in October 1974, so if the bones from this site were buried in August, these could not possibly be their bones. The team leader explained that there was no way to date the site so precisely. Later, when the relatives had left the lab, she remarked that this question—unlike those of the skeptical man—seemed to resist the facts of death; the woman seemed to hope there had been a mistake in the identification, a mistake that would allow her to conserve the possibility that her relatives might still be alive.

After the presentation of archaeological findings, K., a physical anthropologist who had worked on the case, presented her findings. She explained the basic process of establishing age and osteological sex, the analysis of bone pathologies, and the complex work of associating fragments. This family's missing relatives were three of ten people buried at this site whose identity had been confirmed by DNA analysis; there could be other people whose remains were found at the site, she said, but could not be identified by DNA. A geneticist from CING then explained that, after a preliminary identification of the remains had been made through anthropological analysis, bone samples had been sent to the genetics team for blind confirmation using DNA samples provided by family members—some of whom were in the room. He told the family: *The results were double-checked. It is 100 percent certain that these bones are yours.* The widow of the adult victim began to weep, and then her daughter—his daughter—as well.

Another relative seemed upset at the paucity of the remains. He asked whether the CMP might find "the rest of the bones" someday. The investi-

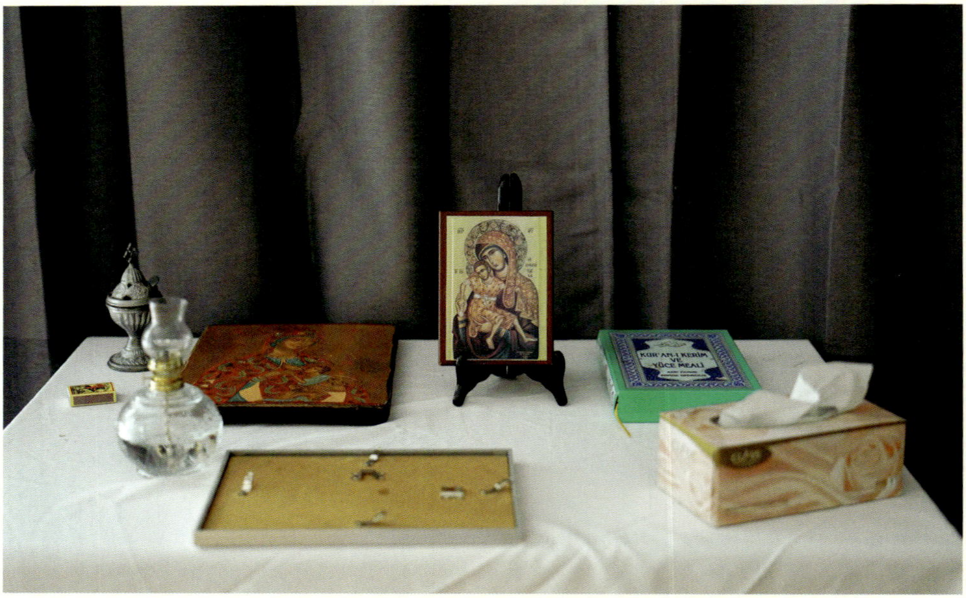


*NO.*

**1.8**

gator agreed it was possible that additional bones might be found at other excavations; if there were reason to think such bones might belong to this family, the CMP would certainly inform them. *But*, he continued quickly, moving toward closure, *that doesn't mean you should keep waiting and expecting at any moment to hear from us*. An elderly relative asked whether the family could learn the names of the other people found in the grave. The investigator told him that was "private information" reserved for the relatives of the other missing persons; the CMP kept this information confidential, to protect the relatives. *It's a matter for them to decide whether they want to tell other people*, he said. *What I can confirm is that the other seven people whose remains were found in the same grave were individuals from your village.*

The investigator then explained the next steps to the family. After the viewing, the remains would be taken from the lab to his office, where he would issue them a document confirming the deaths of their relatives, which they could take to the municipality to get death certificates and make funeral arrangements. On the day of the funeral, if they wished, soldiers would escort the "coffins" to the church. At that time, he would also give them a file on their relatives, with information about the investigation, two short reports with the archaeological and anthropological findings, a photograph of the gravesite, and a photograph of each person's bones. The skeptical relative asked if the reports would show cause of death, and said something under his breath that I could not follow when the investigator said no.



After the presentation of findings, the family was invited to the next room to see the bones. They milled around, looking at the arrays on the tables. The widow continued to cry, comforted by her daughter. Another relative, the adult victim's brother, picked up one of the finger bones, stroked it, compared it with his own, put it back on the table. He counted the bones on each table, shaking his head as if in disbelief. The widow stood in front of her husband's bones, repeating, *We sent them as men, and they came back in pieces!* And then, gesturing to the array in front of her: *Those aren't his bones!*

At the time, I heard the widow's words as a refusal, but I am not sure of that now. It is, I think, irreducibly ambiguous why exactly the elderly brother shook his head, or what exactly the widow meant when she disclaimed her husband's bones. Perhaps the old man did not want to believe the evidence in front of him; perhaps the old woman wanted more bones in order to be sure. An archaeologist I met in the field, who had attended a number of viewings, told me that family members "always ask for skulls," which were found in only about 10 percent of cases. Skulls, he explained, gave relatives more of a "sense of a person" than other bones; they felt they could "see" their person by looking at the underlying structure of his face.[28] In the viewing I attended that morning, the relatives, faced with nothing more than fragments and scraps, did not accede so easily to recognition of the remains. Neither the scientific nor the ritual setting sufficed to connect the remains and belongings these people encountered at the viewing to the people who had gone missing thirty-eight years earlier.

In writing about the forensic identifications of the approximately eight thousand victims of the Srebrenica genocide in July 1995, Sarah Wagner explores the exceedingly complex process by which damaged, disarticulated, and dispersed human remains came to be recognized as the bodies of specific persons as well as communal bodies: Bosniaks, victims of ethnic genocide. Recognition did not always happen, she notes, relating the case of a woman whose "utter rejection of the possibility of her son's death" was not mitigated by a photograph of scraps of his clothing that she was shown by case managers (Wagner 2008, 172). Indeed, on Wagner's account, the process of recognition could be derailed or stalled at any stage, and in the early years of forensic work on the Srebrenica missing, it seemed nearly impossible to many forensic scientists.



Wagner focuses on the distinctive shape given to this process by an innovation in DNA technology in 2001 that enabled the identification of remains that were uniquely resistant to recognition, given the success of the techniques used by Serb forces to conceal and radically mystify the evidence of their crimes. But this "technoscientific production of knowledge," Wagner (2008, 10) argues, could not alone have facilitated the recognition of the remains; the singularity of a person's corporal identity that is achieved through DNA analysis cannot do the psychological work of healing for mourning relatives, nor the cultural and political work of symbolizing loss for a society recovering from genocide.[29] Wagner therefore considers DNA identification of the Srebrenica missing as part of the same story as how families subjectively experienced the remains of their missing relatives and how those remains were commemorated publicly, becoming "emblems for collective categories: victims, enemies, Bosniaks, Muslims, refugees, martyrs" (11)—the latter being precisely the cultural and political work rejected by Damir Arsenijević as a reproduction of the ethnonational categories of genocide itself.

"Recognition is a process of legitimization," Sant Cassia (2005, 213) writes, noting how important it was for Androulla Palma to "recognize [her husband's] bones, to make them hers," when they were finally returned to her after the "desperate" exhumation she undertook at Lakatemeia Cemetery. Recognition was important not only, Sant Cassia notes, so that this long-deferred story could come to a resolution at last (his interpretive reference, again, is Greek tragedy), but also so that Palma could resume her role as her husband's wife in order to mourn and bury him properly, and thereby to resume the "moral person[hood]" that had been disrupted by his going missing and staying missing all those years. Thus, "recognition works both ways," Sant Cassia (2005, 213) says: a grieving relative both performs it and receives it.

The story of Androulla Palma—the experience that has turned into a story—is one of closure: recognition worked by ritual procedure, if with some innovations. Although Palma, on Sant Cassia's account, was profoundly antipathetic to the Greek-Cypriot regime that had kept her in the dark about her husband's fate, she ultimately acceded to a public funeral for her husband at which representatives of the regime officiated; her communal belonging was affirmed along with her husband's. I think there are many stories like hers among the relatives of the missing in Cyprus. But there are also stories that did not resolve in recognition, that persisted after the identification of remains in the suspicion relatives felt that there was too much they did not know. In these stories, the artifacts produced by the scientists were subsumed by a larger story of political secrecy, in which the facts of identification might just be tools of obfuscation.



## Very Transparent

As I noted in the introduction to this book, the forensic teams of the CMP have featured in a number of television broadcasts and documentary films over the years.[30] Images of scientists working with bones had become commonplace by the time of my fieldwork, originating and circulating in a fundamentally different way from the forensic photographs produced in the process of investigation and stored in the CMP's confidential archives. These very public photographs and films of scientists at work participated in a genre of representation that is well established outside Cyprus—in places like Spain, Argentina, Chile, Guatemala, and Bosnia and Herzegovina, where, as in Cyprus, forensic investigations of the missing and disappeared have become public forums for "witnessing" and "memory recovery" (see Arsenijević 2011a, 2011b; Crossland 2000, 2002; Ferrándiz 2006; Ferrándiz and Baer 2008; Nelson 2009; Renshaw 2011; Sanford 2004). Along with the forensic training and the infrastructure of investigation contributed to Cyprus by international agencies is this genre of publicity, which Ferrándiz and Baer, documenting exhumations of leftists killed in the Spanish civil war,

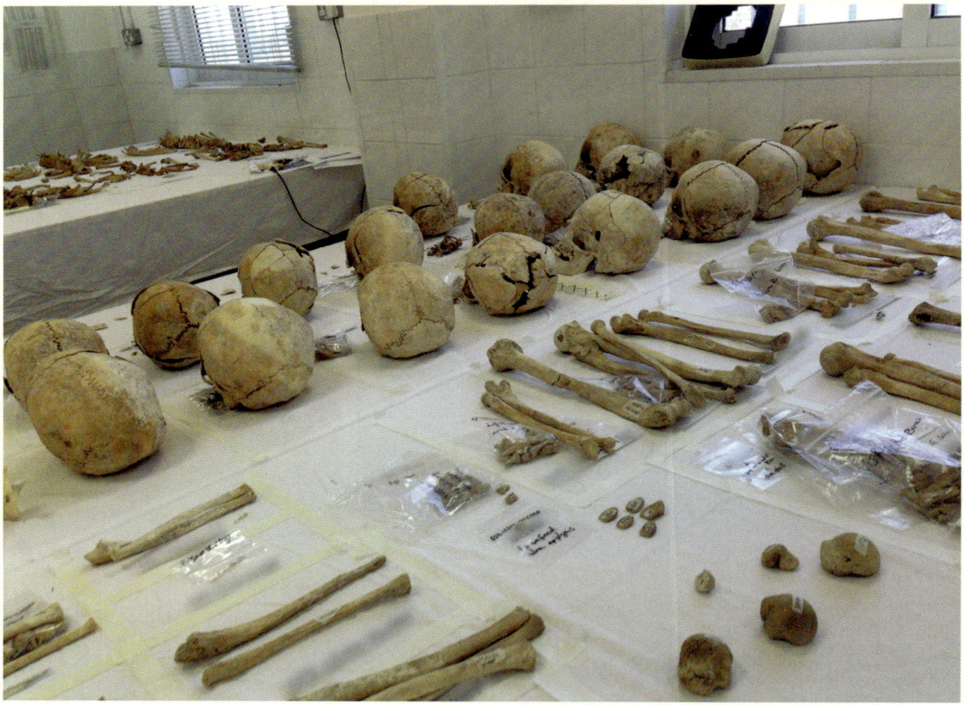

NO.

**1.9**

describe as a "global pool of images of repression, loss, terror and violence" (2008, ¶ 12). This genre features images of mourning women—the Mothers of the Plaza de Mayo in Argentina, for example, mirroring the Mothers of the Missing in Cyprus—as well as images of forensic teams working with bones in a scenario of grim science that Gregory Whitehead calls the "forensic theatre" (1990).[31]

Images of the forensic theater in Cyprus have appeared widely in Cypriot Greek- and Turkish-language newspapers and the English-language *Cyprus Mail*, as well as in American, Greek, Turkish, British, and other international print and online press outlets. Scientists on the forensic teams often brought copies of these newspapers to work, to talk about articles in which they appeared, often by name and in photographs.[32] Z., who had worked both in the field and at the lab, told me, with what I read as embarrassment, that she had been filmed "many times, too many," and she really did not like all the cameras. I was present when camera crews came to the lab twice within the same month to film the scientists as they worked; I was offered a white lab coat to wear so that I could "blend into the background." (I declined.) The scientists were hypervisible, and acutely aware of it.



Early in my time at the lab, I had lunch with a group of anthropologists at the UN cafeteria and discussed their experiences on field excavations. One of the sites had been filmed, and I asked how the filming had come about. P., who appeared in the CMP's commissioned documentary, *Digging the Past in Search of the Future*, told me that many films had been made about the missing and about the CMP specifically. I mentioned a few that I had already encountered, which focused mostly on the Greek-Cypriot missing. P. told me about *Kayıp Otobüs*, a feature-length film that had been shown on BRT, the public television channel in the north, about a group of Turkish Cypriots who went missing in 1964—a case they had worked on at the lab the previous year. V. thought he could get me a copy, though he said it would probably be pirated.

The violence of the 1960s–1970s is represented indirectly in these documentary films. Historically, it has been weeping or enraged relatives, such as the Mothers of the Missing, who have proven the reality of violence in Cyprus in their highly publicized protests at Ledra Palace and other public gatherings. After almost a decade of CMP activity, however, the grief and anger of those directly touched by violence was perhaps losing its evidentiary purchase on Cypriot audiences, who were increasingly cynical about their governments' use of emotive victimhood as propaganda. In this context, the CMP presented a clear alternative to the conventionally ethnonationalist politics that had animated the problem of the missing since the war. The forensic scientists, likewise, presented an alternative representation of the violent past to that of grieving relatives. None of the scientists had been born when the war took place in 1974; in documentary films on the missing, their investment in their work and their relationship with the dead appear to be determined not by personal experiences of violence but rather by the politically neutral, "purely humanitarian" project of putting the dead to rest and helping relatives—their elders—achieve closure. Their demeanor in these films is subdued; they are sober and discreet as they work on the bones. Their affective disposition toward their work indexes the forensic evidence that they cannot disclose to the public. The reality of the violence in Cyprus is evidenced through that indexical representation, rather than by the iconic reproduction of intense grief and anger expressed by relatives.



An important shift had thus been taking place in visual representations of the missing since the advent of the CMP: from relatives to scientists as the important actors, and from personal experience and memory to forensic evidence as the hegemonic form of positive knowledge. Perhaps the greatest significance of this shift lies in how the visibility of the forensic scene in Cyprus—the increasing familiarity of images of excavations, the lab, the bones, the scientists—might affect the experience of relatives of missing persons when they finally saw their person's bones. If a shift was indeed underway in the iconography of the missing, what were the stakes of this shift for their relatives? How did images from the forensic theater of Cyprus mediate their recognition of the bones?

What I have seen and heard of encounters between forensic scientists and relatives of the missing suggests a complex picture. Some relatives indeed seemed relieved to receive the bones of their loved ones and to go through the process of burying and mourning them. F., an archaeologist on a field excavation where I worked, told me that a viewing would go badly only if the forensic team gave a bad presentation. He had presented the archaeological findings for many cases over the years and told me about an especially difficult case where they had found only a few bones. *I spent a long time talking to the family*, he said. *I showed them pictures; I told them all about the methods our team used. We were six or eight people, sieving and wet-sieving, and we looked for months, and this was what we found. The family just kept saying, "Thank you, thank you"—they were very grateful, not suspicious at all.*

Relatives in other cases, however, seemed to have greater difficulty recognizing and claiming the bones. The case files I read contained many stories like this. They included complaints to the CMP written by relatives after a viewing, accusing the scientists of hiding evidence—often, signs of gunshot or knife wounds. In one case, a flurry of letters indicated deep and mounting misunderstandings between the uncle of the missing person in the case and the scientist who had presented the anthropological findings during his viewing. The findings included a gunshot wound in the skull; the anthropologist had apparently shown the uncle the entrance wound, located near one eye orbit, but when he left the room, the man had rolled the skull on its side and noticed another hole. In his letter to the Third Member of the CMP, the uncle accused the scientist of hiding the second hole. He wrote that the viewing had raised a number of unanswered questions, such as why the skeleton was so much shorter than his nephew had been in life; why there was no visible evidence in the remains of a break in his nephew's arm bone that he had suffered as a child; whether his crushed pelvis might have damaged his internal organs; whether his nephew might have been buried alive. In his letter, the uncle insisted that he was not satisfied by the anthropologist's answers to any of these questions and wondered why the scientists who worked on the case had been unwilling to speak about the injuries sustained by other people whose remains had been found in the same grave, which might have given him a better idea of what had happened.



In his written response to these accusations, the anthropologist insisted that the scientists were *always very transparent* with families. He explained that the second hole in the skull was not evidence of a second wound, but rather the exit wound linked to the entrance wound he had indicated to the uncle during the viewing. He noted that relatives were often upset when strangers handled the bones of their loved ones, so he had not wanted to roll the skull over to reveal the exit wound. The extant skeleton was shorter than the victim's body had been in life because the cartilage was now missing. The childhood break in his arm would likely have healed completely, leaving no visible evidence. Finally, he noted, the scientists were not permitted to discuss other cases with relatives, for reasons of confidentiality.

In a second letter to the CMP, the uncle dismissed these explanations and, in stark language, described the anthropologist as "unprofessional" and "untrustworthy." He requested DNA testing of the remains to confirm their identity; DNA testing had apparently not been considered necessary in this case, since the remains bore distinctive anthropological characteristics that made identification straightforward. The uncle demanded DNA results, in order both to resolve his doubts and to bring a case against the Republic of Cyprus before the European Court of Human Rights. *I was traumatized by the viewing,* he wrote. *This experience raised many doubts. I waited forty years, but the viewing that was supposed to resolve my brother's fate has actually made it more confusing.*

Relatives in other cases, in their correspondence with the CMP, expressed similar doubts about the identity of the bones they had seen at their viewings. (Their doubts were no doubt overrepresented in these files, since this is where all complaints from relatives were archived.) However familiar the forensic images of bones might have been to Cypriots, after almost ten years of publicity surrounding the CMP, relatives of the missing did not recognize the remains in these cases. They doubted the identification of their person and suspected the scientists of incompetence or fraud. Images of scientists working with bones might have served effectively for Cypriot publics as evidence of death as such, without serving as evidence of a particular person's death.



I discussed this disparity in the persuasiveness of forensic evidence with L., an anthropologist at the lab who had dealt extensively with relatives. *There are the angry ones, the cynical ones who think we're withholding information from them,* she explained. *There are the upset ones, who ask questions we can't answer. There are the ones who are over it, who are going through the motions but came to terms with the death long ago. Then there are the ones who take a small piece of information and run wild, speculating a whole chain of events and not really listening to us—like the fact that the clavicle was shattered in a certain way, and they come up with the idea that the person must have been shot through the neck, even though there's no indication of a gunshot wound.* I suggested to her that family members were perhaps not comfortable with the lack of certainty that is such a normal and important premise for scientists—that scientific restraint in drawing conclusions is foreign to most people, especially when, for emotional reasons, they want so much to know the whole truth. L. agreed, pointing out that, unlike forensic investigations in other postconflict areas, like Rwanda, the CMP investigations were designed to return as much of the missing person's remains as possible to the families for proper burial. This set up a strange encounter between families and scientists, she said, where remains—sometimes very scant—were treated as bodies, and their return to relatives became a symbolic event.

The first few times she had met with families at viewings, she told me, she cried. *It was very intense,* she said. *But now, I understand the process. I know what has to happen, and I don't feel anything. I had to learn to anticipate the reactions of family members and not allow them to push me into saying things they want me to say. It's very personal—it's not like giving forensic testimony in court.* In her training, she had studied osteology alongside forensic anthropology, including a course in legal frameworks. She had learned in that course how to give precise evidence without exceeding the bounds of

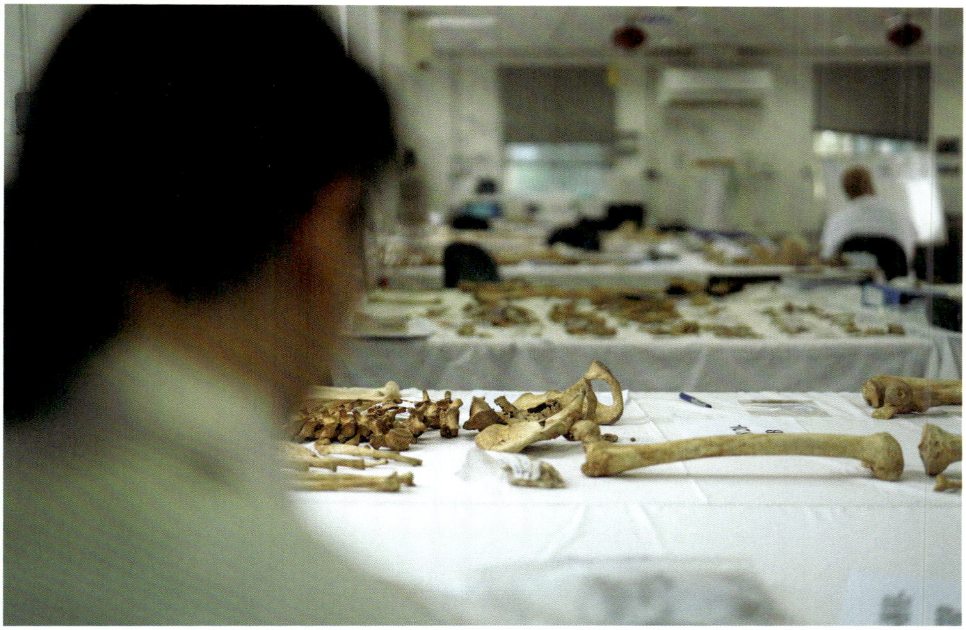

NO.

1.10

what she actually knew from her own analysis. *With forensic testimony, the judge makes a finding and then puts the case away; he doesn't think about the testimony of the anthropologist after that,* she explained. *But what you say to families, you know they're going to take it and carry it with them for the rest of their lives. This will be the information they tell themselves over and over again, whenever they think about the person who died, and that's a heavy burden for us. I feel it very much.*

## Why Humiliate the Dead?



The CMP's mission of closure and healing fostered an ethos of service to the families of the missing among the scientists who worked on their cases. The publicity surrounding the CMP's activities, however, created certain tensions between this ethos of service to families and respect for their rights—especially their right to know. I learned about these tensions first from J., who had served as an investigator and CMP spokesman for many years; he coordinated forensic teams in the south and wielded, I heard, great influence with the Members, though he did not vote in their deliberations. He explicitly positioned himself as an oppositional figure within the CMP, and it was from that position that he extended help to me, arranging for me to work at the lab, to visit excavations, and to attend viewings—as if despite the wishes of the CMP, although the Members had granted me formal permission to do these very things. In our conversations, J. often criticized what he called the CMP's "secrecy," its attempts to control information. *This is all for show,* he said to me when we first met at the lab, gesturing toward the scientists working at computer terminals and tables of bones. *If you ever want to get the real story, come talk to me.*

I did want to get the real story, of course; and so I did talk to J., many times, over many months. He seemed receptive to my work, praising "researchers like [me]" for "revealing, not concealing," and for our disposition to critique. He said he was "humiliated" by the way the CMP went about restricting my access to families and witnesses. He described himself, on the contrary, as "very transparent." And so he seemed to be. Although he worked for diplomats, he was not diplomatic; he expressed himself bluntly, with apparent candor and even rancor. He made himself enthusiastically available for my questions and requests. Over time, however, I came to see these signs of transparency on his part as subtle tactics of mystification. J. invited me to meetings with relatives of the missing but asked me not to mention these meetings to anyone else; he sought conversations with me but asked me not to write about what he said; he gave me copies of confidential documents but asked me to destroy them after reading; he asked me several times, midconversation, whether I was recording him. *I'm telling you these things because I trust you*, he would say, obliging me to secrecy by way of the CMP's secrecy: *If they find out what you're doing, they'll shut you out!*—this, despite the permission I had received from the CMP to do precisely what I was doing.

J.'s politics of transparency were tied to his politics of justice. Despite appearances of political neutrality, he told me, the CMP was an entirely political organization, a "public relations operation" staged for the cameras. In his view, the interest of the organization lay not in determining the truth about what had happened in the past, but rather in bolstering Cyprus's international reputation as a peaceful democratic regime invested in human rights. He condemned the CMP's silence about responsibility for the deaths it investigated, since relatives of the victims never learned what they most wanted to know—namely, how and why their loved ones had died: *No responsibility means no justice. No cause of death means no truth.* He took the position that the CMP's work should be part of a justice process that would ultimately attribute responsibility for the deaths of the missing. *Otherwise, it's hypocrisy*, he said. *The politics of human rights are the dirtiest politics of all. You can't be selective with rights!*



J. pointed out to me that, though the CMP thus did not respect their right to know, it upheld other rights of the grieving families—for example, their right to privacy. The CMP was very concerned to protect the families from unwanted visibility and the kind of exploitation to which, in J.'s telling, they had been subjected by journalists and academics over the years—"vultures," as he called them. *These people, they come to Cyprus for a few days, they stay at the Four Seasons, they do their five-minute interviews with the relatives, they snap their pictures and get their story, and they take off!*

In this light, the greatest hypocrisy of the CMP, J. told me, was its failure to protect the privacy of the dead as it protected the privacy of the living. He had special contempt for journalists and filmmakers who photographed and filmed the bones: *Those TV crews come here and take long panning shots of the bones laid out on the tables, and those are the images people want to see. Those images sell. The CMP allows this. But why do they need to do this? There are so many other parts of this story to film—why humiliate the dead?*

J.'s concern for the humiliation of the dead echoes challenges and protests over the publicity of human remains in a variety of other contexts, from the use of human remains for research and teaching, to the display of human remains for educational purposes in museums and classroom settings, to the circulation of images of human remains in reportage, documentary films, art projects, and sharing on social media.[33] These challenges and protests, when they have concerned remains associated with Indigenous peoples, have often been grounded in tribal ownership of the land where the remains were found, or in claims to kinship with the remains made by living descendants or descendant communities seeking to repatriate them.[34] As Zoë Crossland (among others) notes, kinship on this understanding extends to "cultural affiliation" in cases pursued under the terms of NAGPRA, the Native American Graves Protection and Repatriation Act, a US federal law passed in 1990 with global consequences that are still unfolding (Crossland 2009, 117).[35]



Objections to the storage, study, and display of human remains that are made today in terms of the rights of a descendent community are themselves grounded—in the language of the laws: NAGPRA and UNDRIP, among others—in the dignity of that community's culture.[36] But what of remains that are not dignified by cultural affiliation in this sense? Do the unaffiliated dead themselves, in themselves, have rights? Philosophers, historians, archaeologists, and legal scholars, among others who have considered this question, do not consider it in the particular terms of Indigenous sovereignties, or the even more particular terms of lineage or family, in which so many debates and protests over the disposition of human remains have been waged. The question as to whether the dead have rights has rather most often been raised in the general terms of humanitarian discourse—of human rights and their foundations and implications—in which forensic exhumations and identifications of victims of political violence are authorized, mobilized, and expected today. In this discourse, generic moral concepts of dignity and sanctity often serve as proxies for rights of the dead that do not themselves appear in the language of the law.[37]

Sociologist of law Claire Moon argues that the dead played a crucial role in the development of "humanitarian sensibilities" (2019, 47) and human rights themselves in the twentieth century; she finds their presence in international human rights law pervasive, even though "no single human rights document to date . . . explicitly refers to the human rights of the dead" (43). Moon pieces together references to the treatment of remains in various documents, most especially in the first volume ("Rules") of *Customary International Humanitarian Law* published by the International Committee of the Red Cross (ICRC) in 2005. These and other documents draw from numerous accords and conventions, including the 1929 and 1949 Geneva Conventions and Additional Protocols of 1977, as well as the Rome Statute, the UN treaty that established the International Criminal Court in 1998, indicating general principles that the dead should not be "despoiled or mutilated" (50), that the dead and their belongings should be returned to relatives, and that they should be buried properly. As Moon points out, ICRC Rule 115 "claims to reflect a 'general respect for the dead and their graves,'" requiring—with perhaps surprising specificity, given the generality of their purview—"that the dead be buried according to rites prescribed by their religion, that they should only be cremated in exceptional circumstances, that they must be buried in individual and not collective graves, and that war graves must, where possible, be grouped according to nationality," while Rule 116 specifies that remains must be "identified prior to their disposal" (50).



From all this, Moon concludes that the dead are already treated "*as if* they have rights" (2019, 50, emphasis original). She asserts that the dead cannot claim rights or bear responsibilities, but they can hold rights "insofar as the living behave as if they have obligations towards the dead, treat them as if they have rights, and confer rights upon them in practice" (43). In other words, based on the actual practices of the living, the dead may be said to have rights if they are treated as if they do. If the question as to the status of the rights of the dead is not answered clearly in the body of international law Moon consults, this body of law does clearly ascribe dignity to the dead; this ascription of dignity, she says, is what "turns the rights of the dead into human rights" (50).[38]

This way of thinking about the rights or the dignity of the dead in general that the living have a responsibility to respect perhaps inevitably risks ethical impasses in actual circumstances in which the living may not be able to fulfill their duties to the dead. Layla Renshaw notes such circumstances in which mass graves of the Civil War dead in Spain were excavated and only some remains that were identified could be claimed, mourned, and reburied by living descendants. In any mass grave exhumation, some remains may not be identified; others may be identified but not claimed by any living persons. "Consequently," Renshaw writes, "the opening of [a] grave will unavoidably generate an inequality of outcomes for the dead in the grave" (2019, 527, citing Scully and Woodward 2012). In other words, conceiving responsibilities toward the dead as general responsibilities that apply to all the dead equally may yield harms to the dead that they would not otherwise suffer.

Then, too, general responsibilities toward the dead may turn out to seem, on the contrary, quite specific and inapt when they butt up against mourning and burial practices undertaken in particular contexts. For example, the collective reburials of the dead that have taken place for symbolic and commemorative purposes in Rwanda and Spain contravene the prescription in ICRC Rule 115—expressing a "general respect for the dead and their graves"—that human remains be buried in individual graves.[39] Who among the living could, or should, take the ethical position that these collective reburials are an affront to the dignity of these particular dead?

In his account of the politics and ethics of forensic investigations, *Digging for the Disappeared*, Adam Rosenblatt (2015) shows how humanitarian discourses concerning the dignity and sanctity of the dead came to be so effective globally. He proceeds step by step and site by site, starting from the development of the now-renowned Argentine Forensic Anthropology Team in the 1980s, in their dynamic collaboration with the Abuelas de Plaza de Mayo (though not, as Rosenblatt explores and explains at length, the Asociación Madres de Plaza de Mayo)—an activist group of women whose adult children, while pregnant, had been abducted by secret police during the junta in Argentina (1976–83), and thus who had reason to think they might have living grandchildren. While his historical documentation is concentrated on Argentina, Rosenblatt argues against a case-based analysis of humanitarian forensics and ethics: "It is time," he asserts, "for a historically informed set of reflections on human rights forensic investigation as a distinct, networked *field* of global activism and scientific practice, rather than a loose collection of cases" (8). He dwells at length, therefore, on forensic investigations in Chile, the former Yugoslavia, Poland, and Spain (with even a few brief mentions of Cyprus), tracing expert practices as well as ethical questions and premises "across contexts" (45). Roving thus, Rosenblatt is able to explore what makes humanitarian forensics both highly improvisational, contingent, and place-based, on the one hand, and, on the other, a "global practice" (6), comprising relatively stable and, as he puts it, "networked" scientific tools and procedures, ethical premises and judgments, financial flows and infrastructures, and mobile experts who travel from site to site, doing what they have been trained to do, learning and advising, and carrying with them their past experiences into new scenarios.

It is the ethical dimensions of the forensic enterprise that Rosenblatt examines most closely here, studying the suspicions, objections, and outright protests to their work encountered by forensic practitioners in some contexts—political and religious "counterclaims," as he calls them, to the "moral universalism" of the forensic enterprise of exhumation, identification, and repatriation of the dead. The most famous protest, treated by Crossland, Domanska, and many other scholars as well, is the long-term and ongoing protest of the Asociación Madres de Plaza de Mayo, mothers of missing

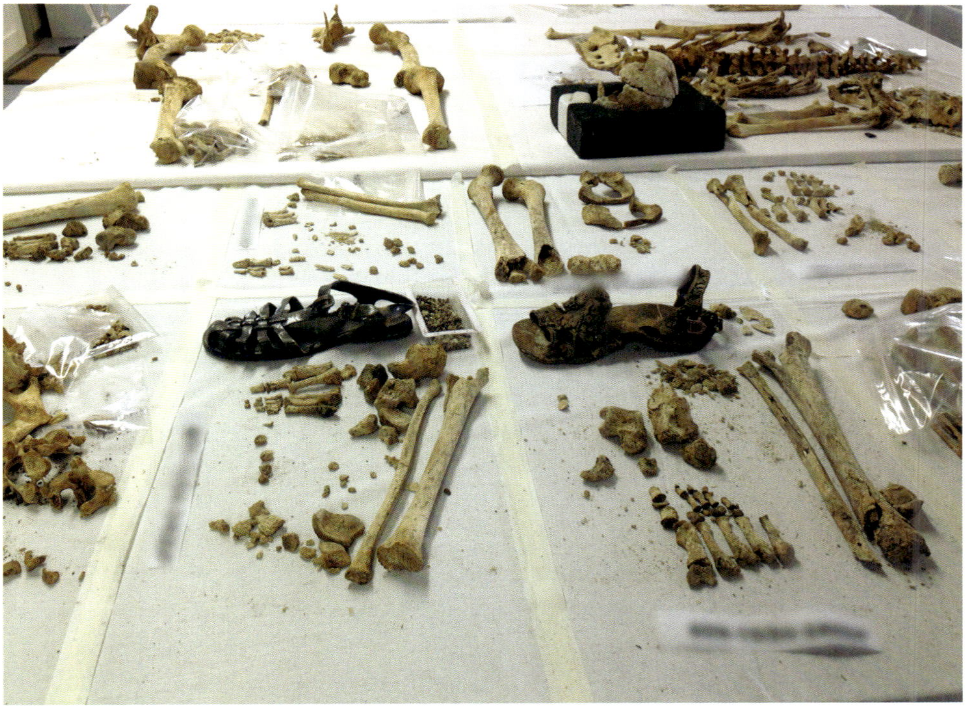

NO.

**1.11**

children in Argentina, who refused to participate in forensic investigations, instead demanding, famously, "aparición con vida"—often translated as "let them appear alive," and often understood as a refusal to accept the remains of the dead until responsibility for their deaths could be attributed. Rosenblatt explores the many registers of this demand, alongside the motives and rationales expressed by another group of Madres who, by direct and deliberate contrast, did (and do) participate in forensic investigations; he is troubled by what he clearly takes to be a misreading of both groups' "political goals" (2015, 106), and a blind celebration and appropriation of the Asociación's refusal by other leftist groups.



More pertinent to the question raised by J. about the humiliation of the dead, however, is Rosenblatt's discussion of the mass grave at Jedwabne, Poland, where the entire Jewish community of the town had been massacred—perhaps by the Gestapo, perhaps by their Polish neighbors—in 1941. Rosenblatt documents the beginning of an excavation of this grave in 2001 that was interrupted and then successfully blocked by Orthodox Jewish authorities—not without pushback from other Jewish authorities as well as the local community—who asserted that the grave and the remains were sacred and must not be disturbed. Rosenblatt duly considers a series of claims about the sacredness of mass graves in this and other cases, warning that we not take these claims at face value (since they might be covers for other motives), nor assume they are local in nature, nor that any particular authority making such a claim necessarily speaks for the dead in question or for the community of the living who are or feel connected to those particular dead, nor that mass graves should necessarily be understood as more (or less) sacred than other graves, nor that all claims about the sacredness of graves are religious in nature.[40]

Indeed, Rosenblatt observes a perhaps impassable disjuncture between what he construes, in the case of Jedwabne, as a definitively religious notion of sacred graves—the notion of an otherworldly place where the dead rest and should not be disturbed, a space delimited by rules that privatively establish the worldly order—and what he calls the "moral category" of sacredness (2015, 146) operative in human rights discourse, which is attributed to the universal human person and by extension to human remains. He sees little prospect of harmonization between these two notions of the sacred nor, by extension, of progress in debates among differently positioned "stakeholders" (e.g., 6, 14, 22) as to the ethical means of dealing with mass graves.

Returning to J.'s question—*why humiliate the dead?*—I still wonder what moral attitude toward the dead or dead bodies motivated his outrage: what specific or generic notions of sanctity, dignity, privacy, and respect (among possible other notions) played into his complaints. The remains of the missing in Cyprus were not entangled in the ethics and politics of Indigenous sovereignty and affiliation, but questions about the handling and display of human remains raised in Indigenous repatriation claims were also raised, at least for J., by the hypervisibility of the Cypriot remains.

These questions recall to me the taboo on seeing sacred objects in classic anthropological studies of ritual and secret societies. In this light, I recall Émile Durkheim's fashioning of totemism from Spencer and Gillen's extractive archive of ethnological photography in colonial Australia. In his writing on Arunta and Warramunga piacular rites, Durkheim paid special attention to the ritual role played by human corpses and bones; as "the deceased is a sacred being," he observed, these mourning and burial rites were especially dense with proscriptions on touching, seeing, or even speaking the name of the dead: "everything that is or was in contact with [the dead] is in a religious state that precludes all contact with the things of profane life" ([1912] 1995, 393).



While bodily materials, including bones, were not themselves totemic, in Durkheim's view, he described several piacular rites in which such materials were treated as totemic by analogy or proximity. In one Warramunga "rite of cloture" described by Spencer and Gillen, for example, following several days of totemic ceremonies, a long bone of a deceased man that had not yet been buried with his other bones, having been "wrapped in a bark sheath," was held by the last of a group of women to crawl under the open legs of "ten decorated men," through a trench that had been dug near a spot on the ground where totemic designs had been drawn. After the last woman emerged from the trench with the wrapped bone, the bone itself was broken and buried, thus ending the ceremony and the period of mourning (Durkheim [1912] 1995, 399). Durkheim construed the contiguity between the trench through which the bone traveled and the totemic designs on the ground nearby, and the burial of the bone in that ground, as symbolically significant; the bone of the deceased man was implemented in this piacular rite, he suggested, as totemic objects were in other kinds of rituals, in order to "act upon the religious powers or forces of nature" and "appease those powers that are ill-disposed toward men" (407). Practices of self-cutting and other forms of self-mortification on the part of the living in piacular rites involving the corpse or bodily materials of the dead were, for Durkheim, tantamount to a "sacrifice to the dead man" (406), who, being no longer human but rather part of the natural world symbolized by his totem, was now feared and treated as sacred.

In *The Nervous System*, Michael Taussig offers a visual representation of the nonuniversal representability of such sacred objects, taking totems from

Spencer and Gillen's archive as examples. Parsing Durkheim, Taussig dwells on the abstraction of these symbols carved into wood or stone or painted on bodies, signifying a totemic animal or plant; the abstraction of these designs is mimetic but not figurative, he says, calling attention to themselves as signifying something other than what they ostensibly represent: "The mark, which bestows sanctity, is in itself not only sanctifying but is more sacred than what it represents—the totem, animal species, whatever" (Taussig 1992, 123). In a text box framed thickly in black, without any image inside, he writes, "This empty space is where I would lik[e] to have presented Spencer and Gillen's drawing of the frog totem because it seems to me next to impossible to get the points about representation across without this amazing image. But my friend Professor Annette Hamilton, of Macquarie University, Sydney, tells me that to reproduce the illustration would be considered sacrilege by Aboriginal people—which vindicates not only the power of the design but of the prohibitions against its being seen, strenuously noted but not observed by Spencer and Gillen themselves" (124).



Taussig thus reads the power of such sacred objects as a function of their exclusivity to ritual elites, implying that respecting taboos on their being touched or even seen by anyone else entails respecting the social hierarchies of gender and age by which totemic societies were structured. That these taboos were "noted" but not "observed"—which is to say, respected—by Spencer and Gillen in their photographic records suggests that they understood themselves to be outside the social world in which the proscription of these objects to Indigenous women and uninitiated men exerted so much power, enjoyed by Indigenous men of status.

These taboos find a postcolonial inflection in the digital archives of Indigenous knowledge being invented in contemporary Australia, and explored by Elizabeth Povinelli as Indigenous experiments with archival power: experiments, as she puts it, with "domiciliation, territorialization, and authorization of historical knowledge" (2011, 154). These archival projects variously limit access to Indigenous cultural and historical knowledge; some, through user protocols, make access to images of totemic objects contingent on the Indigenous ancestry of the user (as well, in one case, as "seniority and gender," 162); while another, conceived by Povinelli and her collaborators, would make access to stories of a Dreaming site and associated images contingent on the user's proximity to the site, through geotagging. These projects thus make the position outside Indigenous society arrogated by Spencer and Gillen one from which it is impossible to see; they digitally enforce the taboos, while admitting "'you-the-stranger'" into the social world of Indigenous Australians in which "all people, except 'you,' have a place based on territorially embedded kinship and ritual relations" (157). The point of this enforcement is not the enhancement of power for those who belong through restrictions on those who do not; nor is the digital architecture of these projects, Povinelli explains, "merely a set of protocols for circulating knowledge" among those who have access (160). For Povinelli's collaborators, this architecture is rather a means to "create and maintain the cosubstantiality of forms of being" (160) through knowledge: a kind of learning and connecting and becoming that depends on who you are, what you are, and where you are in relation to others.

While Povinelli does not address this issue directly, it seems to me that the exclusion of "you-the-stranger" from this knowledge may be precisely what prevents "you" from understanding why "your" exclusion is not equivalent or comparable or translatable to the exclusion of Indigenous women and uninitiated men from this knowledge. In any case, Povinelli's reframing as "social skin" (2011, 162) of what Taussig, borrowing from Durkheim, calls *taboo* makes it easier to see that all exclusions are not equal, all forms of secrecy are not equal, and thus that "doing justice" to the secret, in Taussig's words, might entail defacing it in some cases, but keeping it in others. Both ask us to consider who "we" are in regard to sacred objects, and suggest that the answer to that question might help us understand, too, the nature both of our desire to look and of our obligation not to look.

In light of this social-symbolic understanding of the sacredness of bones —and more to the point, images of bones—the CMP could be seen as an elite with the power to restrict access to historical knowledge. The Members had a proprietary relationship to the images of grave sites and bones generated by the forensic teams; they oversaw an immense archive of forensic photographs—thousands of images. But these images cannot be reprinted here; they are encrypted and stored in the CMP's database, and no one at the CMP has the right to reproduce or transmit them. Only scientists working on a case and relatives of the missing person in question would ever see these images. Even relatives were shown only a small selection of photographs: an image of the grave site after the excavation was complete—none of the active exhumation, when bones were still visible in the ground—and an image of the bones arranged in the form of a skeleton, as far as possible. One investigator told me that families could be traumatized if they were exposed to photographs of bones as they were found in situ in mass graves, dispersed and disarticulated. Indeed, I had seen many photographs of skeletons in situ in the archives and had noted how different the bones looked after analysis, each one visible, clean, laid out on a white table in a rough approximation of a body, if not quite to scale. The archaeological reports usually contained many photographs of a grave, unexcavated or in the process of excavation, showing bones looking uncannily like dead people, practically enfleshed: in the midst of action or in fallen positions, heads above feet, arms raised above heads or wrapped around others, bodies twisted to one side or the other, jaws open. Equally upsetting to relatives, however, according to this investigator, were photographs of bones being handled by strangers, even the scientists who worked with them so carefully. Before a viewing, the CMP psychologists, who counseled families during the course of an investigation, often showed relatives photographs of the bones arrayed on a lab table, in order to prepare them for what they would see in person. The photographs were intended to encourage their recognition of the bones.



This power to disturb carried by images of bones contorted, exposed, and handled by strangers, lay behind the prospect of "humiliating the dead" raised by J., I think; humiliation was the other side of sacredness, on his reckoning. But his reckoning was not universal nor even, necessarily, representative of a local or Cypriot perspective. Shortly after my conversation with J., I discussed the sacredness of bones with a friend, a Greek-Cypriot scholar who had written widely on the Cyprus conflict and the culture of division. I repeated to him J.'s assertion that photographing and filming the bones of the missing amounted to a "humiliation of the dead." My friend reacted with surprise and suggested that the prospect of humiliation might just be a pretext—something J. had said because he did not want me to film or photograph the bones, for other reasons. I said I thought that was likely, but I was also concerned that I might be missing something important about people's attitudes toward the dead in Cyprus. *I suppose that very religious people might feel that way about bones*, he said, *but I don't think it's a widespread attitude.*

Months later, I asked another Greek-Cypriot friend, a photographer and curator, for her thoughts on imaging and displaying bones. She told me about a presentation she had made at a conference some years earlier, in which she had projected an archival photograph—not from Cyprus—of a warehouse where old bones were stored in boxes. A member of the audience had pulled her aside after the presentation to say she had been very upset by the photograph. *It was disturbing to her to see the bones in such a state*, my friend said. *The thought hadn't even occurred to me. Obviously, I wasn't disturbed in that way.* She had heard about such controversies years ago, she said, in American museums that displayed Native American remains to the public, before NAGPRA was passed. The perspective on sacredness that J. had expressed was located, by my Cypriot friend, in the United States.

In Cyprus, the remains of the missing were considered the property of relatives, but images of the remains were not protected by any law—only by the CMP's policy of confidentiality. Did a viewer's vulnerability to being disturbed by these images depend on her relationship to the dead? Or did the bones carry, for some Cypriots, a more diffuse significance? If the bones were indeed sacred, their sacredness—again, I am following Taussig here—was created in the act of revealing them; the moment they were seen was the moment their symbolization of the dead was effected, "bringing matter to life," as Taussig (1999, 43) puts it.[41] The "sympathetic magic" (24) of mimesis opened a live circuit between the dead and their remains. I suspect that this is the desecration at stake in the publicity of the bones, as J. saw it: a humiliation of the dead. For him, this humiliation came not from exhuming and examining the bones, but rather from photographing and filming them, and circulating those images in the public eye. The question posed by the sacredness of the bones in this context, then, is whether that sacredness commands our respect, as J. insisted, or whether, on the contrary, our participation in the revelation and visual publicity of the bones might "do justice" to the secret they represent—that is, the violence at the heart of the Cyprus conflict, which, like any public secret, is not a secret at all. What secrets are we keeping, and whose secrets, if we decide not to show images of the bones—to file them away and keep the door locked?



In their work on mass grave exhumations in Spain, Francisco Ferrándiz and Alejandro Baer examine how the "production, circulation, and experience" of images of mass violence, and especially of human remains in situ in mass graves, have become "crucial elements" in the "recovery" of historical memory, both in Spain and in other locales (Ferrándiz and Baer 2008, ¶ 7). Their assertion is that these morally and semiotically complex images are not only documents of a process of forensic knowledge making, but also tools of that knowledge making in their own right. In their work with relatives of the dead whose remains have been recovered in this process, Ferrándiz and Baer note that "many . . . are truly committed to the task of 'visibilization'—both in a metaphorical and a literal sense" (¶ 19), including photographic recording and memorialization of the exhumations. On the other hand, they report the resistance of some relatives to the opening of graves and the "attendant public exposure of the bones"; these people, Ferrándiz and Baer observe, "resent certain forms of representation of loss and pain, which they view as lacking in the 'appropriate dignity'" (¶ 19). Despite these protests, the visual publicity surrounding exhumations in Spain has become "normalized," according to Ferrándiz and Baer, and these images ever more "mainstream" as they have entered into "mass media formats" (¶ 23). They have even "enter[ed] the sphere of photo artistic expression," following a "progression from document to icon, to memory-art that pleads for remembrance" (¶ 11).

By "memory-art," Ferrándiz and Baer may have in mind the work of artist Francesc Torres, who was among the first to photograph the exhumation of a Spanish mass grave in its entirety. In his introductory essay to his photo book, *Dark Is the Room Where We Sleep*, Torres (2007) tells the story of how he became involved in the 2004 excavation at Villamayor de los Montes, where it was thought thirty to sixty Republicans had been killed and buried in September 1936.[42] (Ultimately, the remains of forty-six men and boys were recovered.) It was not the first grave he investigated, but it was the first he photographed. *Dark Is the Room* contains dozens of full- and half-page black-and-white images of the dead, many painfully intimate close-ups, others wide-angled to show the massive scale of the grave and the number of bodies, all graphic and confrontational: full and partial skeletons in situ in the grave; bones held in the hands of volunteers on the excavation team; skulls with jaws open, full of dirt; bones commingled with rocks and sticks; so many bones. These images are interspersed with black-and-white portraits of the living: elderly villagers, the remains of whose relatives or neighbors were being disinterred; younger relatives, who were not alive at the time of the massacre but had heard stories and retold them to Torres and members of the Association for the Recuperation of Historical Memory, who attended the exhumation of remains; the young volunteers themselves, carefully performing the labors of excavation; curious children from neighboring villages who happened by and enlivened the events. Also tools and documents, landscapes, and gatherings, including a series of color images of what Torres titles "The Return": the ceremony held in July 2006, when relatives assembled with the exhumed remains, now identified and placed in coffin-like boxes, to read out the names of the dead and rebury them together in a collective crypt.

Torres's book also contains a section, "Identification Process," that is more archive than photography. It contains papers from the regional prison, dated 1936, concerning the men who were later murdered at Villamayor de los Montes, and photographs of those men well before they were killed. It contains, as well, documents from the forensic analysis of the remains: photographs and measurements of teeth, bone fractures, and other identifying information; and the final results of the identifications. The dead have no privacy here: they are named, their faces shown in life, their devastated remains depicted and described in the most clinical detail.

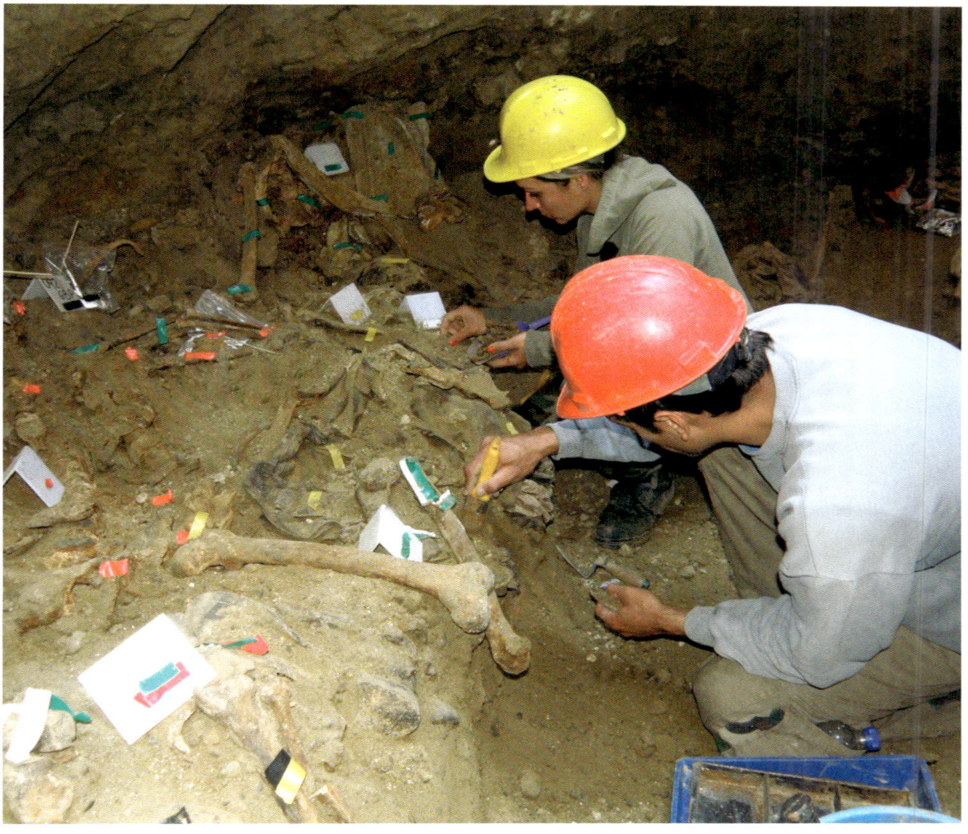

NO.

1.12

In her reflections on Torres's works from Villamayor, Ofelia Ferrán calls them "memory projects" (2013, 117), as his documentation of the recovery of historical memory in these works is itself memorial in nature. Ferrán acknowledges that these photographs belong to a "canon" of images of the exhumed dead, victims of enforced disappearance and mass violence.[43] The circulation of these images, she argues, has formed a "global context" whose "effects" in specific instances may include, in Brett Ashley Kaplan's words, "'unwanted beauty,'" referring to representations of the Holocaust; or in other instances, "compassion fatigue."[44] But they may also, as in the case of Villamayor, in her view, effectively subvert repressive silencing by reclaiming the public space where so much political violence took place, prominently imaging practices of digging and displaying the dead in that space (Ferrán 2013, 128, 129).



Beyond this effective subversion of political secrecy, for Ferrán, Torres's graphic photographs also establish an "imaginary bond" between the dead and the living; they "embody the 'civil contract of photography,'" in Ariella Azoulay's term, demanding of the viewer a "civic skill" in reading the suffering of the victim depicted therein and understanding that suffering as political in nature—an understanding that carries a responsibility for those who behold the injustice of it (citing Azoulay 2008, 14). For Ferrán, Torres's photographs of the exhumed Civil War dead "embody" this civil contract "because they allow both the viewers to see the true dimensions of Francoist violence and its victims to look *at us* from the images" (2013, 131–32). When we look at these photographs, in other words, what we see is the dead looking back at us, obligating us to know their suffering and to redress it.

Renshaw, working in the same context in Spain, concedes that images of mass grave exhumations are "vulnerable to misinterpretation" in that they may "become aestheticised or de-contextualised" (2019, 533). Emphasizing the many sources and uses of these images, from forensic documentation to "historical awareness," she notes that the line is "porous" between images of remains "that are produced to record the physical evidence, to capture it, or to explain it to others" and those that "become aestheticised to convey a certain emotional or political message about the dead . . . particularly through the selection and assemblage of images" (533). She takes the position that it is the absence of a truth commission that brings these risks of decontextualization and aestheticization into play; without a collective process for seeking truth and justice, she cautions, people will take photographs and circulate them by their own methods and for their own reasons, as a "diffuse, citizen-led way of publicly airing and judging the events of the past" (533). In this light, aestheticization seems the lesser harm, and one that might be offset by the robust contextualization of these images within well-documented narratives of what took place.

In a different setting—one that is even more pervasively mediatized than the mass grave exhumations in Spain—Francesc Torres writes of the "complex problem" generated by the "decent, perfectly comprehensible" censorship of images and videos of victims of 9/11 plunging from the Twin Towers to their deaths, which he connects to the secreting of remains and artifacts of the Twin Towers in Hangar 17 near JFK airport, the site of his photo essay (Torres 2015, 151). "I would suggest," he writes, "that the first silent testimony of any act of violence is the victim's body. Without the emotional impact of its sight, the tragedy becomes an abstraction, an enigma that will never be fully resolved either for the relatives or . . . for the people of the country" (151). 

Here, I come finally to my own decision to include images of the bones of the missing in this book. I will tell the story later of how I was denied permission to photograph or film the forensic work I witnessed and shared at the CMP's lab and on field excavations. For now, I will just make clear that the images of bones that appear in this book are not mine. It was easy enough to acquire them; the CMP supplied a few, with permission, and others were taken by a friend whose social skin is different from mine. But acquiring photographs and publishing them in my book are acts of different ethical orders. I decided to publish them advisedly, by which I mean that I took J.'s outrage seriously; the last many pages offer some evidence of this, I hope. But in the end, I am not at all convinced of the existence of any particular, local, or culturally Cypriot ethics of respect for the dead—or for living relatives and other loved ones—that proscribes showing images of their remains in public, especially when they are not identifiable (as they are not, here). Nor do I feel compelled not to show these images by a decontextualized humanitarian concern for the dignity of the dead in general. Finally, since the CMP circulates such images routinely as part of their own publicity efforts, I do not feel bound, as part of my agreement with the CMP, not to publish them, especially as the CMP supplied some images to me for this purpose. That I am publishing other images of bones in the custody of the CMP that the CMP did not supply to me may not sit well with the CMP, but whatever offense I cause by doing this is not an offense to the dead.

My affirmative inspiration for publishing these photographs has two sources. First, I think these images perfectly dramatize the conundrum of public secrecy that I face in this work. I do not wish either to keep or to expose secrets about the violence that produced all these bones. Publishing these images frees me from the position of keeping secrets that I believe J.

(perhaps in good faith) was pressing me to take, but since the photographs contain no information that could be used to identify the dead or the circumstances of their deaths, neither am I exposing any secrets—at least of the kind that would be meaningful to a (hypothetical) truth commission. What these photographs do, I think, is to exert an obligation to knowledge upon everyone who sees them; if not, as Férran has it, because the dead look back at us and demand that we know what they have suffered, then because to deny what we see—to not know it—is an atrocious, insupportable complicity. They visually realize the stakes of the forensic knowledge that my interlocutors at the CMP were after. We do not learn the facts from these photographs—that is, identifying information, or the cause or circumstances of death—but they show us the *artifacts*. They show us how the facts are made.



Second, images like these had already, by the time of my fieldwork, been mediating Cypriots' knowledge of the past for some time. In the previous section ("Very Transparent"), I described a shift that had been taking place in the visual representation of the missing since the CMP began its investigations in 2004: from relatives to scientists as the important actors, and from personal experience and memory to forensic evidence as the hegemonic form of positive knowledge. Photographs of mass grave exhumations and of bones laid out on lab tables had come to dominate the public iconography of the missing, for the most part replacing images of grieving relatives holding photographs of the missing that had been so prominent in the 1970s–1990s. The archive of images in this book shows that shift, and by providing that visual story as a context, I hope to provoke thinking about how these photographs of the graves and bones of the missing in Cyprus are both like and not like other photographs—Francesc Torres's, for example—of other mass grave exhumations and other lab tables, other "forensic theatres." Thus I offer these images here as a sort of dialectical fulcrum for thinking the particularity and generality of mass violence, and of the ethical commitments entailed by our responses to it.

## Lost Heroes of the Republic

As occasions for the dead to be recognized and mourned, private viewings at the lab were linked to the public funerals for the missing that had been taking place, sporadically, since the CMP began to return remains to relatives in 2007. The advent of the dead on these occasions was untimely; one viewing followed another and one funeral another, erratically, in a temporality unrelated to the time of death but determined instead by the opaque order of priorities according to which remains of the missing were sought and examined—opaque not only to the relatives but also to the scientists, who got their orders "from above," as they often told me.

In Cyprus, as in some other postconflict contexts where forensic investigations have become a key process in collective reckoning with the past, the recovery and reburial of missing persons was displaced from the political register of public accounting and criminal justice, and entrenched instead in the psychological-therapeutic register of mourning and healing (Crossland 2000, 2002; Ferrándiz 2006; Ferrándiz and Baer 2008; Renshaw 2011; Robben 1999).[45] The public funerals of the missing whose remains had been found did little to disturb this paradigm. The funerals were public events, to be sure; they were televised and covered in newspapers, and attended by hundreds of people, including representatives of the president, at least in the south. Yet it was the grief and loss of families that was publicized and—through a familiar equation of family with nation—a position of collective victimhood rather than collective responsibility that was promoted on these occasions.[46] While viewings at the lab were conducted away from the public eye, emotionally fraught on all sides and running the risk each time of reaching an end other than closure, these public funerals ritually tied the dead to the political order of division.



Those events share some features with the public funerals of bones of the "nameless dead" killed in the last years of World War II—Serbs, Muslims, Croats, partisans, and royalists—that were conducted during the breakup of the former Yugoslavia in the 1990s, in Katherine Verdery's (1999, 97) classic study of the political lives of dead bodies. Verdery shows how these bones of the long dead, whose memory as "ethnic" or "national" was suppressed during Tito's regime, were exhumed from caves and shallow mass graves in the early 1990s and reburied under intense publicity. She considers their burials as consecrations in ethnic terms of the very soil under contestation by Serbs, Croats, Muslims, and Slovenes in their fight for pieces of the Yugoslav territory—and thus as symbolic claims that instigated further warfare, authorized by accusations against newly national enemies of past genocidal violence. In this way, she argues, the burials of the bones effected a sort of "time compression" (115) between past and present in historical narratives of these ethnonational groups.

The sacredness of the bones of the missing in Cyprus, similarly, was linked in public funerals to an understanding of the missing as ethnonational war dead, claimed by the state as sacrifices.[47] In this light, Sant Cassia describes a public funeral convened for a Greek-Cypriot soldier whose remains were located and identified by Physicians for Human Rights in 2001 (before the CMP initiated operations). The minister of defense, representing the Republic of Cyprus, spoke at the funeral of "twenty-seven years of 'unjust, inhuman and unethical punishment' of the dead. These [remains] were the 'sacred bones of the dead who had been sacrificed'" (Sant Cassia 2005, 221). In framing the death of this soldier as a sacrifice, the minister consecrated his bones as symbols of the dead, not only indexing his individual death but also, and more important for the Republic, metonymically representing all those who died in the conflict.

I attended one of the funerals for the missing in the spring of 2012. This had been arranged by J., who told me the funeral would be "very public, very religious." Two people were buried that day: a woman and man, wife and husband, already grandparents when they were killed by Turkish soldiers in August 1974, along with all the other elderly people from their village. Their remains had been transferred a few weeks earlier from the lab to the CMP office in south Nicosia, in small coffins with crosses affixed to their sides, a Greek flag wrapped around the foot ends and the Cypriot flag around the head ends, with its golden emblem of the island of Cyprus placed in such a way that it would lie directly over the skulls inside, next to white tags bearing the names of the dead. Inside the coffins, the remains were contained in plain white cloth sacks; the skulls were wrapped separately in white cloth to prevent their movement. A smaller, plain box held artifacts from the mass grave where the remains had been found, painstakingly associated with the bones by an anthropologist at the lab. These artifacts would be buried along with the remains; in other cases, J. told me, relatives kept the artifacts in their homes, as precious mementoes. In this case, the forensic scientists, unable to get adequate samples from immediate family members, had not been able to identify the male victim's bones through the regular DNA testing procedure, so the CMP had disinterred the man's father's bones, buried many decades earlier, which provided enough genetic material for a match. His bones would be reburied together with the remains of the son.

Once the remains had arrived at the CMP office, a forensic pathologist had issued an official death certificate, which the living relatives would need to file with the municipality. Before the funeral, one of the relatives had signed a transfer form to accept the remains and had been given in return a packet including summaries of the anthropological and archaeological reports for the case, as well as sketches and photographs of the excavation site and the bones themselves.

The funeral was held late on a Saturday morning, in the grand new church of a neighborhood that had once been a suburb of Nicosia but was absorbed by the city as it expanded southward in the 1980s. Two soldiers from the Republic's army escorted the remains to the church and remained throughout the service, standing at attention next to the coffins. These were positioned with their head ends toward the iconostasis, next to a stand displaying photographs of the deceased. Several cameramen filmed the event from the front of the church. Hundreds of mourners were already seated when I arrived, and dozens more flowed in for almost an hour. I found a seat about halfway back, next to an elderly woman who leaned over and asked if I were a covillager of the deceased, whispering: *I don't recognize you!* I explained that I was a "stranger" (*ξένη*) but had met the family and wanted to pay my respects. People sat or stood as they liked, greeting one another, catching up, talking all through the service with the exception of a few prayers in which they joined, and the hymn at the conclusion of the service, which most seemed to know by heart.

After the priests had sung the liturgy, several speakers addressed the congregation from a podium in front of the sanctuary: a representative of the president of the Republic, a representative from the Pancyprian Organization of Parents and Relatives of Undeclared Prisoners and Missing Persons, and finally, the daughter of the deceased. When she concluded her remarks, the officiant introduced the dozen or so people seated just in front of the sanctuary, naming their positions as representatives of political parties, village associations, even someone from the CMP. These guests were named as they walked up to the front of the church to kiss the icon beside the coffins and then place wreaths on the coffins.

After the service ended, I walked with the CMP representative to the cemetery, just down the street, and waited for the funeral party to arrive. A group of soldiers passed by, carrying the coffins to the grave site, followed by many others—family members and guests—who held wreaths as they awkwardly picked their footing through the narrow lanes between stone vaults in the ground. The grave was a family plot, a stone vault like all the others in this cemetery, topped with a marble slab bearing the names and the birth and death dates of the couple, with framed black-and-white photographs placed on a shelf above the headstone. An assistant to the priest unwrapped the coffins, removing the flags and wreaths. The vault had been opened beforehand and the soil dug from the grave piled into a container next to it. Two cemetery workers lowered one coffin into the vault and then the other directly on top of it. The priest, holding an incense vessel, sang a prayer, splashed oil from a plastic bottle over the boxes, and then tossed the bottle into the vault. He was handed two bowls of κόλλυβα (a traditional funeral dish made from boiled spelt or wheat berries); he threw a handful from each into the grave, then the bowls themselves. A photographer snapped shots of the entire process from close-up. The priest took a spade and dug a bit of soil from the pile, poured water on it, then washed the mud into the vault. He handed the spade to the cemetery workers, who shoveled the rest of the soil into the vault, smoothing it over before maneuvering the heavy marble slab over the grave to seal the vault.

In terms of the CMP's mission, this was a successful public funeral, centered on grieving relatives and a community of covillagers who had been dispersed by war, now reunited in mourning. It was a performance of closure, many years after the disappearance of the old couple. Their daughter, the only member of the family to deliver a eulogy, had spoken of her parents with deference and affection, pausing to collect herself as she described the pain of not knowing what had happened to them all those years, and expressing her faith in their delivery to God, now that she was able to bury them properly.



Some relatives of the missing were more ambivalent about their public role as victims, however, as I heard from U., a friend whose uncle had been one of the missing persons on the official Greek-Cypriot list. His remains had been found and identified a few years earlier, and U.'s father—the man's brother—had attended the viewing along with some of their other relatives. U. told me, *My father was really surprised and confused by this experience, how religious it seemed, like a funeral. He went there expecting to collect the bones in a box or something, but there they were, all laid out on the table like a skeleton, with candles, a photograph, and everything. I remember he told me how strange it was to see the personal effects: buttons, a wallet, shoes, things like that. It was a strangely religious experience for him.*

U. saw that his father had been "compromised" by the whole process, from the viewing to the funeral, which had been attended by soldiers and the mayor: a very public event that was photographed and covered by the media in a "very sentimental tone." *He was basically coerced into participating*, U. said. His father did not have the option not to participate, so strong was the social pressure to accede to this heavy symbolization of his brother as a "lost hero" of the Republic. U.'s father was a leftist and antimilitary, so this symbolization had put him in a very difficult position. Given this experience, U. wondered if the process of identifying and returning the remains of missing persons might not heal the wounds of the past; on the contrary, he said, it seemed to reopen those wounds, to reduce grown people—the relatives of the missing—to the children they had been when their loved ones were lost, even though they were older now than their missing persons had been then. U. described the posture of his uncle's relatives at his funeral:

*slumped over, submissive, childlike.* It might be true that some relatives felt comfort and closure when they received and buried the remains, he said, but on a broader social level, the heroization of the missing enacted by the CMP was of a piece with the politicization of the missing that had previously been pursued by the state in its concealment of the names and its refusal to investigate.

In more recent years, too, some relatives of the missing in both the north and the south have gone to elaborate trouble to bury their dead in ways countervailing the ethnonational character of official funerals. Another friend of mine, a member of the Bicommunal Initiative of Relatives of the Missing and Other Victims of War that had formed in 2005, posted on Facebook her reaction to such a funeral, held in 2017 in a southern village just a few minutes from the buffer zone, organized by another Greek-Cypriot member of the Bicommunal Initiative for his brother. She wrote:



> A piece of his hand, the bone from his elbow to his palm, is all that is left of X., the brother of my friend, who had been "missing" since 1974. Today, after 43 years, they buried these meager remains. The ceremony was simple; my friend and his siblings didn't want politicians, nor flags, nor armed forces (unfortunately, the last two came despite his wishes; the deceased was entitled to this, they said, because he was a soldier). But my friend spoke. He said that the number of the "missing" has increased instead of decreasing over the years, bringing votes upon votes to generations of political candidates who have built careers upon the pain of the people. He spoke about the Turkish-Cypriot missing whom they hid from us and still hide from us, and he also spoke about his friends who came from "the other side" to stand by him at this difficult moment. As had stood by him, for so many years, the "Bicommunal Initiative of Relatives of the Missing and Other Victims of War." People like T., who lost his parents and siblings to Greek-Cypriot massacres. And yet he was here. My friend also said that he had been expecting at least to bury these remnants of his brother under conditions of peace, with a solution [to the Cyprus Problem] in place. . . . But where [is the solution]? That, too, they have taken from us, those who pointlessly shout empty slogans from afar.

Such overt contestations of official narratives of the missing and the political interests behind those narratives, especially on the Greek-Cypriot side, were rare during the time of my fieldwork. But it seems to me they indicate the existence of critique behind the scenes, too—that is, in the ostensibly private space of family conflicts, hidden from the cameras; in affective experiences of irritation, abrasion, and suspicion; in grumbling that might be recuperated and spoken louder by those with more distance from the coerced role of grieving relative. How could the story of any missing person in Cyprus be closed, without a claim for justice? How could the death of any missing person be assimilated into the social order, when the body politic itself remained divided?

In their analysis of public rituals commemorating the missing and unknown dead, Sant Cassia and Verdery end their analysis at the ritual performance—perhaps presuming the efficacy of the performance in assimilating death into the social order and symbolically reconstituting the body politic. By striking contrast, Meira Weiss (2002, 69), writing about public funerals and other ritual commemorations in Israel that framed the deaths of soldiers as sacrifices "necessary for national life," approaches these performances as *attempts* at symbolic reconstitution made by official state actors and in official state discourses of heroic sacrifice. Weiss seems to me less interested in the success of these attempts (which she duly documents) than in their failures, which she finds in criticisms of Israel's "moral integrity" by some grieving relatives of dead soldiers, and in art exhibits curated and featuring works by other grieving relatives that were designed to "attack . . . the standardization and commodification of bereavement" in Israel (80, 81). She traces the failures of these public rituals, as well, in her own affectively charged counternarrative to the "all-too academic writing" in which she analyzes them (78); in italicized passages that interrupt her writing of the main text, she confesses her perverse enthrallment by the loss and grief experienced by the families with whom she conducted ethnographic research, her self-censorship about their criticism (any criticism) of the Israeli national project, and the wound to her "Self" made by one of the curators (84), who perhaps clued her into the necessity of distancing herself from that project.

In the case of U.'s uncle, the forensic investigation conducted by the CMP had not only failed to effect healing and closure for U.'s father; it failed as well to satisfy U.'s cousin—the dead man's son—though for different reasons. U. called this cousin "the black sheep of the family": a right-wing nationalist police officer in a family of leftist intellectuals. He had attended the viewing of the man's remains at the CMP lab along with U.'s father, and he told U. afterward that he found it "suspicious" that the scientists would not say that Turkish Cypriots had killed his uncle; he thought they were withholding information. Within one family, then, the public consecration of this missing person as an ethnonational martyr failed as a ritual performance in two converse ways. Too much was said about the Cyprus Problem, and the consecration seemed coercive and overdetermining; too little was said about the Cyprus Problem, and the consecration seemed cursory and presumptive, casting doubt on the scientific identification of the bones. This death thus slipped through and exposed the weak graft precariously attaching the private mourning of the family to the public mourning of the nation—weak not because family was pitted against nation, but because family was split by nation.

## The Bones Become More Human as We Look at Them



One day at the lab, I followed Y., the lab's forensic photographer, as he hurried from table to table. He was taking multiple photographs of the bones and artifacts from a case, then uploading the best pictures into the database so the anthropologists working on the case could add captions and incorporate the images into their reports. Y. took individual photos of each item associated with the missing person as well as photos of the "whole body"—that is, as much of an entire skeleton as possible. He did the same with the artifacts, photographing each scrap of clothing separately and then placing the scraps in a meaningful array. He pointed out to me the case he was working on now, bodies from a family grave: a father, mother, grandmother, and two small children. He had created a folder in the database where he could put the photos of their bones and artifacts together—*like a family album, in a weird way*, he said.

That day, Y. got some help from K., an anthropologist, who had noticed he was having trouble figuring out how the scraps of clothing fit together. K. knelt on the floor next to the white sheet where the fabric was laid out and within half a minute had reconstructed almost an entire shirt, assembling scraps from the front and back, the breast pocket, the sleeves, the collar, the buttons. Y. whistled and praised her skills. K. replied that she liked working with the artifacts; it reminded her of housework and her family. *If you do enough laundry, you understand how clothes are put together*, she said, smiling, gesturing toward the old torn shirt on the floor. For whom was this old shirt repaired and summoned into the present? K., along with Y., me, and others in the lab who had gathered around for a moment, were the only audience for her deft handiwork. It was a fleeting moment; the shirt would be disassembled shortly afterward, the pieces placed in a plastic bag and set aside for a viewing with the relatives at some point in the future. Of the shots taken by Y., the best one would be uploaded to the digital case file, where, in all likelihood, no one would ever see it.

The care K. put into piecing the shirt together, which she likened to the care she put into doing her family's laundry, also mirrored the care she put into piecing skeletons together from bones and bone fragments, the analytic procedure that every anthropologist undertook when "working on a body." The scientific process of associating and ordering bones and bone fragments was oriented to the visual recognition of bodies. Ironically, perhaps, the anthropologists conducted their analysis "blind"—that is, without external references such as the case files of missing persons, which usually contained photographs of those persons from the time they went missing; descriptions given by relatives, noting habitual activities like smoking or forms of labor that might have left traces of repetitive motion on their bones; and unique physical traits or medical conditions that might aid in identifying their remains. Working first without such antemortem data, anthropologists proceeded by areas of the body, locating all the pieces that belonged to each limb, the hands and feet, the pelvis, spine, skull, teeth, and other parts, organizing them as far as possible in the form of a skeleton on a table. They ascertained whether the bones considered "associated" by the archaeologists who had bagged them at the excavation site did indeed belong to the same individual, and then they tried to associate any unassociated bones from the site with that or another individual. They measured each bone in several ways, using different metrics for different kinds of bones and bone features.[48] They provisionally determined the age, osteological sex, stature, bone pathologies, and nutritional health of the individual; they noted abnormalities like growths and discolorations, as well as indications of breaks and wounds.



Once this picture had been painted in the abstract, the anthropologist working on a body would consult the archaeological report from the excavation that had yielded the remains, as well as team members working on other bodies from the same grave site, in order to associate the skeleton with a specific case file. S. told me that, after she finished an anthropological report, she would look at the antemortem data to see how close she had come to the information already known about the individual in question—his or her age, stature, medical conditions, habits, work. *That's the fun part!* she said, laughing. These were, after all, "just bones," in the context of analysis that she likened to solving a mystery. In another sense, however, the bones were deeply and intimately known by the anthropologists who worked on them. Not only when and how the person had died, but also much of who he or she had been in life, was written on the bones.

*We're surrounded by death,* C. remarked, another day. She asked me if I found it strange to be in a room "with all these bodies around." I told her it did not feel strange to me, but perhaps that was because I knew nothing about the people whose bones these were; it might be harder if I understood more about who they had been before they died. *We don't know much about them, either,* C. told me. *The archaeologists usually know a lot more, since they sometimes have contact with witnesses at the site. They know the reasons why the site is being excavated, the expected number of bodies, where they came from.* I said it seemed to me the anthropologists learned things about these victims that other people could not know, even their closest family members and friends. Even though the bodies were strangers, anthropologists knew all about their illnesses, their injuries, and their habits. *That's true,* C. said. *The bones become more human as we look at them.* 

For anthropologists at the lab, the work of building a person from fragments was a scientific process of restoration and reconstruction. Yet, as C. suggested, this might also be a rehumanization of the dead and, as such, a summoning of emotion and memory, or a semblance of memory. In this imaginary dimension of their work, the anthropologists were in a sense acting as proxies for the relatives of the dead, consigned to guesswork rather than memory, but nevertheless conjuring a person. The association of information from a file with an array of bones was an act of imagination: enlivening the bones with an image of the person. In this, the scientists—more than the relatives, ultimately—were the ones who could see a missing person in his or her bones.

I recall in this connection a visit to the lab by the Third Member of the CMP, who accompanied a foreign ambassador and guests on a tour of the facilities. He introduced the visitors to K., one of the team leaders, who gave them an overview of the forensic work undertaken at the lab and then a few details of the specific case her team was working on at the time. The visitors walked around the lab, looking at the bones and asking questions of the anthropologists at each table—about the effects of soil conditions on the remains, about the different colors perceptible on the surface of the bones, about the different signs of injury. Later, when the visitors had reassembled by the front door, one of them asked the Third Member why so many of the anthropologists were women. He said he didn't know, but guessed it might have to do with the "sensitivity" of their work and the fragility of the bones: *It takes a caring person.*

In what sense were these scientists feeling or showing care as they made their observations, measurements, and analyses? Advancing a "care ethics" perspective on forensic work, Adam Rosenblatt suggests that it is the very

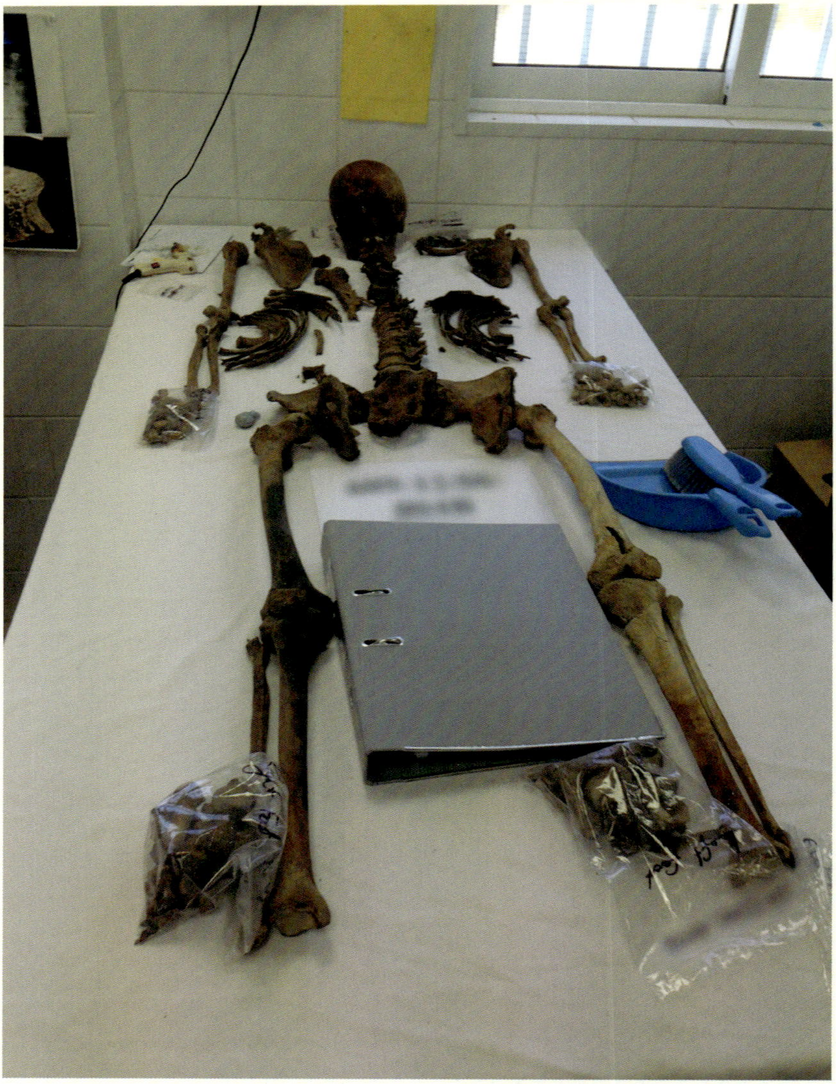

NO.

**1.13**

tactility of this work that demands and capacitates a forensic ethics of care for the dead. He describes forensic ethics as those that arise from and respond to the "importance of touch" in "a world of intimate touches, glued fragments, and regretful cuts" (2015, 175, 174). Even "washing and preparing the clothes for viewing . . . is an intimate act of care" (176), he writes, observing that articulating bones and restoring skeletons as far as possible are "caring actions" that "create real changes in the conditions and status of dead bodies" (177). These actions acknowledge the value of the "integrity" of the body (188), he explains, which may matter when forensic workers cede care of the body to relatives or others who will mourn and bury it: "The forensic investigator, from a care perspective, seeks the integrity of the dead body *as a body and a beloved*. She sees the work of care as a form of repair and knows that a few bones or locks of hair—however useful for ascertaining the identity of the deceased—are far less adequate, as objects of care, than a full body" (183).



Recovering full bodies from their graves and restoring whole skeletons in the lab "as far as possible," as I so often heard scientists say, was indeed the goal of their work, if an ideal rarely reached. In many cases, the meager array of fragmented remains made it difficult for relatives to accept that this was the body of their missing person. Scientists told me that families often expressed a strenuous wish to bury a whole body, as they feared an incomplete body could not rest in its grave; some were disturbed, too, by the idea that pieces of their loved one's body might still be buried somewhere, abandoned. In light of these wishes and fears, while the scientists may have been caring for the dead by working to restore the integrity of a body, they were also, and perhaps more deliberately, caring for the living.[49]

Not just anyone was positioned to care in this way, however. The imagination of careful women caring for bones that was expressed by the CMP's Third Member was promoted as well on the CMP website. The scientists who appeared there in photographs of the lab were almost exclusively women. During the time I spent at the lab, two men worked there, on a team of twelve; another joined shortly before I left, along with another woman. Men were much better represented in CMP photographs of field excavations. A clear visualization of gender was at work in these representations: men along with women were shown doing the adventurous and dirty work of toiling in the fields, lifting buckets, wielding shovels and picks, operating machines, climbing hills, and descending into wells; while scenes of the lab, white and pristine, were populated by women in white lab coats, working alone, eyes cast down on the bones they handled dexterously yet tenderly. Their eyes and their hands were the forensic tools that mattered.

Such images of scientists performing this work contained a tension between scientization and sacralization, between naturalization and humanization. The sober demeanor of the anthropologists, and their generational and temporal remove from the events of violence, did not fit the image of grief and mourning long established in the iconography of the missing; but it was precisely these forms of remove that qualified them as scientists and legitimated their proximity to the bones, an intimacy that might otherwise have been jarring or even wounding to relatives of the missing. That these strangers were women, already positioned for Cypriot audiences to perform the work of care, perhaps tempered the pain of estrangement from the bones that mourners might experience on seeing them treated so clinically.[50] Moreover, this work was secluded in the protected if not private space of the lab, far from the public space of state funerals that were dominated by the presence of (male) clergy and politicians.



In both scientizing and gendering forensic work in this way, images of women anthropologists working on bones depoliticized the knowledge of violence that the bones materialized, reaffirming the CMP's "purely humanitarian" stance of political neutrality. Perhaps—as I read it—this representation was meant to persuade resistant publics to accept the difficult work of the CMP by framing the forensic encounter with bones as continuous (or at least consistent) with traditional rituals of washing and examining bones before burial—rather than as an encounter with the violence that produced the bones and that continued to cause so much pain.[51] But whatever the design of this representation, and whatever its effects, the intimacy that scientists developed with the bones was more than a representation. For many who worked at the lab, it was a creative process—a labor of imagination—as well as a work of care.

Imagination and empathy are not equivalent, and I would not collapse them into a "care ethics" perspective on forensic work in the manner of Rosenblatt, much as I think this perspective aptly captures the situatedness of many forensic workers in contexts of competing moral claims to the dead or responsibilities for the dead. But I do not presume that the scientists at the CMP, in doing their careful work, were caring specifically for the dead, nor that they attributed personhood to the bones in their custody at any stage in the forensic process; conjuring a person from bones as an act of imagination does not require an osteo-ontology of personhood. As I noted earlier, what permitted the bones to "become more human" as the scientists looked at them was not necessarily a visual semblance—the visualization of whole bodies by way of the articulation of skeletons ("as far as possible"). Even in cases where very few remains were found, scientists could see much about the person in disarticulated bones and bone fragments that would not look human to anyone else. The technical skills of identification were also talents of imagination. It was this capacity to read bones, to imagine and conjure people, that positioned scientists to travel with these time machines—to encounter the past through their association with the dead. Those associations were constructed through unconventional means: not through kinship or friendship, but sensorially, through the intimacy of vision and touch.

## Outside of Time



When I first visited the lab, and K. showed me around the facilities, she took me last to the viewing room. She pointed out the coffins in the back of the room, plain wooden boxes with crosses on the sides. *Those are for Greek-Cypriot remains,* she explained. *For the viewing, we will put up icons and a cross and some candles for them. We don't do anything like that for the Turkish Cypriots. Greek-Cypriot families sometimes bring a priest, but Turkish Cypriots almost never bring a hodja—maybe it's happened once, in all these years.* I asked why, and she shrugged: *Greek Cypriots are more religious!* Later, I described this viewing scenario to a Greek-Cypriot friend, who said it made perfect sense to him: *On the Greek-Cypriot side, we have the Christian tradition of resurrection, which comes with the hope of return. The missing have always been seen with this hope of returning to life. Now that they're being found, and it's clear they're gone, people see them as sacrifices, as martyrs. So their recovery has to be treated as a religious ceremony. On the Turkish-Cypriot side, that's just not an issue.*

This dichotomy between Greek Cypriots and Turkish Cypriots in the matter of religiosity is reproduced by some anthropologists of Cyprus who attempt a comparative or cross-border perspective. In his ethnography of the missing, for example, Sant Cassia (1999, 2005) cautiously compares the imagery of suffering in the north and the south. Associating Greek-Cypriot photography featuring grieving relatives with "Christian iconography," he declines to draw a similar connection between Islam and Turkish-Cypriot photography of atrocity, which he interprets as documentary realism rather than allegory.[52] The distinction between religious Greek Cypriots and secular Turkish Cypriots is read here in terms of divergent cultural features that preceded and survived the division between south and north, rather than as political effects of that division that have worked to authorize and intensify it for the last fifty years.

I am inclined toward the latter view—that is, toward understanding religiosity as a political index of division—given the extent to which religiosity was identified as a political threat by my Turkish-Cypriot colleagues and friends. I first encountered this sense of threat when I attended the state funeral of Rauf Denktaş, former president of the TRNC, with several Turkish-Cypriot anthropologists from the lab.[53] A secularist and rigid Kemalist, Denktaş had fostered close ties between the TRNC and Turkey until the last few years of his presidency, when the referendum on the Annan Plan focused popular resistance to Turkey among Turkish Cypriots and growing support for reunification with the Republic. The day after the funeral, I caught a ride home from the lab with one of the Turkish-Cypriot anthropologists who had not attended. I told her about it, and she asked if it had been "very religious." I was not sure how to respond; I said it was the first time I had witnessed a Muslim prayer. She laughed: *We don't do that often—we're not very religious!* By then, I had heard this refrain many times. In my time at the CMP, religion was rarely a topic of conversation, and when it came up among Turkish Cypriots, it was usually in the context of a discussion about Turkish settlers, whom they often described as peasants or laborers and "very religious"—the bearers of Islamic tradition as well as signs of growing Turkish power in the north.[54]

This came across to me clearly one morning at the lab, when Y. was checking headlines during the coffee break. He read out loud to me the news of a double murder in north Nicosia. The owner of a large supermarket chain in the north and his wife had been found dead the night before, and the *Kıbrıs* newspaper had received a text message from the purported killers, claiming responsibility. The message, from a group called Tura, claimed the group had demanded money from the man and killed him and his wife when he refused; they would likewise kill anyone who refused to support them. Y. had never heard of this group before: *I'm shocked! Where did they come from?* He explained that Tura (*toughra*) was the name for an Ottoman seal, so they must be a religious group.

Y. related the details of the story to the others at the table in Turkish, and then in English so as to include a few Greek-Cypriot colleagues who were sitting around. He told us, *My sister was saying to me last night that she's going to take our grandmother and move to our old village! My grandmother's been saying this for a long time.* Their old village was in the south, near Paphos; his sister was thus implying that they needed to escape the north and its increasing Turkification. Riding home later that day, Y. told me that Turkish Cypriots were afraid Turkey would annex northern Cyprus; there had been talk of making the TRNC the "eighty-second city" of Turkey. I asked if he was really afraid of this; it seemed so unlikely, especially given Turkey's bid for membership in the EU, and he agreed. *But there are so many people from Turkey living here now, we feel outnumbered. We could never win a vote like that!* In Y.'s commentary, religiosity in Cyprus was directly connected to the division as a matter of demography, democracy, and sovereignty; it was a way of marking the precarity of Turkish Cypriots, outnumbered by Turkish settlers as well as by the equally religious (and much more numerous) Greek Cypriots.

The perception at the CMP that Greek Cypriots, unlike Turkish Cypriots, would experience their encounter with the bones of the missing in a religious register may be linked as well to the importance of mortuary practices in Greek Orthodox tradition. Connections between ritual practices of exhuming and reburying bones and the exhumation and reburial of the remains of the missing were more commonsense in the Greek-Cypriot context, where bones were already saturated with meaning, even if Greek Cypriots did not actually practice exhumation and reburial in cases of natural death.[55] The cultural aesthetics of corpses and bones in the ethnography of death in Greece open a way to understand the forensic context in Cyprus in symbolic—though not necessarily religious—terms.[56] 

Ethnographers of Greek mortuary rituals emphasize the element of time as a symbolic operator. In accounts of these practices, the mourning ritual of lamentation, followed by the funeral and burial of the corpse, is fulfilled some years later by the exhumation and reburial of the bones, usually in a family or church ossuary. At stake in the intervening time is the decomposition of the flesh, a natural process—dust returning to dust—facilitated by the body's burial in the ground in a plain wooden coffin; the Greek Orthodox Church has never authorized cremation or embalming (Danforth 1982, 48; Panourgiá 1995, 188, 197). According to Neni Panourgiá (1995, 191), writing about death in contemporary Athens, the fear that a corpse might not return to dust, but instead remain "undissolved" or "partly decomposed," motivated some families to postpone exhumation for years after the normative period, ranging from two to five and in some places up to ten years. Once the remains had been exhumed, on her account, they might be reburied in the same grave along with other remains, or in an ossuary belonging to the family, the church, or the municipal cemetery. Panourgiá notes "horror" on the part of her Athenian interlocutors at the thought of having the bones of their loved ones reinterred in a collective ossuary—"the fate of paupers" and a "matter of indignity to be avoided at all costs" (184), avoided by those without permanent burial plots by constructing family ossuaries or vaults within large urban cemeteries.

In the rural village in central Greece described by Loring Danforth, on the other hand, it was customary to rebury bones in the ossuary at the village church. This ritual, he argues, marked the beginning of the depersonalization and abstraction of the dead, no longer named individually but recognized and cared for collectively by the community as a whole (Danforth 1982, 134). The interval (or "liminal period," as Danforth has it, 43) between burial and exhumation was a time of fantasy, according to both Panourgiá and Danforth; during that time, Panourgiá (1995, 177) explains, the living might "play" with the notion that the dead person might still be alive. Only exhumation and reburial, and the destruction of the original grave in that process, would render the complete separation of the dead from the living (Danforth 1982, 133, 150; Panourgiá 1995, 189). The brief passage of the dead back into the domain of the living in the exhumation ritual was, thus, an "illusion," Danforth suggests; on his account, exhumation could only be "disjunctive" in its "promis[e] to return that which it cannot" (65). He recounts the experience of a woman whose encounter with the bones of her father forced a recognition of his death that she had, until that moment, acknowledged only outwardly: "One woman reported that prior to the exhumation of her father . . . she was excited and impatient. She felt a sense of eagerness and anticipation. She thought she would see her father again—alive. She thought she would feel joy, but when she saw only his bones, her hopes were crushed. The joy she had anticipated was transformed into grief and pain" (65).



In her ethnography of death work performed by women in Inner Mani, Greece, C. Nadia Seremetakis likewise depicts mourners in their approach to exhumed bones as yearning for connection with the dead: "Burial interrupts visual contact with the dead. Exhumation restores that contact. . . . This can be a moment of shock, loss, and extreme grief for the exhumer who finds the dead 'unrecognizable.' Exhumation then constitutes a re-encounter with the dead in a new and alien form. . . . When they return, the search of the senses for the recognizable begins" (1991, 187–88).

Exhumed bones would be considered "clean" if they were white and dry, signifying moral purity, according to Danforth, who traces a "symbolic association between the soul and the bones of the deceased" (1982, 49). In a corpse that had not entirely decomposed, bones might be yellow, brown, or black; they might retain pieces of decomposing flesh or hair; they might exude an unpleasant smell. In such cases, Danforth suggests, the dead person had not yet entirely separated from the domain of the living; the condition of his bones was evidence of his "binding" to life and earth by sin (52). Citing Lawson's 1910 monograph on modern Greek folklore, Danforth notes that those dead persons most likely to persist in the world of the living as revenants were "those who had not received proper burial, those who had met with a violent death, those who had died under a curse, those who had led particularly evil lives" (126). He thus reads the exhumation of bones in public as a form of "social control," an exposure to the moral approbation of the community: "'[The bones] didn't come out well.' . . . 'He didn't have a good soul.' . . . 'The earth didn't forgive him.' . . . '[It's] a sign for the world to see'" (50–51).

Seremetakis frames the reading of the bones as a more complex divination—not a reproduction of the community's moral judgment mediated by religion, but rather a vision beneath the surface of the present into heterogeneous time: "Exhumers who expose and discuss blackened bones and white-yellow bones also endow the dead with time or separate the dead from time. The exhumed black bones with residues of flesh are tied to the past. They have remained static and *outside of time* and show no purifying transformation in time" (1991, 229).

Seremetakis is wary of Danforth's assertions of the finality and stabilization of death symbolized by exhumation and reburial. In dreams, in memories revived by encounters with other dead people, in symbolically resonant events like births and weddings, she finds the dead "haunting" everyday life and "defamiliarizing" the social order long after death rites are performed (Seremetakis 1991, 14). With this focus on the instability of the dead, Seremetakis develops a theorization of "ritualization" to situate death rituals in their ongoing, everyday, nonpublic, transgressive, cooperative, improvisational, open-ended practice: "The concept of ritualization moves the analysis of death rites away from performances fixed in time and space and resituates it within the flux and contingency of everyday events" (47). "Deritualization," on the other hand—a concept she coins to capture the fixation and institutionalization of symbolic practices, and their location in public space—is thus associated with modernization and its fragmenting and marginalizing effects on ritual.

With this vision of ritualization, Seremetakis refuses any alignment between mortuary rites and religious practices. She discerns instead the "antiliturgical character" of women's death work, expressed in conflicts between women and (male) clergy in Inner Mani, and in the literal distance between mourning ceremonies conducted exclusively by women in the home and public funerals conducted by priests at church that were attended by (male) leaders of the community (Seremetakis 1991, 6, 161). Panourgiá likewise insists that death rites in Athens were neither formalized nor prescribed by the church, even if they were widely thought to be so. Knowing the "rules

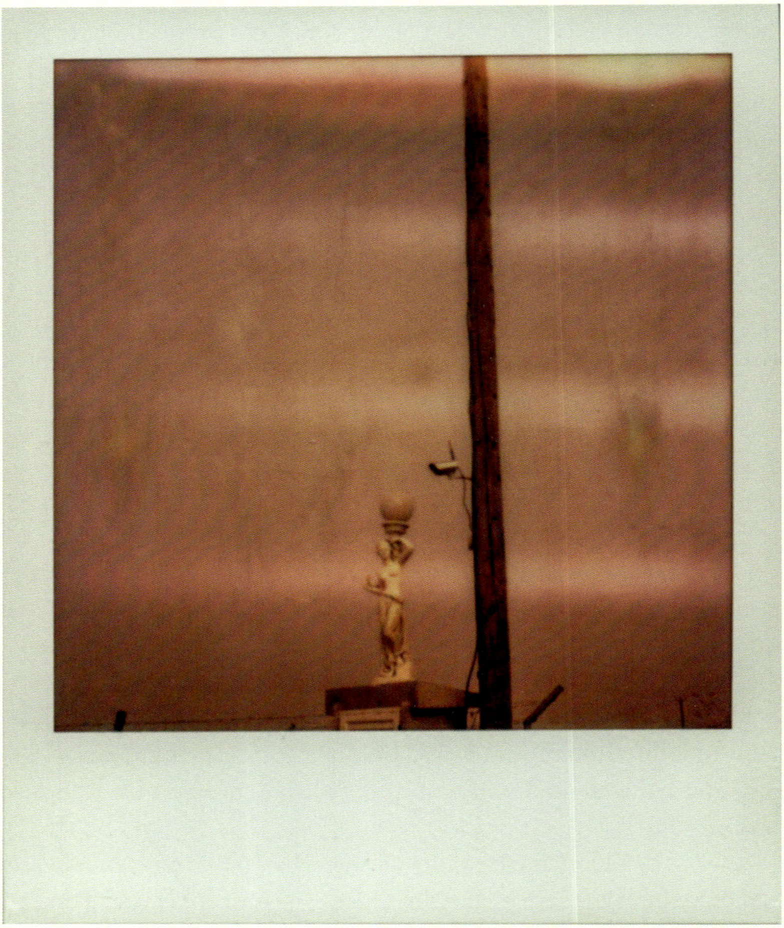

NO.

1.14

that govern" exhumation, for example, was a sign of being a "good Christian," she notes, yet those rules were "set not by the Church but by custom" (Panourgiá 1995, 190, 188). In the practices of preparing and burying the corpse, and of exhuming and reburying the bones, she finds evidence of the "personal, almost casual relationship of Greeks to religion and the organized church, in contrast to their intimate, almost organic, relationship with ritual" (98).[57]

Deritualization—for Seremetakis, a process by which ritual is fragmented and marginalized by modern institutions of medicine and law, and by formal religious institutions in secular societies—can perhaps help to account for the transformation and invention of death rituals in modern scientific practice. In this vein, Aslıhan Sanal, writing about organ transplantation and anatomy dissection in Istanbul, theorizes the "rites of passage" performed by Turkish medical professionals in order to transform dead bodies into noble humans whose body parts can be recuperated ethically by the living. Following Arnold van Gennep's schema for rites of passage in burial and reburial practices, Sanal identifies, in the practices of surgeons and anatomists, the successive stages of separation ("invention" of human identities for corpses), transition ("purification" of corpses through medical techniques and moral symbolization), and incorporation ("diffusion" of body parts into the living) (Sanal 2010, 146, 175). These rituals continually risked failure, she argues, because they required the invention of a "transitional phase" for corpses, between death and burial (135)—a disruption and dislocation in the proper order of time and space through which the living become dead and are then reborn in the afterlife, in Turkish Sunni Muslim thought. The rituals operated by transplant surgeons overcame this risk, she says, successfully transforming brain-dead people into donors: heroes and heroines who had made a noble sacrifice of their bodies for the common good. The rituals operated by the anatomists, however, remained "incomplete," as they attempted to transform the unclaimed corpses of psychiatric patients into public servants who advanced medical knowledge for the good of society.

Sanal (2010) shows how this transformation was forestalled by the anatomists' own inability to forget where these bodies had come from, and the abject state in which the people whose bodies they were had lived before they died. By inventing identities for the bodies, and by treating them in a "very caring and tender" manner, anatomists tried to "humanize the dead" (138, 139)—partly, Sanal suggests, in order to protect themselves from the trauma of witnessing the indignities these bodies had sustained both in life and in death, including the violence the anatomists themselves were doing by cutting into them and cutting them up, "violating their integrity" (141). The objective of such violation, understood as a social good by anatomists, was the production of medical knowledge; but it was not only a better understanding of human anatomy that they gained from working on these bodies. They learned, as well, the "secrets of the naked body, the secrets of insanity," and "secrets of everyday violence," internalized by anatomists as "personal knowledge" (147, 148).

The growing intimacy that anatomists developed with the bodies brought with it a more intense "internalization" of their "tainted meaning," to the point, Sanal says, that the anatomists began "inhabiting the uncanny" (2010, 147, 148). She argues that the suspension of cadavers in this transitional space and time could not be resolved, because the "diffusion" rituals by which these dead bodies became usable parts remained hidden in the shameful, polluting space of the dissection lab, an underfunded and low-status space within an elite state medical college. Sanal explains that, despite the "public service" the cadavers performed in helping medical students become good doctors, the "trauma, secrecy, and invisibility" of dissection could not become public (176); unlike the brain-dead donors with whom transplant surgeons worked, cadavers could not be incorporated by the living so long as the living suppressed their knowledge of the violence that had produced them.

In light of these ways of thinking about death in modernity, and the status and value of dead bodies and remains, it is more helpful, I think, to interpret the scientific practices of exhumation and analysis at the CMP in terms of alienated, fragmented, and unsuccessful ritual than in terms of Turkish Islamic or Greek Orthodox Christian traditions. The temporally erratic advent of the missing as dead in Cyprus introduced complex time into the forensic process and, with it, a kind of indeterminacy in forensic methods of closure. For Seremetakis, the proper time of ritual is not fixed but discontinuous and open-ended, accommodating repetition and improvisation. The time of death, likewise, is heterogeneous, "outside" the chronological time of history and biography; bones can retain their flesh, the natural process of decay notwithstanding, and the dead can return to the domain of the living in the form of ghosts, memories, dreams, and descendants. The scientific process of analysis and identification conducted by scientists at the CMP, as they tried to discern the effects of life and environment on buried bones, took place in equally complex time. The intimate knowledge of the dead these scientists developed always contained some imagination of who they had been in life; what they had done, witnessed, and endured; and how they might be related to the living. This was both a scientific and a moral imagination, even if scientists felt uncomfortable with the moral dimension when it came to managing encounters between the bones and the relatives of the missing.

Crucially, these scientists were not conscripted in traditional death work, like the Inner Maniat women who feature in Seremetakis's ethnography; they were not dealing with death in the everyday context in which she situates ritualization. They were confronting not death but murder—violence, trauma—even though they were not permitted to determine its causes or circumstances. The scientists understood that what relatives wanted to know, and demanded from them, could not be answered by their findings; the acutely political dimension of their death work forestalled symbolic closure. The ritualized closure of death and time attempted by public funerals was, then, in a sense, a falsification of the ambivalent and indeterminate attempts the scientists made to know and to humanize the dead.



## Endless

In Cyprus's "forensic theater"—Whitehead's term for a generic scene of clinically sanitized and inspected mass death, arranged as if staged for the cameras—the scientists were subjects of publicity. In images of forensic work, their affect and demeanor were almost incidental features of the background, receding from the bones and the graves that occupied the foreground. The often-intense emotions they in fact experienced at work did not figure in public representations of this forensic scene. Their emotions were unrelated to personal memories of the dead, but, as many told me, the toll their work took on their bodies and psyches, and their contact with the dead as they conducted that work, were experienced as deeply personal.

Excavations demanded intense physical labor—difficult enough during the rainy winters, when archaeologists often worked in cold, heavy mud, but exceedingly so in summer, when temperatures reached into the midforties centigrade. *You do the best you can,* A. told me: *You wear a hat, you put up sheets to cover the trenches, you take your lunch in the shade. But it's very difficult.* C. told me she had become a sort of "zombie" on her last excavation. *I just worked and worked and worked. I lost all mental focus on what I was doing. It wasn't until I was transferred to the lab that I realized I'd been in a state of shock. It felt normal at the time—it's what everyone was doing—but in reality I was being pushed to my limit.* The difficulty of physical work was compounded by dangers of all description: spiders and snakes, unstable footing, collapsing trenches, buried explosives. Quite a few archaeologists had suffered accidents, stumbling down a mountainside, falling into a trench, getting hit by a digging machine, cutting a hand on rusted metal in the ground. Health and safety standards were "evolving," O. told me: *We figure it out as we go along! It's very improvisational.*

At a recent meeting of the field teams, a debate had developed about the necessity of special suits, masks, and gloves for archaeologists working in toxic environments—for example, on well excavations where, digging into wet layers of soil, they might contract infections from rotting animal remains or even human corpses. *It's exciting,* F. told me. *That's what I love about it, working outside, dealing with the environment. That's what I was trained to do.* Sometimes, however, it was less exciting; it could be mind-numbingly boring and tedious. One team working on a well excavation had spent several weeks sitting in their trucks, waiting for a ramp to be built into the well so that they could descend safely and start digging. *It's always the same,* said L., a team leader at the site. *It's tedious and it's frustrating. What gets you through it are your friends. You get to know each other very well in a situation like that!*



The discovery of remains, which came with great excitement and the satisfaction of making a find, also cost archaeologists dearly. *I wonder sometimes what the work we're doing here is doing to us,* P. remarked at lunch one day. She told me about her experience at an excavation where remains were recovered of an infant, three children, and an old woman. *How could someone kill babies and children?* she asked. *This is something sick.* She told me that was the only time she had felt so disturbed at an exhumation. T. said that, in the beginning, when he was first working on excavations, he would get upset; thoughts would pass through his mind about who the people might be and how they had died. P. agreed: *I remember one grave where we found a man and woman. Her skull was resting on his shoulder and his arm was around her. I thought that maybe the woman crawled up to the man as she was dying and he hugged her, for comfort. I saw that image in my mind for a long time afterward.* T. described a different grave where a group of soldiers had been buried. Their bodies were recovered with their hands behind their backs but clasped together, he said, as if they had all been holding hands when they died. L. said, *It's natural to get upset when you see things like that. We're surrounded by it all the time.* At her first dig, she told us, she saw the skeletons in the ground and broke into tears. *You get used to it,* T. said to me. But P. disagreed: *You bury it in your unconscious and that's how you get used to it, but it's still there. I wonder sometimes what this is doing to us, over time, seeing so much and burying it.*

They learned to "bury it" in the lab as well as the field. Y., the photographer, who was educated in art history and had worked as an art photographer before joining the CMP, came to his job without any forensic experience. He told me he had found it very strange at first to be shooting so many bones, day after day, but it quickly became "normal." He spoke of the strange semiconsciousness of death and violence invited by the forensic scene: *The work we're doing here, it's probably taking a toll on us even though we don't know it. I think once I stop working here, after a few years, then I'll realize the trauma I've been through.*

When I first began visiting the lab, T. was working on a new body, from which he had mostly fragments to work with; even the whole bones were not in good shape. He told me he was having a great deal of trouble sorting the fragments into piles of like parts and then gluing the pieces together to restore the original shape of the bones so that he could measure them. *This case is bringing me so much stress,* he said. It was the first body he had handled alone; he had worked alongside a more experienced anthropologist for his first month at the lab and had gotten a lot of coaching from her along the way. *There are so many fragments in this case—how will I ever get it done? The stress follows me around; I think about work when I'm at home. I even dream about it—like, yesterday, I was putting ribs together, and I saw them in my dreams last night.* He showed me a clump of black, brittle, peat-like substance, which he thought was brain material with a little hair caught in it. The room heater, a massive machine mounted high on the wall next to his table, started up just then and nearly blew the material away. T. grimaced and hurried to put it back in the baggie.

A few weeks later, I chatted with T. about his new project. He had recently been assigned to sort through the unassociated artifacts from a large case on which an entire team at the lab had just begun work. The case involved forty-three individuals, presumed to be Turkish Cypriots, all the males over fifteen years of age from a village in the south, who had been rounded up and taken away on buses in August 1974. The gravesite found by the forensic team contained the remains of only one of two busloads of these people; it was still "unknown," T. told me, where the people on the other bus had ended up. The excavation team suspected that the grave was at least a secondary burial site and perhaps a tertiary site, meaning the bodies had been moved at least once from their original grave. The remains had therefore been recovered mostly as "general body parts"—that is, unarticulated bones (not in correct anatomical position) that were unassociated with particular individuals. Whole skeletons were exceedingly rare for this site, which made the work of the anthropologists all the more difficult.

In addition to the thousands of unassociated bones and bone fragments, almost five hundred artifacts had been bagged and stored. T.'s job was to remove them from their bags, wash and dry them, compare them with the inventories filed by the field team, and correct or expand those descriptions. He was going through the artifacts one by one, studying and measuring them, compiling a list with multiple categories so that he could start trying to match pieces of whole artifacts together and then associate the artifacts with the bones. He showed me a piece of rubber from the sole of a shoe that was found with some foot bones. If he was able to put that piece together with others recovered from the grave in order to make a whole shoe, then he could try to match the shoe to the individual whose foot bones were buried in the same grave. He held up a few other items from the array: a large men's eighteen-karat gold ring, engraved with a crescent and some letters; several sets of buttons; pieces of cloth; foil paper from a cigarette box; some unsmoked cigarettes. *This is very difficult work,* he said, *because there are so many artifacts and I have to stay very focused on the details in order to match them. But*—he smiled—*I'm getting used to the pressure.* He reminded me how overwhelmed he had been when I first met him, right after he had been transferred to the lab. *When I started, those first few weeks, I would lie awake at night wondering how we would ever get through all these bones. There were so many. They weren't even associated yet—it just seemed endless.*



## Whether a Genocide Has Taken Place

Up until the moment of provisional identification, an anthropologist who had worked so intimately and intricately with an individual's bones would not know his or her identity—nor, therefore, his or her ethnic identity. And yet, having communicated with the archaeologists who had exhumed the remains, and with the investigators who had located the site, the anthropologist might know at least the general story of how the remains had ended up in that place and, therefore, a presumption of the victim's ethnic identity as either Greek Cypriot or Turkish Cypriot. Damir Arsenijević, writing in the aftermath of the genocide in Bosnia and Herzegovina, describes the moment at which remains are identified as the moment when "it" becomes "who"—"a moment of decision; a moment of naming" (2011a, 194). His concern is to interrupt that moment, to recapture the bones of the dead from the multiculturalist politics of reconciliation that identify and consecrate bones in ethnic terms:

> The scientist, the bureaucrat and the priest assume the perspective of the perpetrator of the crime. For it is in the fantasy of the perpetrator that the executed person is the ethnic *other*. . . . But whose bone is the bone? Does it belong to the perpetrators who killed and buried the bodies? Does it belong to the family members of the missing persons? Does it belong to the diplomat in whose country peace in Bosnia was brokered? Does it belong to those, like me, who feel ashamed and wince every time the bone is touched? Yes and no. It belongs to all of us. It is a societal thing. It is thus precisely because the suffering and death which resulted from genocide are the effects of the politics of terror and, as such, are pre-eminently a public matter. The emancipated process of becoming a subject can only take place when the subject is freed from the shackles of a victim position or any other position that is merely focused on the interests of a particularist identity. (194, 195)



Such identitarian interests weighed on scientists at the CMP, too, who were hired as representatives of either the Greek-Cypriot or the Turkish-Cypriot community in the postconflict game of balance, and who were tasked with the identification of bones that were themselves taken as communal representatives. In relation to the bones, then, scientists were positioned as either covictim or perpetrator. V. described to me the perversity of this positioning during a visit some members of a Greek-Cypriot group had recently made to the lab. One of the visitors, a woman who was about his father's age—therefore a teenager in 1974—and who knew he was Turkish Cypriot, had gestured across the whole room of bones laid out on tables and said to him, *Imagine, Turkey did all this!* V. told me he had felt that he could not say to her that there was not a single Greek-Cypriot bone in the whole room—that the bodies belonged to Turkish Cypriots killed by Greek Cypriots in 1964. He had kept quiet, but the experience had left him with a terrible feeling, as if the woman were accusing him of violence. *It's like we're being punished!* he said. *Turkish Cypriots have never denied what happened in 1974, but Greek Cypriots deny what happened before, to us.* He could not understand how someone of this woman's age could deny that there had been "trouble" in the early 1960s: *She was old enough to have lived through it!*

V. told me that story one morning just before Easter, when CMP employees would have a week-long holiday. (I learned that, in addition to two weeks off in August, all CMP employees had week-long holidays for both Easter and Baïram, the big religious holidays for Greek Cypriots and Turkish Cypriots, respectively—in the name of balance. *We don't take any of the bad nationalist holidays on either side*, an archaeologist told me, laughing—no holidays commemorating war heroes, for example; the religious holidays were considered cultural rather than political in nature, and therefore inoffensive.) Some of the anthropologists—those who would not be celebrating Easter during the holiday—were exploring vacation itineraries online during their midmorning break. Z. was looking into a trip to Izmir, and V., who had visited the city many times, asked if I had ever been. I had, and told him my impression of its flatness, its shoddy and anonymous modernist architecture, so unlike nearby cities such as Boursa—which made sense, I said, since the old city of Smyrna (now Izmir) had been burned to the ground in 1923 and rebuilt after the disastrous Greek campaign to reclaim Asia Minor from the Ottomans. D. chimed in, *Let me ask you: who burned Izmir?* I said, *That depends on who you ask!*



This comment stirred a conversation among several of the anthropologists. V. and D. were of the opinion that it was the Greek soldiers who had set fire to villages in Anatolia and then Izmir as they fled from the Ottoman forces in defeat. L. said this made no sense to her, since at the time the city was under Greek control and would have been retained by Greece if Prime Minister Venizelos had not made the mistake of trying to claim more land in Asia Minor. D. agreed that the whole Greek campaign in Anatolia had been a terrible mistake; what they disagreed about was who had destroyed Izmir. He told us he had heard that it was actually Armenian gangs who had burned down villages in Anatolia and killed the women and children left behind by their Turkish husbands who were serving in the army, and then moved on to Izmir.

I felt oddly stung by this comment, wanting to correct D.'s perspective on history, in which I heard ugly echoes of anti-Armenian propaganda and genocide denial. I told him I had studied the burning of Smyrna and had never come across a version in which Armenians were responsible; to my knowledge, the Armenian quarter of the city was the first to burn, and almost all the Armenians living there had died, so it was difficult to understand how Armenian gangs could have done it. But I had certainly come across accusations against both the Greek and Turkish armies. D. kept his patient demeanor as he continued to argue that the Turks had not burned Izmir. L. grew more visibly frustrated and upset, laughing uncomfortably: *Enough! No more talking about history!* She told D. that they both—she in Greece, he in northern Cyprus—had been given only one side of the story in school. *It's not our fault; it's how we're taught,* she said. *When you tell me what you've learned, I get upset, because I've learned the opposite!*

The conversation might have ended there, but Z., who was still online, mentioned the headlines she was reading just then about the French law banning denial of the Armenian genocide, which had recently been struck down by the French supreme court. D. wondered why the court would come to that decision unless it was to acknowledge that there had been no genocide. L. contended that the court's decision had been based on the constitutional protection of free speech: *You can't legislate what people are allowed to say. It's absurd to try and forbid people from saying things like this, even when they're obviously wrong.* V. pointed out that in Germany, it was illegal to deny the Holocaust. I suggested that was a different context, one where the prohibition was enforced in the same country where the genocide had taken place; contemporary Germans, descended from the perpetrators of the genocide, were now forbidden to deny it. At that moment, passing by, the lab manager, who had served in the Bosnian army during the war in the 1990s, told us that his country faced the same impasse: *When your population is made of the people who committed genocide and the people targeted for genocide, it's impossible to agree on whether a genocide has taken place—even if everyone knows it.* D. asked L. directly if she thought a genocide against the Armenians had been carried out by Turkey; she demurred, trailing off in a comment about different perspectives on history. 

As it turned out, though, D. was after a different point. He argued that it was the Ottoman army, and not the Turkish, who had killed the Armenians: *The events took place in 1915, years before the Turkish Republic was founded. How can Turkey be blamed for this?* He reiterated that he thought Armenian gangs had been killing civilians and burning down villages throughout Anatolia at the time: *Of course, the Ottoman army would try to kill them!* L. argued that taking up arms to fight the Ottoman soldiers was a natural reaction to oppression on the part of Armenian civilians; she drew a comparison with Chechens today, and the Russian army who had branded them terrorists. D. acknowledged that Armenians had been targeted, and a million people could not have been killed by accident: *This happened on purpose. But my question is: can the Turkish government be blamed for it?*

For Arsenijević, if "becoming a subject" is the only path opening toward a "hopeful politics after genocide," this becoming requires not only the liberation of survivors from their ethnic identities as perpetrators or victims, but more: a rebuilding of relationships among the living and the dead—a reinvestment of bones in their relations with others, to make up the gap between the remains of the dead and their names, their "full identity and history" (2011a, 194). In the lab, it was bones from 1964, ethnically misnamed, that triggered the movement of these scientists from their workplace in 2012 to mass death in the burning of Smyrna in 1923, and onward, to the dying days of the Ottoman Empire and the Armenian genocide in 1915. These movements in time, across sites of ethnic memory crucial to these scientists' understanding of themselves as inheritors of either a Greek or a Turkish legacy of violence, were inflected by their work on the artifacts of death in Cyprus, and their unstated and utterly habitual understanding of the two-sidedness of conflict and loss demanded by that work. Their relationship to the bones of the Cypriot missing introduced a kind of indeterminacy into the legacies of violence that they had inherited and that they read back onto the bones. In their debate about those legacies—one of the few open arguments I witnessed during my time at the lab—they positioned themselves with deliberate distance, even if they could not sustain it; and in doing so, they participated, if only momentarily, in a reorganization of ethnic history.



## We All Have the Same DNA

The connection or distance the scientists felt to the ethnic histories of violence they had inherited—that is, what it meant to them to carry the legacy of those histories—described a complex understanding of relatedness and belonging that mattered in the scientific register of their work as well. Ethnicity operated in the forensic context as a genetic tie of kinship, in the form of DNA evidence. In the viewings and subsequent funerals of the missing, this tie entailed for relatives both the right to claim remains as property and the obligation to overcome their grief and accede to the end of the story.

But this genetic tie was more malleable and erratic as forensic evidence than it appeared in public representations of the CMP's work. In the lab, I learned that in many cases, the greatest difficulty anthropologists faced in making an identification was not the anonymity of the remains but their relatedness. Often, multiple victims from a burial site came from the same village, which implied close kinship and coethnic status. When the victims were so closely related, Z. told me, it was nearly impossible to distinguish them by DNA analysis using the reference samples of living relatives. She described another case in which the remains of two sisters had been found in the same grave. The sisters were so similar, in terms of their anthropological traits as well as their DNA, that they could not be distinguished forensically. The remains of both women were returned to their relatives, who buried them in the same grave, as they had been found.

Yet this kind of kinship—reckoned separately for Greek Cypriots and Turkish Cypriots, given the apparent impossibility of intermarriage, accepted as a premise of social life in Cyprus by almost everyone I knew—

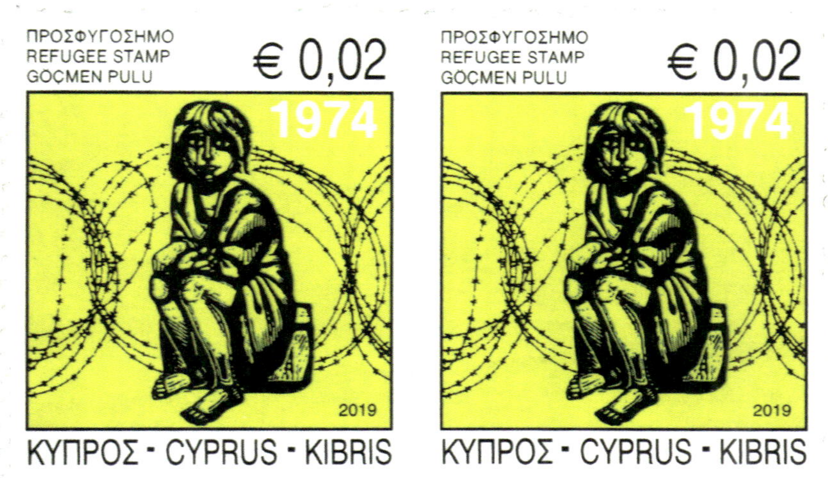
ΠΡΟΣΦΥΓΟΣΗΜΟ
REFUGEE STAMP
GOÇMEN PULU
€ 0,02
1974
2019
ΚΥΠΡΟΣ - CYPRUS - KIBRIS

NO.

1.15

described a much narrower conception of relatedness in the lab than genetic ancestry. I had heard many times, from Greek Cypriots and Turkish Cypriots, that Cypriots were all one people: *We all have the same DNA!* The ethnic populations of the island could not be identified genetically. Indeed, there seemed to be a sense of great genetic diversity among the lab scientists themselves, who had all been DNA typed when they were hired by the CMP so that any material they left on the bones they handled could be excluded from DNA identifications. When they got their results, a few of them consulted a website where ethnic ancestry could be evaluated using DNA results. T. had obtained results using only a European database, which showed Polish and French as well as African ancestry for him. He explained his French background by way of the Lusignans who had ruled Cyprus from the twelfth to the fifteenth centuries. His African ancestry was more proximate, personified in his grandfather, who was "really Black," he said, "African, a Muslim holy man"; he believed African slaves had been brought to Cyprus by the Romans, and a Black population, from which he descended, had resided on the island ever since. O. had consulted a database that included all of Asia as well as Europe, and her results indicated ancestry in Asia Minor as well as Iran, India, and Egypt.



While the scientists thus reckoned their own ancestry in rather broad terms, they viewed the genetic identity of the missing through a narrower lens. Explaining how they used "reference groups" in their analysis of bones, P. told me they were limited to the "white European" population: *Cyprus should have its own metrics for reference, since it's an island and we have a unique, isolated evolutionary history. The population is very different from American and western European populations. But we don't have the data.* I asked why the CMP anthropologists could not collate the data they were recording in the case files in order to develop population-specific metrics; V. had suggested they would be able to record this data without any identifying information that might compromise the confidentiality of analysis. But P. explained that there was no mandate for data collection within the CMP; its investigations were conceived as a strictly limited humanitarian mission, not as a research project with broader implications for knowledge about Cypriot society.

The DNA databank used by the CMP contained only samples contributed by relatives of known missing persons on the official list agreed upon by both sides. The samples of Turkish-Cypriot and Greek-Cypriot relatives were collected separately by different agencies in the north and the south, and then submitted to the Cyprus Institute of Neurology and Genetics. The databank did not contain samples from all the relatives of the missing, however, since some were unwilling to participate. Explaining to me the

DNA-testing process established by the CMP, K. offered several reasons for this reluctance: *Some relatives don't want to accept the death, so they avoid the whole investigation. Then there are some who believe they'll stop getting money from the government if their relative is confirmed dead. Since the war, they've received subsidies if they are the spouse or child of a missing person. It's not true that they would lose the subsidy if the person is found. But they don't trust the government.*

## We All Have Darkness in Our Hearts



The mistrust of government that reverberated in the refusal by some relatives to participate in the investigations, or to recognize the remains of their missing persons, expressed deeply embedded and well-worn dispositions of suspicion among these victims and heirs of political violence. But this mistrust might also have expressed what remained unspoken in encounters between relatives and scientists: namely, the relatives' own experience of violence, which was not always limited to victimhood.[58] The same people who assembled for a viewing of bones might themselves be keeping secrets about what they saw, or heard, or did.

O. raised this issue in telling me about a difficult excavation in north Nicosia on which she had worked a few years earlier. The case involved only one individual, buried in 1974 near an olive tree in the backyard of a house near Ledra Palace. Investigators had gathered conflicting information from witnesses, who identified the victim as either Turkish Cypriot or Greek Cypriot. The house belonged to an elderly Turkish-Cypriot woman and her husband, who lived there with their daughter. According to O., they were a wealthy family and had lived in the house since the early 1960s. *They were the least cooperative people I've ever dealt with,* she said. *When we're excavating in a village or a town, people in the neighborhood come by all the time to watch, and they tell us how they admire the work we're doing. They compete to bring us things—water, snacks, coffee.* In this case, however, the old couple resisted. They had grudgingly given permission to the CMP to excavate the lot next door, which they also owned, but the team had not found any remains there. A witness had pointed out the olive tree in the backyard of their house, but the old couple did not want the CMP to excavate there. *They said they didn't want their yard ruined,* O. said. *So we had to agree to a lot of restrictions.*

The team was given only a month to complete the excavation, in a very narrow space, and the CMP contracted to pay for repaving the driveway and any repairs to the property. *They didn't like us being there—they didn't let us into the house at all. People usually welcome us in; we're allowed to use their bathrooms and kitchens, and they do it gladly! Not in this case. We had to walk all the way to Ledra Palace to use the restroom.* Thinking the old woman might feel "accused" by the CMP, O. told me, the Turkish-Cypriot members of the team repeatedly assured her that she was doing a good thing by letting them do their work—that it was an honor for her, that she was not in any trouble. But she kept saying it was impossible that someone was buried there. *She was just ashamed*, O. said. *They must have been there when the body was buried, since they lived there at the time. They paved the driveway right over the grave.*



In the end, the team found remains quickly and were able to excavate an entire body within the allotted month, not without some damage to the property. The body belonged to an elderly man; his dentures had survived better even than his bones, and I could see them clearly in the close-up photographs of the skeleton in situ. Several of his bones were sampled for DNA testing, but no matching relatives were found in the databank. His remains were never identified, and they ended up being stored in the annex at the lab.

*The information is out there*, an investigator told me. *We haven't gotten very far in the last forty years, but it's not because no one knows anything. People know things. Knowledge is everywhere. But there's no political will to bring it out.* Yet the sort of resistance to opening up the graves of the missing that O. had encountered in the old couple in Nicosia was not fixed; it was dynamic and unpredictable. The same investigator told me that the relatives he worked with had often been holding on to their pain for so long that they had become "hardened," an existential state that, in some cases, entailed extreme political views—virulence against people from "the other side" and resistance to reconciliation. At the moment when their missing relative was found, however, and they were preparing to bury the person at last, they would sometimes "soften," and "want to connect with 'the other' on a basic human level." They would become willing to acknowledge the violence done to "the other side" and talk about what they knew.

At moments like that, the investigator said, relatives had shared information with him about possible locations of a burial site in their village; or, even if they said they did not know anything, they suggested the names of people who might. *People don't talk to me because I work for the CMP*, he insisted. *They talk to me because they trust me, they see I'm not playing games. And maybe for them it's a catharsis. They've been living for so long with what they did that it's a relief to say it. At the time when they did what they did, they believed in the ideology that they were saving their country and harming their enemy. But later, when they come back to reality, the ideological motivation comes apart, and they're troubled by what they've done. Who can they go to? They can't go to their priests; they can't go to the police or the authorities, because very likely those are the same people who gave them their orders. So who can they go to? People like this, who have gone to the point of killing another human being, and maybe more than once, maybe many times—people like this are very sensitive; they have good antennae; they can feel you. They can tell when you're trustworthy. They're very suspicious of politicians, for the same reason, because they can sense bullshit. With these people, we aren't acting as investigators, we're acting as priests, as confessors. We talk to all kinds of people—killers, rapists, fascists, Greek Cypriots and Turkish Cypriots. I try to find the cracks in them and let some light shine through. We're all killers, we all have darkness in our hearts. We're all capable of these things, under the right circumstances.*



## Nonknowledge

The sense the investigator conveyed of such diffuse responsibility for the violence of the past was obscured—had to be obscured—by the narrative framing of healing and closure promoted by the CMP and by the sacralization of bones that fortified that narrative symbolically. The CMP quietly contravened the maxim of international governance in postconflict states that truth leads to peace, rigidly delimiting what it meant to know "what happened": that is, to be certain of death without knowing its cause and circumstances. At the same time, the CMP avidly promoted transparency in its making of forensic knowledge. In the context of UN governance in Cyprus, the ideology of transparency signified a kind of proceduralism that would, in theory, ensure the legitimacy of the peace process. Apart from the Nicosia Bicommunal Wastewater Treatment Plant, the CMP was the only major bicommunal project to operate in Cyprus since the war in 1974.[59] The Members of the CMP framed their project as a sort of canary in the coal mine: a tentative model for bicommunal cooperation that might work in other sectors of development and reconciliation in the future.

Certainty of the death of missing persons is not nothing. Many relatives of the missing whose remains were found have acknowledged their relief in having this certainty at last. Some have said that they somehow knew all along that their loved one was dead, but now, with forensic evidence, they "really" knew. That recursive space of knowing what one already knows is, as Sant Cassia (2005, 219) argues, the space of the public secret in Cyprus. This is not empty logical space; it is occupied by the positivity of nonknowledge: specifically, quantitative information about the bones of missing persons that would confirm their deaths. For many relatives, this information was not an adequate substitute for a persuasive story about the death they cared so much about and had carried as a possible truth for so long. Thus, for some, nonknowledge obstructed the hypothetical path from truth to peace projected by the UN's ideology of transparency, even as it kept that path open for others—those who accepted the resolution of their case but continued seeking to know more.



The forensic knowledge produced by the CMP was thus part of a dynamic of conflict management: a dynamic between "non-knowledge and authoritative knowledge," as Adriana Petryna (2002, 39) argues about Soviet interventions after the nuclear accident at Chernobyl, Ukraine, in 1986.[60] Petryna examines the "constructed nature of the unknown" in Soviet nuclear scientists' reports, which claimed that appropriate metrics for assessing the damage were "unavailable" or "not designed for these levels of radiation" or "destroyed or lost" in the accident (38–39). Their not knowing the information such hypothetical tools could deliver facilitated scientists' attempts to placate public anxieties by working with other tools that radically downplayed the extent of the disaster. In a similar way, scientists at the CMP knew what not to know, but their not-knowing had the positive character of producing rigorous data to ascertain the identity of remains and thus the deaths of specific missing persons.

Nonknowledge about the missing had radically changed character when the CMP began its investigations in 2004. Before the advent of the CMP, as Sant Cassia has shown, the dominant narrative of the missing in the south was about not knowing their fate; this narrative held open the prospect of their survival. In the north, by contrast, the missing were presumed dead, but not knowing the when, where, and how of their deaths barred public mourning (Sant Cassia 2005). These framings were contradictory, or at least incongruous, but they shared the logic of indefinite deferral of knowledge about the deaths of the missing. The production of that knowledge by the CMP since 2004 has created symbolic murk around the missing, undermining these dominant narratives—confirming the deaths and permitting mourning—while blocking the development of a common narrative of collective responsibility for violence. Thus, even as the possibility emerged for the missing to be mourned as dead, a kind of narrative indeterminacy was carefully guarded by the CMP.

Yet fragments of the old narratives continued to carry a charge, even if they no longer cohered and the old political structures no longer authorized them. The CMP was set up to resolve contestations over the facts of historical violence through the findings of forensic science, guaranteed as politically neutral consensus by the ethnic balancing of forensic teams and of the committee membership itself. Forensic science emerged in this formation as a terrain of politics, where the increasingly old conflict was continually reinscribed in the production of new knowledge. Rather than serving as the conditions for a collective and shared understanding of the past, neutrality and balance seemed rather to operate as covers for the positioning of relatives of the missing in the long-standing politics of division. The presence of a Third Member in this field of positions—the embodiment of an invasive and overweening international community, functioning as mediator if not tiebreaker—only amplified the suspicions of those positioned on either side of the divide that the CMP's investigations were not, in fact, neutral. But the CMP's failure to stabilize the meaning of the bones left a hermeneutic opening yet to achieve narrative closure—an opening for Cypriots to reflect on the meaning of the deaths of the missing for them today, on what kind of mourning would allow them to move on, and on what kind of truth they might still want to know.



Public accounting and private mourning are not intrinsically incompatible processes in Cyprus; indeed, they might reinforce and supplement each other. It is possible, too, to oppose the priority placed by the CMP on mourning over accounting, without assuming that a public accounting process—such as a truth and reconciliation commission—would necessarily promote recovery and reunification in Cyprus. Many truth and reconciliation commissions have been criticized for failing to yield peace, justice, and healing, especially in cases where amnesty has been transacted for testimony, as in postapartheid South Africa.[61] Truth and reconciliation commissions foreground truth in the form of individual narratives; victims, perpetrators, and witnesses tell their stories and are supposed to be relieved of pain and guilt in the process. The investigations of the CMP might seem to take the opposite course, obstructing narrative and producing nonknowledge of death, foregrounding mourning over truth. Yet the truth production administered by truth and reconciliation commissions entails its own distinctive forms of nonknowledge. As J. said to me, *TRCs are about individuals, not about structures. They don't touch the structures. They aren't about truth, so they aren't about justice. They're a joke.* By "structures," he explained, he meant the planning and coordination of violence on a large scale, and the concealment of evidence afterward—processes that he saw occurring "dialectically" on the local level, the state level, and the international level. The truth and reconciliation commission model of reckoning with violence indeed constitutes a different approach from the closure model of the CMP; but, as J. indicated, the distinction between these models does not turn on revealing versus concealing truth. It turns rather on the different parameters these models place on truth (individual, structural) and the different possibilities for mourning and justice they open up.

In his insistence on the right to know vested in relatives of the missing, J. aligned human rights with a particular conception of justice, denigrating the proceduralist ideology of transparency promoted by the UN via the CMP for contributing to the political foreclosure of responsibility in Cyprus. The conception of responsibility he invoked was juridical, referring to war crimes and human rights, and thus, at least implicitly, a national or international system of criminal justice. A number of cases regarding the missing in Cyprus, structured by this conception of responsibility, have been brought against both the Republic of Turkey and the Republic of Cyprus in the European Court of Human Rights (ECtHR) since the 1980s.[62] Usually, these cases have originated in claims lodged with the CMP that, unsatisfied by the CMP during its decades of inactivity, were then referred to the ECtHR.[63]



These cases include the interstate case *Cyprus v. Turkey*, brought in 1994 and decided in 2001, in which Turkey was found to have violated the rights of several Greek-Cypriot claimants to know the location and disposition of their relatives, missing in action since the war in 1974.[64] In *Varnava and Others v. Turkey*, a case brought by a group of Greek-Cypriot claimants in 1990 and decided by the ECtHR in 2009, the court found in favor of the claimants on most counts. However, two cases brought by Turkish-Cypriot claimants against the Republic of Cyprus in 1989, *Karabardak and Others v. Cyprus* and *Baybora and Others v. Cyprus*, were rejected by the ECtHR in 2002 on the grounds of the claimants' ostensible failure to adhere to the "six-month rule" governing cases of enforced disappearance.[65] In the domestic space of litigation, several civil cases have also been brought by Greek Cypriots against the Republic of Cyprus—for example, *Palma v. Cyprus* and *Passia v. Cyprus*, both decided in favor of the claimants by the Supreme Court of the Republic of Cyprus in 2012.

In some of these cases, the right of claimants to know the fate of their missing relatives was connected with other questions produced and sustained by political division, including the right of refugees to return to their homes on the other side and their right to the property they had left behind. In this light, the historical unfolding of the problem of the missing in Cyprus can be seen as part of "the process by which human rights have been used to translate political claims in legal language" in Cyprus, as Demetriou and Gürel (2008, 26) describe this history of legal innovation at the supranational level, enhanced by the occupation of Cyprus by UN peacekeeping forces since 1964 and especially by the accession of Cyprus to the European Union in 2004. The question of the missing thus cannot be disaggregated from the emergence of the litigating subject as a social-political form in Cyprus. Cypriot litigants do not necessarily hold a specific concept of legal or criminal responsibility in mind when they bring cases against the state, be it Cyprus or Turkey, but such a concept persists as precisely that form of responsibility foreclosed by the CMP investigations and its rhetoric of transparency. In all the court cases named above, the knowledge relatives sought under their right to know concerned the location and disposition of the remains of their missing person—not the circumstances of the person's death, nor the identity of the killer. It is a profoundly restricted kind of knowledge, matching exactly the kind of knowledge produced by the CMP, whose investigations since 2004 have come to obviate additional litigation.



But more has been created by these lawsuits than a forum for making and satisfying demands for knowledge of death. I recall here Loraux's focus on lawsuits as the most threatening kind of memory prohibited by amnesty, since the bringing of evidence (in the form of memory) to sue for justice (in the form of punishment) could only nourish and amplify conflict in the city. In the shadows cast by the forensic investigations in Cyprus lie murky but intense yearnings for justice where it has been rendered unspeakable in forensic terms. Suspicions that more could be known are given voice in court, even if the framework of agreement between the two regimes does not permit such knowledge to surface there. In this sense, right-to-know litigation in Cyprus has helped to engender secrecy as a position maintained by the defendants in these lawsuits—that is, the state regimes in the north and south. But this litigation has also opened up an imagination of justice as a kind of claim made on the state by its citizens, on both sides of the divide.

In becoming litigants, grieving relatives of the missing have retained the symbolic authority of their losses authorized by the state, while transforming the state's withholding of information into their victimization by the state. Their right to know has become a right to sue. This movement of demands for justice from the field of politics into the juridical domain might indicate a broader process of judicialization in Cyprus, as Demetriou and Gürel (2008) suggest—a process in which, as Comaroff and Comaroff (2006, 25, 22, 26) put it, "politics itself is migrating to the courts," part of the growing "culture of legality" or "fetishism of the law" coinciding with the rise of violence and lawlessness in postcolonial societies, though not only there. Judicialization, in their telling, represents a new reckoning of the responsibility and accountability of the state itself that is emerging through litigation undertaken by citizens, often in class actions combining elements of criminal law, human rights law, and tort law (Comaroff and Comaroff 2006, 27). This reckoning is particularly urgent and compelling, they note, in states where jurisdictions are multiple, unclear, or in the process of being "remap[ped]"—not only in places where the vertical sovereignty of the state is redistributed across or contested by the "horizontal, partial sovereignties" of corporations, criminal organizations, and religious, nationalist, or otherwise communal groups, but also in places such as Cyprus, where courts with supranational jurisdiction supplement or supplant state courts (33, 40).



One of the dangers of judicialization envisioned by its critics is the reduction of conceptions of harm, responsibility, and entitlement to the bodies and claims of individual litigants. This reduction obscures structural harms, collective responsibilities, and social reciprocities that would, in theory, be properly and more effectively addressed in the field of politics—not merely electoral politics, but also revolutionary and social movements that take the state as their target. Thus, for Comaroff and Comaroff, judicialization marks a "displacement" into the juridical domain of conflicts that, in other times or places, would properly be pursued and mediated "in parliaments, by means of street protests, mass demonstrations, and media campaigns, through labor strikes, boycotts, blockades, and other instruments of assertion" (2006, 3, 26).

Right-to-know litigation in Cyprus, it seems to me, invites a reconsideration of this idealization of politics as the proper field of justice.[66] Such litigation may well signal a trend toward the judicialization of politics; after decades of ineffectual public protests, the demands for knowledge brought to court by relatives of the missing in Cyprus, articulated in terms of human rights and harms, do indeed risk the occlusion of other victims of the conflict and other forms of harm besides the loss of a relative. Yet the excess suffering, longing, and suspicion expressed by right-to-know litigation—conditioned by the impossibility of tying responsibility to forensic evidence in court—may convey an understanding among relatives of the missing that politics in Cyprus are not what they should be: not a field of justice, that is, but rather a vortex of secrecy.

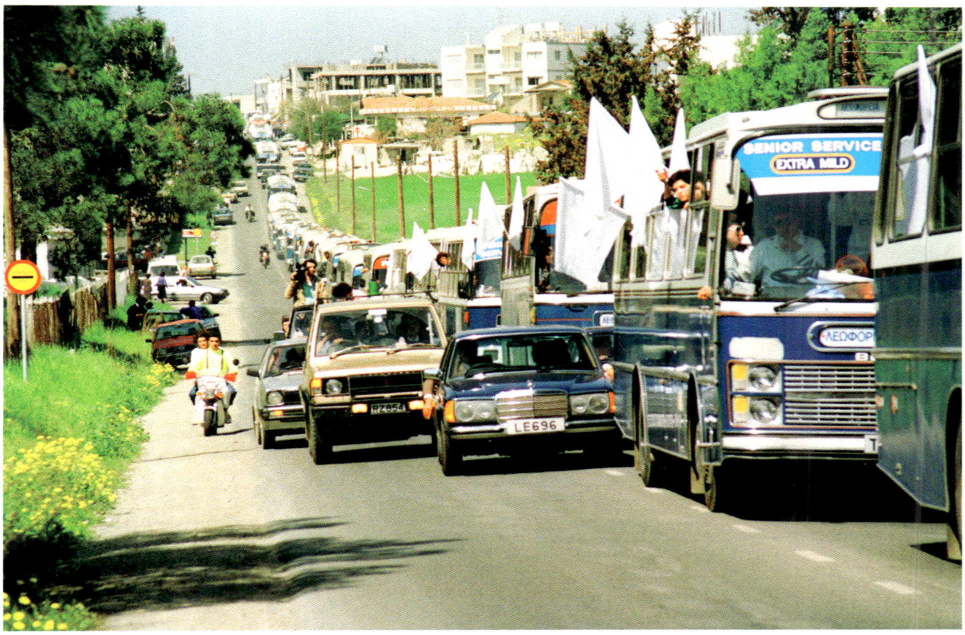


NO.

**1.16**

## Let Me Rest

Writing about the "inevitably controversial" exhumations of the remains of perhaps 100,000 opponents of Franco who were executed and secreted in mass graves during and after the Spanish Civil War, Francisco Ferrándiz wonders, "Does anthropology have any business getting mixed up with suppressed memories, the historical schemes of victors, war monuments, skeletons, and mass graves?" (2006, 7). He makes a subtle, complex, and (to my mind) persuasive case for anthropological research on the forensic process, noting the importance of studying the long and ambiguous afterlives of "social trauma" and the "social responsibility" anthropologists carry toward the dead that is distinct from the responsibility of grieving relatives (8). After all, as Diane Nelson (2015, 71) reminds us, "there are dead with no survivors"—one among many reasons it might be impossible to identify and count remains.



Victoria Sanford (2004, 211ff.) takes a different but equally strong stance of truth telling and "witnessing," working with forensic anthropologists on exhumations of clandestine graves in Guatemala, while collecting testimonies from survivors and conducting research in state archives, in order to help compile a robust record of genocide for the Commission for Historical Clarification. Diane Nelson, also writing about Guatemala after genocide, suggests there is reason to tread carefully on this terrain, which she finds shifting constantly underneath the "double relation between error and truth"—a relation between the two-facedness of "duplicity" and its other, "transparency." In Guatemala's history of violence, she writes, in which civilians—Indigenous people, leftists, others—were forcibly and massively recruited into the state's counterinsurgency campaigns, the very conditions of knowing about violence are radically unstable (Nelson 2009, 27, 14).[67]

With this caution about being "in the know" in mind, I have tried to figure out an orientation that I consider ethical toward writing about the forensic knowledge produced by the CMP in Cyprus—much of which was defined bureaucratically as "confidential," and some of which struck me as "private" or "off the record," according to an admittedly muddy and "relatively tacit" mix of "ordinary ethics," in Michael Lambek's (2010, 2) felicitous phrase, along with ethnographic research ethics and specific strains of regulatory ethics. During fieldwork, I saw much more than I have written about here, but my decisions about what to write and not write—and specifically, about what to consider confidential—indicate only one ethical register operating in my text. Another is indicated by what Taussig (1999, 69, 68) calls the "empirical" or "technical" questions (as distinct from the "political problem") raised by secrecy—questions about the reliability and rationale of ethnographic research conducted with interlocutors for whom suspicion and dissimulation might be political tactics (in which an ethnographer could be unwittingly enrolled) or survival strategies (which an ethnographer could unwittingly impair). It may be that "the bones don't lie," as Nelson (2015, 65) heard from a forensic anthropologist working at La Verbena cemetery in Guatemala City, as he was trying to disaggregate the remains of people killed and illicitly dumped in the ossuary during the civil war from those ritually deposited there after natural death. But the bones do not speak for themselves, either. Attempting to speak for them carries risks—of making mistakes, of doing violence—that I am not willing to take.



Throughout the time I worked with the forensic teams, I had formal permission to see the materials in the CMP archives, to talk with employees and participate in their work; and I had formal permission to write about what I learned. That permission, however, was treated by some within the CMP as provisional and contingent on their personal discretion, like a gift, or on a transaction, where something was expected from me in return. Even more puzzling, I was denied permission to film or photograph any CMP activities, despite their already hypervisibility. I had come to Cyprus with all my film and sound equipment and an idea for a documentary film project on forensic investigations. I was hoping to begin observational filming with the forensic teams at the beginning of my second summer of field research. By the time I requested permission, I had already been working with the forensic teams for many months, in both the lab and the field. I had learned a great deal about how the scientists produced and shared their knowledge, about their employment relations, and about the local and international politics of the CMP. I had discussed my film project with several of the scientists, who seemed to think it was a good idea so long as it did not involve interviews with them. The CMP had granted me practically unlimited access to the textual artifacts of its forensic work: missing persons reports, archaeological and anthropological reports, results of DNA analysis, chain of custody forms for each transfer of remains, internal letters among scientists and CMP Members, death certificates, press releases, and so on. I had learned about the scientists' formal and informal procedures of analysis, including the print and online manuals, databases, and computational tools they used; I had read the files of open and closed investigations; and I had studied the digital architecture of the database in which all information about the cases was recorded, including the massive archive of field and lab photographs. I had been present at meals, staff meetings, debates, and conflicts, and involved in spontaneous interactions of all kinds. There was little I had not seen.

It came as quite a shock to me, then, when my request to film the forensic teams was summarily and flatly denied. The Members offered me no explanation, and I did not seek one through formal channels, though I asked colleagues on the forensic teams to help me speculate. One suggested that I had been denied permission because I had wanted to shoot observational footage rather than interviews, which would make it harder for the CMP to "control the message." Another thought it was because I had argued with one of the assistants on the committee and burned an important bridge (which was no doubt true). Several pointed out that, because I was American, I would be understood by the CMP as inherently suspect. There was strong resistance, too, to any photographing or filming on the part of J. and those on the committee he could persuade.



All of these reasons seemed to me plausible, but only partially explanatory. As a researcher, I had become embroiled in the same dynamics of secrecy and transparency that I was pursuing as an object of inquiry. I was being positioned by my interlocutors—differently, by different people—as someone who would respect their secrecy or, instead, violate it in accordance with my own research ethics. Certain interlocutors—like J.—seemed to hold both expectations simultaneously. I thus came to see special stakes in doing research with this organization that extended beyond the ethics of ethnographic research and the complex attachments, boundaries, and obligations that anthropologists always negotiate in fieldwork. Secrecy, rather than being a distinctive feature of the CMP as an organization, or of the local context as perceived from outside, was instead immanent in a critique of the politics of division in Cyprus that I learned to develop with my interlocutors, even if we were mobilizing that critique toward different ends.

But if publicity is not the right alternative to secrecy, then what is the alternative to publicity? Perhaps it is to leave the bones where they lie. As I discussed earlier, Ferrándiz documented this sentiment among early opponents to the exhumations in Spain: "Exhumations were described by some . . . organizations as an 'erasure of genocide' or even a 'second killing' of the victims. A number of manifestos circulated on the internet suggested that the exhumations were being done for media attention and personal profit, undermining the powerful denunciation of injustice inscribed in the buried bones, silent witnesses of the atrocities" (2006, 9).

In Argentina, too, widespread resistance to exhumations of the disappeared expressed political claims for justice by the activist branch of the Mothers of the Plaza de Mayo. Antonius Robben documents the evolution in the politics of these Mothers from demands to know the fate of their missing relatives, akin to the right-to-know claims made by Cypriots, into full-blown opposition to exhumations. Despite the "anguish" of not giving proper burials to their loved ones, he reports, some of the Mothers came to understand mourning as a form of depoliticization and thus refused the coercive presumption of death made by the postjunta government in order to "keep the wounds inflicted by the disappearances open and to resist a national process of forgetting" (Robben 1999, 106, 104)[68]—though, as I noted earlier, Adam Rosenblatt complicates this narrative about the Mothers considerably. Zoë Crossland (2002, 121) likewise construes the position of the Mothers not as a refusal to recognize the deaths of the disappeared, but rather as an attempt to maintain their absence as such in the public eye until accountability for their deaths could be established. The Mothers' slogan, *aparición con vida*, announced their rejection of forensic investigation as a project of knowledge rather than justice—"producing 'only bones'" (Crossland 2000, 153)—or what Avery Gordon (1997, 115) calls "knowledge without acknowledgment." Crossland cites several Mothers expressing indifference to human remains: "'We already know that thousands of *desaparacedos* were secretly murdered and buried. The exhumations don't tell us anything we don't already know'" (Crossland 2002, 121); and, "'The bones don't interest us. What are we going to do with bones?'" (Crossland 2000, 153).[69]



Although no comparable movement against the forensic investigations of the missing has developed in Cyprus, I heard a number of relatives express their wish to leave the bones in peace, and a few scientists as well. For these people, to not excavate was not to conceal evidence; on the contrary, it was a way to preserve evidence. For some, like N., the archaeologist who argued against excavation and exhibition, this meant the preservation of history; for others, it meant the preservation of situated testaments to violence. *The whole island is a graveyard*, one archaeologist said to me at the beginning of an excavation: *Anywhere you look, there could be bones*. In her ethnography of Lapta (Lapithos), a formerly mixed village in the north, Rebecca Bryant captures this morbid attunement to the artifacts of violence beneath the visible surface of things, some known through discovery and others only by rumor: the bodies of an entire family murdered and thrown into a well in 1963, a mass grave in the village square, another mass grave under the monument at Five Mile Beach where the Turkish army launched its attacks in 1974, even a hidden arms cache found by accident during the renovation of a house in the old Greek quarter (Bryant 2010, 188–91). Holding on to this open sensibility to death—to its diffusion and its scale—might, for some, be a better way to face Cyprus's violent past than the forensic closure of individual cases.

A Cypriot filmmaker I knew, who had publicly criticized the Republic's use of the Mothers of the Missing for propaganda and had filmed a journalist conducting investigations with witnesses and relatives of the missing, told me he had often wondered if it wouldn't be better just to leave the bodies where they were: *The dead person, if he could talk, he would say, "Leave me be! Let me rest."* He told me about the experience of an old friend of his from childhood, whose uncle had been killed in the war. *They found his bones*, the filmmaker told me. *And when they gave them back to my friend, they had a big funeral. It wasn't what my friend wanted at all. The politicians spoke their words; the priests spoke their words; there was a big crowd. After it was over and everyone left, I talked to my friend about it. He said he would rather the remains had stayed where they were than to have all this happen.*



The visibility of the bones raises two distinct problems related to secrecy in Cyprus. One problem, linked directly to prospects of justice and a political settlement, is that of secrecy on the part of the CMP, which destroyed and concealed evidence as it produced evidence. The other problem is the privacy of the bones—the right of the dead not to be seen—and the power borne by images of the bones to traumatize or mystify when they circulate in the public eye. These two problems of secrecy converged in the way that images of bones worked as evidence in Cyprus. They circulated as signs of transparency without revealing any forensic knowledge, beyond confirming what everyone already knew: that thousands of people had gone missing and died forty to fifty years earlier. Could the truth effects of these images ever exceed their capacity to reproduce secrecy? Or, as J. suggested, were they "just for show"?

At this point, at the conclusion of part one, I would like to venture some tentative answers to these questions. In these pages, I have explored the drama of revelation performed by the CMP, turning on careful efforts at both publicity and secrecy. The discovery and identification of human remains by CMP scientists gave many relatives of the missing the satisfaction of knowing what they had always known, without really knowing it; yet their desire to know what they most wanted to know—not the mere fact of death, but the how and why of it—remained unsatisfied. For some, the conviction that there was much more to know was fortified by suspicions that the CMP was concealing or ignoring evidence even as it disclosed evidence.

It is not my aim to argue against those suspicions, nor to affirm them, even if I have found myself taking both positions at various points in my conversations with scientists and relatives. In writing ethnographically about the CMP, I have tried, in Sedgwick's terms, to show both paranoid and reparative orientations to the forensic knowledge project the scientists were pursuing, and thereby to show the complex oscillation between secrecy and becoming that they, as "custodians of memory," were enacting. This oscillation makes room, I think, both for critical analysis of the history of secrecy in Cyprus and for an anticipation of the future that diverges from the repetition of that history. In a different idiom, this might appear as an oscillation of myth and history, as Claude Lévi-Strauss ([1978] 1995, 40) presents them in *Myth and Meaning*: myth being "static," comprising combinations of a closed set of elements, in contrast to the "open system" of history. As soon as he offers this distinction, however, Lévi-Strauss begins to unwrite it, showing the very same range of both variation and repetition among lineage accounts by Native Canadians and historical accounts of French and North American wars. "I am not far from believing," he writes, "that, in our own societies, history has replaced mythology and fulfils the same function, that for societies without writing and without archives the aim of mythology is to ensure that as closely as possible—complete closeness is obviously impossible—the future will remain faithful to the present and to the past. For us, however, the future should always be different, and ever more different, from the present, some difference depending, of course, on our political preferences" (43).



The vanishing distinction Lévi-Strauss finds here between myth and history turns on the "aim" or the "should" of those undertaking to express them: either to reproduce the past with a little difference or to create "ever more" difference. He identifies that normative stance not as a cultural feature—since all of "us" are included in his "should"—but rather as a political disposition. Archives, in his imagination of history, operate like the artifacts I have been writing about here: objects with the capacity to stop time in its repetition and overdetermination, and to open experiences of uncertainty, possibility, and difference. Archives are also unlike these other artifacts, of course. The bones of the Cypriot missing have distinctive, organic qualities that qualify them to tell time—and in telling time, they impinge in specific ways on the emotions and imaginations of the people who work with them. These artifacts can become human; they can become ethnic, and then unbecome it; they can become the effects of histories of conflict outside (yet still inside) Cyprus. Their activity is vitally political.

Arsenijević writes of the disturbance exerted by bones, imagining himself at the edge of a mass grave, wanting to "bear witness to anything resembling a human" and finding a "limit-experience" of the human in "the unpleasant corporeal remainder that, after genocide, stays with you, one which resists all the ideological mechanisms of quantification, identification, burial and sacralising—the excess of scattered bones, the dead-but-alive organic matter" (2011b, 166). I hesitate to suggest that the resistances bones bear to being successfully scripted in the CMP's drama of revelation and its narrative of closure are immanent in the matter itself—as Bennett (2010, 3), for one, argues for the "force" or "vitality intrinsic to materiality," exceeding complete semiotic capture.[70] In telling time, in killing time and filling time, the artifacts of the missing in Cyprus did activate such affective charges in the scientists, relatives, and others who held and beheld them, I think; but I do not presume that these affective charges preceded or exceeded the meanings these people made of them. The force operated by the artifacts of the missing lies rather in their capacity to slip between semiotic captures, to condense multiple temporalities and thus to accommodate discrepant meanings. They are in the right place at the right time to make things happen. But what they make happen does not depend on them alone.



I think back, here, to the argument N. made against excavation, that spring afternoon on the mountainside—his assertion that *history doesn't belong to us; it belongs to future generations*, and his contention that the CMP should be preserving mass graves until proper excavations could be done. *People in the future will have better tools*, he said. *They'll know what to do.* And then, G.'s response: *How long should we wait?* It had already been fifty years, then, since the first violent events whose aftermath these young scientists were confronting. At the time of this writing, it has been almost sixty.

Perhaps, among those technologies to come that N. imagined, among those better tools to be wielded by future generations, might emerge new narrative tools as well—new ways of linking the present to the past, new ways of finding meaningful footholds in the flux of time. Perhaps we will know the time has come to use those tools when we discover that we already know what to do with them.

# 2

# Documentary

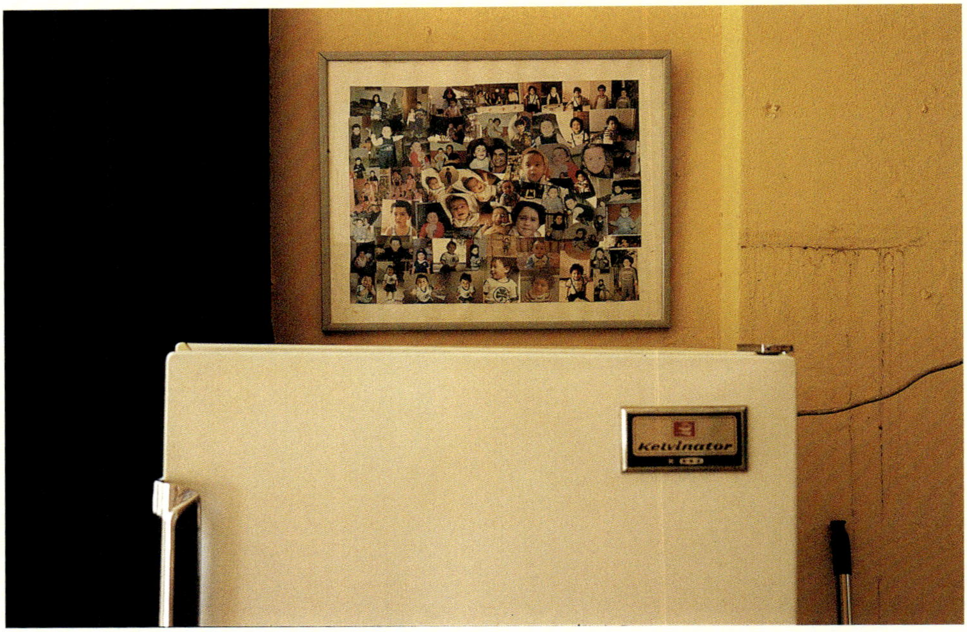


NO.

**2.1**

A crystal image of time destroys the past,
a full moon of forgetting, to save the future.

—Alev Adil, “The Eclipse Begins”

## An Impossible Thing

I first heard of the documentary film *Digging the Past in Search of the Future* in a conversation (in English) over lunch with some CMP archaeologists, early in my time at the lab. *I was in that film!* P. told me. *You can see me in the opening scene, in the background.* C. pointed out that their friend B. "starred" in the film, in a long interview conducted at an excavation site in Kyrenia, a port city on the northern coast, where he was working as a team leader. *He speaks very poetically about the work we do,* C. said, noting that the film had been commissioned by the CMP as a sort of "advertisement" for its humanitarian mission.



B.'s interview in the film follows a sequence shot at a large excavation—at that time, the largest ever undertaken by the CMP—where deep trenches had been dug into an old riverbed on the outskirts of Kyrenia. The remains of thirty-eight individuals had already been recovered by the time this footage was shot; B., standing at the edge of the trench, explains that more are expected, judging from witness information. The camera dwells on the piles of rock, dirt, and mud being deposited on the dry riverbanks by digging machines, and the rhythmic sifting of this dense material by two archaeologists, outfitted in bright yellow full-sleeved coveralls to shield them from the cold and damp. B. is asked how it feels to find bones during an excavation. He speaks thoughtfully, in English: *You feel this pain when you reach the bones or you start recovering them, because you remember that this was a living being, once. He had a family, he had a life, he had dreams. You feel this sadness inside you—it doesn't matter who he is, or from where he is coming. [ . . . ]*[1] *You don't give yourself [over] to your feelings. You shouldn't do this; it's not the professional way. Feel it, keep it inside you, but at a level, and show respect to the remains.* Scenes of such respectful work—exhuming, sieving, and sorting; washing, measuring, and matching—frame the encounter between the living and the bones of the dead as a difficult yet transformative experience for many subjects in the film.

Directed and edited by Michael Georgiades, *Digging the Past* is the product of a collaboration between the CMP and The Elders Foundation.[2] Although quite a number of documentary films made in recent years address the missing and the work of the CMP, *Digging the Past* is one of the very few in which excavation sites, the lab facilities, and CMP scientists themselves are named and fully shown. At the time of my fieldwork, the thirty-five-minute film was available for streaming on the CMP website, and the DVD was routinely distributed with CMP promotional materials; it was an official self-representation.

It follows the trip to Cyprus made in 2008 by three of the Elders: Lakhdar Brahimi, Jimmy Carter, and Desmond Tutu. These senior statesmen visit two excavations and the CMP lab in the company of four Cypriot teenagers—a strictly balanced group of two girls and two boys, two Greek Cypriots and two Turkish Cypriots, who express great admiration and respect for their mentors in a series of on-screen confessionals. The film thus overtly stages generational distance and connection, mediated by the meetings of the group with a number of CMP scientists—about a decade older, on average, than the teens—and two middle-aged Cypriot men who, as young children, had lost their fathers. Generation shifts with these subjects, crossing through moments of historical time: moments of violence in 1964 and 1974, moments of discovery and mourning in the early 2000s. The generational theme wends through many conversations between the Elders and the teens, who talk about "suffering from the mistakes of the past made by other generations" and reiterate the necessity they feel, as young Cypriots, "not to let it happen again."



That necessity is dramatized in one of the later scenes of the film, following the group's meeting with the head anthropologist at the lab, who has walked them through her analysis of a set of remains arrayed before them on a table. Desmond Tutu asks the anthropologist about an apparent gunshot wound in the skull she is holding. The next cut is to a confessional with Idil, one of the Turkish-Cypriot teenagers, standing outside the lab. Visibly distraught and rushing her words, she describes (in English) her panic upon seeing the wound in the skull: *I was down when I saw the gun hole in the remains. And then I decided to look around to escape from the gun hole and I saw the other one, as a part of another remain, and another one. I saw three of them, and most of them were not only one hole but more.* Her frantic attempt to get hold of herself by seeing something other than broken, ruined bones conveys the efficacy of the bones in generating an experience of arrest in chronological time—outside the narrative of death and reconstruction presented by the anthropologist—and of dilation in the present moment of Idil's shocking encounter with these artifacts of death.

The intensely visual nature of this experience, for Idil, is doubled here by its recording on film, which both thematizes and performs visualization. This double vision is exploited more fully in a scene toward the end of the film featuring Veli Beidoğlu, a middle-aged Turkish-Cypriot man whose father, a bank manager in Famagusta, disappeared in May 1964 and was presumed killed by Greek-Cypriot militia. Seated with the group in the viewing room at the CMP lab, Beidoğlu speaks (in English) of his encounter with the bones of his father, recovered recently by the CMP:

> Coming here and seeing it, it was like, looking at the bones and, you know, the remains, with the holes here and there, it was very emotional. [ . . . ] It was a very emotional moment, that it was actually happening, because I never thought, in my lifetime, that I was actually going to be in that position of actually recovering my . . . because there was so much. . . . It was an impossible thing, that, one day, when I was growing up . . . that it was going to happen. Because all forces were against it! Nobody wanted this thing to come to . . . to come out in the open. Everybody was trying to keep it under, both sides, because they didn't want to own up to their responsibilities.



Beidoğlu's fraught monologue, full of hesitations and repairs, captures the recursion of the archaeological process in the visualization process, linking the unearthing of the bones of his father to the "coming out" of the truth of his death that had been buried for so long. Beidoğlu's "emotional" encounter with his father's bones thus accrues second-order value as a record of truth seeking and truth making: the production of a visual record of the very process of discovery and revelation in the CMP's work.

The easy transpositions of archaeological metaphors of time—"burying" and "digging" the past—into the visual register of documentary film here suggest a symbolic affinity between bones and images, graves and archives, which turns on the emplacement of film amid the ruins of war. Thus, although bones stand as perhaps the most powerful artifacts of violence in *Digging the Past*, the film actually opens with a sequence filmed in the dead zone of old Nicosia: a "dead space of silence and soldiers," as the narrator puts it, speaking over images of the ruins of bombed-out and abandoned buildings, crumbling into piles of rubbish and the rampant overgrowth of weeds. Such scenes appear in many recent Cypriot documentary films; their emphatic visualization of ruins, barrens, bones, and graves establishes and privileges our visual access to the material debris of war and time.

As I noted in the introduction, the archaeologist Shannon Dawdy connects the interest she observes in "ruins, materiality, and 'thingness'" among scholars across the social sciences and humanities to an "emerging fixation on time itself" (2010, 761, 762). The aestheticization of ruins has a long history in Western art and science, she argues, tied to a modernist ideology of linear, progressive time defined by its "rupture" from antiquity, which positions ruins within nostalgic or tragic visions of the past. Dawdy moves not to de-aestheticize ruins and other archaeological "things" but rather to displace the modernist fixation with progressive time they evince by engaging with the nonmodern (nor postmodern) "clockpunk" aesthetic developed by global "urban youth and online communities" (766). What typifies clockpunk, in her reading, is the "temporal folding" ingrained in its material culture, including practices of salvaging and recycling, and integrating antique devices with digital and cyber technologies, in ways that give the lie to the "self-deception of modernity as always new" (766, 763). With Walter Benjamin's *Arcades Project* in mind, Dawdy imagines ruins themselves as clockpunk formations, like those "artifacts of vintage modernity" theorized by Benjamin as dialectical images, whose material presence survives their use-value, rendering them rich "semiotic vessels" that collapse and reorganize time (777, 768). The ruins of contemporary cities—yielded by postindustrial depressions, natural disasters, and the neglect or active social engineering of urban communities—stand as vital clockpunk artifacts, for Dawdy. The shift away from the "temporal ideology" (762) of modernity that she proposes enables a perspective on such ruins that is neither progressive nor dystopian, but that comprehends decay and demolition as complex historical processes that open nonlinear experiences of time for those who inhabit and study them.



Dawdy's clockpunk sight line, trained on the material-aesthetic qualities of artifacts that inspire complex temporal experience in those who deal with them, comes close to what I have in mind with the concept of artifactuality. Here, in part two of this book, I examine the complex operation of nonlinear time in Cypriot documentary films—in their visualization of artifacts like ruins and bones, but also in their incorporation of archival images to represent memories of war as well as the time before: family portraits, village scenes, pastoral and urban landscapes. Perhaps more significant than these material-visual imbrications in documentary films, however, is their treatment of archival photographs and film as artifacts: as materials subject to decay and decomposition, materials that can be scratched and warped or otherwise altered by accident or design; and that, in all these ways, record and tell time, and give intractably partial witness to what they show.

As an opening gambit to this part of the book, I suggest that when we consider archival images as artifacts in these ways, and visual archives themselves, we may better sense the resonances between forensic and documentary knowledge projects, which entail specific processes of destruction in the very practices by which knowledge is produced. In part one, I examined the destruction of knowledge through the anonymization and classification of witness testimony and other evidence about violent incidents, as well as the destruction of graves, and of history and culture more generally, in the exhumation and recovery of the bones and belongings of the missing. In part two, I examine the destruction of history in the process of seeking and using archival material in documentary film. This process, as I show, is a kind of repetition of the destruction of memory in the very formation of archives themselves: through (psychic) repression and (political) suppression, as on Derrida's (1995) account in *Archive Fever*, or, from a filmic vantage, through the framing out (and thereby the creation) of what Barthes (1982), in *Camera Lucida*, calls the "blind field" beyond the frame.

In the last few sections of part two, I explore the artifactual techniques employed by some Cypriot filmmakers to tap into the creative potential in these processes of destruction: not only by blurring generic boundaries between documentary and fiction film—for example, by using archival material in fiction films, or fictionalizing events from the archival record in documentary films—but also by deliberately altering archival material to draw attention to its mediation of memory, or "faking" archival material to emphasize how much archives do not tell us about the past. I understand these techniques as artifactual in the sense that they involve the reuse and recontextualization of objects that have survived from the past—artifacts—to engage viewers in an experience of moving in time that opens the question of their belonging to time.



In that sense, archival images thematize temporality in the same way as the bones and belongings of the missing that I explored in part one. Unlike those forensic artifacts, however, which can only be recognized or rejected, archival images are not defined by their singularity or burdened by their sanctity. And they are not destined to be reburied. They can be digitized and copied; they can be edited and doctored; they can be played with. In treating these images as artifacts, I venture, Cypriot filmmakers have found radical potential in the visual archive that bones do not offer: materials for imagining a different world to inhabit—not an altogether different world, but one made from the same past as the present one, with a future yet to be determined.

## My Own Archive

In July 2012, I spent a witheringly hot day at the house of my friend M.'s aunt in Güzelyurt (Morphou), in the north. The house had belonged to a Greek-Cypriot family before the war, and was allotted to M.'s grandparents in 1975 by the emergent government in the north as compensation for the loss of their house in a nearby village, which had been turned into an army camp the year before. M.'s aunt told us the story as we helped her prepare lunch, mostly in Turkish, with M. translating as needed for me; but she also spoke to me partly in Greek, which she had learned from other children in her village when she was very young. She described what it was like when the problems started in 1963. *The Greeks didn't give us any trouble,* she said, and then quickly amended, *Well, they attacked other villages, but they didn't come into our village. We were never in danger inside the village. But once the army made it into a camp, we had to leave.* It was the first time M. had heard some of this story, she told me later: *I really don't know much about my family's village or how they moved here. We don't talk about these things. I just have vague ideas.*

After lunch, M. took me to see the little house in back, behind some lemon trees and a small herb garden, where her grandparents had lived until they had both passed away the year before. The house had not been used since then, she told me, but it was full of her grandparents' furniture, clothing, pots and dishes. M. said her mother and aunt often talked about cleaning up and repairing the place so that it could be used, but they had not brought themselves to do it yet. 

In the hallway running the length of the little house was an immense china cabinet with glass doors. M. told me her grandfather had been the one to post family photographs all over the glass, wedging them into the edges of the wooden door frames or taping them into position, overlapping to make room. M. pointed out to me all the people she could name in the photos: her own parents at their wedding; herself as a baby; her grandfather, now gone; her uncles and aunts, some of whom lived abroad and had not been seen in decades. Laughing, she tried to guess the names of those people she did not recognize. In one black-and-white photo of three young soldiers, M. identified her uncle and two of his friends, one of whom had been killed in the war in 1974. Most of the images were black and white; the few color ones were faded and browning in the heat. M. remarked how, as a child, she had loved this cabinet, the one place where the many generations of her far-flung family were ever collected together. "Visiting" the photographs whenever she came to the house to see her grandparents, she said, she had come to think of them as "family treasures."

M.'s fond attachment to these treasures might have been less remarkable if the china cabinet had stood in her grandparents' original home in the village that her aunt still called hers, though she had not seen it in almost forty years. But within living memory, this house had belonged to others—another family, Greek-Cypriot, who had been forced to abandon it and move to the south, leaving many things behind. The china cabinet might have been one of those things, although M. did not say so and perhaps did not know. The otherness of the house somehow enhanced the intimacy of the photos, both kinds of things enclosed within the "vague ideas" M. had long held of how her family had come to live here.

This quality of vagueness links M.'s cabinet of photographs to the losses experienced by Cypriots who lived through the violence of the 1960s–1970s. Many of these people, who had lost their homes and all their personal belongings to fires, bombings, and sudden evacuations or escapes, often expressed a yearning to collect any material trace of those times—especially photographs—in order to anchor their memories and attachments to their lives before the war. *Parallel Trips*, a 2004 documentary film by Derviş Zaim and Panicos Chrysanthou, dwells on this link between losing and collecting as it materializes its own archive, recording the testimony of Cypriots who survived violence and displacement some thirty to forty years earlier. Petros, a middle-aged Greek-Cypriot man who appears as a central character in the film, expresses an archival yearning in the opening sequence. "Because I'm so attached to my village and my house," he says to the camera (in Greek), "I've tried to make my own archive—to find recent photographs of my village, of our house and our neighbors' houses." He holds up a file marked "My House," containing a large map he has constructed by pasting photographs of the houses in his village along the roads he remembers and has drawn onto the map in colored pencil. He indicates the location of his childhood home on one of these roads, leading off the edge of the map. "Many different photos here, I'm very attached to them," he says. "I take good care of them. I don't want to tear them. No matter what the solution will be, these photos are a reminder of my house and my village."



Petros's memories emerge through brief scenes over the next thirty minutes of the film, intercut with stories from other survivors of the 1974 massacre at Palaikythro (Balıkesir) that he had witnessed as a ten-year-old child. He recalls being rounded up with other children and women from the village by Turkish soldiers, hearing others being shot nearby, tending the wounded, and finally being bused to a refugee camp in the south. Later in the film, he appears in the present, playing and baking bread with his three children in the courtyard of a new house, somewhere else.

Salih, a Turkish-Cypriot man also featured in *Parallel Trips*, seems to feel a similar longing, even awe, for photographs of the past. He relates his memories of his father's death in an explosion in 1957 and of fleeing his village with the rest of his family in 1963 after an attack by Greek-Cypriot extremists. "We left our place," he says. "We left our home. We left our memories. We left our photographs. In short, we left everything we had. [ . . . ] I have no photos that date before '63. They must have been burnt, damaged. They've all disappeared. Not only our photos but also our memories have been lost." In the house in Nicosia where his family moved as refugees, along with furniture and other belongings of the Greek Cypriots who had lived there before, he found a photograph of a military officer shaking the hand of another officer over a table with a British flag laid across it. Salih explains that he will keep this photograph "in order to return it to the owner, to him or to his children."

In the film, both men are fixated on photographs—their own and those belonging to others—not only to ground their attachment to their homes but also to imagine a future: for Petros, a time when he might reinhabit the house he has lost; for Salih, a time to meet the former owner of the house where he now lives. In ethnographic studies of loss and memory in Cyprus, too, the ownership and the fate of personal photographs left behind during the conflict feature as vital, material links between past, present, and future, as between Greek Cypriots and Turkish Cypriots. Yael Navaro, for example, relates the experience of Latife, a Turkish-Cypriot woman living in a house in Tashkent that had belonged to Greek Cypriots before the war. The Settlement Office in the north had given the house to Latife, along with her husband and baby, after they had fled their own village, hearing of massacres of Turkish Cypriots in nearby villages. They left all their belongings behind. Latife tells Navaro how she took the furniture and clothing she found in her new house as well as neighboring ones; she had no problem with "loot." Yet Navaro observes the exquisite care Latife took of these objects, and the house itself, in everyday acts of cleaning and polishing, arranging and rearranging, which Navaro interprets as signs of moral ambivalence about Latife's act of appropriation. In the arrays of family photographs with which Latife has decorated the living room, Navaro (2012, 181, 191) finds attempts to "personalize" the space and turn it into a home—and more, to assuage unspoken "guilt" at having taken someone else's home, to exorcize the ghosts that now haunt that "melancholic" space.

Navaro writes, too, of another Turkish-Cypriot family living in an appropriated house in Güzelyurt, to which they avoided making major repairs or changes during their thirty years of residence, since, they said, the house did not belong to them and could be taken away at any time. Navaro dwells on the relationship the members of this family developed with the house's former occupants, whom they partly imagined and partly reconstructed through documents and especially photographs left in the house. They showed Navaro (2012, 187–88) a series of images of one of these former occupants, a woman they called "Christina": as a child in a school uniform, in her wedding dress, with her baby, standing inside and outside the house. More than the furniture and clothing left in the house, and more than the house itself, these images crystallize their fantasy of this woman, animated by their compassion for her and their hope to meet her someday. In this house, where "Christina" exists not as a ghost but rather as a real person to whom the family feels deeply connected, no symptoms of guilt or melancholy plague their inhabitation.

Rebecca Bryant also writes of Cypriots living in appropriated houses who confronted, in different ways, the photographs they found upon moving in. She classifies photographs and other personal belongings that are "inseparable from the owners" as "remains," distinguished from other kinds of household objects and from homes themselves (Bryant 2014, 686). Such remains, she argues, could not be appropriated or transformed by new inhabitants of a house, who either destroyed them or saved them but put them away, "unable to destroy them but also unable to live with them" (692, 687). Photographs, in particular, she suggests, are tied to their subjects, to the temporality of their lives and to their mortality. She notes several cases in which the new occupants of appropriated houses burned the photos they found inside, eliminating the possibility of any future connection with the former owners (Bryant 2010, 78; 2014, 18). On the other hand, she writes of Fadime, a Turkish-Cypriot woman living in an appropriated house in the north, who tells Bryant she saved the "three or four" wedding photographs she had found there and kept them safe for years afterward. At some point, the former owners of the house, Greek Cypriots who were not permitted to cross the border, sent some English friends to visit their old house, and Fadime sent the photographs back with them. When the checkpoints opened a few years later, the former owners came themselves to thank Fadime, who had been living in their house for over thirty years by then (Bryant 2010, 76–78; 2014, 26ff.). Bryant implies that the wedding photographs formed grounds for identification between the two women, "both brides," if not grounds for lasting friendship. In Fadime's gesture of kindness and compassion—saving another person's photographs—Bryant sees a kind of "stranger" intimacy, where mutual recognition and respect are premised on anonymity and distance (Bryant 2010, 78; 2014, 28–29). With Barthes, she perceives the special capacity of photographs both to "particularize" the subject depicted and to "generalize" the significance and value of that subject through the generic representation of their "humanity" (Bryant 2014, 692, 693).

In Bryant's and Navaro's accounts, the relationships these finders of photographs developed with the subjects of the photographs entailed both a personalized imagination of the original owners of their houses and a complex identification, across ethnonational lines as well as across time. This is not generational time, but rather the time after war, shared by members of the same generation. These relationships resemble but also diverge in important respects from the intergenerational relationships Marianne Hirsch describes under the term "postmemory": a highly charged, highly mediated tie to the past experienced by the descendants of those who have lived through violence, such as the children and grandchildren of Holocaust survivors whose artistic productions she examines. Hirsch describes this kind of tie as a mode of recognition and recollection of violent events that is "distinguished from memory by generational distance" and "from history by deeply personal connection" (1997, 22). On her account, postmemory combines close familial attachments to older family members with painfully "'indirect knowledge'" of their experiences (Hirsch 2008, 106, quoting Hoffman 2004, 25), generating an urgency in the children and grandchildren of survivors to know everything that happened, along with a recognition that such knowledge is elusive, if not impossible.



Inherent in postmemory, Hirsch (2008, 104) indicates, are unexamined assumptions about the "inheritance" or "transmission" of memory, and the danger of "appropriating" the stories of survivors as one's own memories. Considering artistic works that address the Holocaust, and the special role played by photography in these works, she questions the family as the pregiven and primary site of postmemory. She examines the ways in which "anonymous" and "public images and narratives" (112) of violence and the time before come to mediate or even script intimate family memories—and, conversely, how "private" family photographs and narratives may be integrated into "cultural" or "archival" memory, so that "less-directly affected participants can become engaged in the generation of postmemory" in their artistic and political expression (111). Hirsch identifies this dynamic between the "familial" and "affiliative" forms of postmemory with, respectively, the indexical-iconic and symbolic registers of photographs (114, 116). It is in the oscillation between these registers, she suggests, that the particularized "who" and "mine" of an image come to be appropriated as the generalized "we" and "ours."

Following this line of Hirsch's thought, I see a close connection between the ways in which Cypriots displaced from their homes by war apprehended the photographs they found in the houses they appropriated, and the ways in which Cypriots of the postwar and later generations apprehended archival images from the war and the time before. Both kinds of images grounded identifications that exceeded genealogy and familial transmission, extending to "strangers" who nevertheless shared an intimate history of violence and displacement.

The very familiarity of personal photographs as a genre in Cyprus—especially wedding and family portraits—depended on such identifications. But these identifications were at work as well in another familiar genre: war photography. Photographs of paratroopers, bombings, soldiers with guns, am-

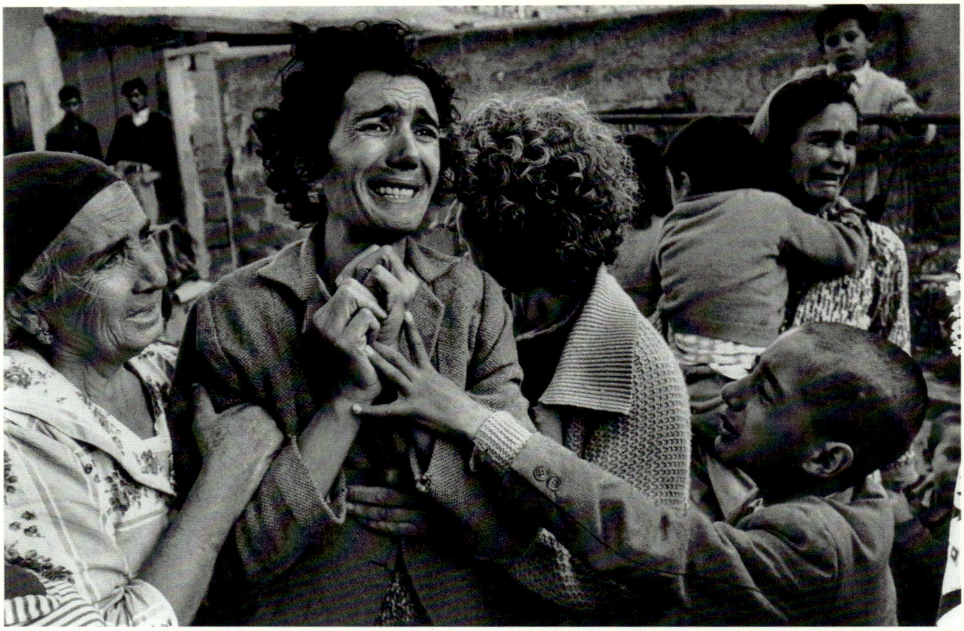

NO.

2.2

bulances and corpses, unarmed people running through streets and living in refugee camps had all found a secure place in the iconography of the conflict by the time I was doing my research. In addition to newspapers and television programs, these images were popularized in Cypriot war museums, several of which were built in the 1960s and 1970s, and others as recently as 2010. The display of photographs in these museums, as several scholars have noted, served the nationalistic purposes of celebrating the military victories of each side and reaffirming each side's status as the victim of the other's atrocities. Yiannis Papadakis and Paul Sant Cassia, both writing before the opening of the checkpoints in 2003, emphasize the common subjects—military personnel, missing persons, refugees—along with the divergent modes of display in the National Struggle Museum in south Nicosia (founded in 1962) vis-à-vis the Museum of National Struggle in north Nicosia (founded in 1982). They note, for example, the "romantic style" and religious symbolism employed in Greek-Cypriot paintings and photographs, in contrast to the "realism" and absence of symbolism in Turkish-Cypriot images (Papadakis 1994, 404; Sant Cassia 2005, 133).[3] Sant Cassia develops his analysis along these lines, extending beyond museum displays to the wide range of archival images published by the Press and Information Offices (PIOs) in the north and south. He characterizes Turkish-Cypriot official photography by its emphasis on "documentation" that is "almost forensic," featuring graphic images of wounds and the "presence" of corpses that underline the "certainty of death" (Sant Cassia 2005, 150, 141, 137, 150). This mode of representing suffering stands in direct contrast, he argues, to the recursive and open-ended structure of official Greek-Cypriot images of "absences," such as the ubiquitous photographs of women and children holding photographs of their missing sons, husbands, and fathers. Such "absences" emphasize uncertainty, he contends, and thus depict the ongoing conflict as a "continuing drama" in Greek-Cypriot nationalist ideology (Sant Cassia 2005, 133, 135), as opposed to the coercive closure of "putting the past behind us" in Turkish-Cypriot nationalist ideology.



Alexandra Bounia and Theopisti Stylianou-Lambert also compare the two "struggle" museums in Nicosia, as well as several others—the Museum of Barbarism (founded in 1966) and the Peace and Freedom Museum (founded in 2010) in the north, and the Museum of Commando Fighters of Cyprus (founded in 2010) in the south—where photographs were similarly instrumentalized to affirm nationalist narratives of the conflict. While Papadakis and Sant Cassia focus on the divergent styles of photographic representation in the north and the south, however, Bounia and Stylianou-Lambert call attention to common techniques of presentation across the five museums, noting how the choice of black-and-white or color photographs, the attribution or not of authorship, and the identification of subject, place, and date work to reinforce the "authenticity" and "accuracy" of the images on display in all the war museums. Such tactics of display, they argue, share the premise that photographs are "a mechanical reproduction of reality," and therefore that the archiving work of museums amounts to a "salvation of memory" (Bounia and Stylianou-Lambert 2013, 3, 4, 10).

In their analysis of photographic displays in these museums, Papadakis, Sant Cassia, and Bounia and Stylianou-Lambert all explore the intimacy between photography and nationalist ideology, which sustains popular memory of one-sided and unavenged suffering. For Sant Cassia, this politics is the evidentiary "scaffolding" of photography "as an official incontestable approach to the past and as the legitimating medium of official reality" (2005, 148). The two new museums examined by Bounia and Stylianou-Lambert manifest a strong continuity with this scaffolding built in the older museums. It would seem not only that these museums reflect and reinforce one another's strategies of visual representation, but also that they all draw on photographic repertoires that exceed the context of museum display. In this vein, Bounia and Stylianou-Lambert cite Papadakis's earlier writing about his visit to the Museum of Barbarism in the north, when he was struck by the familiarity of photographs of refugees—familiar to him not from representations of Turkish-Cypriot experiences of displacement to the north, but rather from Greek-Cypriot experiences of displacement to the south. "These images are indeed familiar," Bounia and Stylianou-Lambert write: "Not these *specific* images, but this *type* of image" (2013, 16).

But perhaps these specific images, as well. Papadakis (1994, 408) remarks on the striking similarity of certain photographs displayed in the two "struggle" museums; one image of a dead man in a street, he notes, was even displayed in both museums, although the two versions were captioned and contextualized in incompatible ways. Bounia and Stylianou-Lambert (2013, 13–14) likewise observe discrepant captions for identical photographs in different museums, including one of the most famous images of the entire conflict, featuring a Turkish-Cypriot woman grieving her lost husband at Gaziveren; this photograph, taken by British photojournalist Don McCullin, won the 1964 World Press Photo of the Year award. I have heard that it is often misidentified in the south even today as an image of a Greek-Cypriot woman taken in 1974, in part because the image has circulated in propaganda materials misidentifying it as such immediately after the war and in annual commemorations of the war ever since.

The generic legibility not only of "this *type* of image" but also of "*specific* images" is precisely what makes the realism of war photography dangerously misleading—an argument pursued by Susan Sontag in *Regarding the Pain of Others*. Describing the way images of "dead civilians and smashed houses" may "quicken hatred of the foe," Sontag warns:

> To those who are sure that right is on one side, oppression and injustice on the other, and that the fighting must go on, what matters is precisely who is killed and by whom. . . . To the militant, identity is everything. And all photographs wait to be explained or falsified by their captions. During the fighting between Serbs and Croats at the beginning of the recent Balkan wars, the same photographs of children killed in the shelling of a village were passed around at both Serb and Croat propaganda briefings. Alter the caption, and the children's deaths could be used and reused. (2003, 10)



The generic familiarity of personal photography and war photography across ethnonational lines and across time in Cyprus was perceived by some Cypriot photographers I knew as both a political and an artistic problem. The challenge to see Cypriot history in a new light, or to see a different history from the one apprehended through familiar genres, was the motivation for the organizers of *Re-envisioning Cyprus*, a photography and multimedia exhibition held in December 2010 at the Pantheon Gallery in south Nicosia. The exhibition was staged to mark the fiftieth anniversary of the independence of the Republic of Cyprus, cohosted by the University of Nicosia and the Cyprus University of Technology in Limassol, with funding from the Republic's Ministry of Education and Culture. The editors of the exhibition catalog describe the contributors as members of many generations and as practitioners of many arts and sciences, representing "anthropology, social sciences, art history, literature, cultural theory and visual arts." Their common aim, they wrote in their introductory essay, was "a wish to see Cyprus with our own eyes (whoever we are, citizens or visitors) and with our own minds, rather than through officialising lenses or narratives." They pursued this wish either by, on the one hand, "excavat[ing] past images"—an archaeological metaphor emphasizing the affinity between archival images and buried artifacts—or, on the other hand, by "produc[ing] new ones" (Loizos, Philippou, and Stylianou-Lambert 2010, 7).

Contributions of the "excavation" kind featured images that seemed to belong to familiar genres but revealed new subjects—as in the photographs of impromptu family gatherings and studio portraits commissioned by Cypriots from the 1930s to the 1980s, collected in Nicos Philippou's alternative "photo album" to explore Cypriot identity and self-representation through modern, urban themes and settings; or the archival images of child laborers and their families in Cyprus, assembled by Loucas Antoniou to illuminate the growth of small businesses in Cyprus as well as the mining industry, farming, housework, and labor strikes, in the early decades of the twentieth century. Contributions of the "production" kind featured new images of familiar and highly symbolic places—such as Theopisti Stylianou-Lambert's photographs and video stills of tourists engaged in self-photography at the Rock of Aphrodite, displacing "official" promotional images to reveal a space of play with self-image and performance; or Orestis Lambrou's series on the old airport of Nicosia, an icon of Cypriot modernism that was built in 1970 and abandoned in 1974.[4]



The exhibition opened on December 8, 2010, with a speech by the Republic's then-minister of education and culture, Andreas Demetriou, who had been instrumental in its funding. G., one of the organizers, explained to me that, until recently, institutions did not exist in Cyprus to support this kind of work. He credited Minister Demetriou, a leftist academic who had introduced controversial curriculum reforms during his tenure, with an understanding of the importance of a "critical view" and "multiple ways of imagining ourselves." Although the *Re-envisioning Cyprus* exhibition did attract a number of critics, G. said, he did not fear a broad reversion to nationalist attitudes among the Cypriot population, given the broad swell of new thinking that was rising: *Once the book is opened,* he said, *it can't be closed again!* He compared the present moment—it was then 2012—to the period of cultural tumult in the 1920s–1930s, with the rise of the left as an intellectual movement and then as a labor movement: *That was a period of intense contestation of ideas, unofficial views, creativity, knowledge, and modernizing movements in Cyprus, in all kinds of ways, including technology. It wasn't until the 1950s that Cyprus became so conservative, with* EOKA, *the rise of nationalism, and the republic of priests led by Makarios.*

S., another of the organizers, told me more about the critical reactions provoked by *Re-envisioning Cyprus.* Several Greek-Cypriot newspapers, she said, reported visitors' complaints about the absence of the conflict from the installations: *They thought, "How could the Ministry of Culture and Education support this exhibition as a view of Cyprus on its fiftieth anniversary?" But that was the point. We were very tired of the Cyprus Problem, and we were looking for ways of approaching Cyprus since independence that weren't completely dominated by it.* Particularly troubling to some visitors, she told me, was the installation by the German photographer Johanna Diehl, who presented a series of images of mosques in the south and churches in the north. Some Greek-Cypriot visitors were offended, S. said, miming their complaints: *"We take care of their mosques but they destroy our churches—how can they be shown in the same neutral light?"* These visitors—not the majority, S.

insisted—were so attached to the images they already knew of Cyprus that they literally could not see it otherwise. What they expected to see—what they wanted to see, according to S.—were signs of conflict and suffering.

## Stills

A month-long exhibition of Panicos Chrysanthou's photographic works opened on a dank evening in January 2012 at the Eirini gallery, on the southern edge of the dead zone in the center of Nicosia. The exhibition, amounting to a retrospective of Chrysanthou's entire corpus, was a sign of the transformation of the dead zone itself. Writing about several major art exhibitions staged in and around the buffer zone since 2005—most organized by foreign curators, working with foreign and some Cypriot artists—Haris Pellapaisiotis describes this transformation of the area "from a 'no-go' military border to a 'threshold' or an 'in-between' space," demanding its rethinking as "liminal," "suspended," "porous," and "common" (2014, 221, 222).[5] Chrysanthou's exhibition was designed with such a rethinking of place and borders in mind.



The gallery space was brightly lit and crowded with visitors, young and older—many of the same people I had seen at cultural events elsewhere in Nicosia. They chatted and pointed as they moved through the gallery. Speakers were assembled for a panel at the front of the room, connected by microphone to two video cameras recording the proceedings. In Greek, Chrysanthou welcomed the audience and opened the panel, saying that he was not entirely sure why he had wanted to do this exhibition. *It has to do with seeing life in the dead zone*, he suggested. He introduced the speakers. A few were politicians, friends of Chrysanthou, including a functionary in the Ministry of Education and a member of the municipal water board, who commented on the relevance of his work to the Cyprus conflict.

A historian, taking a different line, "facing the future rather than the past," as she put it, offered brief remarks that both addressed Chrysanthou's works directly and recontextualized them. What she wanted to speak about, she said, was Occupy the Buffer Zone (OBZ). This movement represented the first time that she had seen the anger and resentment surrounding the Cyprus conflict turn into a political vision and a culture. She read aloud from OBZ's recent press release, which positioned the buffer zone as a place for culture to be created. Venues like Eirini, she proposed, like OBZ itself, were contributing to the "resuscitation" (αναζωογόνηση) of the dead zone, transforming it from a space of death and impasse into a space of life and culture, activity and activism. For her, this possibility expressed the relevance of OBZ to Chrysanthou's work, and of Chrysanthou's work to politics and culture in Cyprus today.

Later, Chrysanthou replied directly to her remarks: *Culture stopped in 1974!* he exclaimed, indicating that perhaps it was just now beginning again. Cyprus had been a very difficult place to make art, he explained, not just because Cypriots constructed political obstacles to artistic expression, but also because they did not value or understand art. *But it's still very important to try and make art,* he said. *I have a lot of hope in that process.*



An anthropologist on the panel addressed Chrysanthou's works in differently political terms. He framed Chrysanthou's films as works whose theory was also their practice: collaboration (συνεργασία) between Greek Cypriots and Turkish Cypriots described both his production process and the theme of his films. He pointed out that Chrysanthou employed Turkish-Cypriot crews on his shoots; he had codirected *Our Wall* and appeared on-screen in the film with his Turkish-Cypriot friend Niyazi Kızılyürek; he had collaborated with the Turkish-Cypriot director Derviş Zaim in making the documentary film *Parallel Trips*; he and Zaim had coproduced each other's recent fiction films *Akamas* and *Mud* (*Çamur*). His political orientation to the work of making films was thus profoundly bicommunal, long before bicommunalism became a normalized framework for cultural production in Cyprus.

A long, vigorous discussion among the panelists and many in the audience followed these opening remarks. The discussion centered on the Cyprus conflict, only lightly touching on Chrysanthou's works. Audience members challenged the ways in which certain panelists had framed the politics of division or the facts of history. Others reiterated the necessity of reconciliation and looked to Chrysanthou for an inspiring vision of this possibility.

Curious people from the pedestrian shopping area outside the gallery's open doors wandered in and out. Slowly, spectators began to drift away. The panel disbanded and released the remaining audience into the gallery. Many left, and the crowds around the photographs thinned. I was able to stand for a long while in front of a series of images of abandoned villages, including Ayios Sozomenos, a once-mixed village near the Green Line that was evacuated in 1974 after it was bombed by the Turkish air force. Some were stills from Chrysanthou's film *A Detail in Cyprus*, set and shot in this village eleven years later, in 1985. Some were taken on visits Chrysanthou had made to the abandoned countryside outside Paphos and Limassol in 1984, before the film was realized. Others were taken later still, in 1985, 1986, 1988, 1989, 1990, 1991, 1996, 2009. Many of the same images had been featured in an exhibition of his works in Avesta, Sweden, in 2010, from which an annotated catalog, *Sto-*

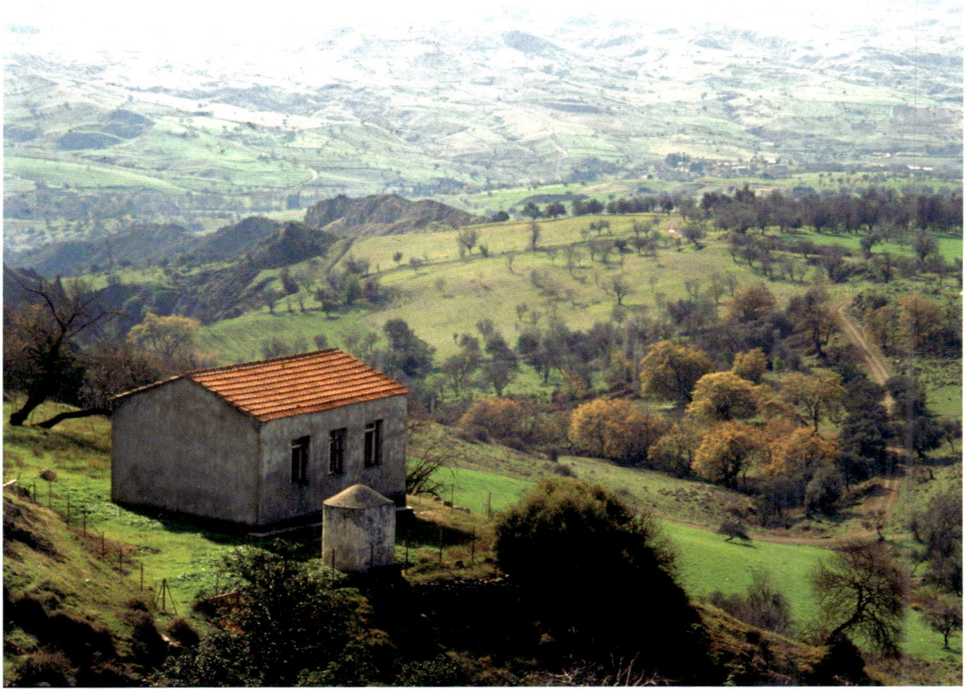

NO.

2.3

*ries of the No-Man's Land*, was published (Chrysanthou 2010). The captions in the catalog disclose the names of other villages that a hasty viewer might take for Ayios Sozomenos: Istinjo, Zacharka, Melandra, Arodes, Phinikas, Vretsia, Falia, Pelathousa, Chrysochou. The text explains that these villages, all located in the south (Chrysanthou would not have been able to visit villages in the north between 1974 and 2003), had been inhabited by Turkish Cypriots before they moved into enclaves in 1964 or were forcibly resettled in the north in 1974; they were never resettled by Greek-Cypriot refugees coming from the north, who stayed away from farming areas in the arid south and moved to larger towns instead, in search of wage employment.

Studying these photographs, I recalled a moment when the panel discussion had fixed on the trope of ruins. The anthropologist, commenting on the aesthetics of Chrysanthou's photographic works, had said, *Death is everywhere in these images. Especially the ruins of the villages, which give me a strong feeling—I don't know what to make of it. Maybe Panicos wants to immortalize [απαθανατίζει] these ruins? It troubles me.* Answering him a few minutes later, Chrysanthou insisted that he did not wish to immortalize ruins: *I'm not in love with death*, he said. For him, the ruins were like graves: *I like graves. They're like spring: there is beauty and life in them, a life that anticipates loss. The ruins express a feeling of melancholy in regard to the future rather than the past. Death comes to everyone and everything, but life continues in other forms, like flowers growing on a grave, and grass growing over an old stairwell in that image*—he gestured toward the photographs of abandoned villages hanging on the wall across from him. The discussion moved on to more overtly political matters.

After the panel, I tarried at those photographs, one abandoned village blending into the next. The names of the villages did not appear on the gallery walls; they did not figure in this iconography of ruin and new life. A few days later, at the screening of *A Detail in Cyprus* in the same gallery, surrounded by these images, Chrysanthou spoke of his experience fleeing his own village as a child in 1974, with his family. Although his village was not abandoned for long—it was soon resettled by Turkish Cypriots relocated from the south—his series of photographs of abandoned villages in the south and along the Green Line fed his imagination of all the villages deserted in an instant during the conflicts, including his own. In his catalog, recounting one of his early trips to this part of the country in 1984, he describes Ayios Sozomenos as a "ghost village":

> It was a great sorrow to roam through the deserted streets in-between walls, which still bore the smell and colours of the people who left. I

> had though the impression that I could feel their pulse. I might not know who lived here and who lived there, I might not know the personal life and private stories of each one, but I felt that I know only too well this very bitter feeling of nostalgia and the deprivation of this very personal and unique space, one's home, which I am sure people from these villages experience. Because I too, had a home somewhere in the "north," with a thousand details that composed a part of my life. It might be, I was thinking, that the house I was born in and through which I got to know the world, is today like one of these houses. Perhaps our own vine, our own lemon tree, our jasmine, perhaps they are blooming still all of their own, as these do here. Perhaps on the wall one can still see the sketch I made. And out of the window one perhaps may still be able to see the same view as I once had.
>
> I could feel the pulse of this village because I had in me the pulse of my own village, which was just like all other Cyprus villages. Perhaps that was the reason that I wanted my camera to touch softly, like a caress, upon these remnants of life. They were the rolling images of homeland through time. (Chrysanthou 2010, 36)



The scale of these photographs, reproduced in the catalog, spans from massive landscapes, showing ruins of buildings in relief against mountain ranges and rolling valleys; to the world of humans, also of the goats and pigeons who have taken up residence in the ruins; to detailed close-ups: wall textures, stairwells and doorways, yellowing photographs in broken frames hanging askew on cement walls riven with cracks and holes, an old farm chair overgrown with grass in the corner of an open courtyard, sunbeams streaming into roofless rooms, illuminating dusty bottles on sagging windowsills and old toys, disintegrating into a hard dirt floor. Some of these are scenes of abandonment; others—like the black-and-white image of a schoolroom in Zacharka, its floor literally covered with tattered books and papers, and a few broken wooden desks and chairs—seem more the afterscenes of violence or vandalism. And then there are the graves, many graves.

In the gallery, I stopped at a photograph of the investigative journalist Sevgül Uludağ, talking with Hayriye Tatit in her home in Güzelyurt (Morphou), an elderly woman when the photograph was taken in 2007; her husband had disappeared forty-three years before. I recognized Uludağ from her work with the CMP and her many appearances at bicommunal events in Nicosia. Later, Chrysanthou told me that he had filmed some of the interviews she conducted with relatives of the missing in the early 2000s. The photograph was a still from this footage. There were, in fact, many stills

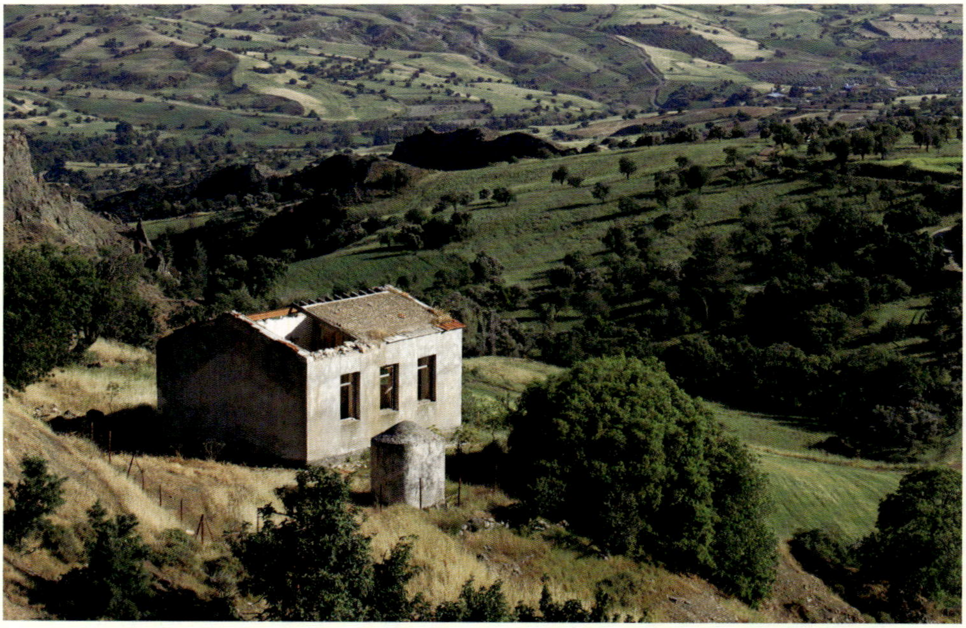

NO.

2.4

among the prints exhibited at the Eirini gallery, including the image to which Chrysanthou had gestured when he spoke of flowers growing on graves—a moment from *A Detail in Cyprus*, shot in the cemetery at Malia village where a simple monument to the Turkish-Cypriot victims of the violence in 1964 had been constructed around six raised stone burial vaults. The same graves appear twice in his catalog: in a black-and-white photograph, taken from behind and above, of two crew members filming the graves on January 18, 1985, showing the well-groomed, hard-packed ground visible around the stone edges of the graves, with a bit of brush starting to creep over the tops; and, on the next page, a bright color photograph of the same graves a few years later, utterly overgrown and surrounded with yellow wildflowers, dated March 17, 1989, and captioned, "Life never stops."



This caption expresses Chrysanthou's philosophy of time as movement, captured within his images of the other kinds of life that flourish in the ruins of human life—flowers, grasses, goats, pigeons—and by constructing sequences of images of the same houses, graves, hills, and faces over time, every few years, accreting now into decades. His decision to display stills from his films alongside his photographs, in the same room where the films would be screened throughout the duration of the exhibition, was a decision not to distinguish as genres the composed images captured in photographs from the images in motion captured on film. The finitude of photographs as representations of discrete, complete moments in time was belied by their mobilization in displays of series or sequences. With his stills, Chrysanthou created photographs not with the camera but by editorial cut, the same storytelling procedure by which he constructed narratives in his films. The stills thus blurred the distinction between photograph and film determined by their different capture of time.

This distinction in the experience of time afforded by different image media is a topic of Roland Barthes's exploration in *Camera Lucida*. Barthes opens the book by expressing his "desire" to discover the distinctive ontology and phenomenology of photography, articulated as a "decision" that he "liked Photography *in opposition* to the Cinema" (1982, 3). In the fragmentary reflections that follow, he proceeds as if by differential diagnosis, evoking film only in order to elucidate, by contrast, the being and experience of photography. Playing implicitly with the structuralist technique of resolving oppositions, the text works through distinctions. The most famous of these, perhaps, obtains between what Barthes calls the *studium* of a photograph—its cultural content, the "details" of life akin to "ethnological knowledge" (28) by which the image educates the viewer about a time and place, and from which the photographer's intentions can be divined—and its *punctum*, a "detail" experienced as an "accident" or "wound," an irreducibly subjective "addition" brought to the image by the viewer, even though it is "already there" (55).

Although this opposition is internal to the photograph, Barthes builds from it an external opposition between photography and film. He develops the notion of a "blind field" as a feature or "power" of cinema: a field beyond the screen of projection from which personae emerge and toward which they progress. Barthes treats this blind field largely as a temporal feature—evoking a time before and after the film sequence seen by the audience—that is distinctive to the experience of time in cinema as opposed to photography. Where film shows time in motion, he suggests, photography, in its "flatness" and "immobility," constitutes total arrest: "motionless, anaesthetized" (78, 57)—death. But the *punctum*, if the viewer can find it, he says, "endows" a photograph with a blind field, "a kind of subtle 'beyond'" into which the imagination of the viewer can move (57, 59). The *punctum*, in this line of thinking, becomes a temporal operator: the finitude of the photograph is shattered in the viewer's encounter with the *punctum*, putting the viewer into motion across time as she looks, imagines, yearns, and fears.



The still is a liminal form that, in a different way, troubles the distinction between photograph and film, posing the question: how can form render time visible? This question animates the short documentary film *Still*, made in 2009 by Alana Kakoyiannis, a filmmaker based at that time in Nicosia, who presents herself, in the film's voice-over, as "an American of Greek-Cypriot origin." The film engages the trope of the filmstrip as it unfolds. In one sequence, two small inset frames show scenes from the old airport inside the UN Protected Area in south Nicosia, including the airport terminal itself, seemingly built from shattered glass and dust. Shrubs grow through broken concrete gates and doorways, and a lone airplane stands, still, where it was grounded on the tarmac in 1974. Kakoyiannis uses the inset technique again a few sequences later: three frames show scenes from the dead zone in central Nicosia—barbed wire and barrels, crumbling houses and old furniture exposed to the sky. As with the airport sequence, these images are not photographs, but rather scenes that endure for several seconds each—time lapses in which nothing happens. These scenes play thus on the dual sense of "still": on the one hand, motionless; on the other, enduring from an earlier time. They are short films of residual places, presented as if they were photographs, immobile and forensic in their documentation of place.

The still takes a different form here from that of Chrysanthou's freeze-frames from his films. Here, the unfolding present comes to look like the "this-has-been" of the photographic image, as Barthes describes it. The possibility arises from these scenes that the blind field beyond the screen is not a space of activity and movement, as Barthes axiomatically presents it, but rather a frozen space in which nothing happens or will ever happen. In voice-over, Kakoyiannis comments on the still quality of this living space: on the cobwebs and bird nests that have infested the old airplane that remains "grounded, still"; on the ruins of abandoned homes in the dead zone, the old chairs and broken plates, "remnants of people's lives" arrested at the moment of their flight, now standing as "symptoms of inertia." "In many ways," she says, "life hasn't moved on for Cypriots." Niki, a Greek-Cypriot refugee of the war—one of two women whose memories anchor the film in a discontinuity between present and past—appears especially stuck, fixated on the loss of her home in 1974 and unable to move into the present. In this, she is unlike her Turkish-Cypriot counterpart, Günay, who speaks of the decades of her dwelling in the former home of Greek Cypriots as a process of work, and who inhabits her borrowed house with a sense of propriety and inevitability, even if she seems more at ease in the lush garden she has built around the house than inside the house itself. In Günay's experience of the time after war, there is a hint of progress, of moving on. Capturing this hint, Kakoyiannis interlaces her stills with visual motifs of movement: rippling water flowing across old maps of Cyprus, ribbons tied to stalks of wheat blowing in the wind. Much is still in this film, but something is moving.



The blind field in *Still* is not only a temporal feature of images; it may also be understood as a social field, composed of relationships, conversations, practices, objects, and stakes—a field of all that is unseen and unknown but that makes its way into our awareness nonetheless, obliquely. Avery Gordon writes, "The blind field is what the ghost's arrival signals. . . . It is precisely what is pressing in from the other side of the fullness of the image displayed within the frame; the punctum only ever evokes it and the necessity of finding it. Yet the blind field is present, and when we catch a glimpse of its endowments in the paradoxical experience of seeing what appears to be not there we know that a haunting is occurring" (1997, 107).

The duration of still scenes in *Still* is the temporal experience of a haunting; it implies the moving life of secrets that survive in the present even as the material world crumbles and decays, creating artifacts that mark time and manifest its processes of decomposition, sedimentation, and breakdown. Suggestions of this movement of secrets beyond the screen emanate from the interviews with Niki and Günay, who often trail off midsentence or look away from the camera, unable or unwilling to complete a thought. The film, in line with documentary conventions, transforms their memories of war and their memories of home into testimony. But there is still room

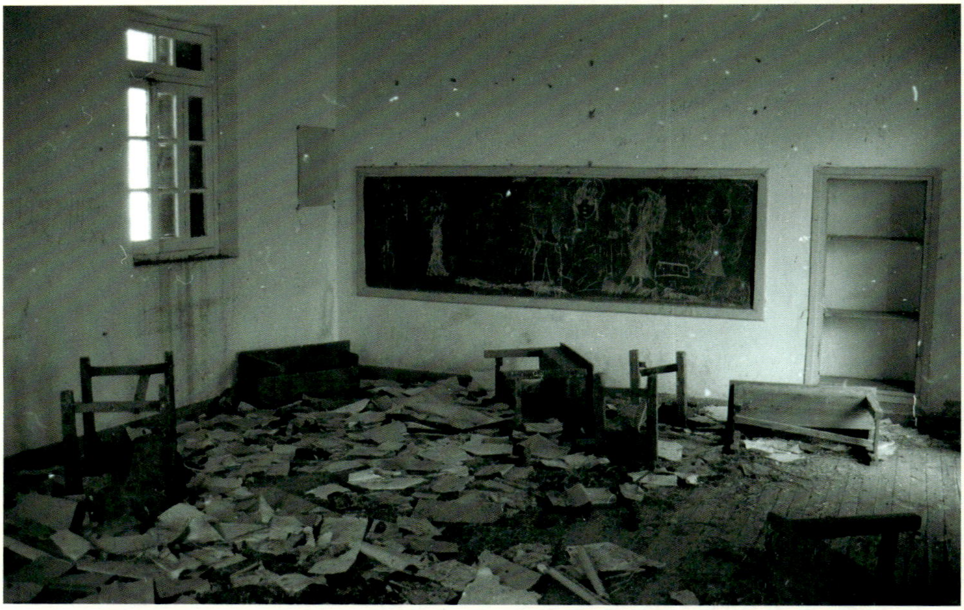

NO.

2.5

for ghosts. Thus the dilation of time in the still scenes—time lapses when, it seems, nothing happens—prepares viewers to attune to the subtle signs of what is happening beyond the frame: there is something yet to be learned and known, a presence of the past that creates anticipation.

## A Brief History of Cypriot Documentary Film



In their account of Cypriot filmmaking between independence in 1960 and the division in 1974, Theopisti Stylianou-Lambert and Nicos Philippou note that film production in Cyprus was limited during this period by the absence of film studios, workshops, and film processing facilities on the island—limitations that also shaped the orientation of Cypriot filmmaking toward Greece, where much of the material recorded in Cyprus was sent for editing and processing. Film production was also restricted, for the most part, to Greek Cypriots, since so many Turkish Cypriots lived in enclaves from 1963 onward, without access to equipment or funds. In Cypriot films that date to the predivision period, the authors argue, Turkish Cypriots were entirely excluded from representations of Cypriot national culture (Stylianou-Lambert and Philippou 2014, 62, 65). These representations largely consisted of bucolic dramas and comedies, featuring mountain and seashore landscapes and scenes of pastoral and village life—an "idealized view of 'premodern' rural life" that Stylianou-Lambert and Philippou describe as a "folk nostalgic paradise" (67, 62). They discuss the production of numerous "folkloristic and touristic" (62, citing Kleanthous 2005, 5) documentary programs for Cypriot television by the Cyprus Broadcasting Corporation (CyBC) in this period, and the "documentary precision" (67) with which even fiction films recorded rural Cypriot life, featuring rituals such as weddings.

What is most remarkable about all of these films, the authors suggest, is the utter absence of any sign of the political events and social and economic changes that Cypriots were experiencing at the time, including industrial modernization and labor struggles in Cypriot cities, and violent conflicts within the Greek-Cypriot community as well as between Greek Cypriots and Turkish Cypriots (Stylianou-Lambert and Philippou 2014, 65, 67, 81). In terms of both what they represented and what they declined to represent, then, Cypriot films of this period resembled "romantic" (69) Cypriot photography of the period to a large extent.[6] Examining the mutual "echo and refer[ence]" between film and photography, their similar focus on "sense of place and ethnonational identity" (63) in representations of Greek-Cypriot culture as Cypriot national culture, and the remarkable overlap between professional filmmakers and photographers, the authors show that film and photography before the division shared both a politics and an aesthetics that derived from colonial representations of Cyprus and persisted for decades after independence.

Following the division in 1974, I found in my own research, documentary filmmaking in Cyprus shifted away from touristic fantasy and folkloristic portraiture, and toward the events of war and mass displacement. Even so, only a handful of documentary feature films about the conflicts of the 1960s–1970s were produced in the years after the war, although a number of documentaries were made for television during this period.[7] It was not until the opening of the checkpoints in 2003 that Cyprus saw rapid growth in the production and consumption of documentary films—the overwhelming majority of which address the Cyprus conflict. With the help of a generous and resourceful friend, I was able to see and acquire copies of nearly all these films and to meet many of the filmmakers. Most had not experienced the events of the 1960s–1970s themselves, or experienced them only as young children, but it seemed to me that the politics and visions of Cypriot life expressed in their films were determined to a large extent by those events. Many new filmmakers were self-described amateurs who had picked up a camera to extend their activist work; thus, after 2003, documentary film became a popular platform for what was often called "peace messaging." Others, however, were trained filmmakers concerned not only with the political efficacy of their work but also with its aesthetic and poetic dimensions.



One of the latter was David Hands, a filmmaker and media producer based in Nicosia, whom I met in July 2012. At the time, he was helping out with DOCYouth Camp, a week-long "boot camp" in documentary filmmaking for young Cypriots hosted by the Cyprus Community Media Centre (CCMC), in which I was involved as a participant-observer.[8] I learned that Hands was a cofounder and partner in the media production company Crewhouse, located a few doors down from the CCMC in the dead zone of central Nicosia. The partners and freelance media makers working at Crewhouse were often hired to shoot or edit footage for other organizations—Cypriot organizations like the CCMC and the Association for Historical Dialogue and Research, and international ones like Greenpeace and the Thomson Foundation—as well as by media outlets such as Al Jazeera, Reuters, the BBC, and Bloomberg. Hands, the child of a Cypriot mother and British father, had been raised in Cyprus but worked for many years as a photojournalist in conflict zones from Bosnia to Israel/Palestine to East Africa; he had both an insider's intimacy with the cultural and political conditions of work in Cyprus and an outsider's comparative sensibility. In addition to his personal film projects and the media pieces he produced for Crewhouse, he was also an experienced teacher, working with local children and with educators who used visual media in their classrooms.

I spoke with Hands again when I returned to Cyprus in 2014. By then, he had finished his master's thesis about bicommunal filmmaking in Cyprus and was willing to talk with me about it. In the thesis, he argues for bicommunal film as a cross-cultural genre defined by its "aim to bridge the gap between two societies that display significant social separation, by promoting an understanding of the other" (Hands 2012, 16). He dates the period of bicommunal filmmaking in Cyprus to 2003; before the opening of the checkpoints, he argues, the north and the south had separate "mono-cultural media landscapes," in which broadcasts from the "other side" were reflexively cast as propaganda (13–14). After 2003, he writes, bicommunal activities and settings became popular subjects for filmmaking, but addressing them demanded "sensitivity" on the part of filmmakers to the incompatible perspectives on the conflict among Turkish-Cypriot and Greek-Cypriot viewers, as well as practical strategies for overcoming the long-standing "social separation" between the two communities (17).



Hands examines the particular problems faced by bicommunal filmmakers regarding audience reactions, the use of terminology and iconic images, selecting language and subtitles, selecting crew members, and funding and distributing films. He makes special note of filmmaking conventions of "fairness," "balance," and "equal coverage" of Turkish-Cypriot and Greek-Cypriot perspectives and experiences (Hands 2012, 19–20). These conventions, he suggests, derived partly from the filmmakers' own genuine desire to reach multiple audiences in Cyprus without offending or patronizing them, but partly also from pressures exerted by funders. In this, filmmakers had a difficult path to tread between funders such as the United Nations Development Programme (UNDP), perceived as advancing a pro-reconciliation, "politically correct point of view," and funding from state ministries, perceived as promoting the "official" point of view, in the north as in the south (32).[9]

When I asked Hands if he considered himself a bicommunal filmmaker, he laughed and held up his hands as if to ward off an attack. He preferred, he told me, to describe himself as "a filmmaker in a bicommunal situation." Earlier in his life, he said, working as a journalist, he had been trained to value neutrality, which he defined as *writing and editing without emotion, just showing what happened and letting the audience make up their own minds.* By contrast, his film work had a point of view and an agenda: *not to turn people into bicommunal activists, but to offer people a different perspective and open them up to new ways of relating to one another.* When we first met, he had just finished a thirty-six-minute documentary film, *This Is Kontea (Κοντέα Εστί),* set in the northern village of Kontea—his mother's village, which her family had left during the war as refugees. He thus felt personally connected to the village, he told me, and got involved in a project to restore a cultural heritage site comprising an Orthodox church, a Catholic chapel, and a mosque in the village square that had been destroyed by time. The village had not been bombed or attacked, but the war had forced people to leave, and these precious buildings had fallen apart in the years since.



Hands had first made a five-minute film about the village to help raise funds from the UNDP for the restoration project. Once the project was underway, he aimed to make an "art documentary" about the restoration, focusing on one character and the many stories of the village that crossed through him. In this early vision of the film, the Cyprus Problem would only appear in the background, in the visible ruins of the heritage site, and in the work of restoration undertaken by Greek Cypriots who had abandoned the village during the war and returned forty years later to collaborate with Turkish-Cypriot residents of the village who had settled there after the war and agreed to participate in the project. Hands shot over the course of five years, he told me, all the while defending his vision of an art documentary against the onslaught of demands and agendas brought by those involved in the restoration project. Slowly, he said, he came to understand that he was not making an art film at all, but rather a straightforward message film about collaboration and conciliation. He ultimately edited the film with this purpose in mind and gave it over to the Heritage Foundation formed by villagers. He told me he had kept asking himself, *How could I think my idea for the film was more important than the work the villagers were doing?* It was impossible for him to sustain an artistic vision when the politics of division pressed on every aspect of his subject. He narrated his decision to change direction as a story of his own enlightenment about the vocation of filmmaking in Cyprus, and his privilege to do "important work."

I heard similar stories from other Cypriot filmmakers, though often they were told with more bitterness and frustration. Funding to support film projects was limited, by any measure, and further restricted by its earmarking—especially by international organizations like the UNDP—for "peace projects" that would emphasize one or another aspect of reconciliation. These limitations on funding not only constrained the politically radical and artistically creative potential of filmmaking but also generated competition among filmmakers that hindered their collaboration and mutual support. In

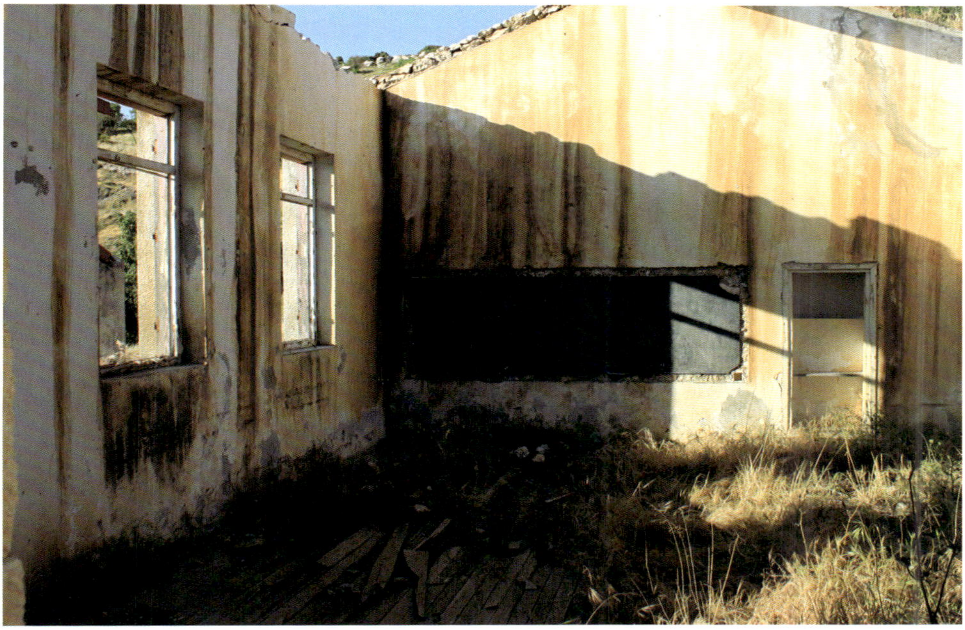

NO.

2.6

this vein, a young filmmaker living in the south told me that he was heartened by how much documentary film was being made at that time by Cypriots, but he worried that their films had "no edge and no heart." Many filmmakers, he said, were obliged to work on others' projects, usually through NGOs or press outlets, and thus contributed production or editing labor without sharing in the vision of the film. Likewise, a friend of mine, an avid consumer of film who had grown up in the north and now lived in the south, acknowledged that documentary films were being made in the north now, as they were in the south, but she insisted they were not any good: *They're not professional. They're not imaginative. They tell a story we already know; it's what the audience expects. These films just don't work.*



Filmmaking was also threatened, according to some of my interlocutors, by the active silencing of nonnationalist perspectives. Accusations of censorship by the state, in the north as well as in the south, were not uncommon. A case in point is *Akamas*, a fiction film directed in 2006 by Panicos Chrysanthou and coproduced by Derviş Zaim. Chrysanthou and Zaim have accused the Ministry of Education and Culture in the Republic of censoring the film by limiting its public screening and television broadcast—a claim contested by the ministry and some people I know in the Cypriot film world—as well as waging a "financial war" against them, ultimately withholding funding that it had contracted to provide during the production of the film. In this controversy, Chrysanthou publicly denigrated the ministry as nothing better than a petty bureaucratic organization without any artistic vision or appreciation for Cypriot culture. Outright censorship was not necessary, he said to me, when filmmakers had to depend on such institutions for support.

Crucial to the production and screening of many of the films described above was the material, technical, creative, and networking support of the CCMC, a bicommunal Cypriot NGO founded in 2009 to foster media access, multiperspectival media, and technical training in radio, television, and film. The CCMC, funded exclusively by the UNDP at the time of my research, was located on the premises of the Ledra Palace Hotel within the buffer zone in central Nicosia, just across the road from the Home for Cooperation (H4C) and a few buildings down from Crewhouse, the international for-profit media company cofounded by David Hands. Members of the CCMC staff explained to me that their organization had begun as a UNDP initiative in order to support the messaging of civil society organizations in Cyprus, all oriented toward peace and reconciliation; its member organizations at the time of my research included Hands across the Divide, the Rooftop Theatre Group, the Green Action Group, and the Association for Historical Dialogue and Research, among many others. The CCMC provided equipment and expertise to any member organization seeking to create videos, social media platforms, press releases, or other media-related tools. It also offered regular training workshops in media production, photography, blogging and podcasting, online activism, and online social networking.

In the early days of the CCMC, I learned, the staff had devised a long list of media makers working in Cyprus—filmmakers as well as those in television, radio, and web design—whom they might enlist as freelance experts or collaborators. But of that original list, only a handful still worked with CCMC by 2012, when I got involved with the organization. It was difficult to raise the funds necessary to produce high-quality films, so talented, professional media makers looked elsewhere for work, often leaving Cyprus altogether. The CCMC staff expressed frustration to me, not only at the difficulty of fundraising in Cyprus but also at the pressures their funders placed on them to emphasize peace messaging. These pressures took specific depoliticizing and often absurd forms: for instance, the requirement always to represent Turkish-Cypriot and Greek-Cypriot perspectives in literally equal numbers in any media project and to avoid using certain loaded terms—such as "human rights" in reference to media access—so as to avoid offense. In the view of one staff member, such balance was artificially contrived and prevented organic collaborations from developing among people based on the interests they actually shared in common. Nor did it make for good stories, he remarked; many peace-oriented documentaries suffered from an "overly dramatic" and rather "humorless" tone. The CCMC's explicit valorization of media transparency ran counter to these pressures, which described a continuum between overt censorship by funders and forms of self-censorship enacted by many of the CCMC's member organizations for fear of attacks by nationalists on either side of the divide.



In the summer of 2012, I attended a planning meeting at the CCMC to discuss some of these issues. Staff members and several freelance media makers who had collaborated with the CCMC in the past convened to sketch out new directions for CCMC programming, to develop strategies for reaching wider audiences and ideas for fundraising so that the CCMC could become more independent from the UNDP, its only funder at the time. The conversation gravitated toward the subject of censorship. It was not only funders who exerted pressure, I learned; one freelancer said that his biggest problem was the board of his own organization, a CCMC partner engaged in bicommunal education, whose members could not agree about the acceptability of any number of terms and phrases, and were given to "falling all over themselves trying not to offend the nationalists," as he put it. Another freelancer said he thought the UNDP and other large funders were getting more used to "sensitive" terms; recently, he had completed a project approved by the UNDP in which he quoted texts from the extremist organizations EOKA-B and TMT, which had been active in the violence of the 1960s–1970s. *That's a big step,* he said. *Maybe they're learning, loosening up a bit.*

With these limitations on antinationalist filmmaking in mainstream settings, such as commercial movie theaters and television channels, special venues for film production and screening proliferated in urban Cyprus after the checkpoints opened in 2003. During my fieldwork, I came to see these venues as spaces of sociality and productivity, where filmmakers collaborated with one another and connected with audiences, and where networks materialized and consolidated among filmmakers, artists, journalists, scholars, and public intellectuals. It was also in these spaces that communities of viewership formed and transformed around particular themes and tropes. These gatherings thus held the potential for collective recognition and synergy around those themes and tropes, but also for repetition and coagulation. David Hands remarks on the latter issue in his thesis:



> Despite . . . growing interest by the mainstream media in bicommunal productions, . . . most of the bicommunal producers still rely on screenings taking place at various organised events, privately hired cinema halls or online screenings. Such events and privately organised screenings have also increased dramatically since the opening of the crossings. Yet, they usually cater [to] the same group of people, composed primarily of individuals who are already convinced of the value of such activities for peace and reconciliation. They also attract the attention of the group of people who are strictly against any interaction between the two communities, but [they are less successful] in getting the "swing audience" interested. (2012, 33)

At the time of my fieldwork, a number of alternative, noncommercial film venues had recently opened in Nicosia. The H4C hosted frequent documentary film screenings following its opening in May 2011. Although English, taken as a common language for Greek Cypriots and Turkish Cypriots, was often used to introduce and discuss these films, H4C had developed a system for simultaneous Greek-Turkish translations by the winter of 2012. The documentary films screened at H4C during this time typically addressed peace and conflict, though not exclusively in Cyprus; some offered a comparative perspective, such as the 2011 film *Twice a Stranger,* by Andreas Apostolidis and Yuri Averof, which examines population exchanges between Greece and Turkey, Germany and Poland, India and Pakistan.

The first documentary film ever screened at H4C set the tone for what followed. The event, in June 2011, was the premiere of *Sharing an Island*, Danae Stylianou's 2011 piece about six young Greek Cypriots and Turkish Cypriots, strangers to one another, who were filmed living together and traveling across Cyprus for five days as they worked through their shared heritage of conflict. In 2011–12, H4C's documentary program also included *Women of Cyprus*, a 2009 film by Vassiliki Katrivanou and Bushra Azzouz, screened in November 2011 and again in May 2012; *The Division of Cyprus*, a 2011 film by the same Greek documentarians who made *Twice a Stranger*, Andreas Apostolidis and Yuri Averof, screened at H4C in May 2012; and *Birds of a Feather*, a 2012 film by Cypriots Stefanos Evripidou and Stephen Nugent, screened in December 2012 (its premiere at the Lemesos International Documentary Film Festival in August 2012 featured in the prologue to this book). In November 2011, H4C hosted the second annual documentary and short film festival With Brand New Eyes: Screenings for an Island, attended by more than fifty people, many of them young and aspiring Cypriot filmmakers. On the program were several short documentaries by Cypriots, including Yetin Arslan and Theopisti Stylianou-Lambert, who collaborated with the CCMC in their productions.



A different kind of screening took place at H4C in June 2012, when the PRIO Cyprus Centre, a Norwegian-Cypriot institute for research and dialogue on conflict and peace in Cyprus, launched its multiyear project, "Internal Displacement in Cyprus: Mapping the Consequences of Civil and Military Strife." With an audience of nearly forty people, PRIO staff disseminated and discussed seven reports and showed one of three short documentary films hosted via YouTube on the PRIO website. These films were made by the same researchers who authored the massive reports on experiences of Greek Cypriots and Turkish Cypriots displaced between 1963 and 1974. The films were the keystone of PRIO's multimedia project, supplementing the reports along with an intricate interactive map of displaced people hosted on the same website. The launch event at H4C was the first public screening of any of PRIO's documentaries.

As I noted in the introduction, H4C was the first institution of its kind to open inside the dead zone in old Nicosia, but kindred institutions had preceded it on either side of the division. Sidestreets, a Turkish-Cypriot foundation for culture and art, was established on the north side of Nicosia's old walled city in 2007. The foundation supports an array of projects such as art exhibitions, art and language classes, artists- and scholars-in-residence programs, and lectures on cultural and political issues. By the time of my fieldwork, it had become the principal venue for art and documentary film

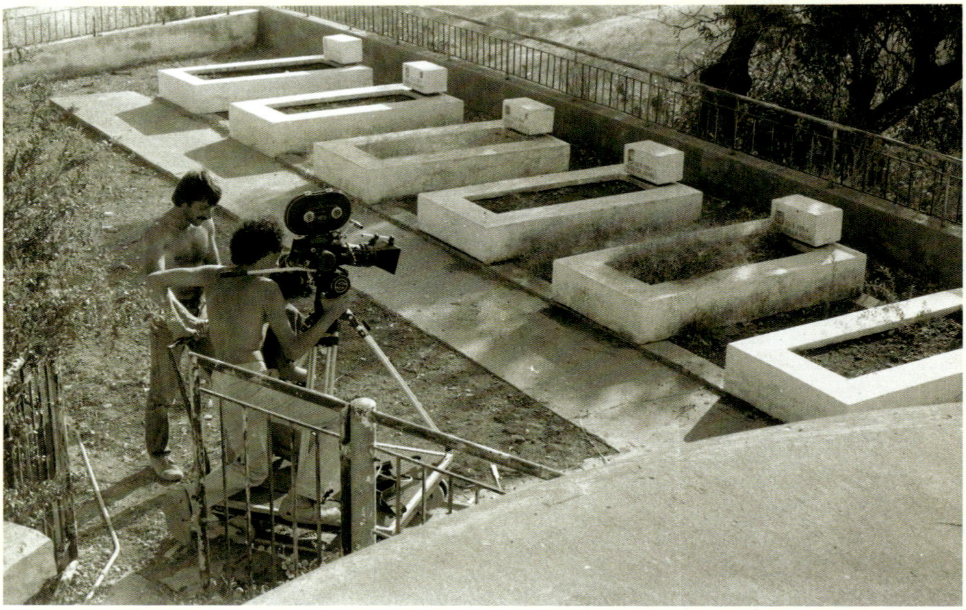

NO.

2.7

screenings in north Nicosia, which included the complete works of Turkish-Cypriot filmmaker Derviş Zaim in April–May 2009; several films from the Festival of the Green Line in March–April 2011; a Tunisian short film series in March 2013; and the simulcast of selected works from the If Kare Squared (IF²) Istanbul Film Festival annually, starting in 2010.[10]

A sort of counterpart to Sidestreets in south Nicosia was the ARTos Foundation, a cultural and research institute housed in the old bakery complex of Agioi Omologites, refurbished in 2003 and opened soon after for theater performances, concerts, film screenings, poetry readings, book launches, and art exhibitions. In addition, the gallery space known as Eirini, or the Peace Room, opened around the same time in a recently renovated Venetian building adjacent to the Ledra Street checkpoint on the south side of Nicosia's walled city. Unlike Sidestreets and ARTos, whose events were organized by the foundations themselves, Eirini was a common space rented out by the municipality for public events: lectures, panel discussions, information fairs, art exhibitions, and documentary film screenings. During my fieldwork, these included *Parallel Trips*, a 2004 documentary film by Derviş Zaim and Panicos Chrysanthou, shown as part of the Festival of the Green Line in April 2011; Chrysanthou's films, *Our Wall*, *A Detail in Cyprus*, and *Akamas* in January 2012; and the 1976 documentary *Cyprus, the Other Reality*, by Lambros Papademetrakis and Thekla Kittou, in November 2012.



Next door to Eirini, between October 2011 and April 2012, an ephemeral venue for documentary film screenings emerged in the building renovated and inhabited by participants in OBZ. Despite the lack of electricity, during the winter months, a number of documentary films were shown on the ground floor of their squat, open to the public, with the help of a generator. At the same time, the Occupy group became a subject for Panicos Chrysanthou, who filmed their dwellings and many of their events. Some participants became skillful documentarians themselves, regularly posting short videos about their activities on their Facebook page—since shut down by Facebook and then reopened under a new name.[11]

Documentary films were also shown regularly at two universities in south Nicosia: the University of Cyprus, the principal public university in the Republic; and the University of Nicosia, a private university on the western edge of the city whose theater, Cine Studio, hosted many art and documentary film screenings, series, and festivals. The northern city of Famagusta hosted the first Famagusta Film Festival in September 2010; several venues for documentary film emerged in the southern city of Limassol as well, including Art Studio 55, which hosted an exhibition of colonial film and photography as part of the Cyprus Film Days Festival in late April 2012. A larger-scale documentary event in Limassol was the annual Lemesos International Documentary Festival, convened each summer since 2006. In August 2012, the eight-day festival held screenings at the historic B Municipal Market—then a performance space run by Theatro Ena—of films such as the Academy Award–nominated *5 Broken Cameras*, a coproduction by Emad Burnat and Guy Davidi, about protests in a West Bank village in the shadow of the Israeli West Bank barrier; *Saving Face*, the 2012 Academy Award–winning short documentary by Daniel Junge and Sharmeen Obaid-Chinoy, about acid attacks on women in Pakistan; and *Children of the Riots*, by Christos Georgiou, about the experience of the Greek crisis and street protests by Greek youth. Coordinated with seminars and workshops hosted by international filmmakers at a nearby hotel, the festival program included films from Cyprus as well as China, Turkey, Pakistan, Finland, Denmark, Germany, Canada, the United States, South Korea, Greece, the Netherlands, Egypt, Russia, Japan, Bulgaria, Palestine, and Poland.



The international framework of the Lemesos film festival—one of several large, state-subsidized festivals established in Cyprus in the early 2000s that began to foster a significant Cypriot cinema viewership, as Costas Constandinides and Yiannis Papadakis (2014, 20) point out—displaced the Cyprus Problem as the central fixation of the documentary genre in Cyprus. Only one of the three Cypriot documentary films screened at the 2012 festival, Evripidou and Nugent's *Birds of a Feather*, addressed the history of conflict in Cyprus. The other two represented, respectively, an outward gaze and a different vision of the locale: the first, *Athenian Mammals*, by Giorgos Apostolopoulos, Ioakim Mylonas, and Panayiotis Fotiou, explored the work and aspirations of musicians and artists in Athens during the economic crisis; the second, Antonis Danos's *Christoforos Savva, 1924–1968*, treated the life and work of the eminent Cypriot artist. In the space of this festival, then, as one of the organizers explained to me, the Cyprus conflict was resituated as one concern rather than the only concern to be addressed by Cypriot cultural production—thus mirroring recent developments in fiction filmmaking in Cyprus as well (Constandinides and Papadakis 2014, 11). This attempt at resituation on the part of the festival organizers expressed a political inclination toward diffusing and reconsidering the politics of division in Cyprus—placing the Cyprus Problem alongside social and political conflicts in many other locales addressed by documentary films shown at the festival. It also expressed, as Constandinides argues in his remarks on the borders in and of Cypriot film, a fraught intellectual and artistic wrestling with pluralism in the very definition of Cypriot national cinema.[12]

## This Empty Folder

A crucial factor in the flourishing of Cypriot documentary film after 2003 was the relative opening of official film and photographic archives to researchers, and the circulation of archival images in public media where they had never before been seen. In the summer of 2010, for example, as the fiftieth anniversary of Cypriot independence was being observed in the Republic alongside the annual commemoration of the coup and invasion of 1974, the CyBC broadcast several documentary films addressing both events. These films included references to violence against Turkish Cypriots during the Greek-Cypriot campaign for independence from Great Britain in the 1950s, as well as footage from the coup backed by Greece in 1974 that led to the Turkish military invasion. In the south, one Greek-Cypriot friend told me, footage of the Turkish invasion was so frequently shown in the years afterward that it seemed part of her own visual memory. Footage of the coup, on the other hand, and the attendant violence against Greek Cypriots and Turkish Cypriots perpetrated by Greek and Greek-Cypriot combatants, seemed much less familiar. My friend, who had been born shortly after the war in 1974, told me she had grown up without any "visual connection" to the coup at all. But in the late 2000s, this connection was, if not commonplace, at least being established for public view in the south.



The limitations of state archives as sources of knowledge in Cyprus had long been a constraint and concern for researchers—a matter not only of omissions due to censorship, neglect, or destruction at the time of archiving, but also of the active restriction of researchers to the archives in the first place by various gatekeepers. Regarding the latter problem, D., an anthropologist who had been conducting research on the division for more than twenty years, told me of a Greek-Cypriot historian he knew who had done extensive work in the state archives of the Republic, but who had essentially been "banned" from those archives, D. said, by the time of our conversation in 2014. D. had his own story about the state archives, a story whose central character was the long-standing head archivist. This archivist had heard somehow—*it's a small place, everyone knows everyone*, D. noted—that D. had crossed to the north back in the 1990s, well before the checkpoints opened, when he had been doing archival research on Cyprus's colonial history. D. went back to the state archives in the south a decade later to locate certain municipal records and was able to find some files on a village he was studying in the north. When he returned the next day, however, the files had been removed from his desk; only one empty folder remained. When D. inquired about the disappearance of the files, the archivist told him that all the records on the village had been lost, except for that one empty folder. *There was nothing I could do about it,* D. said. *Researchers are completely at her mercy, and she can decide to shut anyone out, or just shut the archives altogether. It depends on whether she likes you, and whether she thinks your research is dangerous.* He suggested that the archivist saw her job as safeguarding the Republic from conspiracies to defame it and undermine its legitimacy.



I heard another story about an empty folder from a Cypriot historian who had, similarly, attempted to conduct some research in the Republic's archives. Much of her archival work had been undertaken in British archives on Cyprus in London, she told me, where she had located a reference to a document on British land policy in Cyprus that would have helped her a great deal. The document was listed in the Republic's archives, so she requested it when she returned to Cyprus. *They brought me this empty folder,* she said. *They went to the trouble to bring me this nothing! I was so amazed by this that I tried to take a photo of the empty folder. They practically arrested me. They threw me out, even though there was nothing in the folder that could compromise them in any way, since there was nothing in it at all.* Later, she told me, she returned to London to follow up and found a listing for the same document in the British archives. She ordered it and waited, returning day after day, but the file never appeared, even though all the other materials she requested were delivered to her promptly. *To me,* she said, *this is a very clear sign of secrecy in the archives: a source is listed but it's not really there, or it just never appears.*

"Transparency is not what archival collections are known for," Ann Stoler (2009, 8, 3) writes, reflecting on their many registers of inaccessibility, and the many reasons why information might remain "unwritten" in archives. In the case of the Dutch colonial archives in which Stoler has worked, she notes, accessibility is not a question of the relative guardedness of the archives to researchers: of classified status, formal permissions, or the cooperation of archivists—problems researchers I knew regularly confronted in Cypriot state archives. Rather, she explains, in archives of the Netherlands Indies, "inaccessibility has more to do with the principles that organized colonial governance and the 'common sense' that underwrote what were deemed political issues and how those issues traveled by paper through the bureaucratic pathways of the colonial administration. . . . Knowing what one is after is not always enough" (9). She explores the peculiarly "secret" status of many documents deposited in the archives, finding that the term "secret" functioned as an "administrative label" marking the restricted cir-

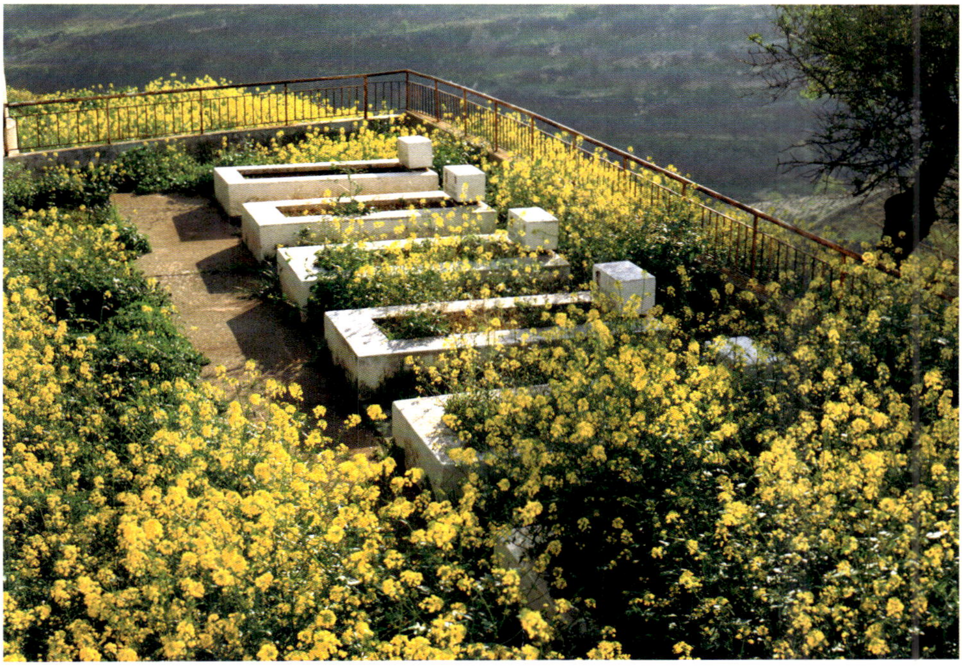

NO.

2.8

culation of documents within the colonial government—one option among others, including "semiofficial," "private," "very secret," and "highly confidential" (13, 26)—rather than a state practice of securing documents from public view. After all, she notes, "many matters" that were marked "secret" in the archives were "not 'secret' at all," but rather quite openly discussed in newspapers and other public forums at the time (11, 15, 17).

Stoler dwells on the multifarious "secrecy" of such documents for methodological as well as historiographical reasons, contending that secrecy exerts a seductive pull on researchers, drawing them into the fantasy that what the state conceals is "its most nefarious intents," even if they know that "codes of concealment are the fetishes of the state itself" (2009, 26)—the ideology of secrecy at the heart of state power, as Michael Taussig has argued. Rather than aiming to expose such secrets in the history of Dutch colonial government, Stoler looks instead to the variegated markings of secrecy in the archive as affective clues to administrators' anxieties about colonial rule, pointing to "unease," "uncertainty and doubt" among colonial officials in regard to emergent or inchoate problems of governance in a complex and rapidly changing environment (28, 4).



In Cyprus, the opening since 2003 might have raised hopes for greater transparency and public access to government records, but the fetish of state secrecy continued to wreak its seduction, and many researchers I knew still faced both blatant and obscure obstacles in their efforts to learn from the archives. Given such personal experiences of obstruction, and the general reputation that state archives had for obstruction, some researchers in Cyprus began to undertake projects outside the state archives to document the events of the 1960s–1970s—projects facilitated by the opening of the checkpoints, which also opened researchers' access to places and people once seen as off-limits. Still, one historian told me that, despite these efforts, documentation of the conflict was "at a very early stage" in Cyprus in comparison to the duration of the conflict, which was going on fifty years by then. She emphasized how protective Cypriots were of the materials they collected; the various groups undertaking these projects did not talk much to one another. *There's no centralization and no cooperation*, she said, *so it's very hard to know exactly what people are doing*. On certain issues, such as missing persons, some journalists had more or less single-handedly created new archives. *But this is just the beginning*, she said. *There are so many obstacles.*

Such irregular and capriciously mediated access to state archives obtained as a condition for research on film and photographic materials as well as documents. I heard many researchers complain, for example, of limited access to the film and photographic archives at the CyBC, the public radio and television service in the south, as well as the PIOs in the north and the south.[13] As Elena Stylianou notes, "The PIO's name itself exercises power as a vast archive of information that has been kept away from the public domain, or at least in darkness," with government archivists carefully selecting certain images for press dissemination to "shap[e] public memory" while just as carefully guarding everthing else (2014, 252). Yet I have also heard many researchers in Cyprus describe their almost complete freedom in these archives—perhaps too much freedom, or the wrong kind of freedom, given the massive volume of uncatalogued materials stored without regard for chronological or topical principles of organization. Despite directives from the European Union regarding the preservation of film as cultural heritage, very little in the way of organization and digitization had yet been undertaken in the state media archives at that time.



One film scholar, E., told me of her difficulties finding old films at the PIO in the south, not because the staff obstructed her research but rather precisely because they were aware of their responsibility to make materials available—especially, she said, to people like her, who were involved in high-profile film festivals and UNDP-funded projects on media literacy. E. had found the staff rather defensive, she said, because they knew they had not taken proper care of their materials. Some of the older film stock had degraded because it was not stored appropriately; she had retrieved one important film that did not have audio, for example. She told me she knew it was not the fault of the PIO staff, as they lacked the expertise and funds to safeguard their materials. She had advised them to hire an expert on film preservation who could tell them what to do and determine whether the materials they had were usable, but they had replied that there was no money for this in the PIO budget. Their archive was supposed to be transferred to the Ministry of Culture and Education—preservation was the ministry's responsibility—but it could not be transferred until it was cataloged. *So the archive is in limbo*, E. said. While the PIO had a catalog of holdings, not everything they had was listed in the catalog, and it was not known which of the listed materials were usable. The staff had not wanted to show E. the catalog, she told me. So, although the catalog was the best indicator of what materials actually existed, she was obliged to work without it, figuring out in advance what to request by title in order for the staff to retrieve it all piecemeal. She advised me to have low expectations if I planned to seek out any archival materials myself.

As for the CyBC, although its collections were beginning to be digitized in the early 2000s, and some photographs, films, and television programs were available for streaming on the CyBC website by 2012, a former archivist there told me that most of its materials were simply "unknown." He described dark, dusty rooms full of unlabeled film cans and piles of prints without names or dates. *They have massive amounts of amazing footage,* he said, *old newsreels and film that doesn't exist anywhere else. But they're not taking care of it. It's getting degraded and falling apart.* He told me the CyBC had been awarded some European funding to digitize it and had people volunteering to come from other countries to undertake the digitization project, such as staff from ERT in Athens (Ελληνική Ραδιοφωνία Τηλεόραση/Hellenic Broadcasting Corporation, Greece's public radio and television service until its closure in 2013). *But they keep saying, "No, it's a five-year project"—meaning, the project will start in five years! It's a mess.*



I discussed my impressions of the trouble with archives in Cyprus with X., who worked in a museum in the south and had done a great deal of research in state and press archives over the years. She laughed and nodded. *Archives are ghostly things here,* she said. *They don't exist! Materials are dispersed all over the place. It's almost like personal collections rather than archives, and they're not organized or cataloged. So you have to build an infrastructure for access in order to get access. It takes a lot of time, and it's endless—you never know how much more there is to do.* She told me about her search for images of the 1974 coup at the PIO in south Nicosia. *They had only fifty photographs,* she told me, *which was ridiculous, since hundreds were taken at the time, and they're known—they're public. They're on the internet.* I asked her what she thought had happened to them. *I have no idea,* she said. *Maybe they were burned, or maybe some politician hinted that the photographs should just "go away," and they've been moved somewhere that no one can find them. It's a mystery.*

She told me, too, about her recent experience with an exhibition project organized jointly by a state gallery in Nicosia and a private organization. Participants were to choose one work from the gallery's collection to write about; some of the works would then be exhibited, along with these new compositions. *They had a catalog, which was good,* she said, *but the catalog did not say where the artworks were located. No one could tell us where they were. There was only one person who knew—she was basically a living archive!—and she had retired.* Ultimately, X. and the other participants were able to locate the artworks, which had been stored without labels in a warehouse outside of town. *We just had to go in and look around. We chose pieces by how they looked, without knowing anything about them. We did a lot of guessing.*

When it came to more overtly political materials, X. said, the problems were worse. She had recently started working on an exhibition piece using archival photographs, and she had sought out the works of a specific photographer, Charalambos Avdellopoulos, who was particularly well known for his photographs of the days following the coup in July 1974. X. had spoken with a journalist who had worked with Avdellopoulos at the time, and who speculated that he had been allowed to enter areas where fighting was taking place, and hospitals where victims were being treated, because he was connected to the coupists or at least to people in the coupist-led government who could offer him protection. I saw some of his black-and-white photographs in a book titled *Cyprus, Days of Rage in 555 Photographs*, published in Nicosia in 1975 (Ioannides 1975). An investigator at the CMP had shown me the book, which he had discovered when he began looking into Avdellopoulos's work for clues to the fate of Greek-Cypriot missing persons. Avdellopoulos was "a right-winger, EOKA," the investigator told me. He explained how Avdellopoulos's works had come to be owned by the *Politis* newspaper. A journalist the investigator knew, who was working for *Politis* some time earlier, had found a large collection of his photographs for sale at a little shop in Nicosia. Since the journalist did not have the money to pay for them, his newspaper had purchased them instead. *But no one knows they're there!* the investigator said.



What it meant for an archive to "be there" was an enigma that X. had confronted in her own research on this collection of photographs. She had a journalist friend at the *Politis* newspaper who had introduced her to the person who was supposed to know about the Avdellopoulos archive. *But that person said she knew nothing, and she sent me to someone else, who also didn't know.* X. was able to find out that some of the archive—not all of it—was digitized, and there seemed to be a catalog for some of those materials. *But the first day, when I went in*, she said, *there was no computer I could use to check the catalog. So I had to come back another day. When I went back, I saw that there was no catalog and no sign of how much material the archive contained.* She asked the woman who was supposed to know about the archive if she could estimate the size of the collection and if she knew what kinds of photographs there were—*No, no, no. She told me I could navigate the digital collection by keyword, but there was no list of keywords they had used to organize the collection, so I had to guess.* X. had only just begun looking around the archive; it would take a very long time, she said, to get a sense of what was in there. What struck her as most curious was that she was able to find only a few photographs by Avdellopoulos—a tiny fraction of his known work. When she asked the supervisor of the collection how this was possible—what had happened to the rest of the archive?—the woman made a gesture and a face suggesting, as X. put it, *Come on! We all know what happened*. What happened, X. surmised, was that the rest of the archive had been "lost" on purpose.

Incidentally, a few years after X. told me this story, I happened upon a digital collection of Avdellopoulos's photographs from *Cyprus, Days of Rage in 555 Photographs* at the PIO of the Republic, in south Nicosia. These were some of the images my friend had been seeking. At the PIO, they were not listed in any catalog; they were located in a series of digital folders organized by year and were not even attributed to Avdellopoulos. When I found them, I thought of something X. had said to me, years earlier: *There's a thread of irrationality running through archives in Cyprus—through what is not there and what* is *there. I'm amazed by what I find, sometimes.*



The ghostliness of the archives was not always a matter of secrecy, then, although in the telling of researchers I knew, it often seemed to smack of secrecy. The inaccessibility of archives, whether deliberately staged or passively resulting from neglect and inertia, shaped the culture of research in Cyprus—a culture of yearning and disappointment, but also of intrigue and virtue, tied to the difficult but important work of exposing a hidden history.[14] That history continued in the very obstructions these researchers faced.

I say "culture of research" to indicate the pervasiveness of these obstructions, which were by no means limited to state or public archives—and thus to open the ambit of secrecy and its many shadings well beyond theories of statecraft. In this consideration, Penelope Papailias's work on archives in Greece is immensely instructive, not least because many of the archival practices she documents in Greece were linked, historically, with archival practices in Cyprus, before and after the division. In *Genres of Recollection*, an ethnography of memory and historiography in Greece, Papailias dwells on the commonsense categories that frame archives as public or private, state or personal, conservative or progressive. Focusing largely on what she calls "personal" archives, defined in contrast to "public" archives constructed and maintained by the Greek state, she argues that such dichotomies, however definitive they might seem to researchers themselves, describe a rather indeterminate division of labor and access. In the archives she explores, including those of oral histories collected in the 1920s and "amateur local histor[ies]" undertaken in the 1990s (Papailias 2005, 44), the personal carries many different contrasts to the public: as parallel, competitor, or challenge. In the very particular history of archiving in Greece, which departs from those of other western European states, Papailias documents the flourishing of personal archives throughout the twentieth century; indeed, she shows, many of the largest and richest collections in Greece today are

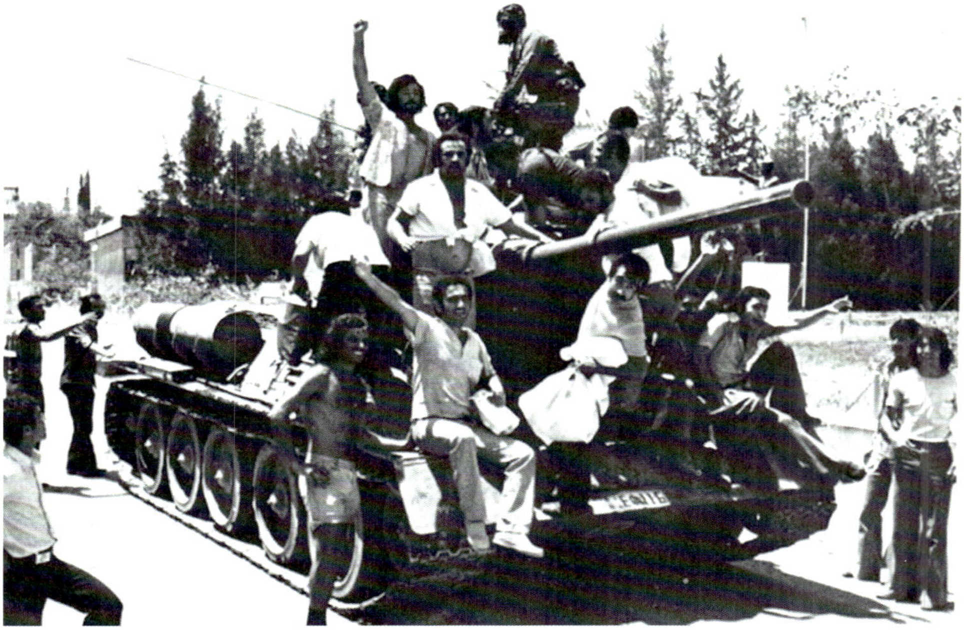

NO.

2.9

held by private institutions and libraries. Papailias accounts for this archival growth in the private sector as a reaction to the perceived "inadequacies" and "gaps" in state archives (30). Some efforts on the part of private archivists, she notes, were geared toward "salvaging" materials neglected by state institutions, and others toward effecting "political resistance" to state narratives (31). Personal archives might thus be positioned as "hiding space[s] in which subversive memories are stored and preserved for possible future disclosure"; yet, just as often, she argues, they incorporate and reproduce the "official taxonomies" and restrictive logics employed by state archives (3).



Conversely, while "hoarding and secrecy" (31) and capricious gatekeeping might thrive among private archivists—who bear none of the accountability to the public that circumscribes state archives, in theory if not in practice—Papailias observes that in some private archives, such the Archives of Modern Social History, drawn from the collections of several leftist political parties, historians have undertaken to "initiate a new kind of archival culture based on scrupulous documentation and an ethics of transparency," underscored by consistent proclamations of "openness" and "accessibility" (32). Yet this ethics of transparency is not a consistent or distinctive feature of leftist archives, either; the Communist Party archives, for example, "remain programmatically shut to outside researchers, reflecting a philosophy of 'closed' archives and an archival culture of restrictions, censorship, and 'top secret' files" (33), uncannily similar to the archives of files amassed by the Greek state on the activities of leftists since the Civil War in the 1940s. Famously, these files were publicly burned by the socialist PASOK government in 1989—ostensibly a gesture intended to symbolize the destruction of state fascism and help Greek society move on from its divisive past, but widely understood, at least by many leftists, as the ultimate seal of state secrecy, destroying all historical evidence of state surveillance and persecution of Greek citizens (Papailias 2005, 32; see also Panourgiá 2009).

Papailias concludes that the status of archives as public or private, state or personal, rightist or leftist, neither predicts nor resolves problems of archival access, nor faithfully describes the novelty of archival materials to Greek audiences. As Hayes, Silvester, and Hartmann (2002) suggest, exploring episodes in which contemporary Namibians were "exposed" to archival photographs from the German colonial period, the opening of archives to the public describes a wide range of affective experiences and dynamic interactions between materials and audiences—in exhibitions, seminars, newspapers, and, I would add, films. It is not in the opening per se but rather in the particular social and political dynamics of those interactions that the potential for learning from the archive resides.

It is with these caveats in mind that I hesitate to describe the period after 2003 in Cyprus as an archival opening for documentarians, despite the many forms of access to archives that did indeed open to filmmakers at that time. With the acceleration of documentary filmmaking in Cyprus since 2003, archival footage was increasingly built into the emerging documentary record, and, in the process, the expanding documentary record reproduced the conditions under which the archival footage was shot, along with all the partialities and exclusions of its original framing. The absence from the archive of what stood outside the frame—what was never filmed, or what film was lost or destroyed—was replicated anytime archival footage was used in a contemporary film.



Filmmakers thus magnified the secrecy and opacity inherent in the archival record in their very attempts to render it transparent—a structural problem of "repression," as Derrida (1995) describes it, in the repetition that defines the archive. For Papailias, too, "repetition remains the most fundamental fact of the archive" at work in multiple dimensions (2005, 17): from what Stoler (2009, 23) describes as the "repetitions, formulae, and obviousness" characterizing documents themselves in their obsessive reiteration of governmental common sense, to the many technologies of analogical replication noted by Papailias (2005, 17, citing Certeau 1988, 72)—"'copying, transcribing, or photographing'"—employed by researchers in their interaction with the archive.

For Derrida, repetition is the very mode by which the archive opens into the future: "there is no future without repetition" (1995, 80). From a positivist perspective, he notes, that future is defined by progress in historical knowledge in relation to the relative incompleteness of the archive, which implies the possibility of completion through the discovery of new materials that "come out of secrecy or the private sphere" (52). It was with precisely this perspective, I think, that many filmmakers in Cyprus did their work, aiming to expose audiences to archival material they had never seen, and to discover and amass new archival material in order to build an ever-fuller picture of Cyprus's history of conflict. From a different perspective, however, oriented not to the normal science of history but rather to the repressive function of memory, Derrida sees the archive opening to the future through its repetition and reproduction in a place exterior to experience—a technological apparatus for archiving memory that he, through Freud, likens to the psychic apparatus of memory itself: the "mystic writing pad" (18–19), a recording apparatus that is also a mechanism for conscious and unconscious censorship. To archive "otherwise," Derrida concludes, is to "recall and archive the very thing one represses, archive it while repressing it" (64). This project requires approaching the archive with psychoanalytic rather than positivist principles of knowledge production, in order to discern therein the "symptoms" of the repression of memory: traces of the "dissimulat[ion] or encrypt[ion]" of that which has been repressed (66).

What would it mean to take such an "otherwise" approach to the documentary archive in Cyprus? A Cypriot photographer and historian I knew told me that it was only recently, within the last decade or so, that scholars in Cyprus had been seriously studying the visual dimension of Cypriot history, thinking about photographs and films as more than transparent evidence of history, and looking at what he called "the agency behind the images." With this question of the agency of images in mind (perhaps a different articulation of the question of archival repression raised by Derrida), I look in the next section at how archival material was used in a number of documentary films to assert the transparency of visual evidence—or, on the contrary, how it was thematized in films that aimed explicitly to experiment with the representation of history. Some documentary filmmakers in Cyprus sought an edge to cut through the evidentiary conventions of using archival material. That such an edge could materialize in repetition might seem paradoxical: what could it mean for Cypriot filmmakers to return to the archive—again—for something new?

Novelty had special stakes for Cypriot documentary filmmakers and audiences, given the archival aesthetics that defined the genre; novelty was a matter not, or not only, of finding new archival material but, perhaps more important, of using archival material in creative ways that would still resonate as knowledge. The knowledge produced in documentary filmmaking continually and indeterminately verged on art, blurring lines audiences might have wished to draw between truth and fiction, even in those films that explicitly aimed to expose hidden truths about the past. This intimacy between knowledge making and art making thus generated a tension between novelty—an object of modernist desire, as Dawdy observes—and documentary conventions of truth telling that many Cypriot filmmakers experienced as constraining.

While the genre of documentary film, as I discussed earlier, was critically important as a social fact in Cyprus, especially after 2003, I do not take this genre as a stable category that is meaningful in itself. My interest is rather in how archival material became artifactual in Cypriot films, and archival material does not distinguish between fiction and documentary genres. Not all uses of archival material in Cypriot documentary films were artifactual; indeed, many of the films I examine here made quite conventional use of archival material without in any way exploring its creative potential as material that mediates memory, gives partial witness to history, and, in its exposure to decay and accident, records and tells time. Those conventional films, as I frame them, form a useful contrast with many others that did employ artifactual techniques to dislodge archival images from the "punctual time" of political utility, in Connolly's (2011, 5) terms, and to open a more "protean" experience for audiences.

## There Is No Meta-archive



One of the earliest documentary films about Cyprus was the 1946 production *Cyprus Is an Island*, shot in Cyprus in 1945 by the British documentarian and film producer Ralph Keene, working with the British novelist and poet Laurie Lee as scriptwriter, and three Cypriots as production assistants: Ahmet Jemal, Polys Constantinides, and Michael Cacoyannis. The last of these, Cacoyannis, in his own time became a well-known filmmaker and, some thirty years later, director of the documentary film *Attila '74*, about the war and its immediate aftermath. *Cyprus Is an Island* was commissioned by the British governor of Cyprus and funded by the British Colonial Office and Ministry of Information. It is a thoroughly colonial production; crafted as a nonfiction educational film, it offers scripted enactments of typical village life, from feasting and dancing to farming and fighting, and charts the many goods of civilization—reforestation of the mountains, irrigation for plains agriculture with the building of a dam, the pacification of "wild" mountain people, the punishment and rehabilitation of brigands and vandals—brought to Cyprus by the British authorities. It contains no indication at all of the labor movement and its suppression in Cypriot cities at the time, nor of the nationalist and secessionist movements brewing among Greek Cypriots, who are—despite mention of the "many faces and many tongues" of the Cypriot population that implies the presence of Turkish Cypriots, Maronites, Armenians, Arabs, and others—the exclusive subjects of the film.

As part of the Cyprus Film Days Festival in 2012, an exhibition on *Cyprus Is an Island* was hosted April 20–29 by Art Studio 55, a multifunctional gallery in downtown Limassol. Curated by the Cypriot photographer Vassos Stylianou and the Cypriot film producer and director Adonis Florides, the exhibition featured a looping installation of the thirty-four-minute film, as well as black-and-white photographs from the book *We Made a Film in Cyprus*, published in 1947 by Lee and Keene. These images included stills from the film as well as photographs of the 1945 shoot in Cyprus, with commentary on the challenges faced by Keene and Lee in their making of the film—notably, the presumptuous editorial interventions of the Ministry of Information in London. The curators of the exhibition in 2012 emphasized that the film, although clearly presented from a "colonial point of view," was invaluable as "one of the few cinematographic records" that existed of Cyprus in the 1940s.[15] That record was conserved by the Colonial Film project, a collaboration between Birkbeck College London and University College London that began in 2007, with the aim of assembling and rendering accessible online a massive collection of archival materials from the British Film Institute National Archive, the Imperial War Museum, and the British Empire and Commonwealth Museum.[16] The Colonial Film website contains information on over six thousand films made in British colonial territories from 1895 up through 1980, with 150 films available for streaming online. *Cyprus Is an Island* is one of fifteen films about Cyprus cataloged in this archive, but the only one that can be viewed in its entirety online.



I visited Art Studio 55 one evening during the week of the exhibition with two friends—one Cypriot, one American, both academics working at a university in Nicosia, who brought with them a fascination with representations of Cypriot culture as well as an ironic sensibility. We wandered around the small gallery space, taking in the story of the film and smiling at the black-and-white images of Ralph Keene, his narrow face shadowed by the brim of a white safari hat, standing knee-deep in seawater or clambering up a rocky hillside, cutting a comically incongruous figure of colonial derring-do. The dramatic sound of the musical score drew us to the back of the gallery, where the film was being projected on a blank wall in front of a few low benches where several viewers were already seated. We arrived when the film was about a third of the way through its run, during a sequence narrating a brewing conflict between Nikos, an honest, hardworking farmer who toiled on the land every day with his family and donkeys, and Vassos, a lazy, solitary goatherd, a "lotus-eater" and ne'er-do-well who allowed his unruly goats to graze in Nikos's field. The musical score suddenly swelled ominously over a montage of close-up shots of goats munching thistly greens, tearing leaves from shrubs, and standing on their hind legs to reach tree branches. When the narrator, in a stentorian English voice, condemned the "sharp, poisonous and insatiable tooth of the goat," the group seated in front of us burst out laughing. My Cypriot friend remarked, *Clearly it was the goats who really caused problems in Cyprus, not the British!* A young man in front of us howled a few minutes later when Vassos, the feckless goatherd, reappeared in his βράκες,[17] sowing seeds in an open field, then standing proudly over the massive dam he had helped to build alongside his erstwhile foe, Nikos, after the prohibition of goats from village lands. "He no longer had his goats," the narrator intoned. "But he had water. He could farm."

The exhibition at Art Studio 55 was designed to explore the status of this film in its relation to the archive. It was, on one level, an object in an archive, cataloged as an artifact of British colonial history; its installation at the exhibition thus marked the present as a postcolonial moment in Cypriot history. But the film was also an archive in itself—not a transparent record of history, but rather a complex and dynamic record of the representation of history. The audience's laughter, and even our mild smiling at the photographic depictions of colonial filmmaking, arose from this historiographical vantage on the archive. Yet this vantage, for all the self-satisfaction it afforded us in the postcolonial present, was unstable. "There is no meta-archive," Derrida writes; with every return to the archive for source material to mobilize in new interpretations and new cultural productions, the archive itself grows, incorporating each new interpretation and production of itself. As its temporal and substantive scope thus expands, he argues, the archive both "gains in *auctoritas*" and "loses the absolute and meta-textual authority it might claim to have" (Derrida 1995, 67–68). The archive exists in the growth of the archive, and the archivist is embedded and implicated in this existence; there is no external position to be occupied from which a secure and objective perspective on the reference of the archive to history could be maintained, nor even the tempting distinction between fiction and nonfiction—between the scripted dramatic sequences of *Cyprus Is an Island*, for example, and its documentary sequences capturing unscripted moments of village life, and shots of the dam and the mechanized production of domestic beer and tobacco, crafted by Keene and Lee as transparent evidence of colonial development but perceived retrospectively, by Cypriots in the room, as signs of absurd colonial fantasy.[18] All of these images were recuperated in the exhibition as artifacts that could themselves be put to work in new productions of art, film, and history, with their own evidentiary and affective purchase on audiences. The curators made an artifactual knowledge project out of this exhibition, showing how archives can be temporal operators: halting the repetition of the past and opening the possibility of difference—"ever more" difference, as Lévi-Strauss wrote—in the future.

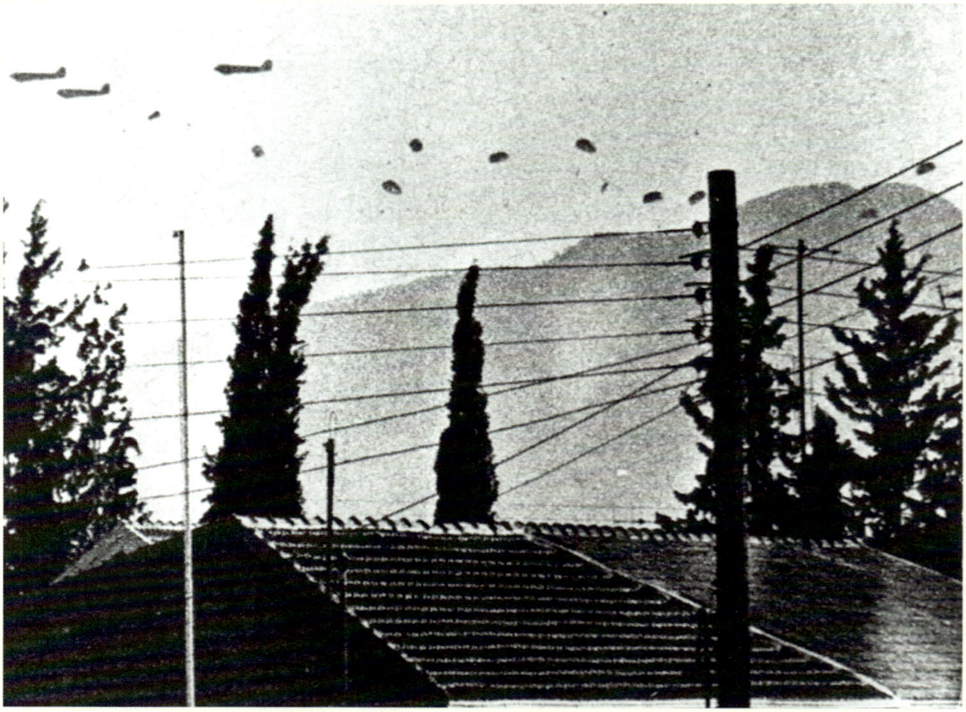

NO.

2.10

## I Didn't Know

In late November 2011, around twenty-five people—almost all women, and including me—gathered for a film screening at the Home for Cooperation. The spacious meeting room and café on the first floor had become popular venues for exhibitions, lectures, gatherings, and other cultural events since H4C's inauguration six months before. This November evening marked the first of several screenings at H4C of *Women of Cyprus*, a 2009 documentary film directed by Vassiliki Katrivanou, a Greek teacher and mediator, and Bushra Azzouz, an Iraqi filmmaker based in the United States, in collaboration with members of Hands across the Divide (HAD), a bicommunal Cypriot women's organization working for equality, peace, and reconciliation. A number of HAD members attended the screening, including several who were featured in the film.



One of these women, Maria Hadjipavlou, a professor of political science at the University of Cyprus, introduced the film. She described its inception in 2004 as a documentary about the referendum on the Annan Plan for reunification and about HAD itself, whose members largely but not unanimously supported the plan and met regularly in the lead-up to the vote to organize actions on both sides of the Green Line. The film developed into something larger, Hadjipavlou explained, as the filmmakers explored these women's memories of violence and displacement during the 1960s–1970s. Their experiences, narrated by Greek Cypriots and Turkish Cypriots who had been separated for so many years by the conflict, and who now yearned to "come together in peace," as Hadjipavlou put it, became the central focus of the film.

Following the screening, a discussion held mostly in English—a native language for only a handful in the room—was led by a HAD member, Nahide Merlen, one of the main characters in the film, whose narration of the bombings by Turkish forces and her childhood experiences in a northern enclave seemed to have brought several viewers to tears. Another HAD member in the audience, identifying herself as Greek Cypriot, said how sorry she was "for all that we allowed to happen," referring to the defeat of the Annan Plan. Several audience members attributed this failure to Greek-Cypriot racism toward Turkish Cypriots. A Turkish academic in the room, who taught at a university in the north, said she wanted to apologize to Cypriots, and especially to Turkish Cypriots, for Turkey's role in the situation. She apologized "on behalf of the Turkish left" for their ignorance about the "realities of this situation." She had come to Cyprus thinking she understood the occupation, she said, but after watching the film, she realized that she "knew nothing before" and now hoped the Turkish left would become much more active in helping to resolve the Cyprus Problem. A young American woman said she thought it would be better if the film could include nationalist or antireconciliation voices, since those seemed to her more representative of the Cypriots she knew; she had seen the film before she came to Cyprus, and it had not prepared her for the depth and entrenchment of mutual hostilities between the two communities.

Hadjipavlou and Merlen fielded this last comment together, explaining that they had wanted the film to have a "positive message" about the possibilities of reconciliation and to represent voices that were normally ignored or excluded in popular discourse: not only women's voices but also voices in support of peace. Yet they had long been aware of their tiny niche and their limited influence. Another HAD member in the audience agreed that they often found themselves "preaching to the converted." *It's always the same people who attend this kind of event*, she said. *If we're lucky, we'll see one or two new people. We never seem to be able to reach outside this small circle.* Other women in the audience talked about a HAD project that had done just that: the Peace Bus, which members would take to villages in the north and the south. On their visits, they would walk around, sit in coffeehouses, meet people and talk—"no lecturing about politics," as one participant explained, simply making introductions between Greek Cypriots and Turkish Cypriots and "getting to know one other." Another HAD member agreed that the Peace Bus was a very successful project. This film, on the other hand, she said, had been more effective at delivering its message of peace to international audiences than to Cypriots.

During the discussion, I was struck by how many in the audience spoke of a new understanding of Cypriot history inspired in them by the film. One woman, who identified herself as Greek Cypriot, confessed that she had never known that Turkish Cypriots had lived for years in enclaves. *I knew in a vague way that they lived in protected areas after 1963*, she said, *but I didn't know that they lived for so long like that, in tents, like refugees, like we [Greek Cypriots] did after the war.* She thanked the filmmakers for making this information available to a Greek-Cypriot audience. Her comment recalled to my mind a sequence midway through the film in which Nahide (Merlen) and Fatma, another Turkish-Cypriot woman who had spent most of her childhood in an enclave, speak of their need for the Greek-Cypriot community to acknowledge its attempted ethnic cleansing of Turkish Cypriots from the island in the 1960s. Seated next to Nahide in a quiet corner of her bookstore, Fatma speaks in English to Katrivanou, who is interviewing her off-camera:

FATMA: I need them to say that, sorry, we did a mistake, we tried to . . . we tried this once, ethnic cleansing. We're sorry on that. This was a mistake; we will never attempt it again. Something like this.

NAHIDE: We need this.

KATRIVANOU: You need an apology?

FATMA: An apology, or to say that, yeah, yeah, we did this, but it was a mistake.

NAHIDE: We need it because we want to live together.

FATMA: Because this is not an invasion, this is not an occupation done by an army. This is what a community did [to] another community. So you need the community to tell you that we did a mistake. We will not attempt it again. It is a mistake; you're our brothers, sisters, whatever it is. But, never [have they said this]. They even deny it, that this happened. Maybe this is the main thing that will bring trust. This is what I'm thinking.



Intercut with this interview footage is a series of black-and-white images —schoolchildren gathered for a group photograph, women working in a backyard garden—and slow-motion black-and-white footage of buildings burning, faceless soldiers throwing grenades, people leaving their villages on foot or in the beds of pickup trucks, crying, hunched over, bandaged, as an elderly woman in a headscarf looks on. The archival material is clearly positioned within the unfolding interview as proof of the events that Fatma and Nahide are accusing the Greek-Cypriot community of denying, and thus as exposing and rendering visible a hidden history that has remained unknown ever since, at least to some Greek Cypriots, on their own admission.

The film makes extensive use of archival material in this evidentiary mode. Katrivanou's interviews with Cypriot women are intercut with old photographs and film footage: images, in black and white and color, of British soldiers checking Cypriots' identity papers in the 1950s; of EOKA rallies against the British led by Archbishop Makarios, later elected president of the newly independent Republic of Cyprus; of Turkish Cypriots fleeing Nicosia in 1963 as their businesses and homes fell to fires set by Greek-Cypriot extremists; of Turkish Cypriots leaving their villages in busloads in 1964; of Turkish Cypriots living in tents throughout the 1960s; of Greek Cypriots living in tents after the invasion in 1974; of Turkish bombers flying overhead, and naval vessels landing at Kyrenia in the summer of 1974; of Greek-Cypriot women and children gathered in village streets, awaiting the return of their husbands, fathers, and brothers taken prisoner by the Turkish army. As the interview subjects speak, or as Katrivanou speaks for them in voice-over, this archival material plays without captions or credits, as if directly illustrating their personal memories.[19] The film returns to the archive again and again, retracing the same events of violence and displacement in 1960, 1963–64, and 1974, following not a chronological narrative but rather the errant trails of different subjects' memories, finding slightly different images to illustrate slightly different iterations of the events. Discrepancies among these iterations are resolved as each story is tied in the same way to archival evidence, rendering them all equally credible.



The archival material in *Women of Cyprus*—marked not only by the grainy, faded quality of the material itself, but also by its presentation in a 4:3 frame inset into the 16:9 frame of the film—includes a series of quotations from other documentary films and television programs. Although any use of archival material entails repetition, an important distinction obtains between the reproduction of archival material from an original source and quotation of archival material as it has been used in another film or television program, which entails an additional stage or layer of mediation (or repression, as Derrida has it) by the director and editor, including more or less witting participation in generic documentary conventions. As archival sources, the film credits list the PIOs in the north and the south, the Greek-Cypriot television channel Mega, and the work of two Cypriot filmmakers: Antonis (Tony) Angastiniotis, a Greek-Cypriot photojournalist and activist whose films, *Voice of Blood* (2004) and *Voice of Blood 2: Searching for Selden* (2005), document massacres of Turkish-Cypriot villagers by Greek Cypriots in the summer of 1974; and Michael Cacoyannis, the Greek-Cypriot film director perhaps best known for his 1964 feature *Zorba the Greek,* whose one documentary film, *Attila '74*, was shot in Cyprus immediately after the coup and invasion in July and August 1974. Sequences from both films are quoted without citation or comment in *Women of Cyprus,* alongside reproduced footage from the PIO archives of events in 1963–64 and 1974—thus seemingly transparently to depict moments of a single, seamless history of conflict, without heeding the discrepant conditions under which this complex visual record had been produced.

I point this out not to criticize the technique but rather to note its conventionality and ubiquity; archival material reproduced (or quoted) without sourcing was commonplace in documentary films made in and about Cyprus, contributing to a densely visual mediation of collective memory in which footage of the events could become familiar to audiences without carrying any particular knowledge about the events themselves nor about what the footage framed out. Thus, while such footage might be recognizably Cypriot, and some audience members might recognize it in precise detail, others might not know in what year or place it was shot, not to mention by whom, or why; it could represent the past both specifically and generically.

Among Cypriot documentary films of the postwar period that have become sources of archival material for more recent films, one of the best known is Cacoyannis's *Attila '74*, which focuses on Greek-Cypriot participants and victims in the war of 1974. Shot in color, and presented in Greek with English subtitles, the film was released in Greece in 1975 by Fox Lorber, an international distribution company, which rereleased the film internationally in 2000 with a new epilogue. It has been widely seen both in and outside Cyprus since its release. Although its presentation of events is unarguably one-sided—apart from the Turkish-Cypriot leader Raouf Denktaş, Turkish Cypriots are never shown or heard in the film—*Attila '74* has been mined for original footage of the war's aftermath by contemporary filmmakers with a more bicommunally balanced eye, such as Katrivanou and Azzouz.



The film opens with scenes of bombed-out, divided Nicosia, its abandoned neighborhoods in rubble. A voice-over by Cacoyannis swiftly outlines the events leading up to the war and the unfolding of the war itself. The film shifts to interviews with Archbishop Makarios, Nikos Sampson (head of the short-lived coupist-led government), and Glafkos Clerides (a Greek-Cypriot politician who briefly held the presidency before the restoration of Makarios, and who was himself later elected president of the Republic); to a high-profile meeting between Clerides and Raouf Denktaş at the Ledra Palace Hotel; and to interviews with Greek-Cypriot soldiers injured by coupists, doctors at a Nicosia hospital who treated those wounded during the coup and the invasion, rape victims at a Nicosia clinic, EOKA-B combatants and supporters, a village priest who had buried most of his covillagers, and two museum directors who had witnessed the destruction of their collections. These interviews are intercut with footage of refugee camps, villages in the south ravaged by the war, prisoners of war returning from Turkey, the incipient Missing Persons office in Nicosia, and the pro-Makarios rally in Limassol where Greek-Cypriot civilians were shot by Greek-Cypriot EOKA-B gunmen in September 1974.

The film uses very little archival material itself: overlaid radio broadcasts from the morning of the coup, falsely announcing the death of Makarios, play in several languages behind Cacoyannis's footage of Makarios walking amid the rubble of the presidential palace, only a few months later; and several short film sequences, cut from CyBC footage, depict the deployment of unidentified soldiers, bombs exploding in Kyrenia, and refugees fleeing their

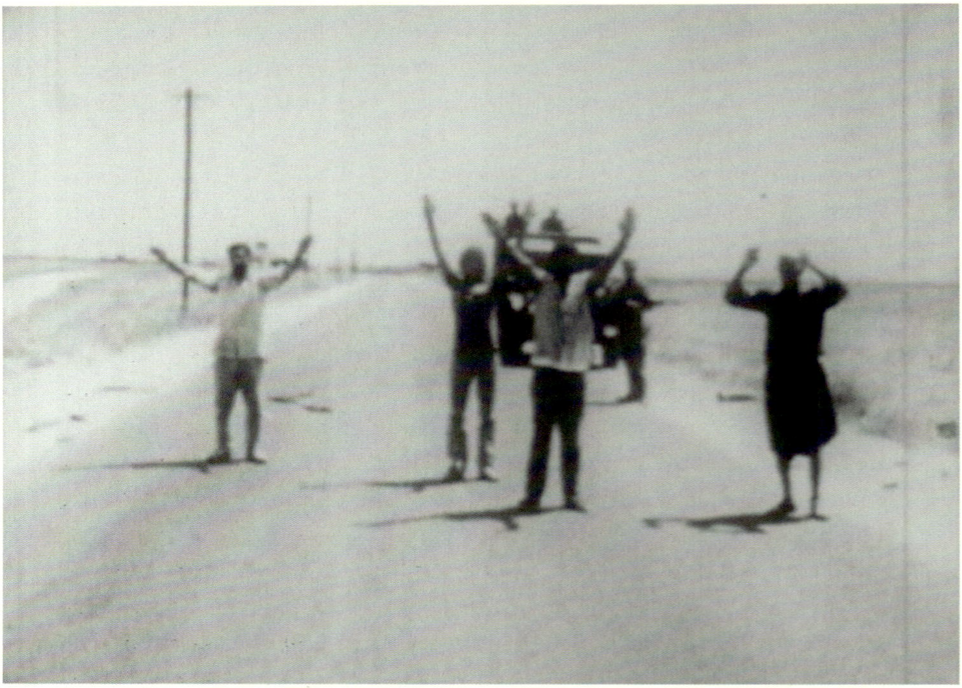

NO.

**2.11**

homes. The proximity of those events to the time of Cacoyannis's filming, a month or so later, establishes an easy continuity between the archival footage and his own. His use of archival material is minimal and unremarkable; it blends smoothly, both visually and narratively, into the unfolding drama of the war he is documenting. It is his original footage—notably, sequences showing refugee life in the camps, crowds awaiting the return of prisoners of war from Turkey, and his interviews with refugee children wounded during attacks on their villages—that has been quoted so extensively in more recent documentary films.

At the H4C screening of *Women of Cyprus* in November 2011, I had a jarring experience: I reencountered an archival moving image in the film, unattributed, that I had already seen in another documentary film, also without attribution. Even the first time I saw this image, it had already resembled other archival images I was then seeing in many Cypriot documentary films. As a novice to the repertoire in the early days of my fieldwork, I was seeing many things for the first time, in a cumulative mode, and I understood that process as one of developing an aesthetic sense of the genre. I was seeing connections and not troubled by how one image resembled another; indeed, in seeing their resemblance—as it appeared to me via the juxtaposition and repetition of archival material in film after film—I created the connections I was seeking. I was enchanted, thus, by a documentary theory of evidence that determined the power of unique archival images to represent generalized experiences. But reseeing that particular archival image at the screening of *Women of Cyprus* in 2011, I became "estranged" from this documentary theory, in the way Shklovsky describes Tolstoy's technique of estrangement, presenting familiar images—familiar, and thus usually experienced as recognized—as if they were being seen for the first time (Shklovsky [1919] 2015, 163).[20] In this estranged way, I saw the archival image as a gambit, a spell being cast—a technique of persuading the audience that one thing was really another. Instead of seeing evidence, I saw how the evidence was made.

In *Women of Cyprus*, this moving image appears in a long archival montage about eighteen minutes into the film. It is a three-second clip of black-and-white footage showing four men in civilian clothes standing in a road with their hands up, held at gunpoint by several soldiers who stand behind them. The men face toward the camera, their backs to the soldiers and their tank. A media logo in the upper left corner of the clip, and its insetting into a small filmstrip-like frame, mark it as archival material; its graininess and half a dozen vertical scratch lines suggest its age. In Katrivanou's voice-over, the image is offered as one of many illustrations of Cypriots taken as prisoners of war in August 1974.

After the screening, I tried to track this moving image down, and I located it in a chain of quotations in a series of Cypriot documentary films. The first of these chronologically was *Trimithi, a Reconstruction in Words*, directed by the Greek-Cypriot filmmaker Andreas Pantzis. Coproduced by the CyBC and the Cyprus Film Council, and recorded in black and white between 1981 and 1987, the film is anchored in interviews with Greek-Cypriot refugees from the village of Trimithi in the hills above Kyrenia (Girne), a port city on the northern coast. Pantzis elicits their memories of the village, the coup, and the war, interrupted at key moments by sequences of archival footage showing soldiers with machine guns, walking down a road toward the camera in advance of a tank; hundreds of tents at a refugee camp; soldiers and tanks deploying in fields; helicopters and bombers filling the sky; warships docking and paratroopers landing; crowds waiting for prisoners of war to return from Turkey, and busloads of prisoners returning to embrace their family members. These archival interruptions situate and thicken the interviews, in which villagers recall in intimate detail their own experiences of the war. In one remarkable segment, an elderly woman from Trimithi tells Pantzis of the advance on the village by Turkish soldiers, as archival footage of soldiers and tanks moving down a dirt road appears for the second time in the film—suggesting, falsely, its depiction of the Trimithi attack that the woman is describing. Such archival sequences only indirectly substantiate the villagers' memories; their juxtaposition with interview footage confers on these fragments a place in the film's story of Trimithi, but not a stable place in a veridical history of the war.

The film is punctuated midway by a disorienting and ominous scene, on which Pantzis dwells for several minutes. The same clip of four men held at gunpoint that Katrivanou and Azzouz use briefly in *Women of Cyprus* appears here in a much longer sequence. Here, the four men are shown being apprehended on a road by soldiers with machine guns and a tank; one of the men, shown from several angles, identifies their home villages in Greek—Peristerona, Gaidoura, Trimithi—before a Turkish officer orders their hands up. This sequence opens with the pulsing repetition of the four villagers putting their hands up, jumps back to the start of the scene, unfolds in slow motion, and then loops several times as the same phrase—"Hands up!" shouted by one of the officers—echoes and reverberates. The next cut is to an interview with an elderly villager, who recalls how Trimithi was taken by the Turkish army, the men separated from the women and children and then killed, their bodies left in the village for the others to find. Pantzis emphatically marks the archival nature of this footage of the men, rendering it in black and white, aging it while also matching it with his own black-and-white palette; the archival sequence runs at an appreciably slower pace than the interview sequences, and the grainy, damaged quality of both picture and sound is exaggerated. As the film proceeds, the archival footage reappears several times, in decontextualized fragments, stuttering and looping like a recurring nightmare, precluding its incorporation into a straightforward visual narrative.

The same scene of the men at gunpoint also appears in *Our Wall*, the documentary film made in 1993 by Panicos Chrysanthou and Niyazi Kızılyürek. In that film, the short sequence plays during a voice-over narration of the coup and the first Turkish invasion in July 1974. Two voices take turns in the narration: one, in Turkish, describes the invasion as a necessary response to the coup in order to restore peace, as footage rolls of a journalist reporting from a field in the north where Turkish paratroopers are landing. Chrysanthou takes over the narration, describing the same events, in Greek, as a shock, a betrayal, a confusion, and a catastrophe. The Turkish-speaking narrator resumes, describing the Turkish military actions as the joyous beginning of a long-awaited dream of peace; but then Chrysanthou's voice-over starts up again, describing the flight of Greek Cypriots from the Turkish army as the scene with the four men at gunpoint flashes up. In this thirteen-second sequence, the voices of the Greek-Cypriot civilian and the Turkish officer are both audible, and the scene plays out in its entirety, at speed. The film cuts smoothly to a scene of several people—presumably though not obviously Greek Cypriot—rushing down a city street, encumbered by belongings.



The same footage of the four villagers arrested on the road appears as well in *In This Waiting*, a documentary film directed by Anna Tsiarta, funded by the Ministry of Education and Culture in the Republic, and screened at the Lemesos International Documentary Film Festival in August 2011. Tsiarta's film takes up the ongoing story of the missing in Cyprus; relatives of the missing, Greek-Cypriot and Turkish-Cypriot, figure as the principal subjects of the film. Long interviews with these relatives are intercut with archival footage of the war and present-day footage of CMP forensic teams working to exhume and analyze the remains of the missing. Tsiarta does not visibly edit the footage of the men at gunpoint, which is presented here in its entirety, in its original color, and at speed—a quick eight seconds, as compared with the thirty-second sequence Pantzis renders from it. Here, what happened to the four men on the road is suspected but not known—an episode in a history of violence conducted in secret and covered up afterward. We learn where the men have come from, but not the circumstances or the site of their deaths. In this film, which focuses specifically and intently on the missing, Tsiarta's use of this footage implies that the four men on the road are in fact among the missing whose recovery by forensic teams is currently underway, as documented in the film. The brief scene is evidence: something happened, even if it is not known exactly what. The footage is a clue that opens an investigation.



The archival fragment in these four films is identical as a source but flexible and varied in its use. In Pantzis's film, the scene has little evidentiary value; it works more to disturb than to document. His film—a one-sided vision of the war, if not a Greek-Cypriot nationalist invective—foregrounds the experience of shock, confusion, and haunting consequent to violence. Tsiarta's film, on the other hand, a bicommunal work of reconciliation and resignation, foregrounds the forensic register of evidence, seamlessly connecting the archival footage of the men held at gunpoint to more recent footage of bones being exhumed, creating a rich ellipsis to suggest what happened in between. In Chrysanthou and Kızılyürek's film, the scene is anchored in contradictory narratives: one, in which the arrest of the men—perhaps not innocent civilians at all but armed irregulars implicated in the coup—appears an act of justice; and another, in which the same arrest of the men portends their cold-blooded, illegal, and secret murder. Chrysanthou and Kızılyürek do not alter the archival footage, as Pantzis does, but their oscillating narration over the intact footage works effectively to undermine its transparency as evidence.

Another rich site of repetition in recent Cypriot documentary films is an episode of mass violence in 1974 whose aftermath was captured by several cameras, Cypriot and foreign. This material formed part of the well-established iconography of violence in the north, but it was not seen in the south until very recently, and it seems to have been the avowed intention of several filmmakers to expose Greek-Cypriot audiences to it. Among these was Derviş Zaim, who collaborated with Chrysanthou on their 2004 documentary *Parallel Trips*, described in the opening credits as "a Turkish-Cypriot/Greek-Cypriot co-production." An early version of the film was shown to a small audience in Nicosia shortly after its release in 2004, and the final version had a public screening at the Eirini gallery during the second Festival of the Green Line in April 2011. The film was made (and set) in 2003, just before and just after the opening of the checkpoints between north and south. It is presented in two parts, each divided into parts. Part one of the film explores two stories of massacres in 1974: the first, at Pa-

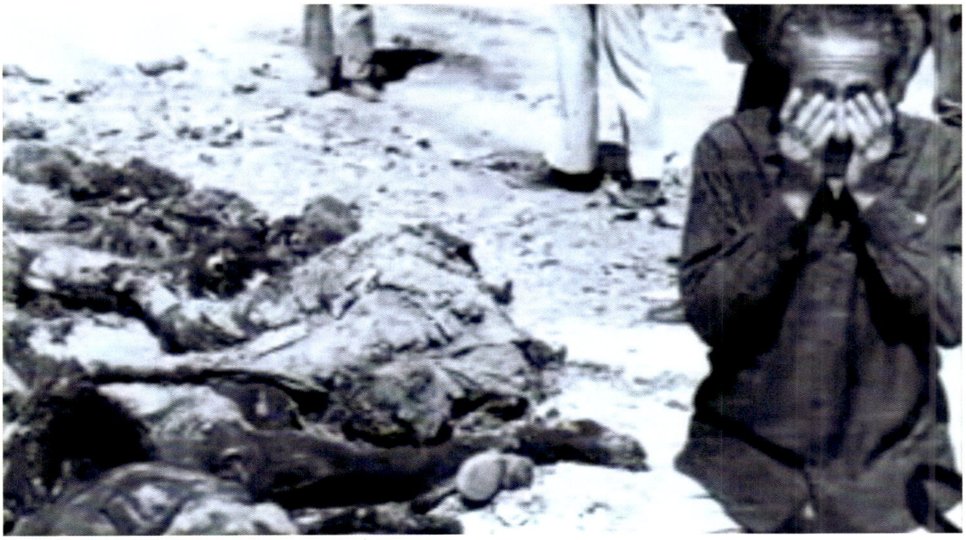

NO.

2.12

laikythro (Balıkesir), where seventeen Greek Cypriots were killed; the second, at the villages of Muratağa (Maratha), Atlılar (Aloa), and Sandallar (Santallaris), where 126 Turkish Cypriots altogether were killed. Part two of the film presents five personae—three Turkish Cypriots and two Greek Cypriots—each of whom was deeply wounded by these events. This structure was evidently designed for balance between Turkish-Cypriot and Greek-Cypriot narratives, even though the narratives themselves persistently upset that balance with the singularity and irreducibility of the deaths, injuries, and losses they communicate.



In a sequence from part one of the film, several unnamed Turkish-Cypriot men who survived the massacres at Muratağa, Atlılar, and Sandallar, interviewed in 2003 at ages ranging from their fifties to their eighties, appear as young men in archival color footage, crying, praying, and staring at the military excavation of the mass grave in Muratağa in 1974. From an interview with one of these men in the present, the screen fades to black, and then fills again with archival footage. The excavation site slowly comes into focus, silent at first; crying is the first sound to arise, and then, in the background, the plinking of shovels striking dirt and the clicking camera of a journalist. The film cuts back to the interview subject, then quickly to a series of archival black-and-white photographs of the survivors, covering their mouths or their noses or their eyes, kneeling by the mass grave or standing at a distance. Another interview subject speaks, drawing the momentum of the film back into the present and holding it there.

The same horrifying scene of the excavation at Muratağa appears in several other recent documentary films. Tony Angastiniotis's films, *Voice of Blood* and *Voice of Blood 2: Searching for Selden*, both feature several long sequences of photographs and footage from the excavation. The two films, narrated in Turkish and Greek, based on Angastiniotis's interviews with survivors of the massacres at Muratağa, Atlılar, and Sandallar, as well as footage from PIO archives, have been widely seen in the north of Cyprus. In the south, they have never been broadcast or publicly screened, and Angastiniotis himself—who identifies as Greek Cypriot (among other things) and is thus taken as a traitor by Greek-Cypriot ethnonationalists in the south—has been the target of press attacks and personal death threats.[21] His films are available on YouTube, where they appear to have found a large audience in the Cypriot diaspora in the UK and the United States.

The first film charts Angastiniotis's investigation of the massacres, intercutting his interviews with survivors and their descendants in the present with photographs of the victims in life and with footage of the mass-grave excavation at Murataǧa in 1974. The same material we see in *Parallel Trips* is treated differently here: sepia-filtered, drastically slowed, and stroboscopically sampled so that it shutters and pulses like an old filmstrip. Archival material is treated just as dramatically in the second *Voice of Blood* film, which opens with a direct address to the audience by Angastiniotis. He attributes to the investigative work he undertook for the first *Voice of Blood* his transformation from a vehement Greek-Cypriot nationalist invested in conflict into a truth teller and insider critic of the Greek-Cypriot side of the conflict. As he speaks, archival footage of soldiers, bombers, fighting, and running in the streets is projected on a screen behind him in a series of rapid, abrupt cuts.



The Murataǧa excavation also appears in *Homeland*, a 2010 film directed by Serkan Hussein and produced by Seren Gazi with the Association of Turkish Cypriots Abroad. Of recent Cypriot documentaries, this film is one of the most densely packed with archival material—much of which has never appeared in films focused on Greek Cypriots' experience of the conflict. Sources include the personal archives of the interview subjects; British and Turkish Cypriot newspapers (*Chening Standard*, *Daily Herald*, *Halkın Sesi*); Turkish-Cypriot and Turkish radio and television outlets, BRT (Bayrak Radio and Television, the national public broadcasting service in the north) and TRT (Turkish Radio and Television); the PIO in the north; and the United Nations archive. The film, narrated mostly in English, with English subtitles for interviews in Turkish, presents itself as a straightforward historical account of the conflict in Cyprus, tracing the bloodshed and the forcible displacement of civilians to decision making by political leaders. The interview subjects, mostly Turkish Cypriots living outside Cyprus, reflect on the origins of the conflict in the colonial period, their experiences of violence, and their lives in the enclaves from 1963 onward. Archival material is presented as transparent evidence of their experiences, pinned to the historical record with descriptive captions and dates. The film dwells insistently on violence, moving through dozens of photographs of Turkish Cypriots killed in 1963–64 and 1974, and film sequences showing homes and shops in Nicosia burning, wounded civilians being loaded onto ambulances, people leaving their villages en masse in buses, corpses in fields and on the floors of houses, public funerals, and the mass graves at Murataǧa and Alaminos. Stock footage of the same scenes of bombers, paratroopers, and Turkish soldiers that appear in many documentary films about Greek-Cypriot victimhood are presented here, on the contrary, as illustrations of the heroic rescue of Turkish Cypriots from Greek-Cypriot violence.

The recycling and reiteration of stock footage among multiple films was only one form of repetition in the Cypriot documentary genre, as I found it. Repetition of archival images and sequences within films was equally prevalent, although filmmakers engaged in this technique to different ends. In *Kayıp Otobüs (Lost Bus)*, a 2007 documentary film by Turkish-Cypriot director Fevzi Tanpınar, for example, the camera returns again and again to personal and family photographs of the film's key subjects, as if to imprint their faces indelibly onto the viewer's memory. The film's scriptwriter, Raşit Pertev, appears several times in the film, speaking about his own memories of the people and events addressed by the film; the photographs, he says, are ones he has collected from friends and neighbors in his village. After its release, *Kayıp Otobüs* screened at film festivals in Antalya, Brussels, Boston, New York, and Washington, DC—not in Cyprus—but found its largest audience on Cypriot television. It was broadcast on BRT on December 16, 2008, and has been rebroadcast a number of times since.[22]



The film treats the story of eleven Turkish-Cypriot men—ten employees at the British military base in Dikhelia, along with a bus driver—who departed the Turkish-Cypriot enclave in Larnaca by bus, heading for the base, on the morning of May 13, 1964, and never returned. This case of missing persons, whose remains were found and exhumed in the nearby village of Oroklini by the CMP in 2006, and identified and returned to the families, is one of the best known among Turkish Cypriots. The "legend" of the lost bus, as Pertev describes it, serves as a touchstone for storytelling and memory work throughout the film, which sticks closely to the events leading up to the men's disappearance, and their relatives' and neighbors' endless speculation and waiting for their return in the months and years afterward. Throughout the film, Tanpınar stages reconstructions of the events of May 13, 1964, presenting slow-motion, sepia-toned sequences of a young boy accompanying his father to a bus stop, the progress of an antique wood-paneled bus down the dusty road from Larnaca to Dikhelia, the detention of the bus and the threatening of its passengers by Greek-Cypriot soldiers with machine guns, and, ultimately, the massacre of the passengers. These reconstructions fade into interviews with relatives of the victims—their wives, siblings, and children—whose memories of the missing men are illustrated with black-and-white photographs of them, working in uniform at the British base or standing for wedding and family portraits. Some of these images, cropped to show only the victims' faces, reappear in the closing credits as the official photographs in their missing persons case files, flashing onto the screen as each victim's name, village, family status, and date of disappearance is typed out on a simulated missing persons form.

These specific and personalized images of the eleven victims mix in the film with stock footage of the conflicts in 1963–64: black-and-white footage of people running down streets or running away from explosions, mothers with crying children, old women staring, soldiers with machine guns and rifles shooting unpictured targets or apprehending people in the streets, state officials marching to meetings, scenes of dust-encased rubble and people living in tents. Tanpınar slows this footage down as the testimony of his interview subjects plays in voice-over, anchoring their personal memories in the historical time implied by the moving images. But the camera always returns to the photographs. In a sequence midway through the film, one woman, the daughter of one of the victims, rues the absence of any personal memories of her father: "You only have a picture of your father in your imagination," she says, emphatically. Tanpınar insists on the significance of photographs to the children of the missing; a minute later, the son of another of the victims, now middle aged, appears next to his own young son as they look together through a photo album. "The children of the missing had their eyes on the road for forty-two years," the narrator explains. The film cuts next to a long segment with a tearful man, son of another victim, framed by black-and-white photographs of his parents and himself as a child, recounting his memories of his father.



In *Kayıp Otobüs*, Tanpınar does not explicitly entertain evidentiary questions about the archive from which he has reconstructed the fate of the lost bus and its passengers. The photographs of the victims, and the stock footage of violent events in 1963–64, along with other visual artifacts such as newspaper pages with headlines about the lost bus, stand as the factual grounds on which other kinds of knowledge might be built—not only Tanpınar's maudlin reconstructions of the day of the disappearance, but also the speculative knowledge accumulated over the years by relatives of the victims. Several wives of the missing men speak on camera about their attempts to learn the fate of their husbands by visiting "mediums," women who read coffee grounds and broad beans, a customary practice of prognostication. They speak of all the rumors they heard in the years after the disappearance, apparent sightings of their husbands, theories about their capture and detention by Greek or Greek-Cypriot troops. These forms of speculative knowledge are swiftly refuted by a short scene halfway through the film, showing footage of the CMP excavation of the mass grave in Oroklini, in a well near an olive grove. A long sequence follows, featuring eight relatives of different victims, discussing their mixed feelings about the discovery of the grave and their burdensome obligation to receive their husband's or father's bones after so many years.

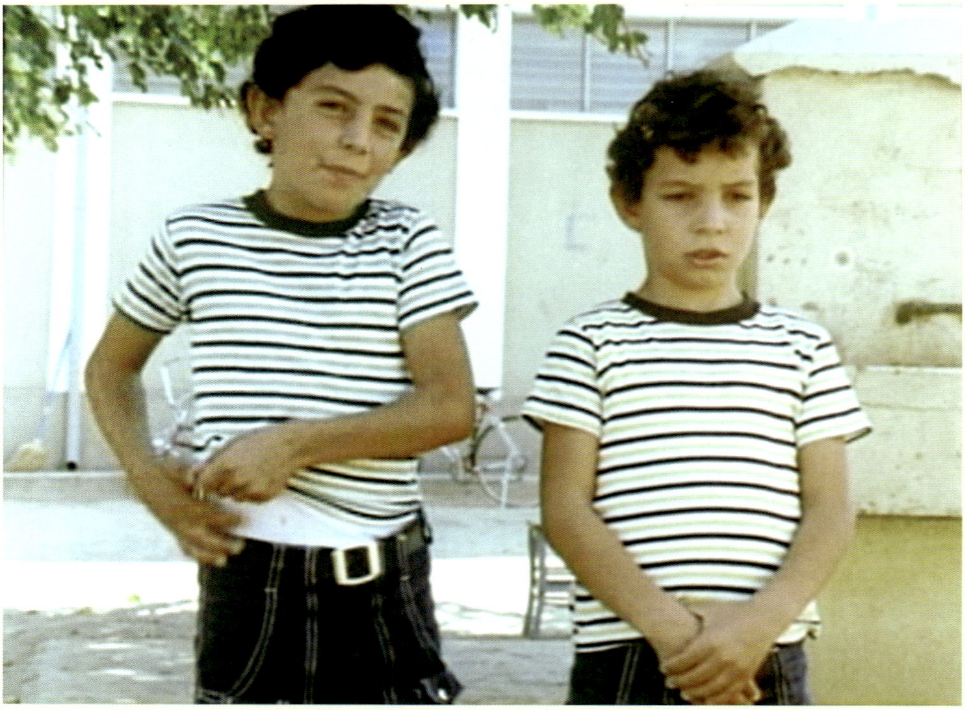

NO.

2.13

*Kayıp Otobüs* trades in many conventions of the documentary genre in Cyprus, including the intercutting of interviews with footage of the events under discussion in order to substantiate the memories of the interview subjects, and the visual differentiation of archival material by altering its color and speed. But the dominant documentary trope in the film is the use of photographs to personalize and concretize the experiences of the conflict rendered by the film. These photographs, and the narratives of interview subjects that accompany them, oscillate between the personal and the generic, counting on the audience's valorization of family bonds and, in particular, the importance of husbands to wives and fathers to children, in order to reckon the destruction of families wreaked by the conflict as a more general destruction of Cypriot society. This mode of eliciting empathy and recognition was not, of course, innovated in Cyprus; it is a long-standing convention of documentary films from many other sites of war and conflict worldwide. But its conventionality did not necessarily undermine its effectiveness or appeal. Indeed, I heard quite a few Cypriots mention *Kayıp Otobüs* as an important documentary film about the missing; many of the Turkish-Cypriot scientists I knew at the CMP had seen it and suggested that I see it. I sensed that, for these people—many of whom had worked on the Oroklini excavation or the analysis of the remains exhumed there—this film was a testament to the importance of their work, which operated on the same level as forensic substantiation of a secret history of violence. The very conventionality of the archival material in the film is what established its efficacy as evidence.



A more innovative use of personal photographs distinguishes *Parallel Trips*, the 2004 film by Zaim and Chrysanthou, from many other Cypriot documentary films of the post-2003 period. *Parallel Trips* does closely follow some documentary conventions of memory and commemoration—for example, lengthy talking-head interviews in which each subject's experience unfolds from beginning to end, anchored by a traumatic event and intercut with B-roll footage of the subject going about the everyday activities of his or her present life. Yet the use of archival material to concretize and enhance the memories of these subjects is striking. As I noted above, many Cypriot documentary films use stock photographs and footage of public events to illustrate the very personal memories of interview subjects who do not actually appear in those archival images. In *Parallel Trips*, on the other hand, archival photographs and footage depict the interview subjects themselves, as they appeared at the time of the events they are now remembering on film, many years later. In part two, for example, Panayiota, the wife of a man who went missing during the early days of the war, here filmed in 2003, in her sixties, appears in an intercut sequence in archival black-and-white footage as a young woman, living in refugee housing with her young son in 1974, recounting how her husband had disappeared only a few months before. Similarly, in part one, Petros, who at the age of ten survived an attack on his family at Palaikythro with several gunshot wounds in 1974, appears as a grown man in 2003; his young daughter is shown thumbing through a book documenting the massacre, pausing at several black-and-white photographs of Petros and his brother Costas as young children, displaying their wounds to the camera. Petros might be familiar to audiences in Cyprus from his interview as a young boy by Michael Cacoyannis in *Attila '74*. His appearance in *Parallel Trips* alongside his brother, Costas, as they also appeared in *Attila '74*, is not a quotation of the earlier film; rather, their retelling of their experience in 2003 summons the archival footage from Cacoyannis's film into the present documentary frame in a ghostly form, while the archival photographs of the two brothers, seen by Petros's daughter in a book, appear in the new footage in material form. This sequence in *Parallel Trips* thus becomes artifactual, visualizing the presence of the past to convey documentary knowledge.



Chrysanthou employs this same technique during a seven-and-a-half-minute sequence in *Our Wall* featuring Fatma, an elderly woman known to both Chrysanthou and Niyazi Kızılyürek, the coproducer of the film. Both men appear in this sequence, hailing Fatma as "Aunt" when they visit her at her home in Potamia (Bodamya). This was and remains a mixed village, located just south of the Green Line; along with Pyla, in the south, and Rizokarpaso, in the north, it is one of very few communities in which Greek Cypriots and Turkish Cypriots continued to live together after the division. In the sequence, Fatma, chain-smoking and dressed in black from head to toe, speaks in Turkish (to Kızılyürek) and Greek (to Chrysanthou), blesses them, and joins them at her kitchen table to talk. Chrysanthou shows her a photograph of her in her youth with a man she identifies as Güney, a man who "took [her] in his arms," as she recalls, tearfully, but who has since "passed on."[23] As she wipes tears from her face with a rag, the scene fades to black-and-white footage, shot decades earlier, of her making the same gesture in a hospital bed, a much younger woman with jet-black hair, but recognizably herself. The scene cuts back to the present, and Fatma recounts, in Turkish, the experience that had put her in the hospital all those years ago. She tells Chrysanthou and Kızılyürek that she was attacked back then in a coffee shop by a man with a stick, who struck her, broke her hand,

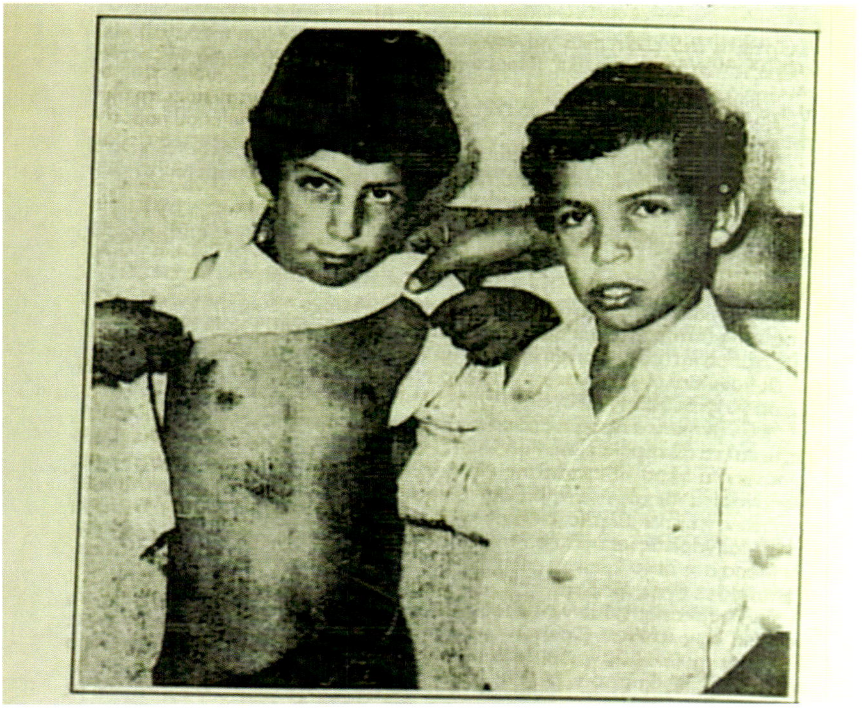

NO.

2.14

and ran off. The scene cuts back to her in the hospital, where she tells the story to Chrysanthou, who is interviewing her off-camera. The story differs here, in the past; in Greek, she tells Chrysanthou that it was three men who attacked her and that she stayed in the hospital for almost two weeks. Once she returned home, she says, she was called back by her doctor, but the village *mukhtar* warned her not to go back because "they were killing Turks" in the hospitals. She was stuck at home for a long time, she says; no one was allowed to visit or speak to her, or help her get to the hospital. Cut to the present, and she names the "TMT rascals" and "those Christian ones . . . EOKA"—"the worst kind of people"—as those who isolated and attacked her in those days because she worked as a cook in a Greek tavern, and "loved Christians and respected them." Speaking now, as an elderly woman who has survived her attack and all the years since, she pleads for opening roads and telephone lines in Cyprus, for connection, for peace, for teachers and parents to show children that "we are all human beings. We must not hate each other." The next cut is to a short archival montage of footage from 1963–64, showing men being equipped with guns, men bandaging other men's wounds, images of buildings destroyed by bombs and fire.

The continuity between that past and this present is complicated but not disrupted by the changing details of Fatma's story of her attack; the clear resemblance between the young and the elderly Fatma, sustained by artful cuts between archival and contemporary footage, anchors her story in history even as it questions the precision and testimonial value of memory. But the movement between past and present does more than render her story historical; it also works an irreducible heterogeneity into the present, as the story Fatma tells now on film contains the past version as well as the present one. What the film shows as difference in the stories is precisely what memory would erase or repress over time. In this case, the archival footage permits the filmmaker to give visual form and, more to the point, material form to that difference: decades-old black-and-white film is physically intercut with new color film, to show not only a historical fact but also the way it was made: artifactually.

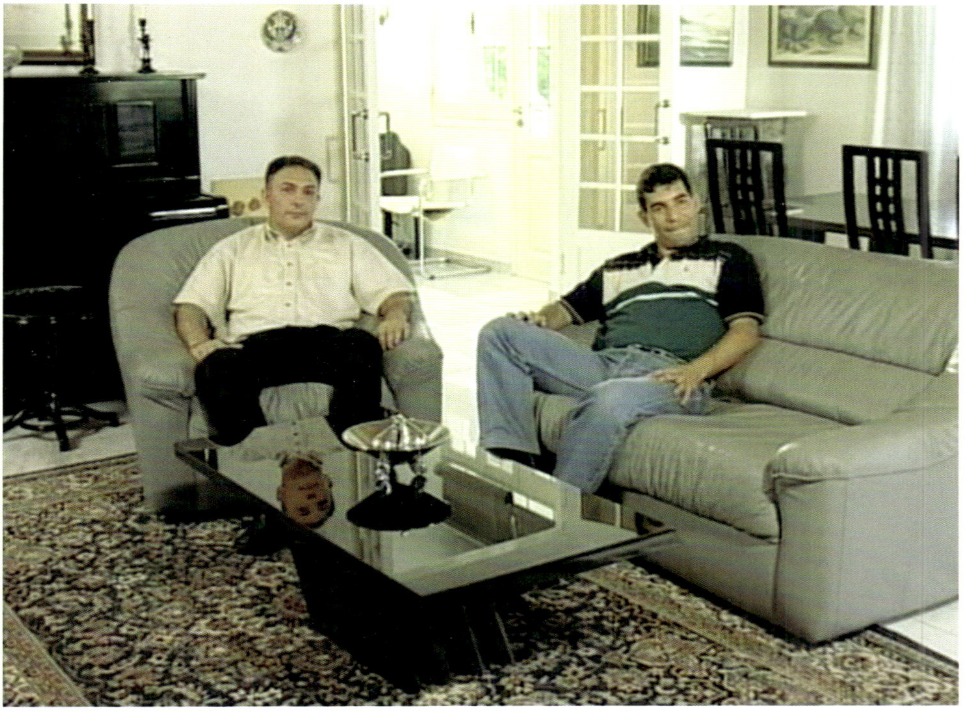

NO.

2.15

## A Crystal Image of Time

In many Cypriot documentary films made since 2003, such as *Homeland* and *Women of Cyprus*, archival material was treated literally and prosaically, without reflection on its conditions of production or its evidentiary status. Some Cypriot filmmakers, however, took a more imaginative and critical approach to archival material, subjecting it to aesthetic processes of damage and transfer, fragmentation and rearrangement. For these filmmakers, archival aesthetics described a creative element in their work as well as a political one; the artifactual techniques they used to transform archival material aesthetically were also a means of experimenting with time and history.



This aesthetic approach to the archive is evident in *Still*, the short documentary by Alana Kakoyiannis discussed earlier. The film opens with the archive. Günay and Niki are the two women who will ultimately emerge onscreen as the principal subjects of the film: a Turkish Cypriot and a Greek Cypriot, both refugees from violence and upheaval (in 1964 and 1974, respectively). Not yet seen in the opening sequence of the film, they speak of their flight from their homes as archival footage rolls, showing people leaving their villages in buses and living in tents, and victims of the violence tended to in a makeshift hospital. The footage is inset in a 7:5 frame within the 16:9 frame of the film. The source material is treated to appear old and frail: grainy, scratched, washed out, slowed down, overlaid sequences generating disjointed passages. The film emerges from this opaque and confusing place of spectral memory into Kakoyiannis's own clear, bright footage of one of the women in the present day, occupying the entire screen and a full spectrum of ambient sound.

This passage from the archive to the present is highlighted by the alteration of the archival material. Kakoyiannis draws from a common aesthetic tool kit here, as Angastiniotis does in *Voice of Blood*: insetting the material into a smaller frame within the screen of projection; altering speed and continuity; scratching, color treating, overexposing or underexposing; stroboscopic sampling to produce shuttering and pulsing; quick cuts and overlays. All these aesthetic devices signal the special status of archival footage as a privileged vision of the past. The source material is artificially aged and damaged to enhance its artifactual quality—to mark its survival not only of the passage of time but also of violent conflict. These artifactual techniques also accentuate the dense mediation of the past performed by these materials: they occlude, fragment, and in other ways distort our view of the past, rather than revealing it clearly and transparently. Kakoyiannis uses stock footage here from the archives of the PIO in the south. Footage like this—even this exact footage—has appeared in a number of other Cypriot documentary films made in the last decade; the distinctive mark of the artist inheres in her visible alteration of the material.

Artifactual techniques have likewise been applied to archival footage in the works of Alev Adil, a poet and a theorist of literature and technology who was raised in a Turkish-Cypriot enclave in north Nicosia before she moved to Great Britain. In a text explicating her "dérive" methodology of art making, Adil notes that hers was "an old Famagusta family" fractured by displacement to enclaves from 1968 to 1974, and thence dispersed to "Istanbul, London, Brussels or Palo Alto"; she takes this complex intergenerational family geography as grounds for her "auto-ethnographic" approach to Turkish-Cypriot and other "border" identities (Adil 2014, 99, 112, 98, 115).[24] In her visual and performance art, Adil uses photography and film to address the experience of conflict in Cyprus. Her collection *An Architecture of Forgetting: Journeys in the Dead Zone*, produced between 2006 and 2008, includes the short film *A Small Forgotten War* and two photographic series, *Dead Zone* and *Havana/Levkosha*, which concatenate present-day images of divided Nicosia in a virtual walking tour through the city.



Adil has also incorporated film footage of Cyprus in a series of multimedia pieces performed in Nicosia since 2010. One of these, *Memory in the Dead Zone*, which Adil performed at Sidestreets in April 2011 and at the ARTos Foundation in March 2012, features stock footage of the war from state archives in the north, as well as home video footage of family gatherings, children playing, friends walking down a quiet neighborhood street. The juxtaposition of such domestic scenes in the lives of strangers with scenes of mass violence that have so insistently framed media representations of the war introduces unease into the domestic scenes and likewise imbues the war footage with an uncanny intimacy.

Adil's performance of this work at the ARTos Foundation in March 2012, which I attended, was part of the collective event Vivid Poetry: *Αλλιώς* [Otherwise], featuring works by Greek-Cypriot and Turkish-Cypriot poets. The main performance space and overflow room were packed with an audience of at least a hundred people: artists and art students, actors, journalists, scholars, writers, and readers. Sequences of film footage, distorted and overlaid, were projected on a screen behind Adil as she read several poems and a performance script. In her poem "Dance the Ruined Map," she spoke of "a secret archive of inherited amnesia," an amnesia that recurred again in the longer poem, "The Eclipse Begins," invoked there as a "feeling" "unreadable" on the "mystic writing pad of history"—the device that Freud (and later, Derrida) offered as an analog or metaphor for the psychic apparatus of memory. Adil's poem wound around this metaphor, drawing history and memory into the same amnesiac space:

The eclipse begins.
The moon covers the sun,
the ghost of the shadow.
"Who are you?"
"Is that you?"
It's so dark ("Euridyce?")
in the golden light.
Disrobing, revealing her nothingness,
facts are more easily forgotten than
feelings.
Guilt replaces desire.
An eternal return
of the destiny written on your forehead,
an unreadable heritage,
the mystic writing pad of history.
Memory causes vertigo,
a vortex of feelings:
desire, altitude sickness, inherited
amnesia.
We mourn the inability to forget.
You remember something has been
forgotten.
A crystal image of time destroys the past,
a full moon of forgetting, to save the future.
I'm waiting for the future,
l'avenir, the one whose arrival cannot be
predicted.
They are ruined maps,
the languages that speak us,
your head on my shoulder,
your hand on my thigh.
The moon covers the sun again.[25]

In the lines of this poem, Adil spoke time and again of memory and forgetting, sometimes in the second person ("you remember something has been forgotten") and sometimes in the first-person collective ("we mourn the inability to forget"), but never in the first-person singular, "I." Nor were the images projected behind her illustrations of her own past. The shifting personae of her text and footage facilitated her exertion of easily forgotten facts, unreadable heritage, inherited amnesia: of a memory that something has been forgotten—not *what* it was, only *that* it was: a memory marking nothing more than the presence of the past.

The central image of Adil's poem is "a crystal image of time"—an evocation, I gather, of Deleuze in his theorization of the time-image in film, where he develops Henri Bergson's philosophy of "pure duration" (Bergson [1913] 2001, 100). What Deleuze calls "crystals of time" or the "crystal-image" is the "indivisible unity" of the actual and the virtual, where the actual comprises the present—time as we actually experience it—and the virtual comprises a kind of subjective reflection of the present: memory or, more precisely, the "virtual image" of "pure recollection," as well as desire and fantasy that constitute our experience of the future (Deleuze 1989, 78, 79, 80). The relation between the times of the actual and the virtual is not reducible to that between "now" and "then," however; as Deleuze explains, the past "does not follow the present that it is no longer, it coexists with the present it was" (79), continuing alongside the present as its virtual image: a sort of mirror image. Thus, he writes,



> the past is constituted not after the present that it was but at the same time, time has to split itself in two at each moment as present and past, or, what amounts to the same thing, it has to split the present in two heterogeneous directions, one of which is launched towards the future while the other falls into the past. . . . Time consists of this split, and it is this, it is time, that we *see in the crystal*. The crystal-image was not time, but we see time in the crystal. We see in the crystal the perpetual foundation of time, non-chronological time. (81, emphasis original)

What is crucial here—what can perhaps unlock Adil's "secret archive of inherited amnesia"—is that, in the crystal-image, the past and present are in a relation of "coalescence" (68, 78), "circuit" (70), or "exchange" (78), rather than a relation of sequence. Linearity is disrupted, and viewers are displaced in time or, rather, placed in many times simultaneously. The crystal-image is thus one of the filmic techniques that Deleuze associates with the powers of the false; it activates, as I noted in the introduction, the "simultaneity of incompossible presents, or the coexistence of not-necessarily true pasts" (131). In Adil's poem, the crystal image of time "destroys the past . . . to save the future." For readers or viewers with a historicist sensibility, who are prepared for a chronological narrative and a personal claim to mnemonic authority, this destruction of the past might seem tragic or horrific, and the future impossible to see without it. For Adil—at least, as I understood her piece; as it

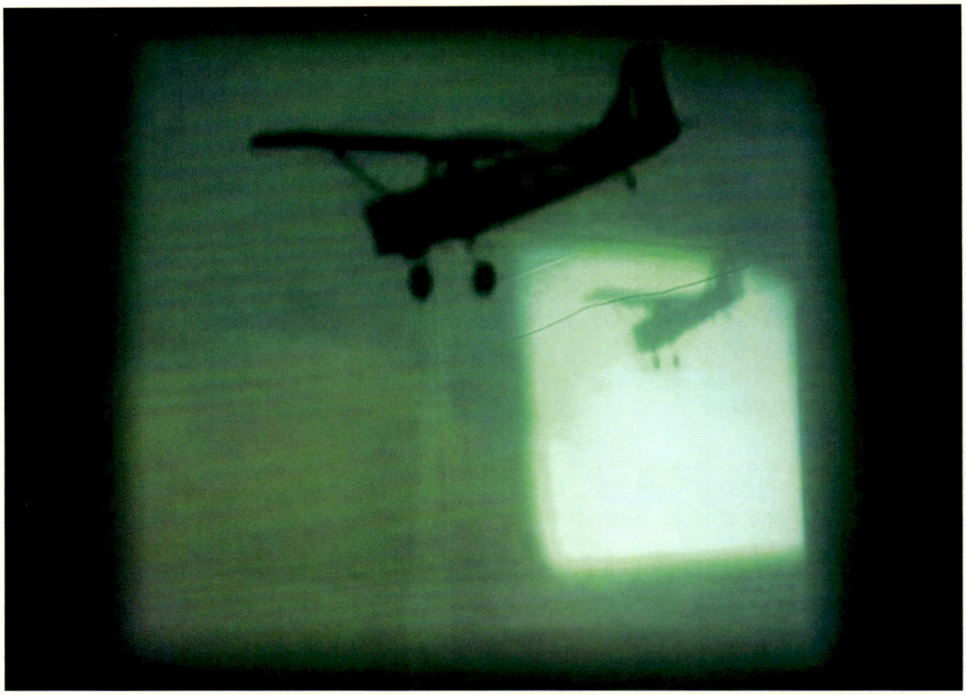

NO.

2.16

worked on me—it creates freedom from the actual; it opens up the possibility of difference, and becoming.

When I spoke with Adil after the performance, she described it to me as an attempt to weave together "the political and the auto-ethnographic." She explained that she did not use material from official archives but rather home videos from the personal archive of a close family friend, who had given her the footage as a gift. Originally on Super 8 film, this footage was converted to low-quality video, which was not only grainy and overly color saturated but also had an incompatible aspect ratio, cutting off the top and side edges of the original frame along with the tops of people's heads. Adil digitized and transferred the video to DVDs, then copied it again. She told me she had deliberately chosen the worst quality video segments and put it through the most damaging processes of transfer in order to emphasize the age, texture, and plasticity of the material. She also chose what she called "the most political" footage from this private, domestic source—such as the scene of a young man smiling into the camera as he holds up a piece of the wall from his house, fractured by bullets. 

By design, then, this material resonated with the generic home videos and family photographs employed in many Cypriot documentary films to construct a nostalgic narrative of peacetime prior to the war. Yet its visual distortion precluded its assimilation to that narrative; its departure from stock scenes of peaceful family life to include evidence of collective violence within the domestic space illustrated the inherently political nature of home. In this, Adil captured the ambivalence of photographic reference to history—what Hirsch specifies as the danger of "screen memories," comparing the use of photographs in two postmemorial works, Art Spiegelman's *Maus* and W. G. Sebald's *Austerlitz*. On Hirsch's telling, Sebald's character, Austerlitz, speaks of the "preformed images" through which "our concern with history" takes shape: "images at which we keep staring while the truth lies elsewhere, away from it all, somewhere as yet undiscovered" (Hirsch 2008, 120, citing Sebald 2001, 72). The capacity of such overly familiar images to obscure truth through misdirection, showing one thing while something else of greater importance remains unseen, describes precisely the trouble of the archive as a proxy for memory.

The power of archival images to disturb memory, to fragment and reassemble outside the structure of a coherent narrative, is mobilized in a different way in *Intramural*, a 2001 documentary film by the Greek-Cypriot director Elias Demetriou.[26] This film, produced by ERT (Hellenic Broadcasting Corporation), was shot in 2001, two years before the checkpoints opened, and set exclusively in the south. It focuses on the division of the island, featuring interviews with a number of Greek-Cypriot scholars, artists, and journalists who comment on the origins of the conflict and its implications decades later, including the absolute mutual alienation of Turkish Cypriots and Greek Cypriots, and the censorship of discussions about any political issues besides the conflict. Toward the end of the film—as the anthropologist Yiannis Papadakis discusses the representation of the Cyprus conflict as a tragic drama in documentary films, critically noting their exclusion of paradox, irony, and humor—Demetriou presents a short montage of stills from *Attila '74* and other Cypriot documentary films, thus building this archival material into his own film, an archive in its own right, through the ambivalence of ironic reference.



A sixty-second sequence early in the film presents archival material in a different mode, one that recalled to me, when I first saw it, the haunting sequence of the four men at gunpoint in Pantzis's *Trimithi*. This sequence opens with footage filmed inside a nightclub in Nicosia; fragmented images of young people dancing flash up and disappear to the rhythms of strobe lights and bass-heavy club music. Intercut with these fragments are photographs of graffiti in Nicosia, passing so quickly as to be nearly illegible: in English, "freedom," "peace," "it is time for the peace," "be happy together"; in Greek, "union," "fuck the Turks," "Cyprus is Greece," "Cyprus belongs to its people," "Ottoman sons of whores," "the only good Turk is a dead Turk," "never slaves."[27] A few seconds elapse, and the graffiti are replaced by other kinds of images, again passing too quickly for viewers to cognize fully: old color photographs of tanks and barbed wire; black-and-white identity photographs from lists of missing persons; a mural depicting prisoners of war held at gunpoint; a black-and-white photograph of a missing person displayed at his funeral; a black-and-white photograph taken inside a building after an explosion, with body parts visible in the foreground; a black-and-white photograph of Mothers of the Missing at a protest, holding signs and photos of their missing sons; a black-and-white photograph of smoke rising over a city skyline; a black-and-white photograph or film still of children in a refugee camp, and another of more children near their tents in a camp; black-and-white photographs from inside and outside a bombed-out building; a black-and-white close-up of a dead man hanging from the broken beams of the building; an engraving of Christ on a cross; a graffito of a swastika.

The documentary and the artistic—murals, photographs, graffiti, engravings—interact here as visual representations of Cyprus's violent history; the "agency behind the images," as my historian friend put it, flattens and spreads, creating a suffocating environment in which the young Cypriots dance, drunken, half-naked, checked-out. Demetriou seems to have designed the disjointed rush of images in this sequence, without commentary or external framing, to mime the experience of flashbacks by survivors of trauma, in line with Freud's theory of repetition compulsion. The viewer who cannot fully perceive the images as they flash up might capture them only in their aftermath—remembering some but forgetting others, seeing words and pictures out of sequence, or blending elements together to construct coherent symbols that did not exist in the original array. The viewer might retrace her memory of the sequence over and over, trying to see the images she did not register on first sight, trying to piece together the meaning that eludes her. Or she might not trust her memory, and attempt instead to reexperience the images, as I did when I first watched the film on DVD, slowing it down in replay, advancing frame by frame, in order to visualize each fragment. Even this attempt at pinning down the images does not reward this viewer's desire for meaning with a coherent history; if she seeks order, she will not find it in this archive.



In *The Migrant Image*, T. J. Demos writes about such compulsive returns to images of the past in the work of several Beirut-based artists who engage documentary film and photography in their representations of the Lebanese civil wars (1975–90), driven by the persistent failure of these images to represent fully that to which they allude. In the context of "state-sponsored amnesia" about the wars (Demos 2013, 193), Demos argues, social and personal traumas have generated partial memories among survivors as well as intense desires to learn about that which remains unremembered and unknown. These mutually constituting motivations have fostered the growth of "an unofficial 'memory culture'" in Lebanon, he explains, in which the symptomatic "psychic effects" of traumatic memory are transformed into creative resources (182, 173). Seizing on the instability and uncertainty of such memory, artists work with the "opacity" of archival images and their insufficiency to represent experience, especially the experience of violence (xx, 172). Demos associates this "resurgence of documentary approaches" in postwar art making with a rejection of the commonsensical evidentiary status of documentary images, and an embrace of the fictive potential of documentary—an orientation to evidence that he dubs "documentary poetics" (xvi, xxi).[28] The artworks he examines install traumatic memory at the heart of the archive of war, deliberately blurring lines between fiction and documentary, objectivity and subjectivity, thus "destabiliz[ing]" the archive as a repository of knowledge and foregrounding art itself as a "historicizing process" (16, 12).

Documentary poetic techniques in this vein include altering, damaging, or compositing archival materials in order to produce an artifactual effect—as in the films of Kakoyiannis and Adil that I discussed earlier. Along these lines, Demos examines the photographic image *Saida, June 6, 1982 (2003–6)* by Akram Zaatari, a Beiruti artist who has also exhibited work in Cyprus (and gave the keynote lecture at the fifth annual International Conference of Photography and Theory held in Nicosia in 2018, which I attended).[29] *Saida*, which was first exhibited at the *Out of Beruit* show at Modern Art Oxford in May 2006, appears to depict one moment during the bombing of the southern city of Saida (Sidon) by the Israeli army during the first day of the invasion in 1982, but it is actually, Demos says, a "digital composite" (2013, 189); according to an expository statement by Zaatari's gallery, he shot six photographs of the event from his parents' balcony at the age of sixteen and assembled them some two decades later in this artwork. His gallery now displays a print of the same composite image, now labeled *Saida, June 6, 1982 (2003–9)* and showing yellow grid lines, described as a "capture" from the ninety-second video Zaatari made in 2002 from the original six photographs he had shot in 1982; the yellow grid lines indicate the progressive movements of the camera during the event.[30] The 2009 version of *Saida* thus makes visually explicit what Zaatari obscured in the 2006 version: the duration of time condensed in the still image that he created by compositing. Demos does not comment on the 2009 *Saida*; it is the 2006 *Saida* that he explores as creative documentation, since it depicts a "constructed event" in a documentary mode that could never have been photographed the way it appears in the work (188–89). Here, on Zaatari's own account, his memory of the event is worked into an imaginative act of spectacularization, authorized morally and politically by his personal experience.[31]



A related approach in documentary poetics entails the crafting of experience-based archival fictions, such as Walid Raad's 2001 video *Hostage: The Bachar Tapes (#17 and #31), English Version*, made with the Atlas Group. This sixteen-minute video contains the filmed testimony of a Lebanese man, Souheil Bachar, concerning his kidnapping and torture in the 1980s, alongside five American hostages. In the reception of the film, much has been made of the fact that Bachar is "played" by a famous Lebanese actor—a signal to Lebanese audiences that the documentary is somehow not real, calling into question the content of Bachar's testimony, even if it partially partakes of a verifiable history (Demos 2013, 191). Although fictive in its personae and testimonial details, Demos contends, *Hostage* expresses more general truths about the uncertainty, terror, and violence experienced by many Lebanese civilians during the wars, and thus contributes to the production of "cultural knowledge" about a suppressed, collective history (193). Indeed, on Demos's reading, by substituting fictive personae for real ones,

Raad opens up the rigid mapping of ethnic/sectarian identity onto victim and perpetrator roles in the wars, thus "facilitat[ing] memory" by unlocking it from the deformative postwar politics of identity (184).

A number of Cypriot artists have, likewise, undertaken documentary poetic engagements with the archive. Elena Stylianou discusses the use of archival objects and images in the works of several Cypriot artists, reflecting on the ambiguous status of such artifacts—factual yet crafted, visible yet not seen—which these artists recontextualize in their projects. For one, she writes, Christodoulos Panayiotou emphasizes "minute particularities" and unconventional lines of sight usually overlooked in visual histories of Cyprus (Stylianou 2014, 251), selecting from "existing photographic archives" a number of uncaptioned and unattributed photographs that have not found a place in the canonical imagery of important political events. Stylianou closely examines his *I Land* series, featuring photographs from the PIO archives, including images of Archbishop (and President) Makarios that Panayiotou juxtaposes with images of everyday "things and people" encountered by the photographers who simultaneously recorded Makarios's official activities (256). On Stylianou's reading, the sequencing of these images in Panayiotou's gallery installations disturbs the organization of historical knowledge by archival categories. These installations thus open up the closed, secretive space of the archive, while "reproduc[ing] and shar[ing]" its authority (254). In the process, she argues, "the official archive becomes a space filled with possibilities" that extend beyond official narratives of Cypriot history. Probing the material and symbolic affinities between bones and images, Stylianou likens Panayiotou to an archaeologist in his encounter with the materiality of the past, and in his desire to "unearth" or "excavat[e] narratives lost or hidden" (243). In her view, it is the secreted nature of these narratives that positions his works of art to partake in the creative potential of the archive.

In light of Walter Benjamin's ([1936] 1968b, 241) famous critique of the "introduction of aesthetics into political life" under Fascism, such aesthetic approaches to the archive in postwar Lebanon and Cyprus raise the question as to how and why art may be political. For Demos, there is no contradiction between the aesthetic and political dimensions of the work of artists like Raad and Zaatari; indeed, he sees the asetheticization of documentary that they carry out as a crucial means of transfiguring collective memory of the civil wars and opening a future that is not already congealed within sectarian politics.[32] The potential of the archive is thus revolutionary even if not revelatory in the positivist sense of exposing a secret history, discovering new knowledge, and adding it to the historical record. The materials utilized by artists like Raad and Zaatari are in any case as often fabricated as found, refusing any equivalence between what is archival and what is historical.

What makes these art projects rather than history projects, Demos suggests, is the artists' aestheticization of the archive; they work perceptible traces of their interventions into the documentary framework, "granting visibility to their subjective processing of past catastrophe" (2013, 187). Indeed, this visibility is a crucial theme of their works, which express the active process of cutting, altering, distorting, fabricating, and repurposing elements of otherwise factual documentation, in a kind of mimetic repetition of memory itself. These modes of artistic intervention constitute specific techniques of archiving on which, as Derrida contends, the psychic formation and recollection of memory depend. They are destructive as well as creative; they conceal while they reveal; and they inevitably leave their own trace even as they mark the loss of what they cannot or will not represent.



"A crystal image of time destroys the past, / a full moon of forgetting, to save the future." In Adil's poem, as I read it, the past that must be destroyed to save the future is the past that has stayed put in chronological time, frozen in events of ethnonational violence and the testimony of personal memory—the memory that "causes vertigo." It is the crystal image of time that gives us access to the past in a different sense: the past that remains present, immanent in the archival footage Adil has employed in her performances, its reflection of the present (and thus its difference from the present) a source of her own creativity. In materializing this past—not only projecting archival footage but also aggravating its material fragility and making its decomposition visible—Adil used an artifactual technique to loop her audience into an experiment with time: an experiment in which the future might be saved from the repetition of the past by making it impossible to predict.

## More Beautiful

In his first film, *A Detail in Cyprus* (1987), Panicos Chrysanthou took the archive as a poetic resource. This film was screened in Nicosia in January 2012, during the month-long exhibition of Chrysanthou's photographic and film works at the Eirini gallery adjacent to the dead zone, which I discussed earlier. The popularity of documentary films in venues like this at the time encouraged, perhaps, a new curiosity about Chrysanthou himself, whose works represented not only a robust realization of Cypriot documen-

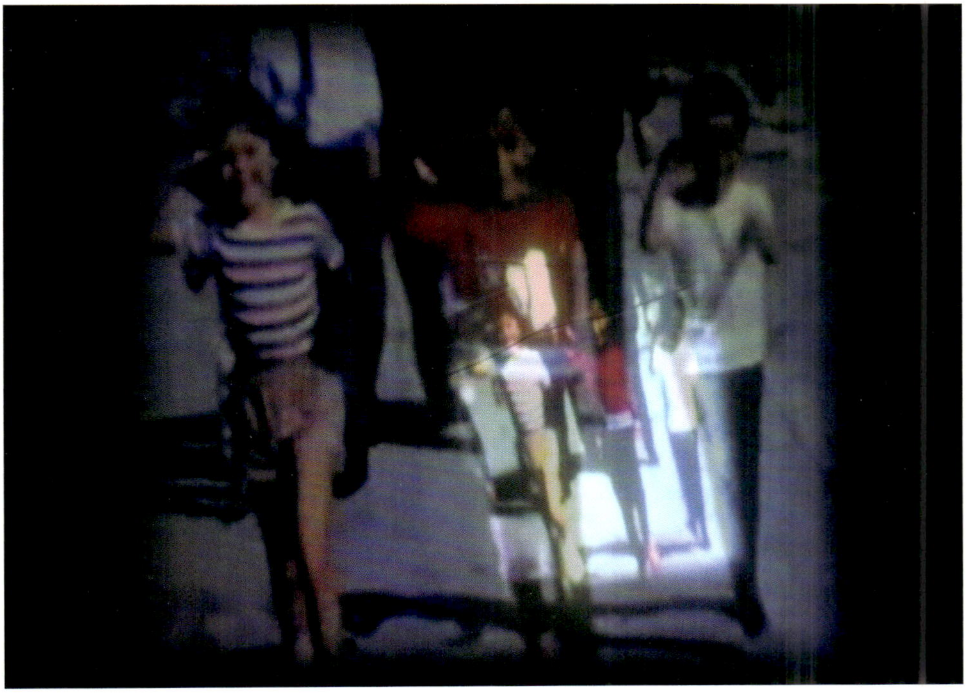

NO.

2.17

tary film as a genre, but also something like a history of documentary filmmaking in Cyprus. His early works, such as *A Detail in Cyprus* (1987) and *Our Wall* (1993)—both novel and quite radical in their time—introduced the Cyprus conflict into the very grammar of postwar documentary film, and vice versa.

I attended the screening that evening in January with perhaps a dozen other people; a few more arrived while the film was underway. Chrysanthou introduced the film in Greek and then in English for the benefit of the few Turkish Cypriots in the room. He told the audience about the production of the film, shot in 1985 at Ayios Sozomenos, a mixed village near what had been established, by then, for more than ten years as the Green Line. The village—which had a majority Turkish-Cypriot population going back to the first Ottoman census in 1831 (PRIO Cyprus Centre 2011a)—had seen two incidents of violent conflict between Greek Cypriots and Turkish Cypriots: one in 1958, during the independence campaign by EOKA in which Turkish Cypriots were targeted; and another in 1964, when violence between Greek Cypriots and Turkish Cypriots forced many of the latter into enclaves, and the village was temporarily abandoned after villagers looted and burned it. In the summer of 1974, bombings by the Turkish military forced the desertion of Ayios Sozomenos for good.



The film takes that history of conflict as its implicit premise. It follows a woman and her young daughter as they travel from their city to an unnamed, abandoned village. Slowly, whimsically, they explore its crumbling houses and rubble yards, stairwells overgrown with brush and dusty rooms full of broken furniture, piles of books, scraps of clothing, old photographs, forsaken belongings of all description. Gradually, other former residents of the village arrive on foot and gather for a feast in the village center as, one after another, they narrate in voice-over their memories of leaving the village permanently in the summer of 1974. Their stories are intercut with long sequences of landscapes and ruins, and the forms of life that flourish in them: birds, flowers, insects, weeds. Occasionally, the mother speaks in a voice-over to her child, inviting her to entertain the possibility of such a return to their village, such a reunion with their lost neighbors—thus positioning the action of the film as an act of imagination, a dream or reverie.

At the end of the film, the audience was slow to ask questions. Chrysanthou introduced Mahan, a Turkish-Cypriot woman who had lived in Ayios Sozomenos, and who appeared in the film with her son, narrating at length (in Greek) her flight from the village during the violence in 1964. A woman in the audience asked her, in Greek, about the neighborliness and love between Turkish Cypriots and Greek Cypriots that Mahan had experienced in her village. Had she met with any of her old neighbors since they left? Mahan replied that she did see a few of them, now and then. Chrysanthou explained that, while Mahan had been born and raised in Ayios Sozomenos, she had married in Dali, the next village over, on the south side of the Green Line. Hers was one of the very few Turkish-Cypriot families to stay in the south after the division in 1974. Mahan explained to the audience, in Greek, why they had stayed: *My husband said, "I've never done anything to anyone. This is our home. Why should we leave?"* She was very afraid for her children, who were ill and close to death when the evacuation took place, and so they stayed with her father in Limassol and raised their children there.

Mahan repeated to the audience some of the story she had told in the film, crediting her Greek-Cypriot neighbors for saving her and her children's lives at several points after the bombings—but insisting, as well, on how terrifying the experience had been for Turkish Cypriots in mixed villages. Chrysanthou interjected, *Imagine Mahan, a Turkish Cypriot living in the south, going on camera saying these things in 1985! Now it seems innocent, but then, it was very dangerous.* He told the audience that he himself had received threats when the film was made and guessed he had "gotten away with it" only because it was accepted at the Berlin film festival, which gave him some visibility and protection. The PIO in the south had coproduced the film, but once it was made, Chrysanthou said, PIO officials told him they were ashamed of it; the cultural institutions of the Republic of Cyprus had never acknowledged the film.



Another audience member asked Chrysanthou why he had chosen to depict the conflict in Cyprus so "indirectly." Chrysanthou replied that he had first conceived the film in a poetic form, through the figure of Adamantios Diamantis, a painter from the village "who has captured so much of Cypriot life in his paintings," and whose massive multipanel works, *The World of Cyprus* (1967–72) and *When the World of Cyprus First Heard the Bad News* (1975), are featured in the film's opening sequence and credit sequence. Chrysanthou told us he had imagined the film unfolding through Diamantis's return to the village ten years after he and all the residents had left; summoned by his presence there, his fellow villagers would slowly, one by one, return to meet him from the remote corners of Cyprus to which they had fled in 1974. Diamantis himself, however, had declined to participate in the film, so Chrysanthou imagined in his place a mother returning to the village and gathering the others around her, and introducing to them her daughter, born elsewhere, in the south, entirely cut off from Turkish Cypriots. Chrysanthou intended the mother's voice-over as a long "lullaby" that would send the young daughter into a dream as her mother put her to bed. *This is an imaginary return. It's the mother's imagination; it's not meant to be "documentary,"* he said, gesturing with air quotes.

And yet the film had a reality effect that tied this imaginary return to the real world and that precluded the film's designation as art or fiction. The characters in the film were actual former residents of the village, to which they actually returned for the making of the film; the memories of leaving the village in 1974 that they recount in the film were, Chrysanthou said, "truthful." He spoke of the film's "reality" by way of the photographic motif, referring to a sequence in which the mother character flips through a photo album that she finds in an abandoned house in the village. Chrysanthou described the contents of the album as "photographs of the past," which he had found in archives in London and Cyprus. In the sequence, the woman turns page after page, revealing a series of black-and-white images: an archaeological excavation in the region, dated 1933; some construction at the village church, dated 1943; a large extended family; the town soccer team; a couple in their wedding portrait; several older couples, Greek-Cypriot and Turkish-Cypriot; all the men of the village gathered for a funeral. Chrysanthou explained that, as the mother turns the pages of the album, she comes across a few photographs that are not yet fixed to pages. These images, he said, depict events that had just happened in real time, "which are not yet part of the past"—for example, an image of a famous musician who visited Cyprus in 1984, and another of Chrysanthou himself during the film shoot at Ayios Sozomenos in 1985. He intended the unfixedness of these recent images in the album to illustrate the process of memory making and to emphasize the ongoing nature of that process, both before and after the events that were the overt subject of the film. These photographs are not yet artifacts, in other words, but they are in the process of becoming artifacts. The film thus visualizes an artifactual mode of historicity, in which the past remains present in material form, available for recontextualization any time the film is seen in the future.



Chrysanthou talked, in this light, about the footage of events in 1964 that he reproduced in the film. This footage, which he found in the PIO archives in the south, was shot not in the village itself but elsewhere in Cyprus; he wanted it to stand in, he said, for what happened in the village in 1964. Black-and-white and color film clips, mostly newsreel, show people running in a panic down the streets of Kaïmakli, a historic neighborhood just outside the old walled city in south Nicosia; men crawling across fields with rifles; men shot dead, their bodies lying on the floors of houses while others stand around aimlessly; men being arrested; wounded men being taken away in ambulances; UN soldiers patrolling village streets; city neighborhoods on

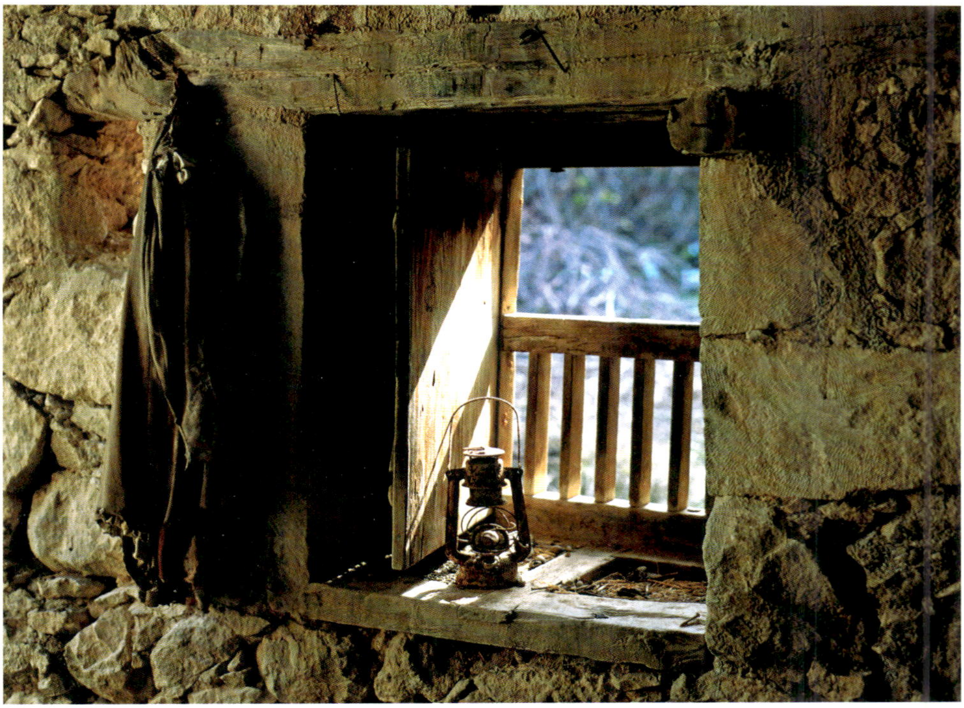

NO.

2.18

fire; airplanes overhead; villagers hugging and kissing their neighbors goodbye as they board buses; buses full of people driving off; graves being dug; coffins in a hearse driving down a city street; women walking out of villages with their children, laden with their belongings; women in black, wailing and holding photographs of their missing relatives up to the camera.

This long sequence, starting about fifty minutes into the film, marks the beginning of the film's ending but recalls as its direct referent an earlier scene shot in the village's overgrown graveyard. In that earlier scene, we see two graves, dated March 10, 1964, and then a whole row of graves culminating in a group headstone, dedicated to "all those lost on February 6, 1964." The relationship between this scene and the later archival sequence determines 1964 as the reality of the film: not only the violence and death at the heart of the conflict in Cyprus—its primary cause—but also the object of the film's documentary ambitions. The murders of villagers in 1964 are positioned here as the past of the events of 1974—the coup, the invasion, and the permanent evacuation of Ayios Sozomenos—which are, themselves, positioned by the villagers as the past of this film as they recount, in 1985, their experiences of those events just over a decade later. What Chrysanthou described as the "poetic form" of the film—the fluid but patterned flow of the past into the present, and the present into the past—counts on a documentary framework in which the audience will receive its archival material. He does not alter the footage, but he imbues it with a dreamlike quality by inserting it into the unfolding reverie of the mother character, as the haunting voice of an old villager sings a lament from the ruined landscape of the present. Chrysanthou explained to the audience: *Using real images like this is more beautiful. It works better with the poetic form of the film to show the past through these images.*



Like other filmmakers working in Cyprus—Pantzis, Kakoyiannis, and Adil, for example, unlikely company in other ways—Chrysanthou accepted the problem of evidence presented by the archive and did not engage in documentary realism in this film. He sought instead to exploit the phenomenological resources of the archive: reworking the material features of archival images and their sequencing to engage the sensorium of the audience, not so much to educate as to disturb and to dream. Even so, this experience depended on the reality of the images he used, if not their realism; as Chrysanthou saw it, "real images" were not only more "truthful" than songs, poems, or paintings, the other forms of art he explicitly referenced in the film; they were also "more beautiful."

When I heard Chrysanthou develop this line of thinking after the screening of *A Detail in Cyprus*, I was not sure how to understand the "more beautiful" quality he saw in the archival material in his film. I thought it had something to do with the gap he left open between the story of Ayios Sozomenos that he was telling in the film—a reverie that harmonized the villagers' experiences of the past with their dreams of the future—and the facticity of the archival material he used in the film, which did not depict the events in 1964 that he sought to capture through that story but rather stood in for them in some way. In that gap between fiction and archival facticity, I thought, perhaps he was trying to open up a possibility of storytelling that audiences could assimilate and make part of themselves, in the way Walter Benjamin ([1936] 1968a) describes storytelling as an exchange of experience.

My confusion led me back to the ghostly scene of the four men at gunpoint, that archival moving image that I had found in so many documentary films about the Cyprus conflict. Chrysanthou had been one of the filmmakers who used it. More than anything else I have seen in Cypriot documentary film, this brief and abrupt scene has stuck with me, marking my frustration with the limits of the archive and all it cannot tell us; but also materializing a vital connection between the visual archive of violence in Cyprus and the forensic investigations of the missing I have been studying. I guess I would say I was "haunted" by it, in Avery Gordon's term. "In haunting," Gordon says, "organized forces and systemic structures that appear removed from us make their impact felt in everyday life in a way that confounds our analytic separations and confounds the social separations themselves. . . . The ghost is just the sign, or the empirical evidence if you like, that tells you a haunting is taking place" (1997, 19, 8).

The moving image of the four men at gunpoint confounded me in just that empirical way, not only suggesting an incident of violence outside the frame—an origin point in the mystery story of the missing—but also, and more difficult to pinpoint and understand, troubling the seductive binaries operated by forensic investigations and documentary film in Cyprus (and perhaps everywhere): privacy and publicity, secrecy and revelation. As Derrida warns in *Archive Fever*, the passage from "private" to "public" is not a passage from "secret" to "non-secret" (1995, 2–3). No matter how many times I saw this moving image—a scene of personal terror, caught on film—and no matter how many times it was shown to audiences, it did not deliver "the facts."

It felt like some kind of resolution, then, when I learned what I now take to be the real story of the four men at gunpoint—or better, the "story of how the real story has emerged," as Gordon (1997, 26) puts it, expressing the threat posed by fiction to the "special truth" of facticity: the threat of eroding its authority. It was a path I had been on for some time by then, so perhaps my discovery was less incidental than it seemed to me at the time. It happened on a visit I made to see Chrysanthou in April 2018, at a small cultural center he had founded with friends in a mountain village near Paphos, where he has lived for many years. I had sought him out a long time before, in 2012, when I decided to focus my research on documentary film in Cyprus; he was then, and remains today, warmly receptive to my inquiries and willing to talk. He has shared with me several pieces of his work in progress over the years, including entries in his ever-expanding "archive," as he calls it, of individuals he has been filming for two decades now: *anyone who is doing something interesting, or who has a quality of openness, who shows something important about Cyprus*, as he once explained to me. He also shared his most recent film, *The Story of the Green Line (Ιστορία για την πράσινη γραμμή)*, which had just been released when he showed it to me in April 2018, though he had already screened it at the Thessaloniki Film Festival in November 2016 and at other venues in Cyprus and the UK.



I had brought my book manuscript with me on my visit, in order to show him sections that addressed his work and to seek his corrections and additions. On the cover page of the manuscript, I had put the still image from *Trimithi* of the four men at gunpoint. As soon as Chrysanthou saw it, he told me what it was. I named the many films in which I had seen the scene but confessed I had not been able to pin the event down in the historical record.[33] Chrysanthou told me he knew what had happened in reality because his own grandfather and cousin were among the four men with their hands up, and they had lived to tell him what took place. Of the four men, Chrysanthou told me, only one was actually killed, though three had been shot. It happened on the Nicosia-Varosha road on August 16 or 17, 1974, he said, right after the second invasion of Cyprus by the Turkish military. Turkish soldiers driving a tank down the road came upon these villagers and stopped them with machine guns. From right to left, Chrysanthou pointed out to me on the still, the four men were his grandfather, who lived; the man who was shot and killed; a sixteen-year-old boy, Chrysanthou's cousin, who was not shot, and told the story afterward to Chrysanthou; and another man he knew, who was shot but survived and also told Chrysanthou about the incident, and whom Chrysanthou had filmed and photographed. Chrysanthou had even made an audio recording of his grandfather telling him about it. He had documented the events as fully as he possibly could.

The short scene captured on the archival footage did not tell the whole story, Chrysanthou told me. A Turkish television crew who had been traveling with other soldiers in their truck down the same road were the ones who filmed what took place: after the four villagers were stopped by soldiers,

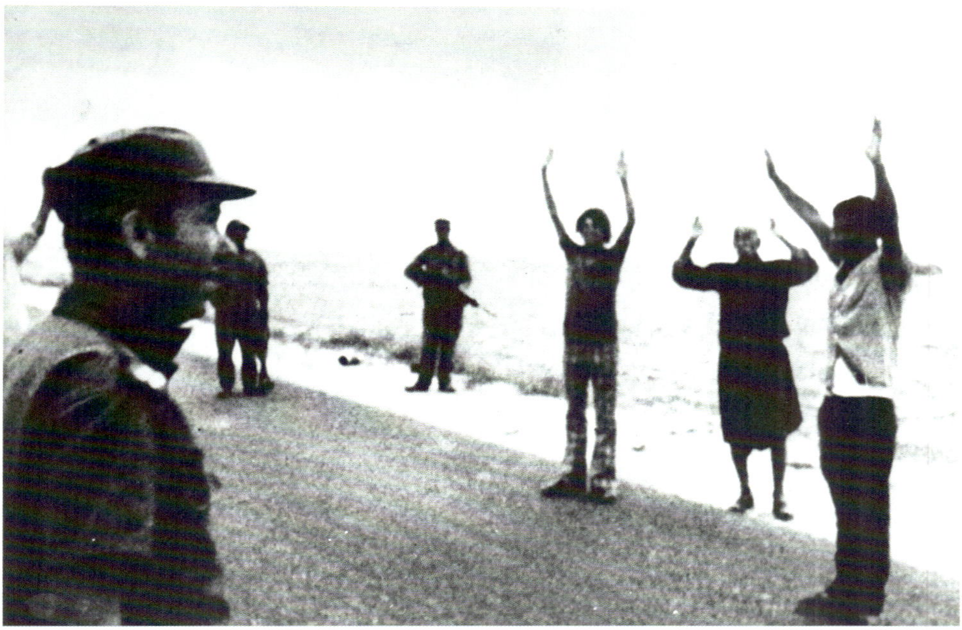

*NO.*

**2.19**

the officer shouted "Hands up!" and then loaded the men onto their truck and drove away. According to Chrysanthou, the soldiers on that truck had already captured eight other people; the whole group was taken to a place where they were lined up and shot. Most escaped and survived, after being treated for wounds, but two were killed, including the second man in the image.

Chrysanthou confirmed that the scene of the four men at gunpoint had been shown many times on RIK, the public television station in Cyprus, as well as on Turkish television. He had gotten the footage from a news agency—now a subsidiary of Reuters—that held a wealth of footage from Cyprus. *I've been dwelling on this event for a long time,* he told me. In his new film, *The Story of the Green Line,* which I watched later that afternoon, he created a dramatic reenactment of both scenes of the event: the capture of the four men on the road that had been filmed by a Turkish television crew, as well as the shooting that took place elsewhere, afterward, beyond the reach of cameras. In *The Story of the Green Line,* these sequences are recorded on black-and-white film—as distinct from the rest of the film, shot in color to mark the present tense of the film's action—and they are presented as a flashback in the memory of the film's central character, Kypros, the persona Chrysanthou created for his cousin, the sixteen-year-old boy who appears in the archival footage. (Kypros is a fairly common man's name in the south but also the Greek word for Cyprus; Chrysanthou was thus wielding a deliberately heavy hand in this naming.) In the film, the flashback is triggered by the now-grown Kypros's return to the spot where the shooting took place and his father was killed.

"Only the movies tell it like it is," Taussig (1999, 6) jokes, making (I think) a reference to *Serpico,* Sidney Lumet's 1973 film about corruption in the New York City Police Department.[34] His joke underscores his definition of the public secret as "that which is generally known, but cannot be articulated" or "spoken" (5, 50). Public secrecy, thus, is not about knowing the secret (because everyone already knows it) but rather about telling it, speaking it, articulating it—publicly. Only a fiction film "based on a true story" could express the truth of police violence and corruption, which everyone already knew.

I thought of this when I watched *The Story of the Green Line,* a dramatic fiction film and not a documentary, Chrysanthou insisted. I asked him why he had chosen to create a reenactment of the four men at gunpoint; after all, he and Kızılyürek had already used the archival footage of the scene in their documentary *Our Wall,* some twenty-five years earlier. Chrysanthou's response to my question was not straightforward. My desire to pin down the event in the historical record intersected with his desire to tell the story of the event; my search ended with his latest film, but in a way I had not expected. I gathered that he felt he could not tell that story with the archival footage—and not only because, in thus attributing facticity to the event (telling the public secret), he would risk censorship or worse forms of protest or retribution. Perhaps more important, the footage did not show what he wanted to tell: namely, the whole story in its coherence, as it had been transmitted to him by his grandfather and others targeted by the shooting—not the fractured and ghostly fragment that survived, in the archival footage, as an index of an unknown event.

His dramatization keyed me into a recognition of the people in that footage, which has circulated on television and in documentary films for decades as a generic representation of violence without attribution or names—without identities, in other words. The dramatization effected a reversal of the evidentiary logic of archival material: the fictionalized scene, rather than the archival footage, is what achieved a specific representation of the four men at gunpoint, as irreducibly unique as reality itself; and in its uniqueness, it became a story.



## What I'd Been Missing

*I definitely have archive fever*, R. said to me, laughing. R. was a teacher and museum educator who had been conducting research in a variety of Cypriot photographic archives for her PhD; I had known her several years by then, and when we got together, we often shared our experiences of doing work in Cyprus. We had been talking about Derrida's essay one April evening in 2014 as we walked through a quiet, leafy neighborhood bordering the southern Venetian walls of old Nicosia. In the essay's title she found a name for her incessant desire to track down new archives and to return over and over to others she had already studied. She described a feeling of "buzzing" and "excitement" as she would sift through the materials she found: *There's something very stimulating about discovering these things!*

But for R., the draw of the archive exceeded the excitement of discovery. She told me about an art project she was working on at the time, for which she had found materials in the Critical History Archive, established by a team of researchers as a joint project of the Association for Historical Dialogue and Research and the PRIO-Cyprus Centre. This archive holds digitized copies of newspaper articles concerning intercommunal conflict during the period 1955–64; it is one of the few searchable, open-access archives in Cyprus today.[35] R. had looked through Greek-, Turkish-, and English-language newspapers from that period, she told me, collecting photographs and other visual materials that related directly to violence—specifically, intercommunal and intracommunal violence against civilians, not only beatings and killings but also other kinds of violence and intimidation, even against children and elderly people. She found stories, for instance, about an incident when villagers took all of a neighbor's belongings out of his house and burned them in the street because he patronized a shop that carried British products, and about an old woman dragged into the town square and held down while neighbors cut off her hair.



*I couldn't believe what I found in these materials*, R. said. *It was a relief to me, in a weird way.* She explained that she had grown up in the Republic, in a society in which Cypriot history was not taught: *In school, the history we learned was the history of Greek civilization.* References to recent Cypriot history were "only very vague," she said—*stories you hear, but you never really know where they come from. But the effects of that history are everywhere—in the division, of course, but also in how people behave, in their values, in how they believe in things. For a long time, for most of my life, I felt there was some big mystery that I didn't understand, something behind what I could see. When I started finding these materials in the archive, I understood that this was what I'd been missing.* It was a relief, she told me, to know that what she saw around her every day had actually come from somewhere—that there was so much evidence of it that one could really see it after all.

What R. called "archive fever"—her desire to search out the truth behind the mystery of everyday life in evidence of a secret history of violence—is one facet of Derrida's conception of archival desire. From the vantage of this desire, secrecy appears as a force of "heterogeneity" or difference, exterior to the archive, that threatens the "consignation" or gathering together of archival materials under the authority of law (the state) and tradition (the community) (Derrida 1995, 2). It is what lies outside the archive, in all senses. For R., this secrecy was a powerful but obscure force of silencing, actively resisted by those who created the new Critical History Archive from extant collections where accounts and images were stored—the accounts and images of people now dead, the real subjects of Cyprus's violent history. Derrida speaks of this "spectral position" of the dead in the archive, which he connects to the position of the psychoanalyst as a screen for the analysand's projections in a transference relation: "It is spectral *a priori*: neither present nor absent 'in the flesh,' neither visible nor invisible, a trace always referring to another whose eyes can never be met" (62, 84). The sense of relief R. gained from this archive came from her encounter with this spectral presence—not knowledge of people's experience of violence, but the exterior trace of memory left by its repression.

"But of the secret itself," Derrida says,

> there can be no archive, by definition. . . . There is no sense in searching for the secret of what anyone may have known. . . . Beyond every possible and necessary inquiry, we will always wonder what Freud (for example), what every "careful concealer" may have wanted to keep secret. We will wonder what he may have kept of his unconditional right to secrecy, while at the same time burning with the desire to know, to make known, and to archive the very thing he concealed forever. . . . We will always wonder, sharing with compassion in this archive fever, what may have burned of his secret passions, of his correspondence, or of his "life." Burned without him, without remains and without knowledge. (1995, 101)



The absence of "remains" and "knowledge" of the secret is a structural feature of the archive that Derrida (1995, 18–19) associates with the other facet of archive fever: its destructive side—an "anarchival" or "archiviolithic" force that he likens to the death drive, a force of forgetting and erasure, of doubt and suspicion, of repression and censorship, in the very recording and repetition of memory. This force, he argues, determines the finitude of the archive: its limits, its exteriority to memory, and the impossibility of knowing all. What Derrida identifies as the "trouble" of the archive—"what troubles and muddles our vision . . . what inhibits insight and knowledge"—is "the trouble of secrets, of plots, of clandestineness, of half-private, half-public conjurations, always at the unstable limit between public and private, between the family, the society, and the State, between the family and an intimacy even more private than the family, between oneself and oneself" (90). This most intimate secrecy, obtaining between oneself and oneself, describes the convergence of the individual and the social in the archive: the synergetic effect of repression (which Derrida presents as an unconscious process of self-censorship) and suppression (which he views as a refraction of law and authority, between the conscious and preconscious control of affect)—the vanishing of "spontaneous memory" in the very process of recording it (28).

In talking with Cypriot filmmakers, and in encountering their work, I came to see the visual archive of violence in Cyprus as a memory apparatus of the kind Derrida indicates: full of rich and vibrant images of the past, but also of absences and mysteries, indices of what lay outside the visible frame

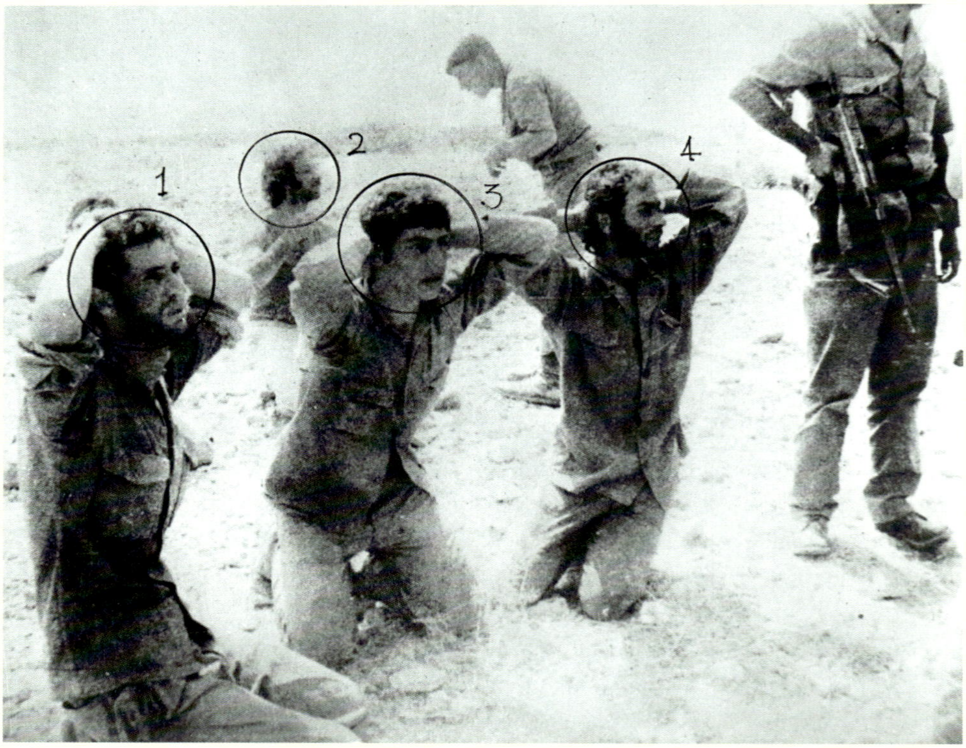


NO.

2.20

and thus traces of both repression and suppression. These archives, as I have argued throughout these pages, were a limited resource for documentary filmmakers who sought to do something new: to tell the story of conflict and division differently, rather than replaying well-worn tropes over and over again. Family photographs and wedding portraits, for instance, appeared in almost every documentary film I saw on the conflict. These images elicited affective reactions in audiences based not necessarily in their own family relationships—which might describe a broader and more complex array of emotions—but rather in a social consensus on the family as a vital object of emotional and social investment in Cyprus. The loss of family members in the conflict, or the rupture of family life caused by displacement, stood as reckonings of the toll taken on Cypriots generally by the conflict, regardless of whether particular individuals experienced them personally. In this sense, the conventional depictions of family that documentary films presented, in the form of archival photographs and home video footage, contained a premeditated affective charge that was released in the viewing of the films—a gratification of expectations that perhaps accounted for some of the appeal of these films to Cypriot audiences.



Stock footage from the war—scenes of bombers, soldiers, ambulances, refugees fleeing their villages and mourning the loss of loved ones—was equally conventional in Cypriot documentary film, as I have noted, but this material perhaps provoked a different affective response. Viewers from the postwar generations came to film screenings informed by their own projects of cultural production: research, writing, theater, art. Their historical knowledge of the conflict was extensive but secondhand; their expertise lay in representation. They engaged documentary films in the mode of postmemory. But these screenings were also attended by older Cypriots: people who had lived through the events of the 1960s and 1970s as adults, and who thus came to documentary films about the conflict with their own direct and vivid memories. These viewers perhaps more easily identified with the subjects of the films, people like them who were being interviewed about their experiences of the conflict. In the discussions that followed screenings, these audience members often spoke of how sequences in a film had stirred their memories. They named the village or city street shown bombed out or burning in archival footage; they recognized the sound of Makarios's voice trembling on the radio after the coup; they recalled what it was like to live in an enclave, or to run from the army, leaving their belongings behind. They took the occasion of a film screening to tell their own stories about leaving their villages, to express the warmth they felt toward their former neighbors and their sadness at losing them, to vent their frustration and anger at the corruption and incompetence of their political leaders after the war. These screenings thus formed fleeting social spaces where intergenerational and intercommunal encounters with the past could take place, mediated by the affective dynamics of identification and catharsis. But the stories recounted by older Cypriots also occasionally led to arguments among them about "what really happened"—thus opening a tension between memory and history, and muddying the evidentiary transparency of the archival footage in the films they had watched together.



These films clearly aimed to expose historical secrets, to highlight neglected dimensions of the conflict, to provoke new reflections on personal and social responsibility for violence and division. The access filmmakers had gained to state archives and private collections since the opening of the checkpoints in 2003—an increasingly long time ago, its singular eruption into postwar time now, itself, incorporated into the even longer history of the division that has survived it—enhanced their possibilities for introducing new knowledge to Cypriot publics. In their aspiration to transparency, opening, and pluralism, these films aspired to a "believable public language of truth," as John Tagg (2009, xxxiii) describes documentary—a language to displace the murky, hermetic, biased representations of conflict in earlier nationalist films. But the archival material in these films depicted only a partial reality, contingently captured on film under conditions unknown to the filmmakers putting them to use so many years later, often in all-too-familiar ways. Intercutting archival material with contemporary footage reproduced that original framing of people and events, rousing the reactions of contemporary audiences within that inherited frame while leaving the frame itself invisible as a repressive force.

Yet the repression itself leaves a trace, Derrida says. And sometimes that trace becomes a groove, a furrow, a wound. (The mystic writing pad—a wax slab under a clear sheet of plastic—is a palimpsest, after all.) When R. told me about her archive fever, she related an experience she had recently had in one of the photographic archives where she had been looking for images of the 1974 coup. *There were so many photographs of soldiers,* she told me, *Greeks and Greek Cypriots and Turkish army. But only the faces of the Turkish soldiers were scratched out. Someone took a pen and scored them, not just scribbling on them but really gouging them out. I don't know why. It could be to protect their identity, in case someone wanted to bring a lawsuit. But it also could have been someone who was really angry, wanting to do violence to those people, who probably don't even exist anymore.* Defacing the archive and leaving a trace—making a new secret by destroying an old one, transmitted nonetheless under erasure.

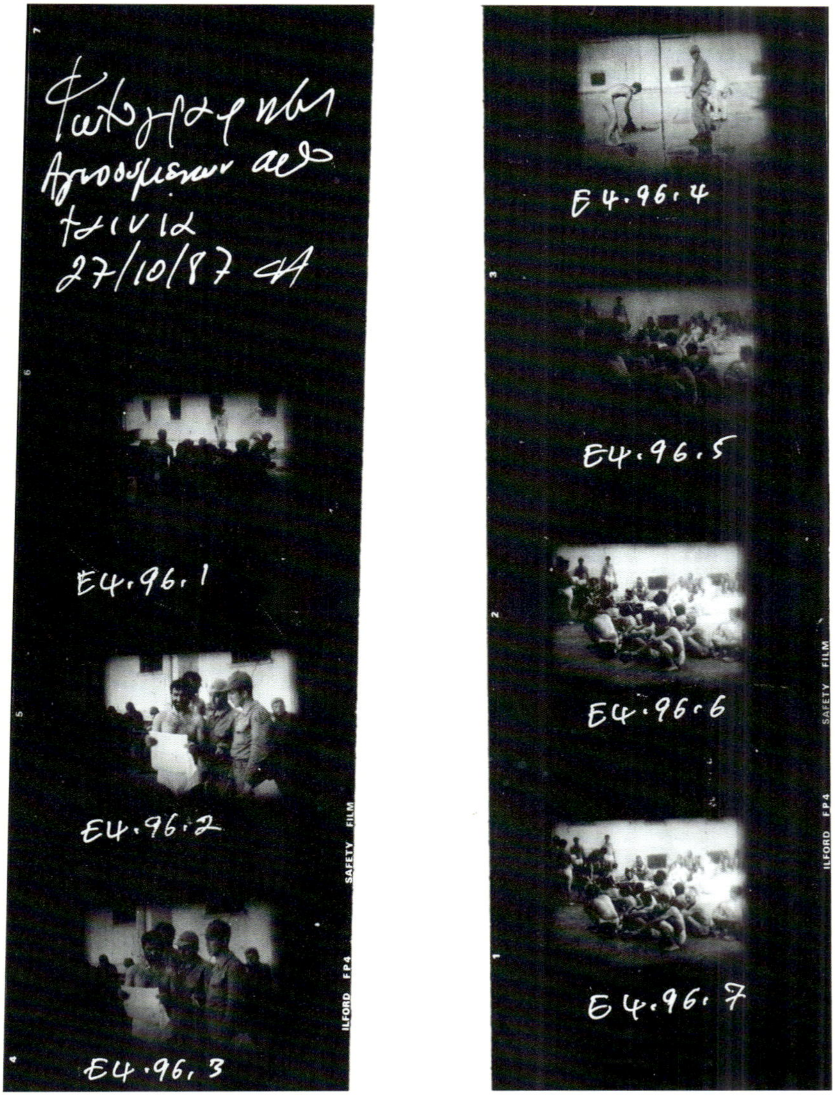

27/10/87
E4.96.1
E4.96.2
E4.96.3
ILFORD FP4
SAFETY FILM
E4.96.4
E4.96.5
E4.96.6
E4.96.7


NO.

**2.21**

## The Cave

The first weekend in April 2012, the night after the police raid that ended OBZ's occupation of the dead zone in central Nicosia, I attended a screening of Derviş Zaim's latest film, *Shadows and Faces* (*Gölgeler ve Suretler*), at Cine Studio, the theater at the University of Nicosia in the southern neighborhood of Ayios Dometios. I went with a Cypriot friend, and we met other friends there, including a professor who would moderate a question-and-answer session with Zaim after the screening. The event had been organized by Panicos Chrysanthou, Zaim's longtime collaborator—they had codirected and coproduced the documentary film *Parallel Trips* (2004); Chrysanthou had coproduced Zaim's fiction film, *Mud* (2003), and Zaim had coproduced Chrysanthou's fiction film, *Akamas* (2006)—though Chrysanthou made it clear in his opening remarks (in Greek) that this new film, *Shadows and Faces*, was not one of their collaborations. Zaim stood and greeted the audience briefly before the film began, telling us (in English) that he was especially happy to attend this event because it was the first time the film would be shown to a Greek-Cypriot audience; he did not want to say too much about it, as he hoped it would "speak for itself."



*Shadows and Faces* delivers a fairly straightforward narrative about the Cyprus conflict, one that would have been—and indeed proved in some ways to be, that evening—quite familiar to Cypriot audiences. It follows Ruhsar, a Turkish-Cypriot girl of about twelve, who is chased from her village along with her father, Salih, by Greek-Cypriot police who are attacking Turkish-Cypriot settlements in the area in 1963 (the date is never pinpointed, only implied). Salih and Ruhsar cannot get to safety in the city, so they make their way instead to the nearby village of Salih's estranged brother, Veli, who agrees to shelter them. Veli's village is mixed; one of the central characters, Anna, is a Greek-Cypriot woman, perhaps a widow, who does not sympathize with the police nor with her own son, Christos, in their raids on Turkish-Cypriot homes and villages. Her allegiance to her Turkish-Cypriot friends moves her to take risks with her own life as she tries, fruitlessly, to protect them. Ruhsar and Salih are separated as they try to evade the police at a checkpoint, and Ruhsar returns to the village alone. Salih's prolonged absence through the rest of the film undergirds the growing tension among the villagers, and between the villagers and the police, which feeds murder after vengeful murder, and ultimately a massacre in the final scenes.

Zaim uses the traditional Ottoman art form of shadow play—known as *karagöz* in Turkish, *καραγκιόζη* in Greek—to insinuate the voice of a narrator, or a chorus, into the action of the film. Shadow puppets appear in the very first scene, where Salih rehearses a play before his daughter, who wants nothing to do with it; he promotes *karagöz* to her as a kind of discipline (*terbiye*, in Turkish) that helps one cultivate one's mind and soul, to master one's dark side. "It has shown me my shadow," he tells Ruhsar, "and that has saved me. It might save you as well, one day." His puppets, the traditional figures of Karagöz and Hacivat, are inanimate pieces of painted metal, yet they speak moral lessons to their audiences at crucial moments. After Salih's disappearance, Veli throws them to the ground, to be discovered later by Ruhsar; they carry bad luck and ill omens; they trouble Ruhsar in her dreams; they are buried, and mistaken for guns; they are dug up and shot; one is placed in the coffin of a villager killed by a policeman; Ruhsar buries them again, for the last time, having escaped with her life to a different village now populated by Turkish-Cypriot refugees. This village is also the site of her reunion with her father, Salih, who performs another shadow play in the last moments of the film, retelling the recent events of their lives as a universal story of ambition and greed: "Perhaps one day a balance will be struck," his puppet sings, "between our minds, our souls and our ambitions. There'll be good people. We'll be good people. And we'll leave the cave without the slightest fear."[36]



The itinerary of the shadow puppets—discarded on the ground, shot, placed in a coffin, buried and unburied and reburied, shifting status from desired possession and metonym of a loved one who is missing to a dark sign of his fate—powerfully recalled to me the bones and belongings of the missing that I had been studying for many months by then. I remarked on this during the intermission to an archaeologist I had met at the CMP who turned up at the screening. *Yes!* she agreed, laughing. *All that digging!*

In the discussion after the screening, Zaim answered questions in English that came to him mostly in Greek, translated for him by the professor I knew; my friend and I noted that he did not give Zaim complete translations of all of the questions, but rather seemed to soften the more pointed ones, or left certain points out altogether. For example, one audience member, a middle-aged man, observed that the film did not seem "balanced," since it only showed violence against Turkish Cypriots perpetrated by Greek Cypriots but did not show what happened to "the other side," which, the speaker noted, "was much worse." The translator left out the last bit and paraphrased, putting the question to Zaim: *Do you think this film gives a balanced or objective picture of the violence that took place?* Zaim replied that he did not think there was "an objective history," only multiple subjective ones, and this film was made from his subjective point of view: *I'm a*

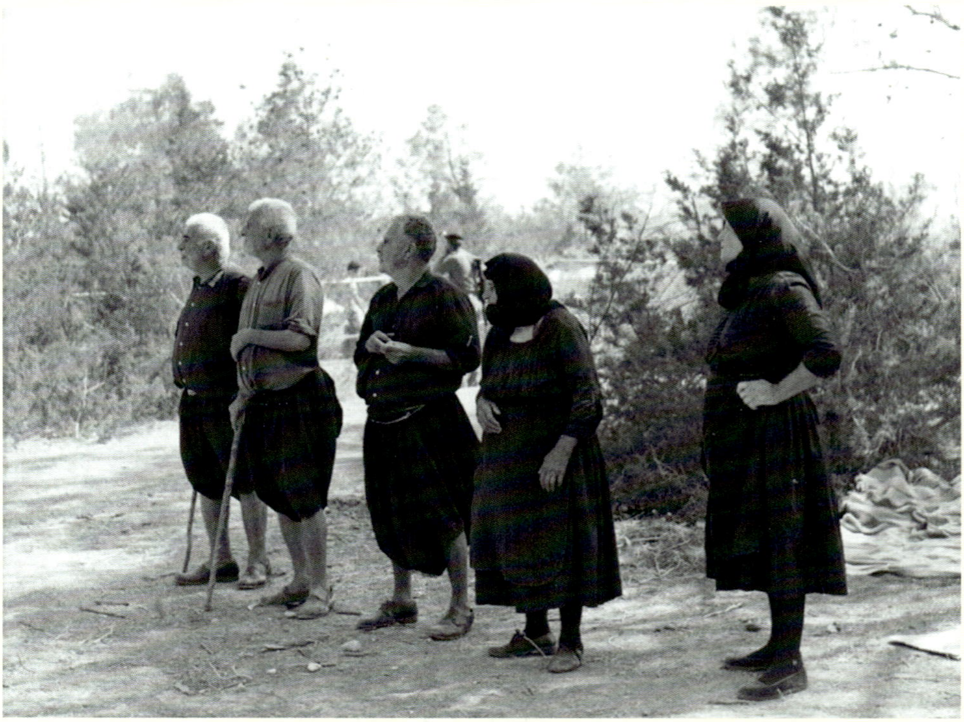

NO.

**2.22**

*Turkish Cypriot from Limassol. That's who I am, and I can't be changed!* He thought there was more value in subjective points of view, he said, and he tried to be as honest as he possibly could in representing his own.

A middle-aged woman in the audience persisted in probing the problem of balance and fair representation, asking (in Greek) what she called a "factual" question: *I've heard many stories about violence at that time,* she said, *stories from Turkish Cypriots and Greek Cypriots, but I've never heard of organized violence on the part of the state. I never heard that the police were involved. Is that true?* There was a pause, and I heard soft laughter in the audience. Zaim, smiling, said only, *Yes!*

Yes. There is no scene in *Shadows and Faces* that represents a specific, discrete event in the historical record of the Cyprus conflict; unlike the scene of the four men at gunpoint in Chrysanthou's *The Story of the Green Line,* Zaim does not fictionalize history here; he does not creatively reconstruct an event from the archive. But the film trades in and counts on common knowledge about the conflict: knowledge conveyed through the telling of stories that Zaim and countless others have heard, with and without names, places, and dates attached. The status of Ruhsar's story might be one of these, or it might as well be one of these; it oscillates, thus, between a uniqueness achieved artfully—fictionally—and a generality achieved by documentary conventions of setting and truth telling.



The opening sequence establishes this oscillation as the basic rhythm of the film. The first moments sustain a close-up shot of a bedsheet billowing and snapping in the wind—a sheet that will recur throughout the film as its central symbolic trope, an opaque screen that divides each character into a shadow and a face, and also unites them. It is the projection surface for Salih's shadow plays, on which a map of Cyprus serves as backdrop; it is also a humble piece of laundry, hanging ever present in the yards of the villagers, simultaneously showing and obscuring their clandestine activities or giving them partial cover as they witness events unfolding. In the opening sequence, superimposed over the rippling sheet, after the production credits and title, and before a word is spoken, three expository intertitles appear, setting the story in historical place and time:

> Until 1960, Cyprus was a British colony composed of Greeks and a Turkish minority. For the most part, the two communities lived in harmony throughout the island. In 1955, Greek Cypriots set up an underground organization, EOKA, and began an armed struggle for union with Greece. Turkish Cypriots saw this move as a threat and formed a counter-organization, TMT. They proposed partition of the island.

> In 1960, a compromise solution of independence was imposed on Cyprus after both union with Greece and partition were rejected. A period of temporary peace followed. In 1963, Greek Cypriots proposed a series of constitutional changes, claiming that the state couldn't function. Turkish Cypriots rejected the proposals.
>
> Tension among Greek and Turkish Cypriots escalated into communal conflict. Being better armed, the Greek Cypriots drove many Turks out of their settlements during clashes over the push for union with Greece.



The last intertitle fades as the sheet blows aside to reveal, in soft focus, a group of police officers in dark-blue uniforms and a few civilians in street clothes, walking out of the yard where the sheet is hanging on a line and down a village road, their backs turned to the camera. The intertitles have already established a documentary code for reading the scenes that follow: the year is 1963, the setting a "Turkish" settlement in Cyprus (in Zaim's term), the police Greek Cypriots. So many documentary films this audience had seen about the Cyprus conflict had opened in this way, even if the communal identities of the characters were reversed. They were thus immediately given to understand that the film was based on a true story, though they would likely not have mistaken it for a documentary; the prominence of overt symbolism, the intent focus on character development, the discernible narrative arc, and the absence of archival material—all generic conventions in their own right—marked it unequivocally as a work of fiction. Yet the film's efficacy, at least for the audience that night in April 2012, lay in its reality effect: *Only the movies tell it like it is.*

And so the discussion continued as a debate about the historical past. One middle-aged man asked, *What do we do about those people who are really responsible for what happened? We all know who they are, and they're walking around today, living in the shadows. How can we bring them into the light?* Another member of the audience spoke up and rejected the premise of his question. *What I found so effective about the film,* she said, *was that it showed that the violence was not just made by a few leaders. It shows how ordinary people got implicated in violence and hatred, how easily hatred was sparked for people who didn't feel it before.* Zaim agreed with her and said he hoped the film showed how looking at our dark sides and coming to terms with our shadows can help prevent us from turning to violence; Ruhsar, for example, among all the characters in the film, has an opportunity to look at her dark side in a serious way. He told us he had not wanted to show a catharsis in the film—such a resolution would have been too heavy-handed—and so he left the question open at the end of the film as to whether anyone learns, and what they learn. This was truer to his own experience in Cyprus, he said.

Zaim had told the audience before the screening that he hoped the film would speak for itself. He must have known that it would not: that he was placing a burden of interpretation on the viewers, and that interpretation might feel to them like taking a side—especially these people, the film's very first Greek-Cypriot audience (as he took us to be). In creating a fiction film, Zaim might have been in a stronger position than a documentarian to craft a story, to assemble the world of characters and symbols from which the story drew its meaning, to direct and calibrate the investments and reactions of the viewers, to offer his dream of a different world to inhabit and entice them to share it. Yet even this dream had an artifactual quality, anchored by objects that survived violence and became temporal operators, recontextualizing the violence in a new story of how what happened had come to pass, and what might yet be coming.



Zaim activates this artifactual historicity not only with the shadow puppets but also with photographs—a familiar tool of documentary knowledge making, including Zaim's own work in *Parallel Trips*. In two brief scenes, the ongoing action of *Shadows and Faces* momentarily freezes in the form of a photograph, immediately reframed by the camera as a feature of the environment in which the action then continues. In the earlier of the two scenes (50:08), it is the courtyard of Anna's house, then empty as Anna makes her way beyond it to Ruhsar's house, that appears as a photograph in Ruhsar's hand just as Anna knocks on her door. The significance of the courtyard, empty now and utterly still but for the soft rustling of a breeze through the leaves of Anna's lemon tree, will not register until the end of the film, when Anna is shot and killed there by Ahmet, Ruhsar's cousin, as she tries to shield her son Christos from Ahmet's gun.

The later scene (1:47:37) opens just after the massacre in Veli's village; Ruhsar and Ahmet tarry, grieving, at Veli's grave, one of ten fresh graves dug at the foot of the village's fortress wall. The camera follows them as they walk away, leaving the village, disappearing behind the turreted curve of the wall, and then it pans back, showing the ground beneath the wall now empty of graves, as if nothing had happened there. The moving image goes still for a moment, and then the camera zooms out to reveal that still image as a poster on the wall of the schoolroom where Ruhsar is staying later that night, along with dozens of other refugees. The still thus becomes a documentary artifact of the village in the time before—not yet associated with the police raids that brought the deaths of so many villagers that day and the displacement of the rest. Just that swiftly, in the blink of an eye—if you aren't watching the film closely, you'll miss it—the present moment in Ruhsar's unfolding day is reframed as the time before; she has now become a refugee, and her experience in Veli's village has become a historical event.

With this artifactual technique, Zaim shows an archive in the process of being made. Ruhsar moves on, finds her father, begins to look at her shadow; but the still image of the village as it was in the time before remains on the schoolroom wall, left behind. Soon it will begin to curl at the edges and decay. One day, we might imagine, momentarily experiencing a dilation of time and our displacement in it, this school will itself have become a crucial site of collective memory for Turkish Cypriots: recalled as a place of refuge in a desperate and dangerous time, now long past; a proto-enclave, the first of many refugee settlements to come; a way station on the impossibly long and twisting path toward a more peaceful future.

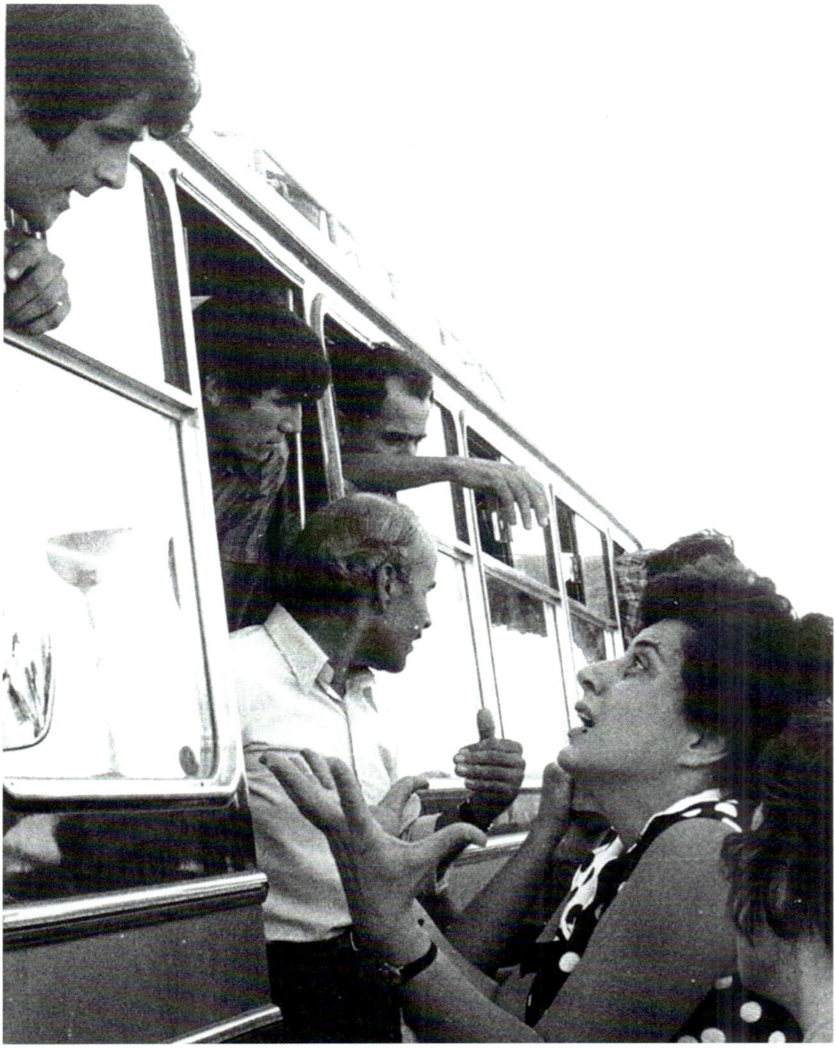

NO.

2.23

# Epilogue. Our Own Ghosts

In her groundbreaking, mind-bending work *Ghostly Matters*, Avery Gordon later wrote, she distinguished haunting from other temporalized modes of experiencing collective and personal violence, such as trauma. In trauma, the repression of violence "jams time" and displaces its experience, through repetition, to later moments; haunting, on the other hand,

> is an animated state in which a repressed or unresolved social violence is making itself known, sometimes very directly, sometimes more obliquely. [In *Ghostly Matters*] I used the term haunting to describe those singular and yet repetitive instances when home becomes unfamiliar, when your bearings on the world lose direction, when the over-and-done-with comes alive, when what's been in your blind field comes into view. Haunting raises specters, and it alters the experience of being in linear time, alters the way we normally separate and sequence the past, the present, and the future. . . . We're haunted, as Herbert Marcuse wrote, by the "historic alternatives" that could have been and by the peculiar temporality of the shadowing of lost and better futures that insinuates itself in the something-to-be-done, sometimes as nostalgia, sometimes as regret, sometimes as a kind of critical urgency. When the something-to-be-done becomes urgent, we feel as if we can't wait any longer for things to change, but of course one does wait, sometimes patiently, sometimes not. (Gordon 2011, 4, 2, 7)[1]

Gordon's (2011, 1) inquiry into haunting developed into "case studies" on transatlantic slavery and state terror in Argentina and Chile in the 1970s—her term "case studies" only hinting at the demanding and deliber-

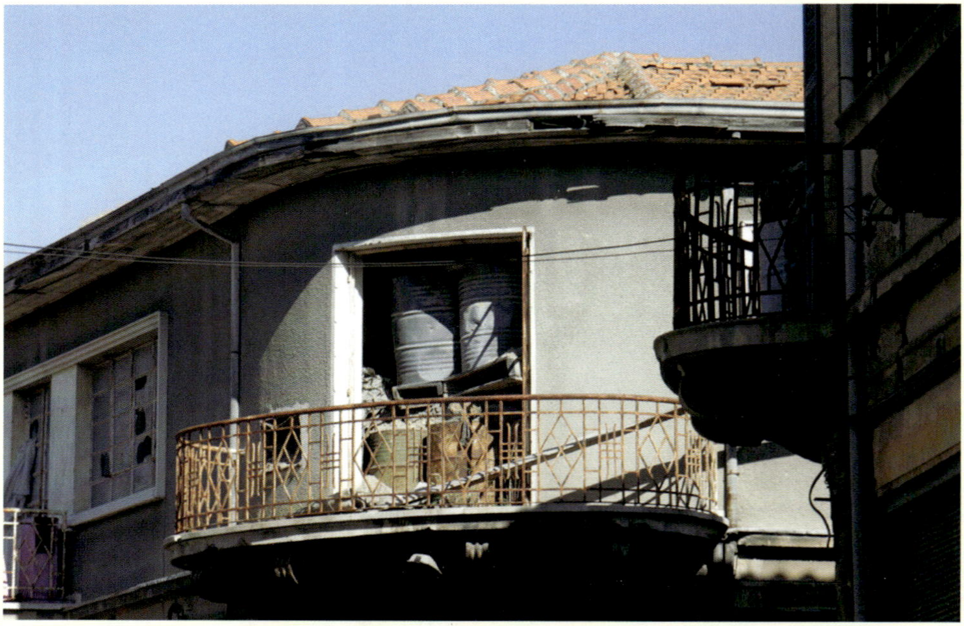

NO.

E.1

ately unorthodox empiricism on which she insists within and throughout her theorization of haunting. Indeed, she argues, it is by studying the experience of haunting that we may "expand the domain of the empirical" where we look for evidence in social analysis, and thereby "take social determination quite seriously" (Gordon 1997, 21). One of the ways to do this, she says, is to "go beyond the fundamental alienation of turning social relations into just the things we know and toward our own reckoning with how we are in these stories, with how they change us, with our own ghosts" (21–22).

I have often thought about haunting as I have written about the knowledge projects pursued by my interlocutors in Cyprus—forensic scientists and filmmakers, primarily, but also teachers, journalists, artists, and yes, social scientists. The very concept of the artifactual, which I have discussed in this book both as a mode of historicity and as the onto-epistemological nature of forensic and documentary knowledge, puts temporal dislocation and empirical evidence into the purview of ethical and political anticipations that recall to me the "something-to-be-done" propelled by haunting, on Gordon's account. And also: the waiting. In hypostatizing the artifactual as a kind of temporal experience and a kind of knowledge project particular (not to say exclusive) to the Cypriot context, I have tried, ethnographically, to expand the domain of the empirical in social science: of what we can sense, study, evaluate, know. In doing this, I do not think I see what my interlocutors in Cyprus do not; on the contrary, I have had to lean into their haunting—their sense that they are missing what they are missing[2]—to figure out what to take as evidence. I have had to learn what they already know and pay attention to how they learn it over and over again. I have taken bones and archival images as objects of my own social analysis because they were already objects of my interlocutors' analysis: evidence that confirmed what everyone already knew[3]—that thousands of people went missing and died fifty to sixty years ago—without disclosing what they did not know but most wanted to know: *What really happened to those people? Why did they die? What is the meaning of this violence?*

In doing this research, I have seen how political secrecy is a black hole, a vast naught, a vortex that draws in and destroys knowledge—"the known unknowns," in Donald Rumsfeld's infamous parlance, opening infinitely into "unknown unknowns." I have tried to avoid miming knowledge production as exposure and thereby reproducing, myself, the ideology of secrecy that works to sustain the impasse of division. I have sought instead to capture the positivities of the knowledge being produced, by documenting the contours and shadings between knowledge and its many obverse sides: what is known in relation to what is suspected; what is disclosed in relation to what is withheld; what is publicized in relation to what is confidential; what is already known in relation to what is truly novel; what is evidence in relation to mere information; what is nonknowledge in relation to overt deception.

Even so, I am not convinced that it is helpful to identify Cyprus as a kind of political context: specifically, a context of public secrecy marked by extreme forms of repression and suppression—not unique in this extremity but keeping company with a limited number of other places (but how many, and which ones?) riven by war and not repaired. Immediately, this marking of the Cypriot context would raise questions about its comparability to the others in terms of scale: the number and brutality of killings and disappearances that took place, the extent of their organization by the state, the distance in historical time of the events in question, the progress in forensic and other knowledge of the events since then, and so on. These are not questions I can answer. Nor can I determine a scale of extremity on which to locate the threshold between remarkable and unremarkable contexts of repression and suppression, and insist that the Cypriot context belongs on the remarkable side.[4] My aim, instead, has been to show how my interlocutors contended with public secrecy in the absence of a public—working on the pretense of a public, or summoning one up in their empathetic solidarity and their productive collaborations with one another, piecing together the evidence as they parried uncertainty as to whether there ever was or could ever be *one* Cypriot society. How far back must they go to give an account of the Cyprus conflict from the beginning? Or was division always there?



In 2014, Good Friday fell on April 18, and for the first time in fifty-seven years, Orthodox services were held at the Church of Saint Georgios Exorinos —the Exiler—in the northeastern coastal city of Famagusta. This highly publicized event arose from the efforts of the Bicommunal Famagusta Initiative, a group of Turkish Cypriots and Greek Cypriots campaigning for the redevelopment of the city—unlikely comrades, these peace activists and property owners, whose interests aligned in this instance if in no other. I had heard about the event during the entire week leading up to Good Friday and decided to go with two friends who lived in the north. On the drive out, one of them, a Cypriot researcher, told me about the history of the church where the services would be held—originally an Armenian church that was given to the Greek-Cypriot community in Famagusta by British authorities in the 1930s. Most of the Greek Cypriots who lived in Famagusta at that time had their homes in Varosha, the district bordering the beach. Varosha was built up in

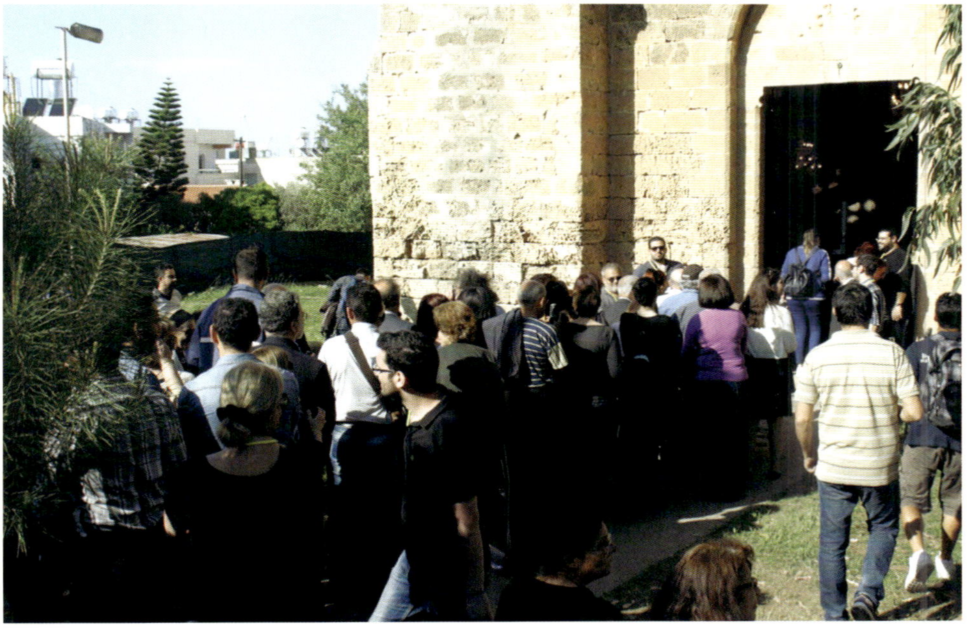

NO.

E.2

the 1960s with high-rise hotels and apartment blocks and came to stand as a symbol of Cypriot modernity and prosperity, as popular with foreign tourists as it was with middle-class Cypriots. In 1974, the Greek Cypriots who lived there fled from the advancing Turkish army, which eventually enclosed the district behind chain-link fencing, stacked metal barrels, barbed wire, and forbidding signs. Varosha stood thus, abandoned, for almost fifty years.

I had visited Famagusta several times over the years, drawn, as many have been, to Varosha's bizarre spectacle of desolation and decay—a modern city shoreline familiar from many Mediterranean coasts, but uncannily so: vacant, rotting, rusting, crumbling into rubble on the sand, thousands of broken windows giving slivers of sight lines into thousands of empty rooms. Visitors kept their distance, deterred from entering by soldiers with machine guns and the prospect of encountering feral animals. I had heard Varosha described many times as a "ghost town"—not a graveyard, like so many places in Cyprus where people were killed and buried in that time of violence. Its loss was mourned, nonetheless.



In the 1950s, my friend told me, no more than 150 Greek Cypriots had lived inside the old walled city of Famagusta where the Church of Saint Georgios Exorinos was located; most lived across the bay in Varosha. It was therefore a very small congregation that was forced to leave in 1957, in fear of retaliation for the first incidents of violence against Turkish Cypriots perpetrated by Greek-Cypriot extremists. The church had not been used since then. My friend, who knew all the stories, made much of the saint's moniker, Exorinos, "the Exiler," laughing at the irony: *People say that if you put dirt from the church courtyard in your neighbor's yard, you can make him leave!*

My other friend told me she had gotten to know some people—architects, urban planners, environmental engineers, permaculture designers, business owners, artists—who were collaborating on the Famagusta Ecocity Project, a multifaceted plan to rejuvenate the city. The project—the subject of a documentary film then being made—entailed opening Varosha, turning the beach area into a sustainable eco-friendly shoreline, connecting Varosha to the walled city of Famagusta and other city districts, declaring the walled city a UN World Heritage Site, and rehabilitating the old port for trade on a limited scale. The Turkish-Cypriot mayor of Famagusta had been working with the Greek-Cypriot mayor-in-exile to support and promote the project, which had given rise to the Bicommunal Famagusta Initiative and ultimately to the Good Friday event we were there to witness.

When we got to the walled city and started making our way to the church, people on the streets kept calling out to my friends, who were well known there, and passed along all kinds of information about the event. We heard that some young Turkish Cypriots who had been protesting early that morning had been detained by the police; that a Turkish nationalist group, including former members of a paramilitary organization active in the 1960s and 1970s, had hung a massive Turkish flag on the building across from the church the previous night. *Once you put up a flag, you can't take it down!* my friend said, laughing. We saw it as soon as we approached the church, billowing in the breeze next to an equally massive TRNC flag, their vibrant reds casting a glow over the entire street. These signs of protest did not disrupt the Good Friday services, however, which attracted thousands of people, almost as many Turkish Cypriots as Greek Cypriots, as far as I could tell. The courtyard through which the effigy of Christ would be carried, covered with flowers, was packed with visitors—worshippers, current residents of the city, former residents and their descendants, curious supporters of bicommunal activity, and dozens of Cypriot and Turkish media representatives with microphones and video cameras. A line formed to enter the church, but many remained outside, seated or standing, talking, waiting.



We, too, stayed for some time, but Christ's effigy did not emerge, and eventually we peeled off from the crowd to head downtown for coffee. A young student whom my friend knew joined us for the walk, and we resumed our discussion of Varosha. He said that he had recently heard Varosha described as a "dead body"; Turkish Cypriots in favor of returning Varosha to Greek-Cypriot property owners were saying, *Why would we want to live next to a dead body?* They wanted to see it developed, used, lived in. My friend told me that attitudes among Turkish Cypriots toward Varosha, like many other abandoned areas in the north, had changed after the checkpoints opened in 2003. For thirty years, they had lived next door to empty houses, sometimes entire empty neighborhoods, without giving much thought to it; the ruins were inert, a matter of indifference. But when thousands of Greek Cypriots began returning to visit, and Turkish Cypriots saw that they still retained a vital connection to these places, the stilled environment was reanimated by the prospect of life.

The shift in Varosha's status from ghost town to dead body turned on this return of Greek Cypriots. In the memories of those Turkish Cypriots who had stayed in Famagusta, or who moved there after the war, the Greek-Cypriot former residents of Varosha were suspended in the past. They had left their traces in the ruins and survived only as ghosts—invisible, perhaps unsettling, but absent.[5] When they came back, aged but very much alive, visible and present, they carried with them their own vivid memories of the city as well as forceful claims to the homes and belongings they had left behind. The city to which they returned could not remain a ghost town; it ap-

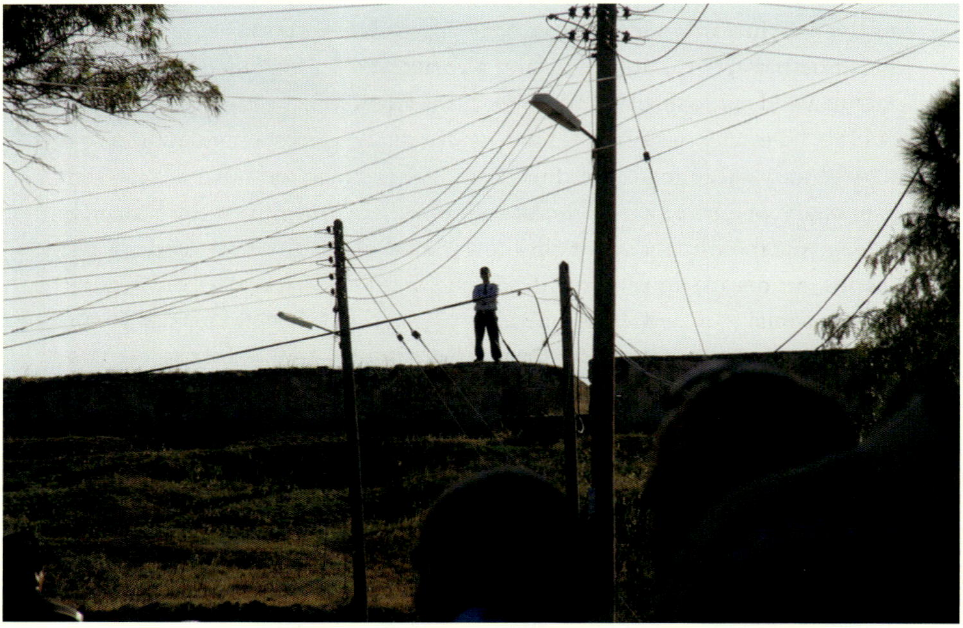

NO.

E.3

peared now as a dead body in advanced decomposition, not empty at all but littered, crammed with detritus, dangerous shards, broken beams, feral animals, foul smells. Valuable beachfront real estate had become worthless; the ruins would have to be torn down and cleared away. No one thought Varosha could be revived and restored to the great city by the sea that it had been before the division. Something new would emerge, or the project of bicommunal reinhabitation and renewal would fail.



From my vantage today, writing these last words in the early days of 2022, the Good Friday event at Famagusta in the spring of 2014, which seemed to me then a moment of opening, could now easily be reframed as just another episode in a long, long narrative of closure. Due to the COVID pandemic, I was not able to travel to Cyprus for almost two years, so—apart from a brief trip in December 2021—it is largely from long-distance talk with my Cypriot friends that I have developed a sense of the present as especially hopeless. The border crossings between north and south reopened only a few months ago, after closing for a year and a half during the worst of the pandemic, affirming widespread mistrust toward the two regimes (but especially toward the Republic, which acted first and unilaterally) that would leap at any pretext to entrench the division; and halting so much of the cross-border cultural and political work that had chipped away at alienation and impasse since 2003. From another perspective, the closures—which did not affect everyday life in significant ways for many Cypriots—may have devastated people's hopes for a settlement by rematerializing the division and proving that, for most purposes, the two communities are not interdependent after all this time but indeed definitively separate. The brief and informal UN-mediated peace talks that had resumed in April 2021 were universally judged a complete failure; the negotiation process was declared "dead" by the Turkish-Cypriot foreign minister.

And yet: the dynamics of emergence and recursion that have characterized the long history of conflict in Cyprus instruct me not to conclude this story, yet. The material and immaterial presence of that long past—its immanence in the ongoing present—unsettles my certainty about the future. The very recontextualization of the Good Friday event in Famagusta that I am in the process of entertaining gives me the form of a future recontextualization of this present moment, with a potentially different conclusion.

In October 2020, the Turkish military took down the barbed wire and fencing around Varosha, and the ghost town was partially reopened for peo-

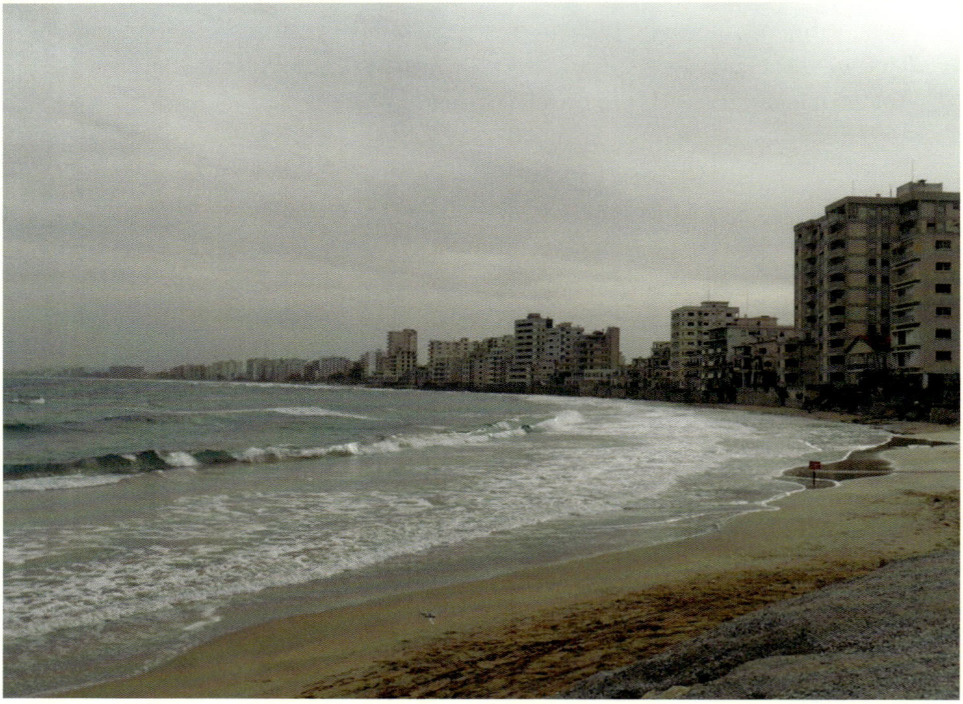

*NO.*

**E.4**

ple to look around, behold the ruins, and pick their way through the rubble to the beach promenade, where they could sun and swim. Since the checkpoints were closed at the time, Cypriots living in the south could not visit, and many protested the opening of Varosha, which they understood as a land grab; the Republic condemned it as a violation of international law, referring to a UN Resolution that required Turkey to turn properties in Varosha over to their original owners, almost exclusively Greek Cypriots. Varosha had been a bargaining chip in the peace negotiations all along; many Greek Cypriots wanted it returned to the Republic in any settlement deal, and it had been offered in many failed deals over the years. Creating new facts on the ground, the Turkish military began cleaning up Varosha, repaving streets and sidewalks, permitting commercial establishments to set up—while also, in theory, opening Turkey up to property claims from Greek Cypriots that had been on hold while Varosha remained deserted and "frozen" under military occupation for the past forty-six years.



In the second phase of the reopening, beginning in July 2021, parts of Varosha were—at least in theory—handed over from military (Turkish) to civilian (Turkish-Cypriot) control. According to media reports, foreign tourists as well as Cypriots have been visiting, prevented from entering roped-off dilapidated buildings but otherwise free to roam and gape. "'It's as if they're performing an autopsy and tourists are coming to witness it,'" one Greek-Cypriot man told an AP reporter; he had fled Varosha with his family as a small child and returned in September 2021 to see his old neighborhood in ruins—but also signs of life, perhaps of threat: refreshment stands, bicycles for rent, bright new trash cans filled with fresh debris.[6]

Is this dead body being autopsied, or is it coming back to life? What does the abrupt recontextualization of Varosha, premised on its revivification—the reframing of a bargaining chip as a land grab—do to the presence of the past in this crumbling, decaying place? What hopes, fears, plans, and resolutions might be born of this moment, if we were to recall not only the time when Varosha was deserted and Famagusta was bombed in 1974—the time in which so much political discourse about this place is stuck—but also that time of opening on Good Friday, seven years ago? What anticipations might such a dislocation in time bring to this place?

This book has explored such questions yielded by the dynamics of emergence and recursion in Cyprus, and perhaps in other places—questions opened up by the experience of time after violence and division, by the dangers and fecundities of ruins and graveyards, by indeterminate shifts in memories and attachments, by all that can be learned from the past and all that remains unknown.

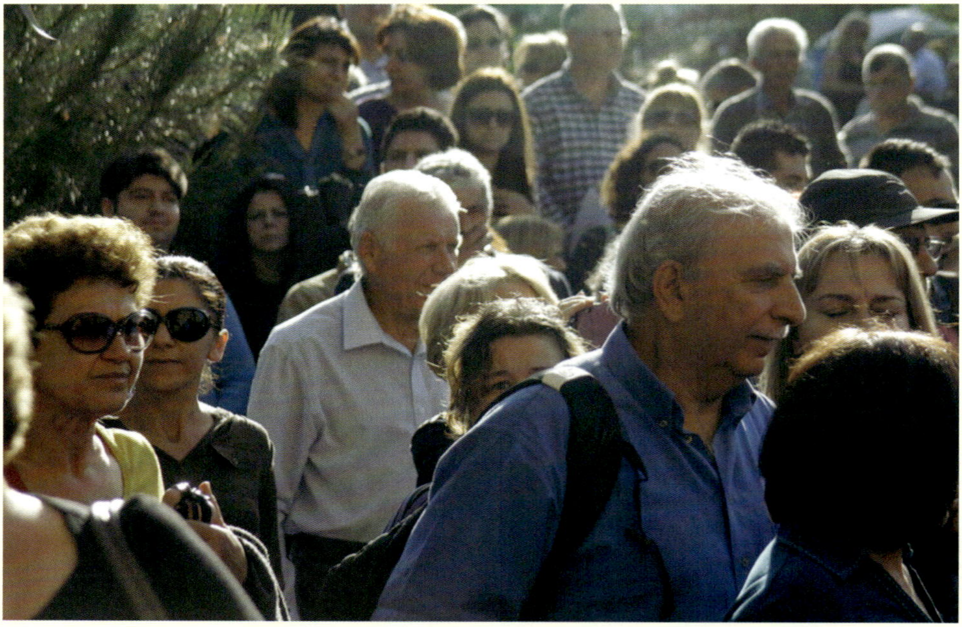

NO.

E.5

# Appendix. Archive

NOTE: All copyrighted images are reproduced with permission. Images labeled "PIO" come from the archives of the Press and Information Office in the Republic of Cyprus and are reproduced with permission.

**P.1**

© Nicos Philippou, *Coffee House Embellishments* (L1010262). 2007.

**P.2**

PIO 34-313-22. Archival note: Takis Ioannides collection, EOKA 1955–59.

**P.3**

PIO E4-053-9_74. Archival note: Exhibition on the Black Bible of the missing (copy). 1974.

**P.4**

© Nicos Philippou, *Sharqi* (3). 2016.

**I.1**

PIO E4-138-003. Archival note: Exhibition on the Black Bible of the missing (copy). 1974. Helicopter during military reconnaissance.

**I.2**

© Nicos Philippou, *Sharqi* (24). 2016.

**I.3**

© Nicos Philippou, *Coffee House Embellishments* (drosia 15.11.06_G6). 2007.

**I.4**

PIO 36-316-23a. Archival note: Takis Ioannides collection, EOKA 1955–59.

**I.5**

PIO 133-B. Published in *Cyprus, Days of Rage in 555 Photographs* (Ioannides 1975), photographs by Charalambos Avdellopoulos and Andreas Koutas. P. 133 (B). 1974. Caption (for this photograph along with two others showing the bombings and fires engulfing the city): Nicosia in flames following its bombing from the air. But the US-made bombers leave only ruins in their wake.

**I.6**

Photograph taken by Robert Vogt. Nicosia (Republic of Cyprus). June 10, 2012.

**I.7**

© Nicos Philippou, *Arizona* (34). 2016–2022.

**1.1**

© Nicos Philippou, *Sharqi* (14). 2016.

**1.2**

Photograph taken by author. Strovolos, Nicosia (Republic of Cyprus). July 28, 2007.

**1.3**

Photograph taken by author. Balıkesir (Turkish Republic of Northern Cyprus). July 28, 2007.

**1.4**

PIO E4-053-009. Archival note: Exhibition on the Black Bible of the missing (copy). 1974.

**1.5**

PIO E4-168-005. Archival note: Exhibition on the Black Bible of the missing (copy). 1974.

**1.6**

PIO E4-168-20. Archival note: Exhibition on the Black Bible of the missing (copy). 1974.

**1.7**

PIO E4-018-012. Archival note: Soldiers arrested by the Turkish. *Günaydın* newspaper, March 15, 1975.

**1.8**

© Committee on Missing Persons in Cyprus (11).

**1.9**

Photograph taken by anonymous visitor (7277). CMP Anthropological Laboratory. 2017. Redacted to obscure identifying case numbers.

**1.10**

© Committee on Missing Persons in Cyprus (13).

**1.11**

Photograph taken by anonymous visitor (7290). CMP Anthropological Laboratory. 2017. Redacted to obscure identifying case numbers.

**1.12**

© Committee on Missing Persons in Cyprus (19).

**1.13**

Photograph taken by anonymous visitor (7286). CMP Anthropological Laboratory. 2017. Redacted to obscure identifying case numbers.

**1.14**

© Nicos Philippou, *Sharqi* (19). 2016.

**1.15**

Photograph taken by author. Postage stamp issued in the Republic of Cyprus, 2019. Author's fieldwork ephemera.

**1.16**

PIO E4-0135-009. Archival note: Exhibition on the Black Bible of the missing (copy). 1974.

**2.1**

© Nicos Philippou, *Off the Map* (16). 2005.

**2.2**

© Sir Don McCullin, Gaziveren (Cyprus). 1964.

**2.3**

© Panicos Chrysanthou, *Stories of the No-Man's Land*, p. 45 (053a). Caption: 06.02.1991. The school of Zacharka village in the springtime. The village had one of the most beautiful schools I have ever seen. Being in nature next to the village seemed to be a paradise for the children. Nobody saved this beauty from the ravages of time and the actions of men.

**2.4**

© Panicos Chrysanthou, *Stories of the No-Man's Land*, p. 44 (054). Caption: 22.04.2010. The school of Zacharka in the springtime of this year.

**2.5**

© Panicos Chrysanthou, *Stories of the No-Man's Land*, p. 44 (055). Caption: 10.11.1984. The classroom of the school of Zacharka.



**2.6**

© Panicos Chrysanthou, *Stories of the No-Man's Land*, p. 44 (056). Caption: 22.04.2010. The classroom of the school this year.

**2.7**

© Panicos Chrysanthou, *Stories of the No-Man's Land*, p. 50 (066). Caption: 18.01.1985. Malia village. Shooting at the monument of the Turkish Cypriots. Filming at the monument dedicated to the dead Turkish Cypriots during the conflict of 1964.

**2.8**

© Panicos Chrysanthou, *Stories of the No-Man's Land*, p. 51 (065). Caption: 17.03.1989. Life never stops. Gravestones in Malia villa.

**2.9**

PIO 085-B. Published in *Cyprus, Days of Rage in 555 Photographs* (Ioannides 1975), photographs by Charalambos Avdellopoulos and Andreas Koutas. P. 85 (B). 1974. Caption: Monday, 15 July 1974, 11 a.m. Tanks manned by officers and men of the Greek Contingent stationed in

Cyprus under the 1960 London and Zurich agreements enter the Nicosia Central Prisons to free 200 members of EOKA B. . . . During the ensuing demonstrations in the prison grounds the released prisoners tore up the Cyprus flag and replaced it with the Greek flag. . . . The tanks manned by Greek army officers played a dynamic part in the opening of the prison gates.



**2.10**
PIO 103-A. Published in *Cyprus, Days of Rage in 555 Photographs* (Ioannides 1975), photographs by Charalambos Avdellopoulos and Andreas Koutas. P. 103 (A). 1974. Caption: With early dawn on 20 July 1974 Turkish transport planes begin dropping paratroops in Turkish held areas from Nicosia to Pentadactylos mountains.

**2.11**
Screen grab, *Trimithi, a Reconstruction in Words*. Andreas Pantzis, 1987. Four men at gunpoint.

**2.12**
Screen grab, *Homeland*. Serkan Hussein, 2010. Excavation of mass grave at Muratağa (Maratha), 1974.

**2.13**
Screen grab, *Attila '74*. Michael Cacoyannis, 1975. Petraki and Costaki in 1974, interviewed by Michael Cacoyannis.

**2.14**
Screen grab, *Parallel Trips*. Derviş Zaim and Panicos Chrysanthou, 2004. Petraki and Costaki in 1974, from a Greek-Cypriot newspaper story.

**2.15**
Screen grab, *Parallel Trips*. Derviş Zaim and Panicos Chrysanthou, 2004. Petros and Costas in 2003, interviewed by Panicos Chrysanthou.

**2.16**
Screen grab, *Memory in the Dead Zone*. Alev Adil. Double screen projection in live performance, 2011.

**2.17**
Screen grab, *Memory in the Dead Zone*. Alev Adil. Double screen projection in live performance, 2011.

**2.18**
© Panicos Chrysanthou, *Stories of the No-Man's Land*, p. 59 (078). Caption: 06.02.1991. Window of Zacharka village. The man of this house left his jacket hanging on the wall when he left. Obviously he thought he was not going to need it any longer. Or did he forget it? Surely he closed the door behind him. But all the doors of the abandoned houses were found open after a few days, and the windows too. The jacket remained there as a ghost in time. I used to see it and take photographs of it for years, always at the same spot, the same shape, in an open house, forgotten, sorrowful. Once I touched it. It had become like iron due to the dust and moisture it had absorbed. On one of my visits it was no longer there; like all remnants of life in the deserted Turkish-Cypriot villages of Paphos. The all-subduing time and the predatory bulimia of people, who picked up even the stones, have gradually removed all that was left behind by the living. They only remain in the memory of

those who lived in these places. And as they move through time and die, the memories go with them to the grave.

### 2.19

PIO E4-053-073. Archival note: Exhibition on the Black Bible of the missing (copy). 1974.

### 2.20

PIO E4-053-013. Archival note: Exhibition on the Black Bible of the missing (copy). 1974.

### 2.21

PIO E4-096-01_07. Archival note: Exhibition on the Black Bible of the missing (copy). 1974. "Photography of the Missing from film, 27/10/87, CA." (CA = Charalambos Avdellopoulos?)

### 2.22

PIO 216. Published in *Cyprus, Days of Rage in 555 Photographs* (Ioannides 1975), photographs by Charalambos Avdellopoulos and Andreas Koutas. P. 216. 1974. Caption: Farmers from Messaoria, now refugees under the trees of the Akhna forest.

### 2.23

PIO 208. Published in *Cyprus, Days of Rage in 555 Photographs* (Ioannides 1975), photographs by Charalambos Avdellopoulos and Andreas Koutas. P. 208. 1974. Caption: Mother and daughter enquire about husband and father. No, he has not been released.

### E.1

Photograph taken by author. Nicosia (Republic of Cyprus). April 19, 2014.

### E.2

Photograph taken by author. Famagusta (Turkish Republic of Northern Cyprus). April 17, 2014.

### E.3

Photograph taken by author. Famagusta (Turkish Republic of Northern Cyprus). April 17, 2014.



### E.4

Photograph taken by author. Varosha (Turkish Republic of Northern Cyprus). December 12, 2021.

### E.5

Photograph taken by author. Famagusta (Turkish Republic of Northern Cyprus). April 17, 2014.

# Notes

## PROLOGUE

1 — I quote here from the English subtitles of the film. My paraphrases of monologues and dialogues in Greek derive from my own translation.

2 — The PRIO Cyprus Centre is a branch of the Peace Research Institute Oslo, an independent Norwegian organization that funds peace-related research in dozens of countries worldwide.

3 — I reproduce here, with a few minor adjustments, the English translation of Yaşin's poem that appears in the film's subtitles.

4 — My translation of the Greek here differs slightly from the English subtitles in the film.

5 — See Christopher Hitchens, *Cyprus, Stranded in Time*, 1989, posted on YouTube by GeezerFellas, August 17, 2019, https://www.youtube.com/watch?v=DwWozRqekUg.

## INTRODUCTION

1 — These official numbers, which reflect a consensus currently supported by the two regimes and taken as a guideline by the Committee on Missing Persons in Cyprus, have been revised multiple times since the division in 1974. See Nelson (2015) on the manifold complexity of counting the dead.

2 — In 1963–64, some 25,000 Turkish Cypriots seeking safety moved to villages or city neighborhoods that were exclusively Turkish-Cypriot; another 100,000 moved into enclaves. In 1974, approximately 45,000 Turkish Cypriots moved from the south to the north, while about 160,000 Greek Cypriots moved from the north

to the south that year. See Bryant and Hatay (2020) and Demetriou and Gürel (2008), who note that some of these figures are contested. Estimates provided by Trimikliniotis and Bozkurt (2012, 3) indicate that the population of Cyprus a decade before the publication of this book was close to 1.1 million: almost 840,000 people lived in the Republic, about 200,000 of whom were non-Cypriot nationals, including undocumented migrants; and somewhere between 300,000 and 500,000 people lived in the TRNC, including 120,000 to 230,000 migrants and settlers. The authors note that these numbers are approximate and contested. See also International Crisis Group 2010.

3 — As in my other writings (see esp. Davis 2012), in this book I use italics to represent the speech of my interlocutors as reconstructed from my field notes; direct quotations indicate my verbatim representation of their speech.



4 — See Demetriou (2006a) on the focus on conflict in social science research about Cyprus.

5 — See Bryant 2007, 2010; Trimikliniotis and Bozkurt 2012. See also Demetriou (2008) on how the process of EU accession formed a space for opponents of reconciliation in the south to consolidate political and social support.

6 — In this book, I use the term "ethnonational" to describe identity formations that take ethnic nationality as their foundation, usually in cases where nationality does not accommodate ethnic distinctions by which a population is meaningfully stratified: for example, "Greek Cypriot" and "Turkish Cypriot" are ethnonational identity formations, while "Cypriot" is not (and "American" is not, as it describes a nationality but not an ethnicity, despite the best efforts of American white supremacists to make it appear so). "Ethnonationalist," on the other hand, describes a political orientation grounded in an identification with one's ethnonationality, explicitly as against other ethnonational identities. Thus, for example, I consider EOKA-B, a paramilitary terrorist group organized around Greek-Cypriot identification with Greek nationality and antipathy toward Turkish and Turkish-Cypriot identity, to be ethnonationalist in its political orientation.

7 — See Bryant (2014), who distinguishes "remains"—personal items left behind by Cypriots who fled their homes, such as photographs and documents, which she sees as "inextricably braided with our stories of the Other"—from "remainders," such as pieces of household furniture, which were also left behind but have a more "ambiguous nature" and lead a "mute existence," even if they may also "come to bear an uncanny quality" (692, 693). My definition of "artifact" straddles this distinction. See part two for a fuller discussion of these objects.

8 — Foucault (1980, 142) reads Nietzsche's genealogical work (especially in the *Genealogy of Morals* and *Human, All Too Human*) as a "challenge [to] the pursuit of the origin," a pursuit that requires faith in the "exact essence of things" and their "inviolable identity" at their beginning, as opposed to the perennial "disparity" and

"piecemeal" fabrication that characterize their discursive reality—including the fabrication of truth itself. Thus, Foucault concludes, "the origin lies at a place of inevitable loss," a place that never existed and cannot be recaptured, "where the truth of things corresponded to a truthful discourse" (1980, 143).

9 — On Latour's telling, the status of "actants" and "propositions" challenges the very "demarcation between epistemological and ontological questions" that we are accustomed to establishing for "analytical clarity" (1999, 141).

10 — See my discussion of Foucault and the concept of truth games in the context of clinical psychiatry (Davis 2012, 54–55). In a short thought piece, "The Political Function of the Intellectual," published in *Radical Philosophy* in 1977, Foucault described regimes of truth in broader terms than those in which he had introduced the concept, as a nexus of power and expert knowledge, in *Discipline and Punish* (1977a): "Truth is of the world: it is produced by virtue of multiple constraints. And it induces the regular effects of power. Each society has its regime of truth, its 'general politics' of truth: that is, the types of discourse it harbours and causes to function as true; the mechanisms and instances which enable one to distinguish true from false statements, the way in which each is sanctioned; the techniques and procedures which are valorised for obtaining truth; the status of those who are charged with saying what counts as true" (1977b, 13).



11 — The *Glossary* was authored by Cypriot journalists Bekir Azgın, Christos Christofides, Esra Aygın, and Maria Siakalli, supported by the Cyprus Dialogue project of the Office of the Organization for Security and Co-operation in Europe's Representative on Freedom of the Media, along with colleagues in the Union of Cyprus Journalists, the Association of the Turkish Cypriot Journalists, and the Ethical Journalism Network.

12 — As superb exceptions, I note Demetriou (2018) and Bryant and Hatay (2020), who develop ethnographically grounded, theoretically powerful comparative theories on refugeehood and de facto statehood, respectively.

13 — See my discussion in part one (in "The Only Terrorist Is the State") on the role of media publicity and especially investigative journalism in the development of the CMP's mission. See Sant Cassia (2005) on the long history of these political strategies before the period of forensic investigations began in 2004. The deception of relatives about the fate of Greek-Cypriot missing persons already known to be dead by authorities in the Republic of Cyprus has, by the time of this writing, been well established. The early investigative work of Cypriot journalists Andreas Paraschos and Makarios Drousiotis, documenting the state's cover-up, was published principally in the *Politis* and *Kathimerini* newspapers in the 1990s and early 2000s, as well as in Drousiotis's book (see Drousiotis 2000). Drousiotis also gave testimony in one of the court cases brought by a Greek-Cypriot "Mother" against the Republic on the basis of her human right to know the fate of her missing husband.

On September 15, 2021, Kyriakos Antoniadis spoke to journalists about the deception on the *Politis* radio station: "We had testimony from witnesses. But the [Missing Persons] Service did not give this evidence to the relatives because they wanted the Mothers [of the Missing] to go to the roadblocks [i.e., the checkpoints between north and south that people could not cross until 2003] with their photographs and cry, so that some people could do their jobs at the expense of the missing. May God never show anyone what I went through during my tenure at the Missing Persons Service.'"

According to *Politis* reporter Panagiotis Chatziapostolou (2021), Antoniadis had been a police officer from 1979 to 1983, and in that capacity investigated the missing after the war, collecting witness information and preparing files on each known missing person. His brother, Savvas Antoniadis, was also on the official list of the Greek-Cypriot missing. (Note that the Missing Persons Service, an agency created within the administration of the Republic after the war in 1974, is not the same as the CMP, the bicommunal agency operating under UN auspices in Cyprus, which was established in 1981 but did not begin investigations until 2004.) See Constantinou 2021 for a fuller contextualization of Antoniadis's comments. For my analysis of "conspiracy theories" about the missing in the context of broader Cypriot discourse on "conspiracy theory," see Davis, n.d.



14 — See the CMP's Terms of Reference and Mandate, accessed March 2, 2020, https://www.cmp-cyprus.org/terms-of-reference-and-mandate.

15 — Cf. Nelson (2015), who meticulously documents and creatively thinks with the different practices and domains of counting (the number of the dead, the value of life, magic money) at the heart of public accounting for the genocide in Guatemala.

16 — See the web adaptation of Neni Panourgiá, *Dangerous Citizens: The Greek Left and the Terror of the State*, 2013, https://dangerouscitizens.columbia.edu/.

17 — See also Fischer (1993), who, in writing on post-Soviet Polish nationalism and postmodern anthropology (among other things), develops several textual forms to accommodate his wide-ranging, multidimensional dialogue with the Polish philosopher Leszek Koczanowicz that took place over several days. In one form, their dialogue is arranged as if the script for a play, organized in subsections by topic; but that form is soon complicated by interruptions, as bits of their dialogue taken out of the ongoing sequence are set into and alongside it. Another form incorporates excerpts from poems that Fischer and Koczanowicz discussed; the excerpts thus become part of their dialogue but also refer to integral texts outside it. In the last few parts of the piece, Fischer stages dialogues on the page that did not take place, between Koczanowicz and authors of variously, intriguingly relevant works who thus appear to be speaking directly to his concerns or responding to his comments. Fischer's experiments here are more obviously and consistently dialogic than that

which I am attempting with the visual archive in my text, but the proliferation and scaling of setting and reference that Fischer accomplishes here are instructive.

18 — As Stavros Karayanni notes in his introduction, Stephanides's "vexed relationship" with English—in which "he found an uneasy home" although it was not the language of his birth or childhood—"yielded an impulse for creative refuge in a multiplicity of languages and cultures," in a distinctively postcolonial mode (Karayanni 2018, 14). This refuge is evinced in the text by fragments of the "Greek Cypriot vernacular," as his translator, Despina Pirketti notes, as well as words and phrases in "ancient Greek, Turkish, Latin, Portuguese, Sanskrit, and other languages," including Spanish and modern mainland Greek (Stephanides 2018, 12, 10).

19 — In *Emergent Forms of Life*, Michael Fischer (2003, 256) thematizes this indeterminacy in the reference of war photography, and the archival desires animating the search for "particular images" of singular events, in his discussion of Polish filmmaker Maria Zmarz Koczanowicz's 1994 work *Traces*, and in Milcho Manchevski's film *Before the Rain*, also from 1994. The setting of the latter is the then-ongoing Yugoslav wars; a character working in a far-off photo archive cannot distinguish "images of World War II concentration camps" from "photos of the former Yugoslavia" (255). Fischer frames this kind of referential indeterminacy in relation to the generic indeterminacy of Koczanowicz's films, and especially *Traces*, which deploys documentary tropes—clips of news broadcasts, archival images of different forms of violence in many different locales—in a fragmented pastiche. "Ethical responses require acknowledging that we have seen this all before," Fischer writes, "and that other worlds . . . continue in parallel time, and that images themselves can be ambiguous as entertainment or tragedy. . . . The immediacy of what is seen or heard is not the whole story, and montage does not itself provide meaning. We need to know what is beyond the frame, how the pictures of the world are constructed, the nature of the archives, the substitutions and variations that make up the grammar (and grammatology) that structures our subjectivities, epistemologies, and apperceptions of what is really going on" (256–57). In drawing parallels between Koczanowicz's film work and the work of contemporary anthropology, Fischer insists on the ethical and epistemological necessity of our engaging with the "increasingly mediated world" in which such images anchor and enliven our sense of reality (257). I take this up at greater length in my discussion of documentary and fiction film genres and tropes in part two.



20 — Arsenejević (2011a, 2011b) pursues this argument; see part one.

21 — See Loizos (2007) on the ambiguities, subtleties, and limits of anthropological, psychological, and historical conceptualizations of "generation" and their relevance to longitudinal ethnographic studies of refugee populations, such as his own multigenerational research with Greek-Cypriot refugees from the village of Argaki (Loizos 2008). Hirsch's (2012) generational distinction between "memory"

and "postmemory" in her examination of cultural transmission and memorialization after the Holocaust is also relevant here.

22 — See the original posting on the Internet Archive Wayback Machine: https://web.archive.org/web/20130724030705/http://occupythebufferzone.wordpress.com/about/obz/. Occupy the Buffer Zone still maintains an active Facebook page, including videos from protests at Ledra Street/Lokmacı over the closure of checkpoints at the beginning of the COVID pandemic in March 2020: https://www.facebook.com/OccupyBufferZone/.

23 — See Stavros Karayanni's (2014) discussion of *Coffee House Embellishments.*

24 — In his 2014 article on *Sharqi,* Karayanni finds and traces the "queer imaginings" of the Cypriot landscape that *Sharqi* engages (273)—which produce a "jarring" "incongruity" and paradoxical plays with hyper/reality through the "medium" and the "tool" of the Polaroid (271), and thereby, he says, "new associations and interconnections between psyche and place, imaginary *topos* and homeland" (269). In these imaginings, Karayanni alights momentarily on the rich and peculiar "encounter" between the landscape depicted in *Sharqi* and that of the dead zone (275): a "strip of land," as he puts it, that "accesses its meanings through bare landscapes and apparent desolation," and that, in hegemonic Greek-Cypriot narratives of victimization by the "perpetrator" on the other side (274), is rife with "signs of conflict" and "lingering evidence of abuse and violation" (274). The landscape of *Sharqi,* on the other hand, while sharing many of the dead zone's ideologically overly symbolized topological and sensorial features, especially its "silence and decay" (275), as well as its alterity to picaresque and touristic dreamscapes of antiquity, villages, sea, and sun that dominate conventional (and commercial) depictions of the Cypriot landscape, nevertheless does not "display visible signs of some established national character" (274). For my purposes, what is most compelling in Karayanni's extraordinarily rich reading of *Sharqi* in relation to the dead zone is his insistence that they both "continu[e] on a trajectory rather than standing still in time, and as a movement and motive that is recurrent, eddying" (275). Thus, he suggests, *Sharqi* engages time as well as place, memory and futurity as well as landscape and homeland—not by "simply" subverting or deconstructing essentialist representations of Cyprus, but rather, and more generatively, by "tak[ing] us across" (277, 275). I find it significant that most of the photographs in *Sharqi* were shot in the dry Mesaoria plains bordering the buffer zone on the Greek-Cypriot side, as it runs from southern Nicosia to the village of Lympia before jutting north again and then due east toward Pyla, a mixed village located in the buffer zone where it meets the shore, which is still inhabited (and still mixed). Thus the landscape captured in these images is a borderland, which Philippou has transformed into a kind of nonplace suggesting rich and numerous references to other places.

25 — See, for example, Neil Hall's (2014) photo essay "Lost in Time: The Cyprus Buffer Zone," and Michael Theodoulou's (2016) article "Tour of the Buffer Zone

in Nicosia's Old Town." See also the exhibition catalogue for UNCOVERED, an art installation that took place in a gallery in the buffer zone but referred to the abandoned airport of Nicosia (Şenova and Paraskevaidou 2011, 9, cited in Pellapaisiotis 2014, 236).

26 — Dawdy (2010, 761) begins this essay by citing the "enchantment" of Alexis de Tocqueville, who "marveled" at the "oddness of new ruins" on the American frontier of the 1830s. I discuss Dawdy's perspective at length in the first section of part two. Cf. Ewa Domanska's discussion of the "'enchantments with things' observable in the humanities of today," which she understands in relation to the growth of "counter-disciplines" and their "'insurrectional' . . . discourses," where "things are perceived as Others who demand their place in discourse" (2006, 346).

27 — "Recent ruins" is Dawdy's (2010, 761) phrase. 

28 — On "melancholic objects," see Navaro (2009, 2012, esp. chap. 7).

29 — The famous line is from L. P. Hartley's novel *The Go-Between* (1953).

30 — Cited and discussed in Connolly 2011, 62.

31 — Deleuze (1989, 130–31) is thinking with Leibniz's notion of incompossibility here.

32 — Deleuze (1989, 141) explicitly equates becoming with the powers of the false.

33 — As Biehl and Locke point out in their widely read 2010 piece, "Deleuze and the Anthropology of Becoming," revised and updated for the introduction of their 2017 edited volume *Unfinished*, "With an eye to the possibilities and noninevitability of people's lives, social scientists must also recognize the thresholds where liberating flights and creative actions can become deadly rather than vital forms of experimentation, opening up not to new webs of care and empathy but to systematic disconnection. . . . Becoming is not always heroic" (2010, 336; 2017, 83).

34 — See also Biehl and Locke, who take inspiration from Deleuze's thinking of becoming—that is, "those individual and collective struggles to come to terms with events and intolerable conditions and to shake loose, to whatever degree possible, from determinants and definitions" (2010, 317). In working through their own research experiences in situations of individual and social crisis, they urge an emphasis on "desire," "openness," and "flux" in "ethnographic efforts to illuminate the dynamism of the everyday and the literality and singularity of human becomings" (318).

### ONE. FORENSIC

1 — See Bryant 2007, 2012; Demetriou 2007, 2018. Demetriou (2007, 987) notes that, within the first three days of the opening, approximately 45,000 Cypriots crossed from one side to the other; in the first three months after the opening,

the Republic estimated that 200,000 people crossed from the south to the north (Demetriou 2006b, 57, citing the Republic of Cyprus Statistical Service report, July 2003).

2 — Demetriou (2018, 1–8) discusses the differential impact this opening had on different people in Cyprus at the time. What was celebrated by many Cypriots as a liberation of their movement—if calibrated differently for Turkish Cypriots and Greek Cypriots at the two ends of any given checkpoint—led to restrictions on the movement of other people, including those working in Cyprus on short-stay visas. Thus "changes in the operations of bordering (the materialities of borders, the apparatus that govern them, and the practices that develop around them) are not evenly distributed across populations" (5). As I discuss in the epilogue, all checkpoints were closed starting in February 2020, ostensibly part of COVID lockdowns in both regimes. The Republic was the first to act, unilaterally closing four of the nine crossings on February 28, 2020; the TRNC closed two additional crossings on March 12, 2020, and both regimes ordered full lockdowns shortly afterward, including bans on international travel. Protesters at certain crossings (especially at Ledra Street/Lokmacı), met with tear gas by police, argued that the Republic was using COVID as a pretext to prevent residents in the south from crossing to buy goods in the north, where they were much cheaper. Over the next eighteen months, some restrictions on crossing were temporarily relaxed for certain groups and then reinstated; for most Cypriots, crossing became practically impossible for nearly a year and a half, until the checkpoints reopened on June 4, 2021.



3 — According to an archaeologist I knew at the CMP, the Turkish-Cypriot side of the CMP had insisted that the Greek-Cypriot side conduct investigations into Greek-Cypriot graves in the south before the CMP could proceed with investigations into Greek-Cypriot graves in the north. According to this archaeologist, Physicians for Human Rights still had a lab in Cyprus in 2012, but no one was working there.

4 — See Kovras 2012 for a detailed account of this breakthrough in the Republic's policy toward the problem of the missing. Two organizations of relatives formed in 1975: the Turkish-Cypriot Association of Martyrs' Families and War Veterans, and the Greek-Cypriot Organisation of Relatives of Undeclared Prisoners and Missing Persons. At the time of my fieldwork, the only organization representing both Turkish-Cypriot and Greek-Cypriot families was the Bicommunal Initiative of Relatives of Missing Persons, Victims of Massacres and Other Victims of 1963–74 Events (otherwise known as the Bicommunal Initiative of Relatives of the Missing and Other Victims of War), founded in 2005. See the section "Lost Heroes of the Republic" for a discussion of funerals for the missing organized by members of the Bicommunal Initiative.

5 — These were the figures reported on the CMP website on their page "Statistics," February 28, 2022, accessed March 10, 2022, https://www.cmp-cyprus.org/statistics/.

6 — EOKA is Εθνική Οργάνωση Κυπρίων Αγωνιστών (National Organization of Cypriot Fighters). In the 1950s, EOKA, a Greek-Cypriot armed resistance group, waged a successful guerrilla campaign against the British—also targeting Turkish-Cypriot civilians and armed irregulars then forming in response to EOKA's actions—with the ultimate aim of uniting Cyprus with Greece. The 1960 Constitution instead established the independent sovereignty of Cyprus and a power-sharing framework for Greek-Cypriot and Turkish-Cypriot authorities. The irredentist movement initiated by EOKA, however, was revived by its successor group, EOKA-B, an overtly ethnonationalist parastate terrorist group that targeted not only Turkish Cypriots but also Greek-Cypriot leftists and even mainstream supporters of President Makarios between 1971 and 1974; their alignment with Greek military officers and Greek political operatives representing the interests of the Greek junta (1967–74) in finally "restoring" Cyprus to its Greek "homeland" led directly to the attempted coup in July 1974 and the war that ensued. See the work of Demetriou (2018, esp. chap. 2), for a rigorous "inventory" of fatalities within the Greek-Cypriot community during this period, and the means by which their counting was mystified by the shifting boundaries of the ethnic category of "other" in reports produced by the UN and the Republic. Thus, Demetriou shows, deaths of Greek Cypriots accountable to "intra-communal" or "co-ethnic" violence in the 1960s through 1974—that is, Greek Cypriots killed by Greek Cypriots—were either not counted at all or counted in such a way as to be easily conflated with deaths at the hands of Turkish Cypriots or Turkish military (2018, 30–31, 37).



7 — TMT is Türk Mukavemet Teşkilatı (Turkish Resistance Organization). See Bryant and Hatay (2020, 11ff.), who discuss the process by which the TMT turned control of the enclaves over to civil authorities that developed in the early years of the enclave period (1963–67; Turkish Cypriots continued to live in enclaves until the division in 1974), while the TMT became a "standing army" concerned largely with security. Yael Navaro (2012, 12ff.) also discusses the TMT's role in governing enclaves and defending them from Greek-Cypriot paramilitary groups, especially EOKA.

8 — Taussig notes how this fantasy stabilizes the ideology of secrecy: "To put it bluntly, there is no such thing as a secret. It is an invention that comes out of the public secret, a limit-case, a supposition, a great 'as if,' without which the public secret would evaporate" (1999, 7).

9 — In 2001, Palma brought a case against the Republic of Cyprus for knowingly concealing information about her husband's death and the location of his body, in violation of her right to know. In June 2012, Judge Michalis Papamichael found in favor of Palma, awarding her €300,000 plus interest from 2001, including €60,000 in punitive damages. See the *Cyprus Mail* article elaborating this decision by Makarios Drousiotis (2012), who testified in the case.

10 — See Paraschos 2012 for an example of such critical coverage in a Greek-language newspaper. I learned of this article when several Greek-Cypriot archae-

ologists at the CMP brought copies with them to the field excavation where I was working at the time; it was a topic of discussion among the team members for many days afterward.

11 — See Taussig 1992, esp. chap. 7.

12 — See Begoña Aretxaga's (2005, esp. chap. 9) troubling of the hyphen in "nation-state," as she considers the perplexing desire for statehood pressed by Basque nationalists in the 1990s.

13 — Perhaps the most persistent and trenchant criticism of liberal theories of the state in anthropology is to be found in Michael Taussig's corpus of works on state fetishism. In spirit possession and shamanic healing (1987, 1997), in the construction and defacement of monuments and symbols (1999), and in the deployment of public secrecy as a weapon of war (1992, 1997), Taussig examines the work of fantasy and ideology that arise from and sediment into political and social forms of power. In these works, the state is a symbolic focus—a sacred thing—at the imaginary center of the pervasive, heterogeneous violence and terror of colonialism, capitalism, and racism. Taking a related but distinct tack, Aretxaga (2005) explores the psychic dimensions of state power in the Basque region of Spain where she grew up under Franco, and where she returned for ethnographic research after the dictatorship. There, she tracks the proliferation of stories about violent events in which the state and its "other," terrorists—that is, the police and the Basque separatists—were locked in an ideological process of uncanny mimesis and doubling, one of whose stakes was the "outlaw" status of the state itself and another, obversely, the separatists' fervent desire to form their own state and thus to become the center of power.

In the past two decades, too, many anthropologists have decentered the state in their analysis, foregrounding the border regions and informal zones of state administration, and tracking the paradoxes and irrationalities of state power. This approach crystallized in the now-classic introductory essay by Veena Das and Deborah Poole (2004) to their edited volume, *Anthropology in the Margins of the State*. Here, they venture to extend the reference of the descriptor "state" to a variety of economic and political activities, sites and techniques and languages of governance, that fall outside classic liberal theories of the state and its rule-of-law discourses on administration, bureaucracy, social order, and military power. Their perspective, powerfully shaped by Michel Foucault's work on biopolitics and governmentality and aligned with his insistence on breaking the juridical equation between state and sovereignty, frames the anthropological theorization of the state as a question of ethnography—that is, of situated attention to the very specific ways in which the state, or the idea of the state, appears in the everyday lives of people at different moments and in different locales.

In contexts of war and postwar "reckoning," to borrow a term from Diane Nelson (2009), anthropologists have also documented the clandestine shape-shifting of state power in the activities of "para-state" forces, such as the paramilitary groups in Guatemala forcibly recruited from Indigenous communities to carry out the state genocide of Indigenous people, examined by Nelson (2004, 2009, 2015) as well as Victoria Sanford (2004); and the Chimès ("ghost" gangs) in Haiti, in Beckett's (2010, 39, 40) account, who were "reportedly formed" by President Aristide as the "armed wing" of his party but then turned against him to stage the coup in 2004.

14 — Whether there was one Cypriot society before the war in 1974—or, for that matter, before British colonialism or Ottoman imperialism—is the central preoccupation of modern Cypriot historiography, according to a study conducted over a decade ago by Mete Hatay and Yiannis Papadakis, who observe the powerful efficacy of representations of history in shaping political subjectivities and promoting "political objectives" (2012, 46). In the post-1974 period, they document the rise of the reunification "paradigm" in Greek-Cypriot historiography—in historical scholarship, if not in history education—which entails a belief in "peaceful coexistence" between the two communities as the norm throughout the history of Cyprus, and frames conflict and nationalism itself as "comparatively recent" developments (37, 38). On the other hand, Turkish-Cypriot historiography, on their account, has for the most part represented division as a long-enduring feature of relations between the two communities, emphasizing the victimization of Turkish Cypriots by Greek Cypriots. Only briefly, during the administration of the left-wing Republican Turkish Party (2003–8), did Turkish-Cypriot historiography and new history textbooks promote the vision of a peaceful, plural but unified Cypriot society whose recent division was largely due to British colonial rule. The textbooks were extremely controversial in the north, Hatay and Papadakis show, and denounced by right-wing newspapers, which pushed the view that "there is no such thing as a 'Cyprus people' or 'Cypriotism'" (45). With the election of the right-wing National Unity Party in the north in 2008, the new textbooks were replaced by renovated versions of familiar nationalist histories. If, for many Turkish Cypriots, there is no going back to the time before division, it may be in part due to the success of right-wing nationalist historical narratives of the kind Hatay and Papadakis document here.



15 — On distinctions and affinities between bones and corpses, see Fontein's discussion of the "agencies and affordances entangled in the affective presence and emotive materiality" (2010, 436) of human remains vis-à-vis dead bodies in distinct historical moments of mass death in Zimbabwe, along with their "complex political efficacies" (2018, 337; cf. Fontein 2014). Fontein observes symbolic contrasts between the "dry bones" of the liberation war dead from anticolonial struggles in the 1890s and the 1950s–1970s, on the one hand, and on the other, the "leaky, tortured bodies" of civilians killed during the 1980s (2018, 337) and the "fleshy, leaky bodies" of people killed in political contestations since the early 2000s (2010, 436). Yet he also observes the mutual entailment of these different kinds of human remains in the "processes by which bones are formed from decaying bodies" in the "passage of time" from burial to decomposition, and in the transhistorical prophecy by libera-

tion fighters in 1896–97 that "our bones will rise again" (2010, 432, 436, 424), which has "entangled" both bones and corpses in Zimbabwe's contemporary "politics of the dead" (2018, 341, 339). Fontein emphasizes the political efficacy of the "unhappy spirits" (2018, 343) of all those killed brutally and unjustly and resting uneasily in unknown graves, which he associates with the "unresolved legacies" of political violence in Zimbabwe, especially in the 1980s (2018, 345). But he also, borrowing from Christopher Pinney's work on materiality, develops the concept of the "'torque' of human substances" to account for the way that human remains themselves both demand and resist "stabilization . . . into recognizable objects and identifiable subjects" through exhumation and proper reburial (2018, 347; cf. Fontein [2014, 130] on the "'torque' of materiality" in Pinney 2005).



16 — From 2004 to 2012, scientists at the CMP's Anthropological Laboratory, after completing their analysis of the remains in a case, would send multiple samples of the bones for blind DNA testing to the Laboratory of Forensic Genetics at CING, a bicommunal, nonprofit institution located in south Nicosia. The results would be sent back to the lab for "reconciliation" with the anthropological analysis, and a final identification would be made by the chief anthropologist on the case. In 2012, the head of the genetics team at CING contested the entitlement of lab scientists to make final determinations of identity, claiming that lab personnel employed improper procedures and stored remains under unsafe conditions. The CMP litigated the case and won the right to transfer the DNA databank to the Genetic Laboratory of the International Commission on Missing Persons (ICMP) in Bosnia and Herzegovina, which has been conducting blind DNA testing for the CMP since 2012. See Vasiliou 2012 for an example of "scandal" reportage of this story in a Greek-language Cypriot newspaper.

17 — The 1960 treaty reserved the airport and two Sovereign Base Areas in Cyprus (the British military bases at Dhikelia and Akrotiri) as "British Overseas Territory." Costas Constantinou (2008, 145, 146) examines the "originary 'exceptionality'" of Cyprus's sovereignty, inaugurated with this treaty, that has discursively conditioned other multiple and "co-dependent" "states of exception" in Cypriot sovereignty, including recognition of the Republic's sovereignty and nonrecognition of the TRNC's sovereignty.

18 — Sevgül Uludağ (2006), a Turkish-Cypriot journalist, conducted extensive research into the Greek-Cypriot and Turkish-Cypriot missing in the north years before the CMP investigations began. This research is compiled in her widely read book *Oysters with the Missing Pearls* (2006), published in Turkish, Greek, and English. See İrvan (2008) on the development and influence of Uludağ's oral history work and "peace journalism." Andreas Paraschos, a Greek-Cypriot journalist, broke the story of the Lakamateia scandal in the *Phileleftheros* newspaper in the late 1990s, which helped trigger the CMP's investigations in 2004 (see Kovras 2008). In his widely read stories about the missing after he moved to the *Politis* newspaper,

he demanded recognition of the Turkish-Cypriot missing as well. More recently, he has become a vocal critic of the CMP.

19 — The percentages represented by the Greek-Cypriot and Turkish-Cypriot populations on the island have been a matter of contention since the British colonial period. Given that census data track citizenship rather than perceived or reported ethnicity, it is very difficult to distill a precise ratio for the Greek-Cypriot and Turkish-Cypriot populations. Members of native minority communities in Cyprus (such as Maronites and Latins) living in the south since the division are counted as citizens of the Republic although they are not Greek-Cypriot in ethnic terms; and a large number of people living in the north who were born in Turkey are counted as citizens of the TRNC although they are not Turkish-Cypriot in ethnic terms. Over a decade ago, Mete Hatay (2007, 44), working from the 2005 census of the Republic and the 2006 census of the TRNC, reported "656,200 citizens (64% of the total population of Cyprus) and 110,200 foreign residents (11%)" in the Republic, and "178,031 citizens (17% in the whole island's population) and 78,613 (7%) foreign residents" in the TRNC. He determined that, "out of the 178,031 TRNC citizens, the current native Turkish Cypriot population (one or both parents born in Cyprus) now numbers 132,635" (47), or approximately 13 percent of the island's total population. Note that these are the de jure figures reported by the two governments and do not accurately represent large numbers of undocumented workers in Cyprus.



20 — Kovras (2008) and Kovras and Loizides (2011) document the consistent policy of the Republic of Cyprus since 1974 to hold the Republic of Turkey alone responsible for the problem of the missing and to acknowledge missing persons only from interstate armed conflict during the summer of 1974. That is to say that the Republic refused to acknowledge the hundreds of Turkish Cypriots as well as Greek Cypriots who went missing at Greek-Cypriot hands during phases of inter- and intracommunal violence starting in 1963 and reaching a peak in 1974. Kovras (2012) explains that it was only after an explicit policy shift in the late 1990s that the Republic publicly acknowledged the official list of all Greek-Cypriot and Turkish-Cypriot missing, which was published in the Republic's Government Gazette in July 2000.

21 — See Crossland 2000 for a history of the Argentine Forensic Anthropology Team (EAAF).

22 — See the CMP's Terms of Reference and Mandate, accessed March 2, 2020, https://www.cmp-cyprus.org/terms-reference-and-mandate.

23 — These comments may have reflected earlier phases of the forensic investigations in the former Yugoslavia, which were focused on evidence gathering—counting the dead and establishing cause of death—rather than later phases, when more effort was placed on individual identification and the repatriation of whole

bodies (see Rosenblatt 2015, esp. chap. 1). In parallel, in her writing on forensic investigations of the disappeared in Argentina, Zoë Crossland (2000) traces the transformation of a criminal-justice scenario into a "closure" scenario more like that in which the CMP operated. After the junta collapsed in 1983, she writes, the newly elected democratic government founded CONADEP (National Commission on the Disappearance of Persons) to investigate thousands of cases of disappearances. Excavations of mass graves were undertaken without the guidance of experts and yielded remains that could not be identified. In response to these failures, the Argentine Forensic Anthropology Team (EAAF) was organized with help from US forensic specialists and produced evidence of large-scale violence used in the successful prosecution of military officers in the mid-1980s. From 1985 to 1990, however, successive administrations issued decrees to pardon the officers; those who had been convicted with the help of forensic evidence were released from prison. Crossland notes that this policy shift necessitated a corresponding shift in the objective of forensic evidence: from seeking justice in the form of court testimony to seeking closure for relatives of the disappeared by restoring their "names and histories" (2000, 152). On a different arrangement of lay initiative and professional expertise, Francisco Ferrándiz, writing about exhumations of the Civil War dead in Spain, notes that grassroots memorial associations have allied with forensic experts "both in order to defend themselves against reciprocal accusations of non-professional conduct and to give their exhumations a more 'scientific' and thus legitimate character" (2006, 9). See also Renshaw (2011, 18–20) on collaborative alliances among relatives, volunteers, and a variety of "experts" in the Spanish exhumations.



24 — Renshaw likewise examines exhumations of mass graves in Spain as "site[s] of image production" (2011, 165). She reports that, during her fieldwork, she observed "intense media coverage" of one particular excavation where a conflict erupted among archaeologists over whether to close the grave during a period of turbulent weather in order to protect the contents from damage and movement, or rather to keep it open in order to be photographed for a national newspaper because "the grave should 'have the greatest possible impact'" (164, 165).

25 — Renshaw (2011, 38) notes that, although relatives of the dead attended and actively participated in the exhumations in Spain, they were largely excluded from the anthropological analysis conducted in forensic labs, as in Cyprus.

26 — ForDisc is an interactive computer program used by forensic anthropologists to classify adults by ancestry, osteological sex, and stature, using different combinations of bone metrics. Licenses must be purchased from the host institution, the University of Tennessee at Knoxville. (The annual license price for ForDisc 3.0 in 2014 was $395.00.) The data that populate ForDisc come from the Forensic Anthropology Data Bank in the United States, contributed by the University of Tennessee and other institutions; the reference population is a small sample of twentieth- and twenty-first-century Americans.

27 — See Navaro 2012, esp. the introduction and chap. 1.

28 — Wagner (2008, 178) and Sant Cassia (2005, 209) both note the importance of skulls in facilitating the recognition of a person's remains by relatives. On Wagner's account, this may be due not only to the visual familiarity of skulls as proxies for faces, but also to the resistance family members may feel to accepting the violence their loved one suffered that resulted in the absence of a head: "Case managers dread cases where the skull is missing because they know how disturbing that piece of information is for family members to hear and for them, in turn, to disclose" (2008, 178).

29 — For case managers tasked with informing the relatives of a missing person about the identification of his remains, Wagner relates, engaging the memories that family members held of their missing person was a crucial step in the process of recognition. In this, visual recognition was sometimes helpful; scraps of a person's clothing found with his remains might trigger a relative's memories about the clothes the person was wearing when he went missing, thus oscillating between "'documentary proof'" and memorial prop (Wagner 2008, 176–77).

30 — See, for example, Piault and Sant Cassia 2003; Angastiniotis 2004, 2005; Zaim and Chrysanthou 2004; Tanpınar 2007; Georgiades and The Elders 2010; Tsiarta 2011; and Evripidou and Nugent 2012.

31 — Ariel Dorfman points to the dependence of this theater on globalization: "We have grown strangely used to them over the last 25 years. . . . Mothers and daughters, wives and sisters, demanding to know the true fate of their men, demanding that they be returned to their families alive. A widespread, almost epidemic, image of tragedy and defiance. . . . Indeed, those marching women brandishing a black and white photo have become so natural to our eyes, so much a part of the mythical landscape of our time, that we tend to forget that there was a time, not very long ago, when photographs did not constitute an automatic ingredient of that sort of protest" (2006, 255–56).

32 — For example, at the time of my fieldwork, Sevgül Uludağ had a running column in the *Yeni Düzen* newspaper covering the activities of the CMP's forensic teams.

33 — David Errickson and Tim Thompson (2019, 304) review controversies over images of human remains posted on social media platforms, such as tourist selfies taken with human remains at Choeung Ek Killing Fields in Phnom Penh, Cambodia, and academic selfies taken with human remains at archaeological excavations. The authors are more directly concerned with the appropriateness of sharing images of human remains for educational purposes, observing the increased expectation in the "digital generation we live in today . . . to immediately image and share what we see with anyone and everyone at any given time" (302), including in classroom and museum settings. They express the urgency of articulating

principles for creating, circulating, and stewarding images of human remains in the digital age and allude to the "best practices" of a number of professional organizations (e.g., the American Academy of Forensic Sciences and the British Association for Biological Anthropology and Osteoarchaeology [302]), which refer to norms of consent and respect. But they stop short of devising rules or protocols and insist on contextualization as a key ethical practice: contextualization in terms of the setting, relevant cultural traditions, and purpose or justification for the display in question, as well as of generational norms regarding the visualization and sharing of experience.

34 — On such claims based on "genetic and spatial propinquity," Crossland (2009, 117) cites Paul Matthews's discussion of "legal issues over whether there is property in the body within Anglo-American law" (Matthews 1983, 202, 218).



35 — See also Nash and Colwell 2020 for a robust overview of anthropological literature on NAGPRA after thirty years. The history of theft, disputed custody, and repatriation of the Native American remains and cultural objects that have been used for research and display in North American museum contexts of course follows closely the history of the settler sciences of anthropology and natural history and their implication in the genocide, forced displacement, and cultural expropriation of Native Americans. Perhaps for this reason, the UK-based archaeologist and curator Trish Biers (2019, 246, 244), citing a study by Nilsson Stutz (2016), notes the much more frequent and much less controversial display of human remains from "archaeological contexts" in Scandinavian and other European museums as compared with North American museums. She sees protests and critiques from Indigenous communities in the United States and Canada to discourage this practice as part of long-term efforts, at least since the passage of NAGPRA, to "decolonise" museums across settler colonial contexts worldwide, including Australia, New Zealand, and the Pacific region (2019, 244). In this vein, Randi Marselis (2016) offers a rich analysis of the collision of North American politics and ethics of Indigenous property and affiliation with Scandinavian discourses of "free speech" and museum practices of community engagement in an article concerning the curatorial choice not to display scalps (rather, the curatorial choice to present the curatorial choice not to display scalps) in a 2012–13 exhibition on Native American culture at the National Museum of Denmark.

In the United States, where extensive litigation has taken place under NAGPRA, the human remains that are repatriated are those that can be affiliated, genetically or culturally, with particular Native American tribes (see Yasaitis 2005 for an analysis of legal cases during the first fifteen years of NAGPRA). Petitions by the living to repatriate remains are thus assertions of recognition: "this is not a stranger," as Zoë Crossland (2009, 117) voices this assertion. As onerous and odious as the process of establishing affiliation has proven to be for many—Native Americans, primarily, but also museums and other federally funded institutions required to identify, inventory, and repatriate Native American items in their collections (see

Bruchac 2010; Colwell-Chanthaphonh and Powell 2012; Zheng 2021; and the debate in *PoLAR* among Schillaci and Bustard [2010], Cordell and Kintigh [2010], and Ousley [2010])—it has also incidentally created the privative category of unaffiliated remains. See Seidemann's very interesting discussion about state legislation enacted across the United States following NAGPRA, seeking to extend protections to human remains found on state or private lands (excluded by NAGPRA), or burial sites "'without reference to ethnic origins, cultural backgrounds, or religious affiliations,'" as described in the Louisiana Unmarked Human Burial Sites Preservation Act passed in 1991 (Seidemann 2010, 201, citing La. R.S. 8:672). See also Midler (2011) on legal innovations permitting certain repatriation claims for "culturally unidentifiable" remains to be made by Native American tribes.

Crossland explores the consequences of the distinction between affiliated and unaffiliated remains: "Those human bodies that remain outside of the community of the living—'unaffiliated cultural remains'—are figured as appropriate subjects for scientific research" (2009, 117), available for advancing archaeological, historical, biological, and cultural knowledge. Taking this privative category as a provocation to question broadly the "treatment of excavated human remains as research materials" (102), Crossland develops an extended comparison between the exhumation and analysis of human remains in archaeological contexts, and postmortem examinations in eighteenth- and nineteenth-century British medical practices of autopsy (dismembering dead bodies to determine cause of death before burial) and dissection (dismembering dead bodies in order to study or teach anatomy)—which, she argues, "reproduce social difference in death . . . through a fluid shifting between different ontologies of the corpse" (104). Connecting these distinct medical practices of examining corpses to modern archaeological and anthropological practices of exhuming and analyzing human remains, Crossland sees multiple ontologies of the body and multiple traditions of dealing with dead bodies in the history of scientific approaches to handling human remains. In this history, rather than a "unified and totalizing" "scientific attitude" of modernist "detachment and objectivity" (118), she instead finds mixed and contradictory practices of differentiation: bodies sorted into those treated as strangers appropriate for objectification and research, on one hand, and on the other, those treated as friends, family, and community members to be buried properly and not dissected, photographed, or studied; also bodies themselves parceled into parts that can be used for research and parts that cannot.

This sorting, Crossland argues, mirrors an ambiguous mix of moral attitudes toward dead bodies: respect for the sanctity and integrity of the body, respect for the wishes of a living person once the person has died, and respect for the benefit to humanity of scientific knowledge, among others. While we might expect science, based on one or another kind of mythologizing, to be enrolled in universalizing, standardizing, generalizing procedures of comparative analysis, Crossland instead shows here practices of differentiating, sorting, and specifying. In the context of eighteenth- and nineteenth-century British autopsy and dissection, the lines of specification were often lines of class; paupers' corpses were readily available (or easily stolen) for dissection, whereas the dead who came from middle-class and wealthy families were rarely even autopsied before their very proper burials. In the context of nineteenth- and twentieth-century North American anthropology and natural history, the lines of specification were often lines of race; it was—and this is of course the crux of NAGPRA—Native American remains that were excavated or stolen, studied, stored, or displayed, largely by white researchers and curators. Crossland suggests, though, that even in these long-enduring situations of entrenched structural hierarchies of class and race, science did not provide a straightforward map of moral attitudes about the body.



Crossland explores how these attitudes might coexist even in regard to one body, as in the notorious case of Ishi, known as the last living member of the Yahi people and storied as the "last wild Indian" when he emerged from the wilderness in northern California in 1911, poor, sick, and alone (see Starn 2004). Ishi was brought to the University of California Anthropology Museum, where he was studied and perhaps befriended (a loaded term to say the least) by the anthropologist Alfred Kroeber, among others, and where he became a "living exhibit" for several years before dying of tuberculosis (Starn 2004, 44). What happened to his body after his death has been the subject of considerable study, debate, and litigation. On Crossland's (2009, 116) account, Kroeber requested in a letter that Ishi's body be cremated, according to Ishi's own wishes, asserting that a postmortem dissection in "the interests of science" was not to be allowed, although a minimally invasive autopsy to determine the cause of death might be permissible. An autopsy in fact ensued, but—perhaps (Crossland indicates) because Kroeber's letter arrived after the fact—Ishi's brain was not cremated with the rest of his remains after the autopsy. It was instead preserved and sent to the Smithsonian Institution for further study, against Ishi's wishes. Thus, his body—which was not and could not be claimed by any living relative or community member, as all the Yahi had been killed in the California genocide decades earlier—was treated as both a friend and an object by the anthropologists who arrogated the privilege of deciding what to do with his remains after his death. Kroeber and the assistant curator of the museum, Edward Gifford, were able to countenance the validity of both the "sentimental" and the "scientific" interests in Ishi's dead body, even if they landed on "the side of sentiment," as Gifford put it (Crossland 2009, 116). Ishi's "mixed" treatment after his death indicates to Crossland the coexistence of multiple ontologies of the body in this early anthropology, and an easy ability for its practitioners to "shift" between these ontologies, "seamlessly and with little clear recognition of doing so" (117), as they performed both their training in "traditions of estrangement" that facilitated the scientific objectification of human remains and their attachment to "newly emerging narratives of human commonality and sympathy" that facilitated their attribution of dignity and even personhood to those same remains (118). What they did not have was an understanding of any Indigenous (or specifically Yahi) ontology of the body that would compel them to respect Ishi's wishes.

36 — Biers (2019) offers a brief overview of international law regarding Indigenous sovereignty over human remains and cultural patrimony. She observes that, though UNDRIP—the United Nations Declaration on the Rights of Indigenous People, adopted in 2007—establishes the universal right of Indigenous peoples to repatriate human remains, it "makes no reference to museums or display" (245). Article 15.1 does establish the right of Indigenous peoples to the "dignity and diversity of their cultures, traditions, histories, and aspirations, which shall be appropriately reflected in education and public information"; along with many Indigenous groups, Biers reads this article as an Indigenous right to collaborate and advise in the use of affiliated remains for research, teaching, and display (245). Yet, Biers observes, while most professional organizations of researchers, educators, and curators have devised ethics codes that reflect these rights, establishing general principles such as the necessity to consult with and/or acquire the consent of the "relevant stakeholder" in their use and display of remains (246, citing as an example the 2010 Code of Ethics published by the British Association for Biological Anthropology and Osteoarchaeology), they are, as she puts it, "vague on specifics"; they do not outline procedures for ascertaining the identity of "stakeholders" or "affected communities," nor how their interests might be weighed against the public interest in beholding remains (the "public interest" is construed, implicitly, as excluding "affected communities"), nor how "cultural affiliation" or "cultural continuity" with remains might be established. For example, she discusses (246) the British Museum's policy regarding human remains, a small part of which reads as follows:

> In the display of human remains at the Museum, explanatory and contextual information will be provided. A written justification for any decision to display human remains shall be retained by the Trustees and shall balance the public benefits of display against the known feelings of
>
> 5.9.1 any individual known to the Trustees as having a direct and close genealogical link to the remains (where these are less than 100 years old); or
>
> 5.9.2 a community which has *cultural continuity* with the remains in question and for whom the remains have *cultural importance* (where they are more than 100 years old).

British Museum, "British Museum Policy: Human Remains in the Collection," December 6, 2018, https://www.britishmuseum.org/sites/default/files/2019-10/Human_Remains_policy_061218.pdf.

37 — The dignity of the dead is the central question explored by Dutch historian Antoon De Baets (2004, 2007) in two linked articles. De Baets closely reads legal and philosophical discourse about the moral and ontological status of the dead in order to develop an ethical stance that he wishes historians to take in relation to the subjects of their research: both the known dead and the anonymous or forgotten dead. De Baets defines the dead, admittedly awkwardly (and with elaborate caveats), as "former human beings" (2004, 134). "Since the dead are not human

beings," he continues, "they do not constitute a category of rights-holders because, unlike living persons, they are incapable of having needs, interests, or duties, or of making choices or claims, either now or in the future" (135). The stance he ultimately takes, then, is that the dead do not have rights, but they do have a special kind of dignity—posthumous dignity—that obligates the living to bear certain responsibilities toward them, including "respect and protection" (139). In large part, De Baets, like Claire Moon (2019), infers the existence of posthumous dignity from the actual practices of living human beings toward the dead, scouring the archaeological and ethnographic record to find instances that he takes to amount to universal evidence of burial rituals and proscriptions on the mutilation of corpses, as well as the body of international human rights law—the Geneva Convention and related treaties in particular—that attain to the same implicit universality.



In his 2007 article, De Baets furnishes a genealogy of the concept of dignity in human rights law and elaborates its implications for the dead. Among the crimes against humanity it enumerates, the Rome Statute of the International Criminal Court, taking the Geneva Convention as a foundation, includes "outrages upon personal dignity," which De Baets takes to mean "humiliating and degrading treatment of persons" (2007, 79). He is clearly troubled by this language, as he has argued both here and in his 2004 article that the dead are not persons. Yet he finds a way to explain this inconsistency, showing that "a new concept—outrages upon the dignity of dead persons—was forged" with a high degree of both contingency and durability in the "Elements of Crimes" drafted for the 1998 Rome Statute to establish the purview of the International Criminal Court (81), in a footnote specifying that unconscious and dead persons could suffer outrages upon their personal dignity. For De Baets, "It is not the dead who suffer the humiliation—for the dead do not suffer anything—but their surviving dear and near. It follows that the dignity to be conferred upon the dead is not human dignity but *posthumous dignity*" (81). This "new concept" of posthumous dignity accurately expresses, on his account, a view that people actually hold that the dead possess dignity by virtue of their "past humanity" (81), the neglect of which "offends the sensibilities of humanity at large" (82).

38 — In counterpoint, Adam Rosenblatt (2015, 155) notes that, in the community of mobile humanitarian forensic workers whom he studies, "rights talk" largely concerns the rights of the living—those who have survived the dead. Forensic scientists, he observes, do not generally speak about the dead as having rights, although certain rights of the dead are actually enumerated in law, as he points out: "not to be trafficked, dissected without consent, or used sexually," all examples of "rights to dignified treatment in death" (159).

39 — See Moon (2019, 50) on the ICRC rule; see Rosenblatt (2015, 30ff.) on Rwandan sites of collective reburial, and Renshaw (2011) and Torres (2007) on Spanish sites.

40 — See Rosenblatt 2015, esp. chap. 3.

41 — On Taussig's (1999, 5) account, in modern capitalist society (distinguished from other kinds of society by the death of god), the sacred does not inhere in things—monuments, flags, paper currencies—but rather is generated by the desecration of those things, an act that "brings a very angry god out of hiding" to condemn the transgression.

42 — A 2008 installation at the Center for Contemporary Culture in Barcelona and the International Center of Photography in New York drew from the same body of Torres's photographic work; it is widely cited today as a groundbreaking documentary art project on political violence. Ferrándiz's (2007) essay in Torres's book, "Fugitive Voices," which is intercalated with Torres's photographs, describes Torres's involvement in the Villamayor excavation.



43 — Ferrán uses the term "canon" here (2013, 128, citing Renshaw 2011, 176).

44 — Ferrán 2013, 127, citing Kaplan 2007; Ferrán 2013, 128, citing Ritchin 2009, 139.

45 — The case of Argentina is mixed, as noted above, since the purpose of forensic investigations shifted from collecting evidence for prosecutions to facilitating healing and recovery among victims' families. The cases of Bosnia and Herzegovina and Guatemala might be counted as examples of prosecution-oriented investigations, although Arsenijević (2011a, 2011b), Nelson (2009), and Sanford (2004) respectively document robust therapeutic rhetorics and practices in those locales as well.

46 — On connections between nationalisms and cultures of victimhood in Cyprus, see Kovras and Loizides (2011), Papadakis (1994), and Sant Cassia (2005).

47 — This is akin to the "appropriation of the dead by the state" noted by Seremetakis (1991, 170) in the displacement or outright exclusion of family claims in the commemoration of the war dead in Greece.

48 — In 2011, when the CMP purchased a license for ForDisc, the anthropologists began duplicating their measurements, recording all the information in their reports and then entering it again in the ForDisc database in order to calculate age estimates, which were then entered into the reports.

49 — Recovering and restoring skeletons in the forensic context is thus a radically different kind of work from what Elizabeth Hallam (2010) evokes as *skeletopoeia*, an artisanal practice of assembling skeletons for medical use that had become a profession for anatomists in Great Britain by the mid-nineteenth century. In Hallam's account, while "deceased bodies enlisted in anatomy have been perceived as extremely emotive" (482), the bones collected for making skeletons at this time "lost their associations with the persons they were once part of" and thus any

"emotionality" that might have arisen from such associations (483). (Hallam notes that these "disconnections" were "made possible through the social and power relations involved in obtaining deceased bodies," 483.) However, she insists, anatomists who became skilled skeleton makers often "emotionally invested" in their work (483) through extended physical, even intimate, contact; they developed "attachments" to the skeletons they produced, in which they saw "traces" and "imprints of themselves": their own distinctive styles of preparation and articulation, as well as the "materializations" of their toil and "endeavour" (483, 484). So, we might say, skeleton makers cared about these bones but did not approach them with an ethics of care.



50 — Rosenblatt notes that "the relationship between gender and care ethics is an area of controversy," as care is associated by some in this ethical tradition with "'feminine' or even 'maternal' thinking" (2015, 239, n24). The positioning of women as caring scientists that the CMP seemed to be attempting in its publicity materials might, of course, have played on generic preconceptions of women as essentially nurturing, though—as I have argued elsewhere (Davis 2017)—in some Greek death rituals women were ritual specialists tasked with exhuming, examining, and reburying bones, and thus, for Greek Cypriots at least, might already have been configured as the appropriate persons to handle bones in a forensic context.

51 — I discuss these rituals in depth in the following section.

52 — Sant Cassia makes this clear distinction: "I suggest that Greek Cypriot representations of suffering are through absences that appear (and I use the word advisedly and cautiously) to bear certain parallelisms to Christian iconography. By contrast Turkish Cypriot representations are through presences, although I would hesitate even further to relate these to Islam" (2005, 133; cf. Sant Cassia 1999, 29).

53 — Denktaş was leader of the Turkish Cypriot community during the enclave period (1963–74) and ultimately president of the TRNC from its founding in 1983 until he left office in 2005.

54 — See Bryant (2010, e.g., 153–54) on the fears and suspicions of immigrants from Turkey (known as "settlers" or "workers") among Turkish Cypriots.

55 — My understanding is that practices of exhuming remains and depositing them in ossuaries, which are normative for Orthodox Greeks, were outlawed by British colonial authorities in Cyprus in the late nineteenth century. Thus, Greek Orthodox Christians in Cyprus are aware of these practices and may think of them as "traditional" in their association with Greece but do not themselves perform them.

56 — On the "aesthetics" of expert knowledge of the dead, see Ochoa (2010, 15), who explores the "sense of the dead" in Kongo-inspired Palo practice in Cuba, "the art of crafting matter into fatefully powerful substances" (13, 2). He writes of his

apprenticeship to Palo practitioners, learning their techniques of listening to the "multifarious discourse of the dead" and intervening into the fate of the living by making and manipulating "healing-harming substances" through the "relay" and "transfers" of "force" (15, 1, 11), which required deep sensory attunement to the matter of which these substances were made.

57 — It is in light of this intimate relationship with ritual among Greek women mourners that Seremetakis develops a critique of the photo essay by Alexander Tsiaras that accompanies Danforth's 1982 text. In Tsiaras's photographs, she sees the distortion and artificial fixation of moments in a mourning ceremony, captured from "unusual and grotesque angles" that do not match the perspective of any participant (Seremetakis 1984, 69). She notes another register of mismatch between Tsiaras's "candid shots" and the "formalized and iconographic postures" performed by the mourners (69)—postures that contrast sharply with the mourners' self-conscious posing for the camera at other moments, disrupting the ritual flow (75). For Seremetakis, this photo essay is documentary rather than ethnographic, as "estranged" as Tsiaras clearly was—by his own report—from the mourners' relationship with ritual.



58 — See Bryant (2006, 2010) on the everyday complicity of Cypriot civilians with acts of violence in the 1960s and 1970s. There is a striking parallel between this kind of complicity in the violence of war and the complicity of police officers and detectives, district attorneys, and judges with the torture of African American suspects by police in Chicago from the 1970s onward, as recounted by Laurence Ralph (2020). He documents the many ways in which colleagues of the torturers in the criminal justice system learned not to know what was happening behind closed doors. See also Dilley (2015), who examines how "non-knowledge" about the children of French colonial officers and Indigenous women in West Africa, as well as about African practices of slavery exploited by those officers, worked to facilitate the colonial enterprise. Dilley details the "social process" (2015, 139) and the networks of relations by which knowledge of these practices on the part of colonial officers was transformed into nonknowledge on the part of metropolitan higher-ups.

59 — The plant, located in Hasoplat (Mia Milia) on the outskirts of north Nicosia, was constructed with UN Development Programme support between 2010 and 2013 to handle increasing volume in the common sewerage system constructed in 1978–80. A documentary film, titled *Manhole*, was made by Aris Kyriakides about the construction and maintenance of the sewerage system in the early 1980s.

60 — See also the introduction by Thomas Kirsch and Roy Dilley to their edited volume, *Regimes of Ignorance*, in which they argue for greater anthropological attention to the positivity of ignorance—for them, a "portmanteau term that embrace[s] various forms of not-knowing (intentional and unintentional), unknowing and secrecy" (2015, 1).

61 — See Scheper-Hughes 2007; Mendeloff 2009; and Payne 2008. Theidon (2013) points to a different but equally counterproductive mechanics of truth and reconciliation in Peru, after the "difficult time" of the armed conflict between Sendero Luminoso, the armed forces of the state, and campesinos in the 1980s and 1990s. Peru's reparations law, passed in 2005, foreclosed victimhood as a legal status for anyone involved in or sympathetic to Sendero Luminoso—thus asserting innocence only for some combatants and victims, and making reconciliation impossible (Theidon 2013, 388–92).

62 — The ECtHR was founded in 1953 to adjudicate violations of the European Convention on Human Rights (passed in 1953). The court's jurisdiction extends to any state that has signed the convention, including all member states of the Council of Europe, formed in 1949. (The ten founding members of the council did not include Greece, Turkey, or Cyprus, although Greece and Turkey joined only a few months later in 1949, and Cyprus followed, after independence, in 1961.) In 1998, signatory states became compulsorily exposed to cases brought by individuals as well as other states (see Demetriou and Gürel 2008).



63 — See the European Parliament's nonbinding Written Declaration 369 on the Work of the Committee on Missing Persons in Cyprus, adopted June 9, 2011. See also the International Convention for the Protection of All Persons from Enforced Disappearance, which was opened for signature by the UN in 2007 and entered into force in 2010. Article 24(2) states, "Each victim has the right to know the truth regarding the circumstances of the enforced disappearance, the progress and results of the investigation and the fate of the disappeared person. Each State Party shall take appropriate measures in this regard" (General Assembly of the United Nations 2010). Kyriakou notes the range of the definition of "victim," here, "as not only the person who is subjected to enforced disappearance, but also as any other individual that has suffered harm as the direct result of an enforced disappearance," including, but "not necessarily," relatives (2012b, 34; cf. Kyriakou 2012a, 87).

64 — Refusal to disclose information about the fate of these missing persons was in fact only one of several violations of human rights on the part of Turkey found by the court in this case.

65 — See Kyriakou 2011 for a detailed critical reading of these decisions. The six-month rule is an admissibility criterion applied to cases coming before the ECtHR; it concerns the period of time after which "domestic remedies" to resolve an issue have been exhausted, at which point the ECtHR may consider a case (Kyriakou 2011, 7). Kyriakou takes issue with the court's decision to apply the six-month rule, or any temporal restrictions, in cases of enforced disappearance. He shows that, while enforced disappearances are considered "continuing violations" in international human rights law, meaning that the violation is considered ongoing until the disappeared person is found, the ECtHR applied "temporal restrictions" on the applicability of complaints, requiring complainants to "make proof of a certain

amount of diligence and initiative and introduce their complaints without undue delay" (3). The *Karabardak* and *Baybora* decisions, made in 2002, concerned disappearances in 1964; the court rejected these applications, arguing that the complainants had not made sufficient efforts to bring the disappearances to the attention of relevant authorities for twenty-five years; and, when they did make applications with the CMP in 1989, they waited another twelve years before deciding that the CMP would never conduct a "credible investigation," finally bringing their complaint to the ECtHR in 2001 (2). The court considered this too late, although in these two cases, it did not set a specific date that it would have considered reasonable. In the *Varnava* case, decided in 2009, where the court accepted the application and decided in favor of the complainants, the disappearances happened ten years later (1974) and the complaint was made in 1990, after a delay of sixteen years. Kyriakou notes that, once the court decided *Varnava*, it seems to have taken 1990 as an unofficial deadline (Kyriakou calls it a "fictitious time limit," 5) for bringing a complaint in any case of enforced disappearance during the Cyprus conflict—immediately dismissing fifty-one applications with very similar factual grounds that had not been submitted by 1990 (6). In addition to the poor foundation in international human rights law displayed by the court's reasoning, Kyriakou is especially concerned by the precedent these decisions set, essentially putting time "on the states' side" (6).



66 — In this, I have in mind the argument Biehl and Petryna (2011) develop regarding the indeterminacies of judicialization. Noting the "overdetermination" of subjects engaged in right-to-health litigation in Brazil by the evidentiary and identitarian coordinates of the judicial system, they nevertheless see "open[ing] up," in the intersections of pharmaceutical markets and judicial processes, "new spaces of ethical problematization, desire, and political belonging" (Biehl and Petryna 2011, 380–81).

67 — See also Theidon (2013, 15) on the dynamics of "duplicity and doubling" attending civilian participation in the Sendero Luminoso insurgency and state counterinsurgency in Peru.

68 — Robben (1999) explains that this refusal was also a legal strategy adopted by the Mothers of the Plaza de Mayo for getting around the statute of limitations placed in 1986 on prosecutions for murders perpetrated during the junta. Maintaining the disappeared as victims of kidnapping rather than murder would keep the window open for depositions and prosecutions, and thus for public accountability.

69 — Gordon (1997, 115) records the same refusals of bones by the Mothers.

70 — In like spirit, Yael Navaro, exploring the relational "embroilment" and "codependence and co-determination" of the "inner and outer worlds" of humans, develops a methodology of sensing to grasp the affects discharged by material

environments—affects that are part of human experience but "excee[d], or g[o] further and beyond the human imagination" (2012, 24, 18).

### TWO. DOCUMENTARY

1 — In quotations from oral speech, including quotations from films, I use ellipses within brackets to indicate that I have left out some part of what was said; I use ellipses without brackets to indicate that the speaker trailed off without finishing a sentence. In quotations from texts, brackets are not used for ellipses.

2 — Formed in 2007, The Elders is an organization of senior world leaders working toward peace and human rights, independent of any government or corporation. See http://theelders.org/.



3 — The chapter of Sant Cassia's (2005) book under discussion here exactly reproduces an article he published in 1999, based on research conducted in the mid-1990s.

4 — The old Nicosia airport has appeared in a number of documentary films, including *Intramural* (Demetriou, 2001), *Still* (Kakoyiannis, 2009), and *Sharing an Island* (Stylianou, 2011). It was also the focus of a major art project, UNCOVERED, in 2010–13. Originally conceived as the venue for the exhibition, the airport—characterized in the exhibition catalog as a space "frozen in time"—was ultimately used instead as the source of "found objects or replicas"; a gallery inside the dead zone of central Nicosia became the installation space for "artefacts, relics, and symbols" from the airport (Pellapaisiotis 2014, 236). See Constantinou, Demetriou, and Hatay 2012 for a discussion of the airport as a contested site of "cultural heritage."

5 — The exhibitions Pellapaisiotis examines in Cyprus were part of a broader movement in the international art world to engage with conflict zones and lines of division. See, for example, *Lines of Control: Partition as a Productive Space*, a traveling exhibition in 2005–9 originated by Green Cardamom, a London-based arts organization. The exhibition began as an exploration of partitioned societies in India, Pakistan, and Bangladesh, and later developed to address similar dynamics of division in North and South Korea, North and South Sudan, Ireland and Northern Ireland, Israel and Palestine, Armenia and its diasporas, and Indigenous societies in the United States. See the project website at http://www.greencardamom.net/html/gc_lines_of_control.html.

6 — See also Eftychiou and Philippou 2010 for a detailed discussion of the romantic tradition in Cypriot photography and its relationship to tourism on the island.

7 — See Kleanthous 2005 for a thorough catalog.

8 — This workshop, organized by the CCMC, brought the film theorist Michael Renov and the documentary filmmaker Alex Rotaru from the University of Southern California's School of Cinematic Arts to lead discussion, production, and editing sessions, along with several Cypriot filmmakers. They also hosted the

American Film Showcase series, promoted as a "cultural diplomacy" project, which entailed the screening and discussion of American documentary films including *Spellbound, Undefeated, Mad Hot Ballroom, Elevate, Rebirth,* and Rotaru's own *Shakespeare High.* The workshop was funded by the US Department of State in association with the International Children's Film Festival of Cyprus and the US Embassy in Nicosia.

9 — The UNDP initiated a "peacebuilding project" in Cyprus in 2005 to "create opportunities for Greek Cypriots and Turkish Cypriots to work together on concrete projects which will benefit all people on the island, while at the same time promoting inter-communal tolerance and mutual understanding" (UNDP 2008, 1). In a partnership with USAID extending through 2013, the UNDP funded civil society organizations, activists, and leaders from both communities (i.e., Greek-Cypriot and Turkish-Cypriot communities) in their efforts to develop bicommunal cooperation toward political and social change.



10 — The Festival of the Green Line in 2010 and 2011 was curated by Panicos Chrysanthou and funded by the Ministry of Education and Culture of the Republic of Cyprus.

11 — See Occupy the Buffer Zone's Facebook page, which includes links to archived former versions: https://www.facebook.com/OccupyBufferZone/.

12 — See Constandinides 2014 for a thorough and nuanced exploration of the problematic of "national cinema" in the Cypriot context.

13 — The CyBC is known in Greek as Ραδιοφωνικό Ίδρυμα Κύπρου (RIK), and in Turkish as Kıbrıs Radyo Yayın Kurumu (KRYK). The CyBC was established as a bilingual radio service in 1953, during British rule, and began bilingual television broadcasts in 1957. It still promotes itself as a pan-Cypriot service, although its offices and archives are located in south Nicosia and most of its personnel and broadcasts are Greek-speaking. It currently broadcasts a bilingual news program, *Biz/Emeis* (Us), which has a small audience in the north, and it employs some Turkish Cypriots. While it is thus not entirely restricted to the south, the counterpart public radio and television service in the north is not a Turkish-language CyBC but rather a different service, BRT (Bayrak Radyo Televizyon), which dates to the enclave period. In 1963, BRT began as a pirate radio service, when Turkish Cypriots, facing intimidation and violence on the part of Greek-Cypriot extremists, pulled out of most government agencies, and the CyBC became, in effect, a Greek-Cypriot service. The television broadcasts of the BRT began in 1976, and it now runs two television channels as well as five radio stations. (Similarly, RIK runs two television channels and four radio stations.)

14 — See, for example, Rebecca Bryant's (2004) first book on Cyprus, *Imagining the Modern.* In the introduction, Bryant documents the transformation of the ethnographic research project she had initially conceived, to be conducted in schools in the

north and south, into an archival project about the history of education in Cyprus, when she was refused permission to conduct ethnographic work in the south. Yet her archival research on education turned out to be just as restricted, though in different ways. Her extensive comparative work in archives in the north and south—including the State Archives of the Republic and the TRNC, and the Archive of the Archbishopric of the Orthodox Church of Cyprus, as well as archives in London and Athens—demanded a reflection on the limits of archival research. Bryant describes the "decade-long history" of her project, with its twists and turns and "barriers," as an education about a "Cypriot history known to Cypriots but not found in books," parts of which "conflicted with what [she] found in the archival record" (2004, ix, 10).

15 — See the "2012 Edition" of Cyprus Films Days in its web archive: https://www.cyprusfilmdays.com.



16 — See the Colonial Film Project website: http://www.colonialfilm.org.uk/.

17 — Βράκες (*vrakes*; singular, *vraka*) are the baggy trousers once worn by Cypriot men, a common trope in stereotypical representations of traditional Cypriot masculinity. Stylianou-Lambert and Philippou (2014) note the production of many "vraka dramas" by Cypriot filmmakers between 1960 and 1974, recalling earlier colonial films such as Keene's.

18 — See the work of Hadjimichael (2019, 162) for a history of this film as "lived experience." By incorporating oral histories many decades later of Cypriots who had appeared in the film—in a sense sketching out its blind field—and by recontextualizing images from the film and text from the accompanying book as colonial discourse, Hadjimichael performs another ingenious expansion of this ever-growing archive.

19 — In his essay "Films of Memory," David MacDougall (1994) reflects on the prevalence in "current social and political documentaries" of this "simple format of archival footage (the sensory) and interviews (the lexical)," pairing testimony with unrelated archival materials "presented quite illegitimately as the memories of the speakers" (261, 265).

20 — I thank Yelena Baraz for suggesting this connection.

21 — Angastiniotis's short documentary film *Memory*, about a Turkish-Cypriot man and a Greek-Cypriot man who fought in Lekfa on opposite sides of the war in 1974, and who met again and became friends and peace activists thirty years later, was screened at Cine Studio (University of Nicosia) on October 11, 2011.

22 — The film is now available through TRT, the national public broadcasting service in Turkey, which entered into a partnership with BRT in 2013.

23 — Chrysanthou identified "Güney" to me as the Kurdish film director and actor Yılmaz Güney.

24 — In the text, Adil assembles photographs from her family archive: a portrait of her great-grandfather, an Imam and poet, taken in 1916; a group portrait of three generations of the men (and boys) in her family, taken in 1936, displaying radically discrepant styles of clothing and accoutrement (signifying the Ottoman, Kemalist Turkish, and European secular worlds they simultaneously lived in); and her own photographs of the dead zone in Nicosia, her childhood neighborhood, taken on her walks through the city in the early 2000s. These images anchor her analysis of the Orientalist, Hellenist, and secular modernist photographic representations of Cyprus by British photographers from the nineteenth to the twenty-first centuries, triangulating "border identities" through these contradictory coordinates of her cultural identity and her British education. They constitute, she says, a "family album" that is "as much of a myth generator as the colonial gaze" in its expression of "mythic regimes inherent in the representation of Cypriot identity" (Adil 2014, 115, 112).



25 — The script of Adil's performance, in English and in Greek translation, was published along with photographs of the event on a now-defunct website: http://www.memorymap.org.uk/projects/alev-artos-foundation. A slightly different version of the poem, in English, appears in Adil 2013 (102).

26 — Demetriou has made two documentaries—*Intramural* (2001) and *Pyla: Living Together Separately* (2004)—as well as a 2011 fiction film, *Fish n' Chips*, addressing the experience of diasporic Cypriots raised in the United Kingdom and their return to the island. *Fish n' Chips* screened at the Rialto Theater in Limassol and in Nicosia during the Cyprus Film Days festival in April 2012.

27 — These are my translations from the Greek.

28 — In a well-known essay, the art historian and art critic Hal Foster seizes on "the archival impulse" established in the international art world by the 1990s, though he carefully notes that this "general impulse is hardly new" (2004, 3). Following these lines, Simone Osthoff, examining contemporary artworks that engage archival materials, observes "an ontological change—from the archive as a repository of documents to the archive as a dynamic and generative production tool" (2009, 11).

29 — Zaatari was one of many non-Cypriot artists who created installations in public space around the dead zone in Nicosia for the *Leaps of Faith* exhibition in 2005 (see Pellapaisiotis 2014, 224–28).

30 — See the page for "Saida, June 6, 1982" by Akram Zaatari on the Sfeir-Semler Gallery website, accessed October 9, 2022, https://www.sfeir-semler.com/gallery artists/akram-zaatari/work?page=19.

31 — See Zaatari's (2006) statement about his archival work in "Photographic Documents/Excavation as Art, 2006."

32 — Haris Pellapaisiotis (2014) takes up the question of aestheticization differently in his essay on the art of the buffer zone in Cyprus. Exhibitions staged in such deeply politicized spaces, he argues, have compelled artists and audiences alike to "engage with the symbols, narratives and meanings which reside within the spaces of the place out of which they operate"; yet such radical emplacement has also created tensions between the political and aesthetic criteria and purposes of art (223). Unraveling these tensions, Pellapaisiotis criticizes international artists and curators for their fascination with and appropriation of the buffer zone, like other places marked by the "signs and scars" of violent conflict (232). In several of the exhibitions he examines, the buffer zone in Cyprus became a sort of fetish for those "who wish[ed] for art to be seen to be political," but whose art was of questionable political value (237). The more obvious effects of these exhibitions, he suggests, were consumerist and decidedly unpolitical: namely, the museumification of the buffer zone and its transformation into an iconic space that could be recuperated in touristic fantasies about conflict zones—part of the process of abstraction by which real places become art spaces (236–37, 234).



33 — Chrysanthou added one to my list: *Cyprus Betrayed* (*Έτσι προδόθηκε η Κύπρος*), a CyBC documentary made by Giorgos Filis in 1975 that has aired on RIK a number of times.

34 — *Serpico* is "based on a true story" written by Peter Maas about Frank Serpico, a whistleblower who reported police crimes to the *New York Times* writer David Burnham and ultimately testified before the Knapp Commission.

35 — See "About the CCHA," Cyprus Critical History Archive: Reconsidering the Culture of Violence in Cyprus, 1955–64, accessed February 3, 2022, https://www.ccha-ahdr.info/about.

36 — This is the English translation of the Turkish as it appears in the subtitles (1:50:42–1:51:20).

### EPILOGUE

1 — Cf. Gordon's (2008, xvi) introduction to the new edition of *Ghostly Matters*.

2 — This phrase is adapted from Gordon (1997, 97).

3 — Gordon, with Sontag (1977), makes this point about photographs: "Photographs furnish a type of evidence. Their declarative verisimilitude convinces us of what we already know or surmise, or proves the existence of something we have doubted, but suspected" (Gordon 1997, 102).

4 — Taussig, stepping back from the dirty war in Colombia that he has just staged as an "example" of public secrecy, notes the "all-consuming banality" of public secrecy that lies at the heart of "a vast range of social powers and knowledges

intertwined with those powers," in "all social institutions—workplace, marketplace, state, and family" (1999, 6, 7).

5 — My description of the former residents of Varosha as "ghosts" is partly inspired by Yael Navaro's (2012) discussion of ghosts in the north as durable "material" features of the postconflict landscape rather than phenomenal apparitions. In developing a Cypriot "hauntology," Navaro takes ghosts to be "what is retained in material objects and the physical environment in the aftermath of the disappearance of the humans linked or associated with that thing or space" (17). Varosha's transformation from ghost town into dead body suggests to me that haunting is not an unqualifiedly durable situation but may itself evolve into something else—decomposition, perhaps, or revivification—depending on the life status of the people whose absence has materialized in the tangible infrastructure of their place, and on how absent they remain from that place. It is in this light that I understand the comment of a Turkish-Cypriot acquaintance who recently pointed out, in a discussion about tokenism in bicommunal initiatives, that Turkish Cypriots might be the "ghosts" haunting Greek Cypriots in their attempts at ethnonational balance in their cultural productions.

6 — Quoting Savvas Constantinides in Associated Press 2021.

# Filmography

## WORKS ADDRESSING "THE CYPRUS PROBLEM"

NOTE: Films are listed chronologically by title, in English—followed, where indicated, by the Greek or Turkish title.

*Cyprus Is an Island*. 1946. Ralph Keene, director.

*Cyprus '74* (*Κύπρος '74*). 1974. Markos Siapanis, director.

*Attila '74*. 1975. Michael Cacoyannis, director.

*Cyprus Betrayed* (*Έτσι προδόθηκε η Κύπρος*). 1975. Giorgos Filis, director.

*Cyprus, the Other Reality* (*Κύπρος, η άλλη πραγματικότητα*). 1976. Lambros Papademetrakis and Thekla Kittou, directors.

*Makarios, the Long March* (*Μακάριος, η μεγάλη πορεία*). 1977. Evangelos Ioannides, director.

*A Detail in Cyprus* (*Λεπτομέρεια στην Κύπρο*). 1987. Panicos Chrysanthou, director.

*Trimithi, a Reconstruction in Words* (*Τριμίθι, αναπαράσταση με λέξεις*). 1987. Andreas Pantzis, director.

*Cyprus, Stranded in Time*. 1989. Christopher Hitchens, writer; produced by Michael Waldman for BBC Worldwide's "Frontiers" series.

*Our Wall* (*Το τείχος μας*). 1993. Panicos Chrysanthou and Niyazi Kızılyürek, directors.

*Manhole*. 2000. Aris Kyriakides, director.

*Intramural* (*Εντός των τειχών*). 2001. Elias Demetriou, director.

*Dead Presumed Missing?* 2003. Colette Piault and Paul Sant Cassia, directors.

*Mud* (*Çamur*). 2003. Derviş Zaim, director.

*Pyla: Living Together Separately*. 2003. Elias Demetriou, director.

*Parallel Trips* (*Paralel Yolculuklar*). 2004. Derviş Zaim and Panicos Chrysanthou, directors.

*Voice of Blood*. 2004. Antonis Angastiniotis, director.

*Which Cyprus?* (*Hangi Kıbrıs?*). 2004. Rüstem Batum, director.

*Voice of Blood 2: Searching for Selden*. 2005. Antonis Angastiniotis, director.

*Akamas*. 2006. Panicos Chrysanthou, director.

*An Architecture of Forgetting: Journeys in the Dead Zone*. 2006–8. Alev Adil, director.

*Lost Bus* (*Kayıp Otobüs*). 2007. Fevzi Tanpınar, director.

*Hidden in the Sand*. 2008. Vasia Markides, director.

*Still*. 2009. Alana Kakoyiannis, director.

*Women of Cyprus*. 2009. Vassiliki Katrivanou and Bushra Azzouz, directors.

*Digging the Past in Search of the Future*. 2010. Michael Georgiades, director; produced by Mediabox for The Elders Foundation.

*Homeland*. 2010. Serkan Hussein, director; produced by the Association of Turkish Cypriots Abroad.

*Shadows and Faces* (*Gölgeler ve Suretler*). 2010. Derviş Zaim, director.

*The Division of Cyprus*. 2011. Andreas Apostolidis and Yuri Averof, directors.

*In This Waiting*. 2011. Anna Tsiarta, director.

*Memories*. 2011. Panikos Neokleous, director, with John Maratheftis and Fetshi Akintzi.

*Memory*. 2011. Antonis Angastiniotis, director.

*Sharing an Island*. 2011. Danae Stylianou, director.

*Third Motherland*. 2011. Costas Constantinou and Giorgos Skordis, directors.

*This Is Kontea* (*Κοντέα Εστί*). 2011. David Hands, director; produced by the Kontea Heritage Foundation.

*Birds of a Feather*. 2012. Stefanos Evripidou and Stephen Nugent, directors.

*The Story of the Green Line* (*Ιστορία για την πράσινη γραμμή*). 2017. Panicos Chrysanthou, director.

# References

Adil, Alev. 2013. "Drifting in the Dead Zone in Cyprus: The Mediation of Memory through Expanded Life Writing." PhD diss., University of the Arts, London. https://ualresearchonline.arts.ac.uk/id/eprint/5851/1/Reid_PhD_Thesis_2014.pdf.

Adil, Alev. 2014. "Developing Identity: An Autoethnography of the Turkish Cypriot Photographic Subject." In *Photography and Cyprus: Time, Place and Identity*, edited by Liz Wells, Theopisti Stylianou-Lambert, and Nicos Philippou, 98–119. London: I. B. Tauris.

Aretxaga, Begoña. 2005. *States of Terror: Essays*. Reno: University of Nevada Press.

Arsenijević, Damir. 2011a. "Gendering the Bone: The Politics of Memory in Bosnia and Herzegovina." *Journal for Cultural Research* 15, no. 2: 193–205.

Arsenijević, Damir. 2011b. "Mobilising Unbribable Life: The Politics of Contemporary Poetry in Bosnia and Herzegovina." In *Towards a New Literary Humanism*, edited by Andy Mousley, 166–80. London: Palgrave Macmillan.

Associated Press. 2021. "'Homecoming' to a Ghost Town Sparks Greek Cypriot Anger." *National Herald*, September 10, 2021. https://www.thenationalherald.com/homecoming-to-a-ghost-town-sparks-greek-cypriot-anguish/.

Azgın, Bekir, Christos Christofides, Esra Aygın, and Maria Siakalli. 2018. *Words That Matter: A Glossary for Journalism in Cyprus*. Organization for Security and Co-operation in Europe.

Azoulay, Ariella. 2008. *The Civil Contract of Photography*. Translated by Rela Mazali and Ruvik Danieli. New York: Zone.

Barthes, Roland. 1982. *Camera Lucida: Reflections on Photography*. Translated by Richard Howard. New York: Hill and Wang.

Beckett, Greg. 2010. "Phantom Power: Notes on Provisionality in Haiti." In

*Anthropology and Global Counterinsurgency*, edited by John D. Kelly, Beatrice Jauregui, Sean T. Mitchell, and Jeremy Walton, 39–51. Chicago: University of Chicago Press.

Benjamin, Walter. (1936) 1968a. "The Storyteller: Reflections on the Works of Nikolai Leskov." In *Illuminations: Essays and Reflections*, translated by Harry Zohn, edited by Hannah Arendt, 26–55. New York: Schocken.

Benjamin, Walter. (1936) 1968b. "The Work of Art in the Age of Mechanical Reproduction." In *Illuminations: Essays and Reflections*, translated by Harry Zohn, edited by Hannah Arendt, 217–52. New York: Schocken.

Bennett, Jane. 2010. *Vibrant Matter: A Political Ecology of Things*. Durham, NC: Duke University Press.

Bergson, Henri. (1913) 2001. *Time and Free Will: An Essay on the Immediate Data of Consciousness*. Translated by F. L. Pogson. Mineola, NY: Dover.

Biehl, João, and Peter Locke. 2010. "Deleuze and the Anthropology of Becoming." *Current Anthropology* 51, no. 3: 317–51.

Biehl, João, and Peter Locke. 2017. "The Anthropology of Becoming." In *Unfinished: The Anthropology of Becoming*, edited by João Biehl and Peter Locke, 41–89. Durham, NC: Duke University Press.

Biehl, João, and Adriana Petryna. 2011. "Bodies of Rights and Therapeutic Markets." *Social Research* 78, no. 2: 359–86.

Biers, Trish. 2019. "Rethinking Purpose, Protocol, and Popularity in Displaying the Dead in Museums." In *Ethical Approaches to Human Remains: A Global Challenge in Bioarchaeology and Forensic Anthropology*, edited by Kirsty Squires, David Errickson, and Nicholas Márquez-Grant, 239–63. Cham, Switzerland: Springer.

Bounia, Alexandra, and Theopisti Stylianou-Lambert. 2013. "War Museums and Photography." In *Does War Belong in Museums? The Representation of Violence in Exhibitions*, edited by Wolfgang Muchitsch, 155–72. Bielefeld, Germany: Transcript Berlag.

Bruchac, Margaret. 2010. "Lost and Found: NAGPRA, Scattered Relics, and Restorative Methodologies." *Museum Anthropology* 33, no. 2: 137–56.

Bryant, Rebecca. 2004. *Imagining the Modern: The Cultures of Nationalism in Cyprus*. London: I. B. Tauris.

Bryant, Rebecca. 2006. "Betrayals of the Past." *Postcolonial Studies* 9, no. 3: 311–24.

Bryant, Rebecca. 2007. "Turkey, Cyprus and the European Division." *Insight Turkey* 9, no. 1: 120–26.

Bryant, Rebecca. 2010. *The Past in Pieces: Belonging in the New Cyprus*. Philadelphia: University of Pennsylvania Press.

Bryant, Rebecca. 2014. "History's Remainders: On Time and Objects after Conflict in Cyprus." *American Ethnologist* 41, no. 4: 681–97.

Bryant, Rebecca, ed. 2016. *Post-Ottoman Coexistence: Sharing Space in the Shadow of Conflict*. New York: Berghahn.

Bryant, Rebecca, and Mete Hatay. 2020. *Sovereignty Suspended: Building the So-Called State.* Philadelphia: University of Pennsylvania Press.
Certeau, Michel de. 1988. *The Writing of History.* Translated by Tom Conley. New York: Columbia University Press.
Chatziapostolou, Panagiotis. 2021. "Κυριάκος Αντωνιάδης (αστυνομικός στις έρευνες για αγνοούμενους): Ήθελαν μανάδες να κλαίνε στα οδοφράγματα, οι μαρτυρίες έμπαιναν στα συρτάρια (ηχητικό)" [Kyriakos Antoniadis (police officer in the search for missing persons): They wanted the mothers to cry at the roadblocks, testimonies were put in drawers]. *Politis.com*, September 15, 2021. Accessed October 9, 2022. https://politis.com.cy/politis-news/32386/kyriakos-antoniadis-astynomikos-stis-erevnes-ga-agooymenoys-ithelan-manades-na-klaine-sta-odofragata-oi-martyries-empainan-sta-syrtaria-ichitiko.
Chrysanthou, Panicos. 2010. *Stories of the No-Man's Land.* Translated by Stavros Marangos. Nicosia: Artimages Cyprus. Photo exhibition catalogue, Avesta, May–September 2010.

Colwell-Chanthaphonh, Chip, and Jami Powell. 2012. "Repatriation and Constructs of Identity." *Journal of Anthropological Research* 68, no. 2: 191–222.
Comaroff, John L., and Jean Comaroff. 2006. "Law and Disorder in the Postcolony: An Introduction." In *Law and Disorder in the Postcolony*, edited by Jean Comaroff and John L. Comaroff, 1–56. Chicago: University of Chicago Press.
Connolly, William E. 2011. *A World of Becoming.* Durham, NC: Duke University Press.
Constandinides, Costas. 2014. "Postscript: Borders of Categories and Categories of Borders in Cypriot Cinemas." In *Cypriot Cinemas: Memory, Conflict and Identity in the Margins of Europe*, edited by Costas Constandinides and Yiannis Papadakis, 207–35. London: Bloomsbury.
Constandinides, Costas, and Yiannis Papadakis. 2014. "Introduction: Scenarios of History, Themes, and Politics in Cypriot Cinemas." In *Cypriot Cinemas: Memory, Conflict and Identity in the Margins of Europe*, edited by Costas Constandinides and Yiannis Papadakis, 1–30. London: Bloomsbury.
Constantinou, Costas. 2021. "Η εξαπάτηση συγγενών αγνοουμένων—'Ηξεραν, αλλά ήθελαν μανάδες να κλαίνε στα οδοφράγματα'" [The deception of relatives of missing persons—"They knew, but they wanted the mothers to cry at the roadblocks"]. *In.gr*, September 29, 2021. https://www.in.gr/2021/09/29/greece/eksapatisi-syggenon-agnooumenon-ikseran-alla-ithelan-manades-na-klaine-sta-odofragmata/.
Constantinou, Costas M. 2008. "On the Cypriot States of Exception." *International Political Sociology* 2, no. 2: 145–64.
Constantinou, Costas M., Olga Demetriou, and Mete Hatay. 2012. "Conflicts and Uses of Cultural Heritage in Cyprus." *Journal of Balkan and Near Eastern Studies* 14, no. 2: 177–98.
Constantinou, Marios. 2006. "Reasons of State and the Constitutional Logic of

Quasi-Stateness: The Post-colonial Contradictions of Cyprus's Integration in the European Confederation." *Postcolonial Studies* 9, no. 3: 295–310.

Cordell, Linda S., and Keith W. Kintigh. 2010. "Reply to Schillaci & Bustard." *Political and Legal Anthropology Review (PoLAR)* 33, no. 2: 378–83.

Crossland, Zoe. 2000. "Buried Lives: Forensic Archaeology and the Disappeared in Argentina." *Archaeological Dialogues* 7, no. 2: 146–59.

Crossland, Zoe. 2002. "Violent Spaces: Conflict over the Reappearance of Argentina's Disappeared." In *Matériel Culture: The Archaeology of Twentieth-Century Conflict*, edited by John Schofield, William Gray Johnson, and Colleen M. Beck, 115–31. London: Routledge.

Crossland, Zoe. 2009. "Acts of Estrangement: The Post-mortem Making of Self and Other." *Archaeological Dialogues* 16, no. 1: 102–25.



Danforth, Loring M. 1982. *The Death Rituals of Rural Greece*. Photography by Alexander Tsiaras. Princeton, NJ: Princeton University Press.

Das, Veena, and Deborah Poole. 2004. "State and Its Margins: Comparative Ethnographies." In *Anthropology in the Margins of the State*, edited by Veena Das and Deborah Poole, 3–34. Santa Fe, NM: School of American Research Press.

Davis, Elizabeth Anne. 2012. *Bad Souls: Madness and Responsibility in Modern Greece*. Durham, NC: Duke University Press.

Davis, Elizabeth Anne. 2017. "Time Machines: The Matter of the Missing in Cyprus." In *Unfinished: The Anthropology of Becoming*, edited by João Biehl and Peter Locke, 217–42. Durham, NC: Duke University Press.

Davis, Elizabeth Anne. n.d. "The Time of the Cannibals: On 'Conspiracy Theory' and Context." Unpublished manuscript.

Dawdy, Shannon Lee. 2010. "Clockpunk Anthropology and the Ruins of Modernity." *Current Anthropology* 51, no. 6: 761–78.

De Baets, Antoon. 2004. "A Declaration of the Responsibilities of Present Generations toward Past Generations." *History and Theory* 43, no. 4: 130–64.

De Baets, Antoon. 2007. "A Successful Utopia: The Doctrine of Human Dignity." *Historein* 7:71–85.

Deleuze, Gilles. 1989. *Cinema 2: The Time-Image*. Translated by Hugh Tomlinson and Robert Galeta. Minneapolis: University of Minnesota Press.

Deleuze, Gilles, and Félix Guattari. (1975) 1986. *Kafka: Toward a Minor Literature*. Translated by Dana Polan. Minneapolis: University of Minnesota Press.

Demetriou, Olga. 2006a. "After Mourning: 'Morning After' Literature on Cyprus." *South European Society and Politics* 11, no. 2: 301–6.

Demetriou, Olga. 2006b. "Freedom Square: The Unspoken Reunification of a Divided City." HAGAR *(Studies in Culture, Polity and Identities)* 7, no. 1: 55–77.

Demetriou, Olga. 2007. "To Cross or Not to Cross? Subjectivization and the Absent State in Cyprus." *Journal of the Royal Anthropological Institute* 13:987–1006.

Demetriou, Olga. 2008. "Catalysis, Catachresis: The EU's Impact on the Cyprus Conflict." In *The European Union and Border Conflicts: The Power of Integration and Association*, edited by Thomas Diez, Mathias Albert, and Stephan Stetter, 64–93. Cambridge: Cambridge University Press.

Demetriou, Olga. 2018. *Refugeehood and the Postconflict Subject: Reconsidering Minor Losses*. Albany: State University of New York Press.

Demetriou, Olga, and Ayla Gürel. 2008. *Human Rights, Civil Society and Conflict in Cyprus: Exploring the Relationships.* Case Study Report WP3. SHUR: Human Rights in Conflicts: The Role of Civil Society. Programme of the European Commission.

Demetriou, Olga, and Murat Erdal Ilican. 2018. "A Peace of Bricks and Mortar: Thinking Ceasefire Landscapes with Gramsci." *International Journal of Heritage Studies* 25, no. 9: 897–913.

Demos, T. J. 2013. *The Migrant Image: The Art and Politics of Documentary during Global Crisis*. Durham, NC: Duke University Press.

Derrida, Jacques. 1995. *Archive Fever: A Freudian Impression*. Translated by Eric Prenowitz. Chicago: University of Chicago Press.

Dilley, Roy. 2015. "Problematic Reproductions: Children, Slavery, and Not-Knowing in Colonial French West Africa." In *Regimes of Ignorance: Anthropological Perspectives on the Production and Reproduction of Non-knowledge*, edited by Roy Dilley and Thomas G. Kirsch, 138–58. New York: Berghahn.

Domanska, Ewa. 2006. "The Material Presence of the Past." *History and Theory* 45, no. 3: 337–48.

Dorfman, Ariel. 2006. "The Missing and Photography: The Uses and Misuses of Globalization." In *Spontaneous Shrines and the Public Memorialization of Death*, edited by Jack Santino, 255–60. New York: Palgrave Macmillan.

Drousiotis, Makarios. 2000. *1619 Ενοχές: Τα λάθη, τα ψέματα και οι σκοπιμότητες* [1619 Guilty: Mistakes, lies, and pragmatics]. Nicosia: Editions Diafaneia.

Drousiotis, Makarios. 2012. "The Exploitation of Human Pain and Suffering in the Name of the 'Cyprus Problem': 'I Could Have Had a Different Life.'" *Cyprus Mail*, December 2, 2012.

Durkheim, Émile. (1912) 1995. *The Elementary Forms of Religious Life*. Translated by Karen E. Fields. New York: Free Press.

Eftychiou, Evi, and Nicos Philippou. 2010. "Coffee-House Culture and Tourism in Cyprus: A Traditionalized Experience." In *Coffee Culture: Destinations and Tourism*, edited by Lee Joliffe, 66–86. Bristol: Channel View.

Erdal Ilican, Murat. 2013. "The Occupy Buffer Zone Movement: Radicalism and Sovereignty in Cyprus." *Cyprus Review* 25, no. 1: 55–79.

Errickson, David, and Tim J. U. Thompson. 2019. "Sharing Is Not Always Caring: Social Media and the Dead." In *Ethical Approaches to Human Remains: A Global Challenge in Bioarchaeology and Forensic Anthropology*, edited by Kirsty Squires, David Errickson, and Nicholas Márquez-Grant, 299–313. Cham, Switzerland: Springer.

Ferrán, Ofelia. 2013. "Grievability and the Politics of Visibility: The Photography of Francesc Torres and the Mass Graves of the Spanish Civil War." In *Memory and*

*Postwar Memorials: Confronting the Violence of the Past*, edited by Marc Silberman and Florence Vatan, 117–36. New York: Palgrave Macmillan.
Ferrándiz, Francisco. 2006. "The Return of Civil War Ghosts: The Ethnography of Exhumations in Contemporary Spain." *Anthropology Today* 22, no. 3: 7–12.
Ferrándiz, Francisco. 2007. "Fugitive Voices." In *Dark Is the Room Where We Sleep/ Oscura es la habitación donde dormimos*, edited and with photographs by Francesc Torres, 50–135. Bilingual edition. New York: ACTAR.
Ferrándiz, Francisco, and Alejandro Baer. 2008. "Digital Memory: The Visual Recording of Mass Grave Exhumations in Contemporary Spain." *Forum: Qualitative Social Research* 9, no. 3 (Article 45): n.p.
Fischer, Michael M. J. 1993. "Working through the Other: The Jewish, Spanish, Turkish, Iranian, Ukrainian, Lithuanian, and German Unconscious of Polish Culture; or, One Hand Clapping: Dialogue, Silences, and the Mourning of Polish Romanticism." In *Perilous States: Conversations on Culture, Politics, and Nation*, edited by George Marcus, 187–234. Chicago: University of Chicago Press.
Fischer, Michael M. J. 2003. *Emergent Forms of Life and the Anthropological Voice*. Durham, NC: Duke University Press.
Fontein, Joost. 2010. "Between Tortured Bodies and Resurfacing Bones: The Politics of the Dead in Zimbabwe." *Journal of Material Culture* 15, no. 4: 423–48.
Fontein, Joost. 2014. "Remaking the Dead, Uncertainty, and the Torque of Human Materials in Northern Zimbabwe." In *Governing the Dead: Sovereignty and the Politics of Dead Bodies*, edited by Finn Stepputat, 114–40. Manchester: Manchester University Press.
Fontein, Joost. 2018. "Death, Corporeality, and Uncertainty in Zimbabwe." In *A Companion to the Anthropology of Death*, edited by Antonius C. G. M. Robben, 337–55. Oxford: Wiley Blackwell.
Foster, Hal. 2004. "An Archival Impulse." *October* 110:3–22.
Foucault, Michel. 1977a. *Discipline and Punish*. Translated by Alan Sheridan. New York: Vintage.
Foucault, Michel. 1977b. "The Political Function of the Intellectual." *Radical Philosophy* 17:12–14.
Foucault, Michel. 1980. "Nietzsche, Genealogy, History." In *Language, Counter-memory, Practice: Selected Essays and Interviews*, edited by D. F. Bouchard, translated by Sherry Simon, 139–64. Ithaca, NY: Cornell University Press.
Fryer, Tiffany C. 2021. "Memorial Alienation, Material Intimacies." Paper presented at the Society of Fellows in the Humanities, Princeton University, February 26, 2021.
General Assembly of the United Nations. 2010. Resolution 47/133: International Convention for the Protection of All Persons from Enforced Disappearance. Adopted December 23, 2010. Accessed October 5, 2022. https://www.ohchr.org/en/instruments-mechanisms/instruments/international-convention-protection-all-persons-enforced.

Gordon, Avery F. 1997. *Ghostly Matters: Haunting and the Sociological Imagination*. Minneapolis: University of Minnesota Press.

Gordon, Avery F. 2008. *Ghostly Matters: Haunting and the Sociological Imagination*. New edition with foreword by Janice Radway and introduction by Avery Gordon. Minneapolis: University of Minnesota Press.

Gordon, Avery F. 2011. "Some Thoughts on Haunting and Futurity." *borderlands* 10, no. 2: 1–21.

Hadjimichael, Michael. 2019. "*Cyprus Is an Island* (1946)—Ethnographic Reflections on a Colonial Documentary." *Cyprus Review* 31, no. 2: 143–65.

Hall, Neil. 2014. "Lost in Time: The Cyprus Buffer Zone." *Reuters*, April 15, 2014. https://widerimage.reuters.com/story/lost-in-time-the-cyprus-buffer-zone.

Hallam, Elizabeth. 2010. "Articulating Bones: An Epilogue." *Journal of Material Culture* 15, no. 4: 465–92.

Hands, David. 2012. "Challenges of Bicommunal Settings to Bicommunal Film Making Process." Master's diss., Cambridge School of Art, Anglia Ruskin University.

Haraway, Donna. 1991. "Situated Knowledges: The Science Question in Feminism and the Privilege of Partial Perspective." In *Simians, Cyborgs and Women: The Reinvention of Nature*, by Donna Haraway, 183–202. New York: Routledge.

Hatay, Mete. 2007. "Is the Turkish Cypriot Population Shrinking? An Overview of the Ethno-Demography of Cyprus in the Light of the Preliminary Results of the 2006 Turkish-Cypriot Census." *PRIO Report 2/2007*. Oslo: International Peace Research Institute (PRIO).

Hatay, Mete, and Yiannis Papadakis. 2012. "A Critical Comparison of Greek Cypriot and Turkish Cypriot Official Historiographies (1940s to the Present)." In *Cyprus and the Politics of Memory: History, Community and Conflict*, edited by Rebecca Bryant and Yiannis Papadakis, 27–50. London: I. B. Tauris.

Hayes, Patricia, Jeremy Silvester, and Wolfram Hartmann. 2002 "'Picturing the Past' in Namibia: The Visual Archive and Its Energies." In *Refiguring the Archive*, edited by Carolyn Hamilton, Verne Harris, Jane Taylor, Michele Pickover, Graeme Reid, and Razia Saleh, 102–33. Dordrecht: Kluwer Academic.

Hirsch, Eric, and Charles Stewart. 2005. "Introduction: Ethnographies of Historicity." *History and Anthropology* 16, no. 3: 261–74.

Hirsch, Marianne. 1997. *Family Frames: Photography, Narrative, and Postmemory*. Cambridge, MA: Harvard University Press.

Hirsch, Marianne. 2008. "The Generation of Postmemory." *Poetics Today* 29, no. 1: 103–28.

Hirsch, Marianne. 2012. *The Generation of Postmemory: Writing and Visual Culture after the Holocaust*. New York: Columbia University Press.

Hitchens, Christopher. (1984) 1997. *Hostage to History: Cyprus from the Ottomans to Kissinger*. London: Verso.

Hoffman, Eva. 2004. *After Such Knowledge: Memory, History, and the Legacy of the Holocaust*. New York: Public Affairs.

International Committee of the Red Cross. 2005. *Customary International Humanitarian Law*. Vol. I: *Rules*. Cambridge: Cambridge University Press.

International Crisis Group. 2010. *Cyprus: Bridging the Property Divide*. Europe Report No. 210.

Ioannides, Panos. 1975. *Κύπρος, μέρες οργής σε 555 φωτογραφίες* [Cyprus, days of rage in 555 photographs]. Photographs by Charalambos Avdellopoulos and Andreas Koutas. Nicosia: Morphotiki.

İrvan, Süleyman. 2008. "Oral History as a Method for Peace Journalists: Sevgül Uludağ as a Case Study." Conference Papers and Presentations, Eastern Mediterranean University, 245–51. http://i-rep.emu.edu.tr:8080/xmlui/bitstream/handle/11129/586/Oral%20History%20as%20a%20Method%20for%20Peace%20Journalists.pdf?sequence=1.



Kaplan, Brett Ashley. 2007. *Unwanted Beauty: Aesthetic Pleasure in Holocaust Representation*. Urbana: University of Illinois Press.

Karayanni, Stavros. 2014. "En-gendering Cypriots: From Colonial Landscapes to Postcolonial Identities." In *Photography and Cyprus: Time, Place, and Identity*, edited by Liz Wells, Theopisti Stylianou-Lambert, and Nicos Philippou, 123–42. New York: I. B. Tauris.

Karayanni, Stavros. 2018. "Introduction." In *The Wind under My Lips/Ο άνεμος κάτω απ΄τα χείλη μου*, translated by Despina Pirketti, 14–26. Bilingual edition. Athens: Rodakio.

Karayanni, Stavros. 2019. "Polaroid Vision: Thoughts on Nicos Philippou's Sharqi." *Cyprus Review* 31, no. 1: 265–78.

Kirsch, Thomas G., and Roy Dilley. 2015. "Regimes of Ignorance: An Introduction." In *Regimes of Ignorance: Anthropological Perspectives on the Production and Reproduction of Non-knowledge*, edited by Roy Dilley and Thomas G. Kirsch, 1–28. New York: Berghahn.

Kleanthous, Alexis. 2005. *Ο Κυπριακός Κινηματογράφος, 1962–2005* [Cypriot cinema, 1962–2005]. Athens: Aigokeros.

Kovras, Iosif. 2008. "Unearthing the Truth: The Politics of Exhumations in Cyprus and Spain." *History and Anthropology* 19, no. 4: 371–90.

Kovras, Iosif. 2012. "De-linkage Processes and Grassroots Movements in Transitional Justice." *Cooperation and Conflict* 47, no. 1: 88–105.

Kovras, Iosif, and Neophytos Loizides. 2011. "Delaying Truth Recovery for Missing Persons." *Nations and Nationalism* 17, no. 3: 520–39.

Krmpotich, Cara, Joost Fontein, and John Harries. 2010. "The Substance of Bones: The Emotive Materiality and Affective Presence of Human Remains." *Journal of Material Culture* 15, no. 4: 371–84.

Kyriakou, Nikolas. 2011. "Enforced Disappearances in Cyprus: Problems and Prospects of the Case Law of the European Court of Human Rights." *European Human Rights Law Review* 2:190–99.

Kyriakou, Nikolas. 2012a. "An Affront to the Conscience of Humanity: Enforced

Disappearance in International Human Rights Law." LD thesis, European University Institute.

Kyriakou, Nikolas. 2012b. "The International Convention for the Protection of All Persons from Enforced Disappearance and Its Contributions to International Human Rights Law, with Specific Reference to Extraordinary Rendition." *Melbourne Journal of International Law* 13:1–38.

Lambek, Michael. 2010. "Introduction." In *Ordinary Ethics: Anthropology, Language, and Action*, edited by Michael Lambek, 1–36. New York: Fordham University Press.

Laqueur, Thomas W. 2002. "The Dead Body and Human Rights." In *The Body*, edited by Sean T. Sweeney and Ian Hodder, 75–93. Cambridge: Cambridge University Press.

Latour, Bruno. 1999. *Pandora's Hope: Essays on the Reality of Science Studies*. Cambridge, MA: Harvard University Press.

Lee, Laurie, and Ralph Keene. 1947. *We Made a Film in Cyprus*. London: Longmans, Green and Co.

Lévi-Strauss, Claude. (1978) 1995. *Myth and Meaning: Cracking the Code of Culture*. New York: Schocken.

Loizos, Peter. 2007. "'Generations' in Forced Migration: Towards Greater Clarity." *Journal of Refugee Studies* 20, no. 2: 193–209.

Loizos, Peter. 2008. *Iron in the Soul: Displacement, Livelihood and Health in Cyprus*. New York: Berghahn.

Loizos, Peter, Nicos Philippou, and Theopisti Stylianou-Lambert, eds. 2010. *Re-envisioning Cyprus*. Nicosia: University of Nicosia Press.

Loraux, Nicole. 2002. *The Divided City: On Memory and Forgetting in Ancient Athens*. Translated by Corinne Pache with Jeff Fort. New York: Zone.

MacDougall, David. 1994. "Films of Memory." In *Visualizing Theory: Selected Essays from V.A.R., 1990–1994*, edited by Lucien Taylor, 260–70. New York: Routledge.

Marselis, Randi. 2016. "On Not Showing Scalps: Human Remains and Multisited Debate at the National Museum of Denmark." *Museum Anthropology* 39, no. 1: 20–34.

Matthews, Paul. 1983. "Whose Body? People as Property." *Current Legal Problems* 36:193–239.

Mendeloff, David. 2009. "Trauma and Vengeance: Assessing the Psychological and Emotional Effects of Post-conflict Justice." *Human Rights Quarterly* 31, no. 3: 592–623.

Midler, Aaron H. 2011. "The Spirit of NAGPRA: The Native American Graves Protection and Repatriation Act and the Regulation of Culturally Unidentifiable Remains." *Chicago-Kent Law Review* 86, no. 3 (Article 12): 1331–61.

Moon, Claire. 2019. "What Remains? Human Rights after Death." In *Ethical Approaches to Human Remains: A Global Challenge in Bioarchaeology and Forensic Anthropology*, edited by Kirsty Squires, David Errickson, and Nicholas Márquez-Grant, 39–58. Cham, Switzerland: Springer.

Nash, Stephen E., and Chip Colwell. 2020. "NAGPRA at 30: The Effects of Repatriation." *Annual Review of Anthropology* 49:225–39.

Navaro-Yashin, Yael. 2009. "Affective Spaces, Melancholic Objects: Ruination and the Production of Anthropological Knowledge." *Journal of the Royal Anthropological Institute (N.S.)* 15: 1–18.

Navaro-Yashin, Yael. 2012. *The Make-Believe Space: Affective Geographies in a Postwar Polity*. Durham, NC: Duke University Press.

Nelson, Diane M. 2004. "Anthropologist Discovers Legendary Two-Faced Indian! Margins, the State, and Duplicity in Guatemala." In *Anthropology in the Margins of the State*, edited by Veena Das and Deborah Poole, 117–40. Santa Fe, NM: School of American Research Press.

Nelson, Diane M. 2009. *Reckoning: The Ends of War in Guatemala*. Durham, NC: Duke University Press.



Nelson, Diane M. 2015. *Who Counts? The Mathematics of Death and Life after Genocide*. Durham, NC: Duke University Press.

Nilsson Stutz, L. 2016. "To Gaze upon the Dead: The Exhibition of Human Remains as Cultural Practice and Political Practice in Scandinavia and the United States." In *Archaeologists and the Dead: Mortuary Archaeology in Contemporary Society*, edited by Howard Williams and Melanie Giles, 268–92. Oxford: Oxford University Press.

Ochoa, Todd Ramón. 2010. *Society of the Dead: Quita Manaquita and Palo Praise in Cuba*. Berkeley: University of California Press.

Ostoff, Simone. 2009. *Performing the Archive: The Transformation of the Archive in Contemporary Art, from Repository of Documents to Art Medium*. New York: Atropos.

Ousley, Stephen. 2010. "Comments on Schillaci & Bustard." *Political and Legal Anthropology Review (PoLAR)* 33, no. 2: 374–77.

Palmié, Stephan, and Charles Stewart. 2016. "Introduction: For an Anthropology of History." *HAU: Journal of Ethnographic Theory* 6, no. 1: 207–36.

Panourgiá, Neni. 1995. *Fragments of Death, Fables of Identity: An Athenian Anthropography*. Madison: University of Wisconsin Press.

Panourgiá, Neni. 2009. *Dangerous Citizens: The Greek Left and the Terror of the State*. New York: Fordham University Press.

Papadakis, Yiannis. 1994. "The National Struggle Museums of a Divided City." *Ethnic and Racial Studies* 17, no. 3: 400–419.

Papadakis, Yiannis. 1998. "Walking in the *Hora*: 'Place' and 'Non-place' in Divided Nicosia." *Journal of Mediterranean Studies* 8, no. 2: 302–27.

Papadakis, Yiannis. 2000a. "Memories of Walls, Walls of Memory." In *Chypre et la Méditerranée orientale—Formations identitaires: Perspectives historiques et enjeux contemporains* [Cyprus and the Eastern Mediterranean—Formations of identity: Historical perspectives and contemporary challenges], edited by Yannis Ioannou, Françoise Métral, and Marguerite Yon, 231–39. Conference proceedings, Université Lumière-Lyon 2 and the University of Cyprus (1997). Lyon: Maison de l'Orient et de la Méditerranée-Jean Pouilloux.

Papadakis, Yiannis. 2000b. "The Social Mapping of the Unknown: Managing Uncertainty in a Mixed Borderline Cypriot Village." *Anthropological Journal on European Cultures* 9, no. 2: 93–112.

Papadakis, Yiannis. 2005. *Echoes from the Dead Zone: Across the Cyprus Divide.* London: I. B. Tauris.

Papailias, Penelope. 2005. *Genres of Recollection: Archival Poetics and Modern Greece.* New York: Palgrave Macmillan.

Paraschos, Andreas. 2012. "Στον βωμό των χρημάτων οι αγνοούμενοι—αδιαφάνεια στη διαχείριση εκατομμυρίων, μυστικά κονδύλια, ρουσφέτια και καριερισμοί συνθέτουν το σκάνδαλο" [The missing on the altar of money: Opacity in the management of millions, secret funds, favors and careerism make the scandal]. *Kathimerini*, April 1, 2012.



Payne, Leigh A. 2008. *Unsettling Accounts: Neither Truth nor Reconciliation in Confessions of State Violence.* Durham, NC: Duke University Press.

Pellapaisiotis, Haris. 2014. "The Art of the Buffer Zone." In *Photography and Cyprus: Time, Place and Identity*, edited by Liz Wells, Theopisti Stylianou-Lambert, and Nicos Philippou, 218–39. London: I. B. Tauris.

Petryna, Adriana. 2002. *Life Exposed: Biological Citizens after Chernobyl.* Princeton, NJ: Princeton University Press.

Philippou, Nicos. 2005. *Off the Map.* Nicosia: Intercollege Press.

Philippou, Nicos. 2007. *Coffee House Embellishments.* Nicosia: University of Nicosia Press.

Philippou, Nicos. 2014. "The National Geographic and Half Oriental Cyprus." In *Photography and Cyprus: Time, Place and Identity*, edited by Liz Wells, Theopisti Stylianou-Lambert, and Nicos Philippou, 28–52. London: I. B. Tauris.

Philippou, Nicos. 2016. *Sharqi.* Nicosia: Nicosia Municipal Arts Centre (NIMAC).

Philippou, Nicos, Theopisti Stylianou-Lambert, and Liz Wells. 2014. "Introduction." In *Photography and Cyprus: Time, Place and Identity*, edited by Liz Wells, Theopisti Stylianou-Lambert, and Nicos Philippou, 1–10. London: I. B. Tauris.

Philippou, Nicos, and Marilena Zackheos. n.d. *Arizona.* Ongoing project.

Pinney, Christopher. 2005. "Things Happen: or, From Which Moment Does That Object Come?" In *Materiality*, edited by Daniel Miller, 256–72. Durham, NC: Duke University Press.

Povinelli, Elizabeth A. 2011. "The Woman on the Other Side of the Wall: Archiving the Otherwise in Postcolonial Digital Archives." *differences* 22, no. 1: 146–71.

PRIO Cyprus Centre. 2011a. "Agios Sozomenos." In *Internal Displacement in Cyprus: Mapping the Consequences of Civil and Military Strife.* http://www.prio-cyprus-displacement.net/default.asp?id=261.

PRIO Cyprus Centre. 2011b. "Peristerona." In *Internal Displacement in Cyprus:*

*Mapping the Consequences of Civil and Military Strife*. http://www.prio-cyprus-displacement.net/default.asp?id=347.

Ralph, Laurence. 2020. *The Torture Letters: Reckoning with Police Violence*. Chicago: University of Chicago Press.

Renshaw, Layla. 2011. *Exhuming Loss: Memory, Materiality and Mass Graves of the Spanish Civil War*. Walnut Creek, CA: Left Coast.

Renshaw, Layla. 2019. "Ethical Considerations in the Investigation and Commemoration of Mass Graves from the Spanish Civil War." In *Ethical Approaches to Human Remains: A Global Challenge in Bioarchaeology and Forensic Anthropology*, edited by Kirsty Squires, David Errickson, and Nicholas Márquez-Grant, 519–39. Cham, Switzerland: Springer.

Ritchin, Fred. 2009. *After Photography*. New York: Norton.



Robben, Antonius C. G. M. 1999. "State Terror in the Netherworld: Disappearance and Reburial in Argentina." In *Death Squad: The Anthropology of State Terror*, edited by Jeffrey A. Sluka, 91–113. Philadelphia: University of Pennsylvania Press.

Rosenblatt, Adam. 2015. *Digging for the Disappeared: Forensic Science after Atrocity*. Stanford, CA: Stanford University Press.

Sanal, Aslıhan. 2010. *New Organs within Us: Transplants and the Moral Economy*. Durham, NC: Duke University Press.

Sanford, Victoria. 2004. *Buried Secrets: Truth and Human Rights in Guatemala*. New York: Palgrave Macmillan.

Sant Cassia, Paul. 1999. "Piercing Transfigurations: Representations of Suffering in Cyprus." *Visual Anthropology* 13, no. 1: 23–46.

Sant Cassia, Paul. 2005. *Bodies of Evidence: Burial, Memory, and the Recovery of Missing Persons in Cyprus*. New York: Berghahn.

Scheper-Hughes, Nancy. 2007. "Violence and the Politics of Remorse: Lessons from South Africa." In *Subjectivity: Ethnographic Investigations*, edited by João Biehl, Byron Good, and Arthur Kleinman, 179–234. Berkeley: University of California Press.

Schillaci, Michael A., and Wendy J. Bustard. 2010. "Controversy and Conflict: NAGPRA and the Role of Biological Anthropology in Determining Cultural Affiliation." *Political and Legal Anthropology Review (PoLAR)* 33, no. 2: 352–73.

Scully, J. L., and R. Woodward. 2012. "Naming the Unknown of Fromelles: DNA Profiling, Ethics and the Identification of First World War Bodies." *Journal of War and Culture Studies* 5, no. 1: 59–72.

Sebald, W. G. 2001. *Austerlitz*. Translated by Anthea Bell. New York: Modern Library.

Sedgwick, Eve Kosofsky. 2003. *Touching Feeling: Affect, Pedagogy, Performativity*. Durham, NC: Duke University Press.

Seidemann, Ryan M. 2010. "NAGPRA at 20: What Have the States Done to Expand Remains Protections?" *Museum Anthropology* 33, no. 2: 199–209.

Şenova, Basak, and Pavlina Paraskevaidou. 2011. "Foreword." In UNCOVERED*: Nic-*

*osia International Airport, Book 1*, edited by Basak Şenova and Pavlina Paraskevaidou. Nicosia: n.p.
Seremetakis, C. Nadia. 1984. "The Eye of the Other: Watching Death in Rural Greece." *Journal of Modern Hellenism* 1:63–77.
Seremetakis, C. Nadia. 1991. *The Last Word: Women, Death, and Divination in Inner Mani*. Chicago: University of Chicago Press.
Shklovsky, Viktor. (1919) 2015. "Art, as Device." Translated by Alexandra Berlina. *Poetics Today* 36, no. 3: 151–74.
Sontag, Susan. 1977. *On Photography*. New York: Picador.
Sontag, Susan. 2003. *Regarding the Pain of Others*. New York: Picador.
Starn, Orin. 2004. *Ishi's Brain: In Search of America's Last "Wild" Indian*. New York: Norton.
Stephanides, Stephanos. 2018. *The Wind under My Lips/Ο άνεμος κάτω απ΄τα χείλη μου*. Translated by Despina Pirketti. Bilingual edition. Athens: Rodakio.
Stoler, Ann Laura. 2009. *Along the Archival Grain: Epistemic Anxieties and Colonial Common Sense*. Princeton, NJ: Princeton University Press.
Strathern, Marilyn. (1991) 2004. *Partial Connections*. Updated edition. Walnut Creek, CA: Altamira.
Stylianou, Elena. 2014. "The Archive as a Space for Negotiating Identities: Defying 'Cypriotness' in the Work of Haris Epaminonda and Christodoulos Panayiotou." In *Photography and Cyprus: Time, Place and Identity*, edited by Liz Wells, Theopisti Stylianou-Lambert, and Nicosia Philippou, 240–63. London: I. B. Tauris.
Stylianou, Elena, and Nicos Philippou. 2018. "Miniature Landscapes: *Sharqi*, the Instant Photograph, and the Re-invention of Cyprus." *photographies* 12, no. 1: 99–116.
Stylianou-Lambert, Theopisti, and Nicos Philippou. 2014. "Aesthetics, Form and Politics in Greek Cypriot Film: 1960–1974." In *Cypriot Cinemas: Memory, Conflict and Identity in the Margins of Europe*, edited by Costas Constandinides and Yiannis Papadakis, 61–90. London: Bloomsbury.
Sztompka, Piotr. 2000. "Cultural Trauma: The Other Side of Social Change." *European Journal of Social Theory* 3, no. 4: 449–66.
Tagg, John. 2009. *The Disciplinary Frame: Photographic Truths and the Capture of Meaning*. Minneapolis: University of Minnesota Press.
Taussig, Michael. 1987. *Shamanism, Colonialism, and the Wild Man: A Study in Terror and Healing*. Chicago: University of Chicago Press.
Taussig, Michael. 1992. *The Nervous System*. New York: Routledge.
Taussig, Michael. 1997. *The Magic of the State*. New York: Routledge.
Taussig, Michael. 1999. *Defacement: Public Secrecy and the Labor of the Negative*. Stanford, CA: Stanford University Press.
Theidon, Kimberly. 2013. *Intimate Enemies: Violence and Reconciliation in Peru*. Philadelphia: University of Pennsylvania Press.
Theodoulou, Michael. 2016. "Tour of the Buffer Zone in Nicosia's Old Town."

*Cyprus Mail*, December 29, 2016. https://cyprus-mail.com/2016/12/29/special-report-tour-buffer-zone-nicosias-old-town/.

Torres, Francesc. 2007. *Dark Is the Room Where We Sleep/Oscura es la habitación donde dormimos*, edited by Francesc Torres. Bilingual edition. New York: ACTAR.

Torres, Francesc. 2015. "9/11: Absence, Sediment, and Memory (Photo Essay)." In *Necropolitics: Mass Graves and Exhumations in the Age of Human Rights*, edited by Francisco Ferrándiz and Antonius C. G. M. Robben, 141–57. Philadelphia: University of Pennsylvania Press.

Trimikliniotis, Nicos, and Umut Bozkurt. 2012. "Introduction: Beyond a Divided Cyprus." In *Beyond a Divided Cyprus: A State and Society in Transformation*, edited by Nicos Trimikliniotis and Umut Bozkurt, 1–21. New York: Palgrave Macmillan.



Uludağ, Sevgül. 2006. *Oysters with the Missing Pearls: Untold Stories about Missing Persons, Mass Graves, and Memories from the Past of Cyprus*. English edition. Nicosia: IKME and BILBAN.

UNDP (United Nations Development Programme). 2008. *Action for Cooperation and Trust: Building Lasting Relationships Islandwide*. United Nations Protected Area, Nicosia, Cyprus.

Vasiliou, Vasou. 2012. "Παιχνίδια με ταυτοποιήσεις—Πληροφορίες ότι κατακυρώθηκε η προσφορά σε ξένο εργαστήρι" [Games with identifications: Sources say the bid was awarded to foreign laboratory]. *Philelevtheros*, March 31, 2012.

Verdery, Katherine. 1999. *The Political Lives of Dead Bodies: Reburial and Postsocialist Change*. New York: Columbia University Press.

Wagner, Sarah E. 2008. *To Know Where He Lies: DNA Technology and the Search for Srebrenica's Missing*. Berkeley: University of California Press.

Weiss, Meira. 2002. *The Chosen Body: The Politics of the Body in Israeli Society*. Stanford, CA: Stanford University Press.

Whitehead, Gregory. 1990. "The Forensic Theatre: Memory Plays for the Postmortem Condition." *Performing Arts Journal* 12, nos. 2–3: 99–109.

Yakinthou, Christalla. 2008. "The Quiet Deflation of Den Xehno? Changes in the Greek-Cypriot Communal Narrative on the Missing Persons in Cyprus." *Cyprus Review* 20, no. 1: 15–34.

Yasaitis, Kelley E. 2005. "NAGPRA: A Look Back through the Litigation." *Journal of Land, Resources, and Environmental Law* 25, no. 2: 259–85.

Zaatari, Akram. 2006. "Photographic Documents/Excavation as Art, 2006." In *The Archive: Documents of Contemporary Art*, edited by Charles Merewether, 181–84. London: Whitechapel Gallery; Cambridge, MA: MIT Press.

Zheng, Christopher. 2021. "31 Years of NAGPRA: Evaluating the Restitution of Native American Ancestral Remains and Belongings." *Center for Art Law*, May 18, 2021. https://itsartlaw.org/2021/05/18/31-years-of-nagpra/.

# Index